THE PROTESTANT REFORMATION IN IRELAND, 1590–1641

The Protestant Reformation in Ireland, 1590–1641

Alan Ford

FOUR COURTS PRESS

This book was typeset by
Carrigboy Typesetting Services
in 10.5 on 12.5 point Ehrhardt for
FOUR COURTS PRESS
55 Prussia Street, Dublin 7, Ireland
e-mail: fcp@ indigo.ie
and in North America for
FOUR COURTS PRESS
c/o ISBS, 5804 N.E. Hassalo Street, Portland, OR 97213.

A catalogue record for this title
is available from the British Library.

ISBN 1-85182-314-x hbk
ISBN 1-85182-282-8 pbk

Printed in Ireland
by ColourBooks Ltd, Dublin.

Contents

Abbreviations

A.D.	G.D. Burtchaell, T.U. Sadleir, *Alumni Dublinenses* (Dublin 1935)
Al. Cantab.	J. and J.A. Venn, *Alumni Cantabrigienses*, part I, 4 vols (Cambridge 1922–7)
Al. Oxon.	J. Foster, Alumni Oxonienses, *1500–1714*, 4 vols (Oxford 1891)
B.L.	British Library, London
Carew Cal.	J.S. Brewer, *Calendar of the carew Manuscripts preserved in the archiepiscopal library in Lambeth*, 6 vols (London 1867–73).
C.S.P.I.	*Calendar of State Papers relating to Ireland*
D.N.B.	*Dictionary of National Biography*
E.A.	The Thirty Nine English Articles
H.M.C.	Historical Manuscripts Commission
I.A.	The Irish Articles of 1615
Leslie, *Raphoe clergy*, etc	J.B. Leslie, *Raphoe clergy and parishes* (Enniskillen 1940) etc., see bibliography
P.B.	J.P. Mahaffy (ed.), *The particular book of Trinity College, Dublin* (London 1904)
P.R.	M.C. Griffith (ed.), *Irish patent rolls of James I: facsimile of the Irish Record Commission's calendar prepared prior to 1830* (Dublin 1966)
P.R.O.I.	Public Record Office, Dublin
P.R.O.N.I.	Public Record Office, Belfast
S.P.	State Papers, Public Record Office, London
U.W.	*The whole works of James Ussher* (ed.) C.R. Elrington, J.R. Todd, 17 vols (Dublin 1847–64)
Ware, *Bishops*	*The whole works of Sir James Ware* (ed.) W. Harris (Dublin 1747–50), vol. i.

Preface to the second edition

THE DEBATE ON THE IRISH REFORMATION

The single most intriguing problem posed by the history of the reformation in Ireland is the failure of the state sponsored religion to take
root in any section of the indigenous population.[1]

With this opening sentence Brendan Bradshaw launched a new era in the study
of the Irish reformation. Previous work had succeeded in establishing an essential narrative framework for reformation history.[2] But, as with all history-writing,
the passage of time rendered more obvious the assumptions that had lain behind
the scholarship, most particularly, in this case, the confessional and even racial
nature of some of the explanations of the failure of the reformation.[3] Bradshaw,
in contrast, provided an escape from narrow chronology and sectarian self-
justification into the much more exciting realms of intellectual history, offering an account of the underlying tensions which, he claimed, effectively ensured
the failure of the reformation during the sixteenth century.

The leaders of the reform programme in Ireland were, he suggested, irre-
concilably divided: first, over the means of spreading the reformation, between
those who advocated coercion and those who favoured persuasion; and second
over the objectives of the programme, some aiming at conformity others at
conversion.[4] Moreover, these conflicts were not merely tactical, they were in
fact a product of fundamental intellectual differences, indeed, of contrasting
anthropologies. The belief in a persuasive strategy of conversion was founded upon an Erasmian, even Platonic, view of human nature, seeing it as essentially good, or capable of good, open to conversion to the truth of the gospel
through reason and teaching. By contrast, advocates of coerced conformity

1 B.I. Bradshaw, 'Sword, word and strategy in the reformation in Ireland' in *Historical
   Journal*, xxi (1978), 475.
2 R.D. Edwards, *Church and state in Tudor Ireland. A history of the penal laws against
   Irish Catholics 1534–1603* (Dublin, 1935); M.V. Ronan, *The reformation in Dublin
   1536–1558 (from original sources)* (London, 1926); M.V. Ronan, *The reformation in
   Ireland under Elizabeth, 1558–80* (London, 1930); W.A. Phillips (ed.), *History of
   the Church of Ireland from the earliest times to the present day* (3 vols., Oxford, 1933).
3 James Murray, 'The church of Ireland: a critical bibliography: part I: 1536–1603'
   in *Irish Historical Studies*, xxviii no. 112(1993), 345f.; Alan Ford, '"Standing one's
   ground": religion, polemic and Irish history since the reformation', in Alan Ford,
   James McGuire and Kenneth Milne (eds.), *As by law established. The church of
   Ireland since the reformation* (Dublin, 1995), 1–14.
4 Bradshaw, 'Sword and word'.

drew upon the much less favourable view of humanity which was an essential part of protestant theology: man was utterly sinful and needed the firm rod of correction to preserve order and discipline. Conversion was something that was wholly a product of God's grace: all that church and state could do was to ensure that people conformed and heard the word preached so that they were exposed to God's grace.[5]

Bradshaw had already suggested that the decisive watershed in the development of modern Irish religious allegiances was the reign of Mary. Prior to that, persuasive policies had had some success. During the reign of Henry VIII the reformation had made considerable progress, at least in securing formal support for royal supremacy. But the attempt to introduce protestantism in the reign of Edward VI showed how reluctant Irish clergy – even those loyal to the king – were to embrace new religious beliefs. The restoration of Catholicism under Mary gave the counter-reformation in Ireland a decisive advantage, which it never lost.[6] In a subsequent study of the urban reformation in the south and west of Ireland in the later sixteenth century, Bradshaw demonstrated how 'the struggle between the reformation and the counter-reformation ... had been resolved by the 1590s in favour of the counter-reformation.'[7] Leaving aside the internal strength of Irish Catholicism, a key factor in the failure of the reformation in the towns was, according to Bradshaw, its association with an anglicising, colonising and essentially coercive strategy during the reign of Elizabeth.[8]

This dissection of the motives underpinning the reformation in sixteenth-century Ireland drew a rapid reply from Nicholas Canny. He claimed that Bradshaw's work was founded upon a fundamental misconception: that the failure of the reformation can be confidently dated to the middle of the sixteenth century.[9] Canny argued that significant members of the Anglo-Irish community in the later sixteenth century conformed to the state church: men such as the Lord Chancellor, Thomas Cusack (1490–1571), or the merchant, Rowland White (d. 1572). Protestantism even made inroads amongst the native Irish, especially in areas such as Thomond, where there was support from local magnates. Such a response, Canny suggested, meant that it was by no means impossible that the reformation might have succeeded in winning over a sig-

5   Ibid.
6   B.I. Bradshaw, 'The Edwardian Reformation in Ireland' in *Archivium Hibernicum*, xxxiv (1977), 96.
7   B.I. Bradshaw, 'The reformation in the cities: Cork, Limerick and Galway, 1534–1603', in John Bradley (ed.), *Settlement and society in medieval Ireland: studies presented to Francis Xavier Martin, O.S.A.* (Kilkenny 1988), 466f.
8   Ibid., 467f.
9   N.P. Canny, 'Why the reformation failed in Ireland: Une question mal posée' in *Journal of Ecclesiastical History*, xxx (1979), 425.

nificant proportion of the Irish people. Indeed, he went farther, and proposed that even if it was accepted that the reformation struck shallow roots in Ireland, the counter-reformation also struggled to obtain the loyalty of the majority of the population. Rather, during the whole early modern period, and even into the mid-nineteenth century, neither the reformation nor the counter-reformation won a 'final victory', but 'the majority of the native population remained outside the structure of the two rival churches, and clung tenaciously to pre-Tridentine religious practice.'[10]

The major service of these two articles was to set the agenda for the debate on the Irish reformation: to identify the key issues of causation and timing – the basic questions of why and when did it fail? But their divergent answers clearly suggested the need for more detailed research on the subject, a challenge which has indeed been taken up over the past two decades.[11] This has resulted in a significant change in the nature of the debate, as some of the insights of Bradshaw and Canny have been adapted and developed, and others questioned and discarded. In brief, Bradshaw's belief in the commitment of the Irish people to counter-reformation Catholicism has been confirmed, whilst his stress upon the contrast between persuasion and coercion has been challenged as too schematic: Canny's insistence that placing the failure of the reformation in the 1550s may be too early has won acceptance, in marked contrast to his claim the religious commitment of the Irish people remained open throughout the seventeenth century and beyond.

Let us take the issue of causation first. Historians have been cautious about developing Bradshaw's distinction between sword and word. Aidan Clarke in an analysis of the first hundred years of the Church of Ireland, conceded that the difference of approach in the sixteenth century was 'perhaps ... philosophically based', but argued that the issue was and obscure and complicated one.[12] James Murray's subsequent examination of the policy of the first reformation Archbishop of Dublin, George Browne, though welcoming the attempt to categorise the intellectual influences that lay behind the actions of politicians and churchmen, suggested that it could also be misleading.

Bradshaw's somewhat exaggerated view that the supporters of the High Commission and the exponents of a coercive military solution to Ireland's

10 Ibid., 450.
11 See the survey in Alan Ford and Kenneth Milne (eds.), 'The Church of Ireland: a critical bibliography, 1536–92' in *Irish Historical Studies*, xxviii no. 112 (1993), 345–62.
12 Aidan Clarke, 'Varieties of uniformity: the first century of the Church of Ireland', in W.J. Shiels and Diana Wood (eds.), *The churches, Ireland and the Irish: studies in church history* (*Studies in Church History*, vol. xxv, Oxford 1989), 110.

political problems were motivated by similar philosophical concerns, gives
the impression that the principle of using ecclesiastical discipline as a
means of enforcing religious uniformity was an intellectual novelty which
required as much formal justification as the notion of conquest. This is
certainly not the case.[13]

Underlying this reluctance of historians to develop Bradshaw's ideas on the
failure of the reformation may be a suspicion of the neat categorisation in
'Sword, word and strategy' of the mentalities that lay behind the persuasive
and coercive reformation strategies. Bradshaw's stark dualism does, it is true,
provide an enticing heuristic tool. No one who has marked undergraduate
essays can doubt its appeal as a way of making sense of the complexities of
early modern Irish history. But that lack of complexity is, in fact, its weakness: it fails to do justice to the sheer messiness of sixteenth century ecclesiastical policy. Bradshaw's almost Platonic belief in the power of overarching
ideals of humanism and protestantism as a means of explaining actions of otherwise diverse groups of politicians and churchmen sits uneasily with the more
reductionist and particularist interpretations favoured by most Irish historians.[14] This is partly a matter of ideological style and intellectual preference.
But the impression that one gains from the recent work on the Irish reformation is that the reasons for its failure were both more mundane and more
complex than 'Sword, word and strategy' originally suggested.

Thus, advocacy of persuasion and instruction could spring from a variety
of motives, some, perhaps, a product of intellectual beliefs, others to do with
pragmatic politics. To Nicodemites or *politiques*, to those wishing to straddle the
religious divide and retain their power and influence, or to those concerned with
the survival of the Dublin polity, the advocacy of persuasion served the useful
purpose of postponing both the imposition of the reformation and the risky
process of forcing people to make a choice between loyalty or Catholicism. Nor
were persuasion and compulsion necessarily opposites. The English model of
the reformation combined the use of propaganda and teaching with the strict
enforcement of conformity. The key difference between England and Ireland
in this respect was that the former possessed both an efficient and effective

---

13 James Murray, 'Ecclesiastical justice and the enforcement of the reformation: the
   case of Archbishop Browne and the clergy of Dublin', in Alan Ford, James
   McGuire and Kenneth Milne (eds.), *As by law established. The church of Ireland
   since the reformation* (Dublin, 1995), 35.
14 Contrast Bradshaw's approach to sixteenth century Irish humanism and its influence on politics in his *The Irish constitutional revolution of the sixteenth century*
   (Cambridge, 1979) with Ciarán Brady's interpretation of the same period in *The
   chief governors. The rise and fall of reform government in Tudor Ireland, 1536–1588*
   (Cambridge, 1994).

system of central and local government and a sufficiently endowed church to ensure that persuasion and compulsion were put into effect. The impossibility, in the chaos of sixteenth century Ireland, of translating official Diktat into religious change on the ground led to that fatal flaw in Irish religious, and secular, policy: 'statute could not create a social reality'.[15] The result was a rather unreal debate within the Irish church about reformation policy – a debate which was artificially prolonged and polarised by the inability of church or state adequately to put either of the options into practice. In fact, as Bradshaw has himself observed, as soon as the protestant reformation in the Church of Ireland got under way in the early seventeenth century, the debate died away, as all members of the Church of Ireland were agreed that conformity had to be imposed with the help of the civil arm.[16]

Where Canny has had an impact is in his attempt to extend the timescale for the failure of the reformation. Not, perhaps as far as the nineteenth century, but certainly into the seventeenth century. Karl Bottigheimer, adjudicating the debate between Canny and Bradshaw in 1985, argued:

> From the 1590s onwards Rome was actively recovering Ireland, and by the 1640s the die was cast. The opportunities which were lost to 'protestantism' in the first century of the reformation would never be repeated ... There was not supposed to be a clandestine, parallel counter-church in seventeenth-century Ireland. And yet it was ubiquitous and seemingly ineradicable.[17]

As a result, it 'seems ... likely that what chance of success the reformation in Ireland might earlier have possessed had been definitively lost by the 1630s.'[18]

Where Canny saw a smooth transition from the sixteenth to the seventeenth century, the evidence of this book, and subsequent work on the Anglo-Irish, would tend to suggest that the turn of the century marked an important disjuncture, a significant change in the pass of confessional self-awareness and distinctiveness. The shift is perhaps most obvious in the case of the Anglo-Irish protestants – that small group in the later sixteenth century who professed loyalty to the state church. The 'protestant' Anglo-Irish of the sixteenth century were a motley band, ranging from those who were genuinely committed to the reformation to 'time serving neuters'. Thus Rowland White did

15 Clarke, 'Varieties of uniformity', 109.
16 Bradshaw, 'Sword and word', 501.
17 Bottigheimer notes that it is still possible that critical changes occurred earlier: it is just that the evidence at present available seems to be concentrated upon the later period: K.S. Bottigheimer, 'The failure of the reformation in Ireland: *une question bien posée*' in *Journal of Ecclesiastical History*, xxxvi (1985), 198.
18 Ibid., 202.

indeed demonstrate a commitment to protestant theology in some of his writings.[19] But Lucas Dillon may well have been a closet Catholic.[20] Much more
importantly, the criteria for membership of the Church of Ireland altered significantly in the early seventeenth century as it adopted a much more polemical tone towards Catholicism, condemning the pope as Antichrist and pressing
for the enforcement of anti-recusancy legislation. The descendants of many of
the sixteenth-century Anglo-Irish 'protestants' were, in consequence, often
Catholic: in 1594 Thomas Cusack's grandson founded that bastion of the Irish
counter-reformation, the Irish College at Douai.[21] Thomas's great-grandson,
Adam Cusack, died fighting for the Confederate Catholics in 1643.[22] Where
an Anglo-Irish man conformed to protestantism in the seventeenth century,
it required a rejection of much of what the sixteenth-century conformists had
stood for.[23]

   If the decisive period was the late sixteenth and early seventeenth centuries,
and if overarching ideological explanations are only a part of the explanation,
how, then do we approach the question of causation? Two important moves
have been made in recent research. First there is a tendency to try to disag-
gregate the complex interaction between Catholic and protestant churches by
looking separately at the internal history of the Church of Ireland. Second
there is a trend towards focusing upon the basic structural and material problems the church faced to see if these could be used to explain the lack of
progress of the reformation over its first hundred years.

THE INTERNAL PROBLEMS OF THE CHURCH OF IRELAND

The key step in breaking down the task of analysis into more manageable parts,
and considering the Catholic and protestant churches singly, before attempt-
ing to assess their complex interactions, was made by Aidan Clarke in a paper

19 Nicholas Canny (ed.), 'Rowland White's "The dysorders of the Irisshery", 1571'
    in *Studia Hibernica*, xxx (1979), 151, 157.
20 Helen Coburn Walsh, 'Enforcing the Elizabethan settlement: the vicissitudes of
    Hugh Brady, bishop of Meath, 1563–84' in *Irish Historical Studies*, xxvi no. 104
    (1989), 374.
21 John Brady, 'Father Christopher Cusack and the Irish College of Douai, 1594–1624',
    in Sylvester O'Brien (ed.), *Measgra i gcuimhne Mhichíl Uí Chléirigh. Miscellany of
    historical and linguistic studies in honour of Brother Michael Ó Cleirigh, O.F.M. chief
    of the four masters 1643–1943* (Dublin, 1944), 99f.; Hubert Gallwey, 'The Cusack
    family of counties Meath and Dublin' in *The Irish Genealogist*, v (1974–9), 597f.
22 Gallwey, 'The Cusack family', 678.
23 I intend to take this point further in a forthcoming article: 'James Ussher and the
    creation of an Irish protestant identity'.

delivered to the Ecclesiastical History Society in 1987. Clarke offered a theoretical justification for concentrating upon the history of the established church in an effort to discover whether it was possible to find within the internal structures and policies of that church sufficient reasons for its failure. This was an important hermeneutical manoeuvre, since it provided a way out from circular arguments about whether the failure of the reformation was a product of the success of the counter-reformation or *vice versa*.

> The premise of this paper is that the failure of protestantism and the success of Catholicism were the necessary condition, but not the sufficient cause, or each other, and its object is simply to recall attention to the existence of very practical reasons why the Church of Ireland should have evolved as it did ... from an inclusive church, claiming the allegiance of the entire community, to one that excluded all but a privileged minority.[24]

This was followed by a dissection of the difficulties and hurdles faced by the sixteenth century Church of Ireland. First amongst these was the ambiguous legacy of the pre-reformation church. While the Church of Ireland inherited the assets of the pre-reformation church, it also inherited its considerable liabilities: most notably a conservative minded ministry with little interest in reformed protestantism – what Clarke describes as 'ill paid, ignorant, crypto-Catholic curates';[25] extensive lay interference in church affairs; and severely limited, even declining, economic resources. Nor was the state in any position to remedy the deficiencies of the church. Controlling as it did only a part of the island, and dependent upon the goodwill of the local elites, the Dublin government was rarely in a position to use the civil sword as Henry VIII or the Lutheran princes had done, to impose uniformity on the people. The insecurity of the state, together with the weakness of the church, therefore, meant that debates over the strategy to be employed had a somewhat unrealistic air: until the fundamental problems of human and material resources were resolved, whichever policy was chosen could not be put into effect.

Clarke's insistence on the fundamental internal inadequacies of the Church of Ireland was buttressed by Steven Ellis's probing of its economic base. Ellis's discovery of an eighteenth-century printed copy of the *Valor Beneficiorum Ecclesiasticorum in Hibernia* enabled him to show how Irish benefices were generally much poorer than their English counterparts.[26] Even in comparison to

24 Clarke, 'Varieties of uniformity', 105f.
25 Ibid., 113.
26 S.G. Ellis, 'Economic problems of the church: why the reformation failed in Ireland' in *Journal of Ecclesiastical History*, xli (1990), 239–65.

Wales, itself the poor sister of the church in England, Irish benefices were miserably endowed, making it difficult to attract well-qualified clergy, and, in turn, severely limiting efforts to implement a coherent reformation policy.[27]

Ellis's article, with its broad comparative sweep, and its suggestion that the financial problems hold the key to the failure of the Church of Ireland, points the way to important new avenues of research. More work first needs to be done on the sources and reliability of the basic source – the Irish valuation. Even in the case of the English *Valor*, which was compiled throughout the country during 1535, the commissioners, despite detailed instructions, used different computational methods.[28] The scope for disparities in the Irish case was immense, for it was compiled over a period of almost a hundred years, reflecting the slow extension of the power of the established church and the state throughout the island. There are, as a result, a large number of additional variables to be taken into account in analysing the Irish *Valor*, most notably inflation, and the huge variation in the value of Irish benefices both between peacetime and war, and before and after plantation. James Murray's precise analysis of the financial background to the diocese of Dublin, which shows just how complex and variable the sources of income were for Dublin clergy in the sixteenth century, suggests that considerable caution is called for when seeking to use official taxation figures as anything other than a very broad generalisation as to the possible value of a benefice.[29] Equally important, Ellis's work focuses attention upon the complicated relationship between lay land (and advowson) holders and the church, which needs to be explored in some detail from the dissolution of the monasteries to the 1630s, possibly, in view of the voluminous sources, on a diocesan scale.

REFORMATION STRATEGY

Though highly useful, economic determinism does not – and, indeed, is not meant to – provide a complete explanation for the failure of the reformation. Even a small number of committed pastors can, as in the case of the Catholic

27 Ellis, 'Economic problems', 251, 257.
28 P.R.N. Carter, 'Royal taxation of the English parish clergy, 1535–58', University of Cambridge, Ph.D thesis, 1994, 27–35.
29 James Murray, 'The sources of clerical income in the Tudor diocese of Dublin, c.1530–1600' in *Archivium Hibernicum*, xlvi (1991–2), 139–60. For an example of the way in which official figures in England can mislead the historian about the actual income from a benefice, see comments on S.E. Lehmberg, *The reformation of cathedrals: cathedrals in English society, 1485–1603* (London, 1988), ch. 7 in Patrick Patrick Collinson, Nigel Ramsay and Margaret Sparks (eds.), *A history of Canterbury Cathedral* (Oxford, 1995), 181.

clergy of the early seventeenth century, overcome considerable handicaps to conduct an effective ministry. There is, in fact, an alternative way of looking at the church's policy in the late sixteenth and early seventeenth centuries: that it failed in its missionary enterprise not just because of lack of resources (though this was undoubtedly a problem), but also because of the way in which it used and directed what resources it had. Indeed, this forms one of the major themes of this book. The evidence of the reconstruction of the Church of Ireland in the early seventeenth century suggests that there was a significant increase in the number and quality of clergy serving in the church, most notably in Ulster, without any increase in the appeal of protestantism beyond English and Scots settlers.[30] Similarly an analysis of the episcopate of the Church of Ireland in the early seventeenth century would, I suspect, show a significant improvement in the quality and ability of the episcopal bench, but again, however, without any commensurate improvement in the church's broader appeal.[31] There can be little doubt that there was a decided shift in the church's pastoral policy in the late sixteenth and early seventeenth centuries which was closely linked to the policy of colonization. The plantation of Ulster, and other smaller ventures, provided the established church at last with willing church-goers, and the church adapted its pastorate to accommodate itself to the demands of settlement and the settlers.[32]

This, of course, strengthened the church's cultural exclusiveness. Here William Bedell, the provost of Trinity and Bishop of Kilmore, provides an ideal case study. Rightly praised for his heroic determination to bring the protestant gospel to the Irish people in their own language, Bedell's death and dramatic funeral, though demonstrating the respect he had won from the local population, have tended to obscure rather than epitomise his achievement. For, despite his strenuous efforts to foster the teaching of Irish at Trinity and to create an indigenous ministry in Kilmore, he had limited success. Trinity remained an anglicising bastion, while few of the native Irish in Cavan conformed to the established church. Hence his inclusion in the pantheon of losers in Irish history.[33] Indeed, for Bottigheimer, Bedell, both in his career and in his comments on Irish religious attitudes, provides conclusive evidence of the way in which allegiances had become fixed in early modern Ireland.[34]

30 Below,
31 I am currently preparing an analysis of the episcopate of the Church of Ireland in the early seventeenth century.
32 Below, ch. 7.
33 Aidan Clarke, 'Bishop William Bedell (1571–1642) and the Irish reformation', in C.F. Brady (ed.), *Worsted in the game: losers in Irish history* (Dublin, 1989), 61–72; Alan Ford, 'The reformation in Kilmore to 1641', in Raymond Gillespie (ed.), *Cavan: an Irish county history* (Dublin, 1995), 73–98.
34 Bottigheimer, 'Failure of the Reformation', 200–3.

The importance of the association between the Church of Ireland and plantation was that, while it gave the church a role, it at the same time narrowly prescribed its extent and inclusiveness – it was part of what Clarke has described as a 'process at once of contraction and increasing purposiveness', which can, perhaps, best be described as protestant confessionalisation.[35] Nevertheless, it would be a mistake to view the Church of Ireland as wholly anglicised. There was an interesting tension, never fully resolved until after disestablishment in 1870, between the tendency on the part of some English clergy to view the Irish church as little more than an imperfect imitation of the Church of England, and the determination on the part of other Irish churchmen to uphold its independence. Though there were indeed periodic attempts to align the Church of Ireland more closely with its English sister, it was until 1800 a separate church, with its own distinct jurisdiction and identity. As a result its commitment to anglicization and its association with colonisation have to be viewed in the wider context of its Irish identity.[36]

THEOLOGY AND PRAXIS

Nowhere was the new confessional awareness of the Church of Ireland more evident than in its religious beliefs. During the early seventeenth century the Church of Ireland came of age theologically, effectively ending the confusion and vacillation of the sixteenth century. The defining moment was the passing of the Irish Articles by Convocation in 1615, a remarkable confession, not just in the Irish but also in the broader British context, identifying itself as firmly anti-Roman Catholic, and going considerably beyond the Thirty-Nine Articles in accommodating puritan and Calvinist concerns, most notably doing what Elizabeth and James I resolutely refused to do – enshrining the Lambeth Articles in an official confession. Recent work has shed much new light upon these developments. Mandy Capern has suggested that the received wisdom that James Ussher actually drew up the articles, which is challenged in chap. 8, below, may have been correct.[37] R.G. Asch has traced the way in which the anti-papist theology of the Church of Ireland translated into demands for firmer measures against recusancy.[38] Further work has also been done on the nature

---

35 Clarke, 'Varieties of uniformity', 117.
36 See Alan Ford, 'Dependent or independent: the Church of Ireland and its colonial context, 1536–1647' in *The Seventeenth Century*, x (1995), 163–87.
37 Amanda Capern, ' "Slipperye times and dangerous dayes": James Ussher and the Calvinist reformation of Britain, 1560–1660', University of New South Wales, Ph.D. thesis, 1991, 113.
38 R.G. Asch, 'Antipopery and ecclesiastical policy in early seventeenth century Ireland' in *Archiv für Reformationsgeschichte*, lxxxiii (1992), pp. 258–301.

of the policy of the Church of Ireland and the way in which it accommodated the ecclesiological and theological ideas not just of puritans but even of
Scottish presbyterians.[39]

The way in which the theology of the Church of Ireland contributed to the
failure of the reformation remains, however, a matter of some complexity. The
relationship between any confession of faith and the attitudes and actions of
church members is difficult to unravel and dangerous to generalise about, and
has, accordingly, generally been shunned by scholars, who have dealt either
with theological ideas in abstract or religious practice on the ground. In chapter 8 it is argued that the predestinarian theology of the Church of Ireland,
when misinterpreted and crudely misused, could be used as an *ex post facto*
justification of the church's failure to broaden its support in Ireland, and this
can clearly be seen in the gloomy accounts of preachers such as Hull, Ussher,
Olmstead, and Jerome[40] about the prospects of salvation for the majority of
the Irish population. Two points need to be stressed about this pessimism.
First, it was theologically unacceptable: no one could confidently identify who
was saved and who was not, or when the ungodly might be saved: that was
God's sole and secret prerogative.[41] Second, the sample of Irish clergymen
who have left us with evidence of their views is limited: caution must therefore
be exercised about drawing large conclusions about the mentalities of Irish
churchmen from small samples. As a result, crude formulations such as 'The
predestinarian theology of the Irish church caused its pastoral failure' have to
be avoided.

Where theology was undoubtedly important was in providing an underpinning to protestant anti-Catholicism. The predominant controversial theology of Trinity College Dublin, and the strongly apocalyptic vision of
Catholicism that many Irish churchmen shared, provided them with a binding ideology that created protestant solidarity by demonising Catholics. Here

39 Alan Ford, 'The Church of Ireland 1558–1641: a puritan church?', in Alan Ford,
   James McGuire and Kenneth Milne (eds.), *As by law established. The church of
   Ireland since the reformation* (Dublin, 1995), 52–68; Alan Ford, 'The origins of Irish
   dissent', in Kevin Herlihy (ed.), *The Religion of Irish Dissent*, 1650–1800 (Dublin
   1996), 9–30.
40 Jerome's career has now been filled out in considerably more salacious detail: Ford,
   'A puritan church?', 61; Steve Hindle, 'The shaming of Margaret Knowsley: gos-
   sip, gender and the experience of authority in early modern England' in *Continuity
   and Change*, ix (1994), 391–419.
41 Indeed James Ussher was one of the leading figures in the efforts made by Calvinists
   in England and Ireland to develop the doctrine of atonement in such a way as to
   accommodate some of the instinctive objections to its exclusiveness by means of
   the idea of hypothetical universalism: see S.J. Clausen, 'Calvinism in the Anglican
   hierarchy, 1603–1643: four episcopal examples', Vanderbilt University, Ph.D. thesis, 1989.

the account in Chapters 8 and 9, below, has now to be read in conjunction with Declan Gaffney's acute analysis of religious controversy in early seventeenth-century Dublin.[42]

CONCLUSION: WAYS FORWARD

The obvious and almost inevitable conclusion of any survey of such a complex subject is that much remains to be done. There is a continuing need for investigation of the internal history of the Church of Ireland: considerable scope remains for locally focused studies and diocesan history; while the 1630s, a period passed over lightly in this book, are just beginning to receive the attention they deserve.[43] But consideration of the internal problems of the Church of Ireland in isolation from developments in Irish Catholicism, though convenient for the historian seeking to compartmentalise analysis and make it manageable, is, however, ultimately rather synthetic. We have already noted the way that the internal problems and policies of the Church of Ireland provide a dynamic that does much to explain the church's failure. Clarke is logically correct when he points out that the success of Catholicism is a necessary condition but not a sufficient cause of the failure of protestantism. But the relationship between the two churches cannot be so easily dismissed. Their parallel development during the period 1550–1640, most notably the way in which they created competing structures founded upon separate parochial ministries, racially distinct congregations, and deeply hostile and antithetic theologies, together with the way that they tackled similar problems with dissimilar results, suggests that a comparative analysis of the two churches would shed considerable light not just upon the timing of the process of confessionalisation but also upon the ways in which the separate churches thought about and defined their mission. Given the overlapping diocesan structures, the template for such comparisons is already there: all that it requires is for historians to start crossing confessional boundaries.

Nor need this comparative aspect be confined to Ireland. Though Irish Catholicism was the most international of bodies, the task of placing it in the

---

42 Declan Gaffney, 'The practice of religious controversy in Dublin, 1600–1641', in W.J. Sheils and Diana Wood (eds.), *The churches, Ireland and the Irish* (*Studies in Church History*, xxv, Oxford 1989), 145–58.

43 John McCafferty, 'God bless your free Church of Ireland: Wentworth, Laud, Bramhall and the Irish convocation of 1634', in J.F. Merritt (ed.), *The political world of Thomas Wentworth, Earl of Strafford, 1621–1641* (Cambridge, 1996); Amanda Capern, 'The Caroline church: James Ussher and the Irish dimension' in *Historical Journal*, xxxix (1996), 57–85.

context of the wider European counter-reformation has only just begun.[44] Was Ireland a backward Celtic backwater, as sometimes suggested by hostile English commentators or Catholic reformers seeking to impose new norms, or might it not be more accurately seen as a not untypical European state struggling to come to terms with the Tridentine reforms? This clearly calls for detailed studies of Irish dioceses, their ministry and its effectiveness, against the background of similar pastoral activity in Europe. Similarly, though Irish protestantism was so clearly derived from England, only Ellis has attempted the difficult task of establishing an accurate basis for comparisons about the economic structure and ministry of the Church of Ireland in relation to its English mother. Here too, the comparison can be extended to the wider, and more complicated issue of relative pastoral effectiveness.[45]

In short, the way ahead for the study of the reformation lies in a greater awareness of the interconnections between the two developing confessions in early modern Ireland, looking at the greater organisational cohesion and religious awareness of the both the Catholic and protestant churches, and the way this manifested itself in deeper and firmer religious divisions. In this process, theology and religious practice subtly merged with racial, cultural, and political developments, producing a complicated mixture of identities and loyalties, the power of which was amply demonstrated in 1641.

Finally a word of warning about the dangers of over precise categorisation. The religious division of Ireland into protestant and Catholic is one of those neat dichotomies which, because, like 'sword' and 'word', it offers the prospect of a clear, straightforward and understandable means of labelling and identification, is instantly appealing to both the writers and readers of history. This book enthusiastically contributes to that process: its main purpose is to identify when the Church of Ireland became firmly and consciously protestant, and to outline some of the main implications and attributes of that distinctive religious identity. But both within churches and between churches there existed significant numbers of people whose commitment to the rigorous observance of the requirements and disciplines of one denomination or the other was traversed and limited by ignorance, stubbornness, self-interest, doubt, even scepticism or ecumenism. Though times of crisis, such as the Nine Years War and 1641, leave us with the impression of indelible hatred and strong

---

44 D.M. Downey, 'Culture and diplomacy. The Spanish-Habsburg dimension in the Irish Counter-Reformation movement, *c.*1529–*c.*1629', Cambridge University, Ph.D. thesis, 1994.

45 This is a difficult topic, where rhetoric can obscure reality: see the contrasting views of Christopher Haigh, 'Puritan evangelism in the reign of Elizabeth I' in *English Historical Review*, xcii (1977) and J.S. Craig, 'Reformation, politics and polemics in sixteenth century east Anglian market towns', Cambridge University, Ph.D. thesis, 1992, 4f.

religious commitment, the tale of everyday life in the 1630s demonstrates that, at the level of the local and particular, it was perfectly possible for Catholic and protestant to transcend the sectarian divide an coexist peacefully. Confessionalisation was, I would argue, firmly established in Ireland during the first half of the seventeenth century, but the two communities, though distinct, had perforce to live in the same island, and, beneath the rhetoric of hostility, accommodations had continually to be made.

Durham, 1 July 1996

Preface to first edition

Religious history has in recent years attracted the interest of several historians of early modern Ireland, who have sought to examine the complex problems posed by the reformation and counter-reformation. Though suggestive, their discussion of questions such as the lack of success of the reformation, the survival of Catholicism, and the growth of the counter-reformation, is still far from producing any satisfactory synthesis. The causation, and even the chronology of each of these three major elements in religious history of the sixteenth and seventeenth centuries has not as yet been convincingly explained. Perhaps one of the problems with some of the recent work in this area has been the tendency to tackle large questions which as yet have not received any detailed attention from the writers of historical monographs and theses. For it is clear that much work remains to be done upon the sources in nearly every area of early modern Irish religious history before one can begin to generalize with confidence about the course of the reformation and counter-reformation. This book is an attempt to fill in some of the gaps in our knowledge of the period by examining in some detail just one aspect of the reformation – the creation of a clearly protestant church between 1590 and 1641.

In writing the book I have incurred many debts of gratitude, most notably to my first history teacher, Ronnie Wallace, to Aidan Clarke who first introduced me to Elizabethan Ireland, and to Brendan Bradshaw, who supervised my thesis in Cambridge. That thesis, with some alterations, forms the basis of this book.

Dublin, 1 July 1984

PREFATORY NOTE

Dates are given in the old style, but the year is assumed to start on 1 January.

Spelling has been modernized in quotations, but no changes have been made to the titles of books.

CHAPTER I

Introduction

The reformation in Ireland began, in a formal sense, with the declaration in 1536 by the Irish parliament that Henry VIII was 'the only supreme head in earth of the whole church of Ireland'.[1] However, in a real sense, it did not get under way until the last decade of the sixteenth century, when for the first time a serious attempt was made to lay the basis for a protestant ministry at a parochial level in Ireland. Up to the 1590s and the early seventeenth century when this attempt began to bear fruit, the ideological impact of the reformation throughout Ireland had been minimal, confined at the most to the English officials and settlers, together with a handful of native protestants. It is of course true that even in England the progress of the reformation from the constitutional and legal concerns of Henry VIII, through the liturgical and doctrinal innovations of Edward VI and Elizabeth, to the effective establishment of a doctrinally aware parochial ministry, took a considerable time. But in Ireland the delay between the formal declaration of royal supremacy, and the enforcement of doctrinal uniformity amongst the parochial clergy, was inordinately long. This work is concerned with that final stage, from the 1590s onwards. First, however, the fortunes of the reformation in the previous two generations must be briefly examined, to discover some of the reasons for its failure to make progress during the period prior to the 1590s.

The essential problem which dogged the reformation throughout the sixteenth century and after was inherent in its very inception: it was conceived in England and imposed upon Ireland as an exercise in dynastic politics. The legislation passed by the Reformation parliament in 1536 had little direct relevance to Irish needs or demands, nor did it take into account the various ways in which conditions in Ireland differed from those in England. The Irish church, in the first place, was a far less centralized institution than its English counterpart. In the later mediaeval period a *de facto* division had arisen in the Irish church, between that part which was *inter Hibernicos*, amongst the native Irish, and that which was *inter Anglicos*, based in the Pale and linked to the Anglo-Norman community. Though not, of course, totally discrete, the two churches varied markedly. The Pale church approximated to English norms in its institutions and clergy. The Gaelic church, however, did not conform to this

---

1   *The statutes at large passed in the parliaments held in Ireland*, 3 vols (Dublin 1786), i, 90; 28 Henry VIII, c.2.

model. Institutionally, the Gaelic church relied upon monasteries as much as cathedrals and parishes as the centre of ecclesiastical power. The system of coarbs and erenaghs introduced a unique semi-ecclesiastical, often hereditary element. Amongst the clergy, abuses were common: celibacy was not always observed, as was apparent from the number of hereditary clerical families; secular concerns distracted many of the secular and regular clergy from their pastoral duties; laymen exercised considerable control over church property and patronage. This latter abuse contributed to the general impoverishment of the church in Gaelic Ireland. This church generally had little to do with the Dublin government or the English king: instead, most of the appointments to important benefices were made by the papacy.[2]

The diffusion of authority in the church made the task of spreading the reformation throughout Ireland difficult. A similar weakness in the secular power was equally, if not more damaging to the reformation. In England the system of political and legal control, which extended down from the Privy Council to the localities, enabled the central government to suppress local opposition to the royal supremacy.[3] The state in Ireland, however, was incapable of establishing or maintaining such widespread social control. Throughout large areas of the island the writ of the Dublin government simply did not run: the remote Gaelic provinces of Connacht and more especially Ulster were *terra incognita* for the authorities. Bordering these regions were frontier areas where such power as the Dublin government possessed was exercised through a judicious combination of persuasion and coercion. Obviously, there was little hope of imposing the reformation upon these areas by official *Diktat*. Even in the Pale, where the authority of the government was effective, the central control over local officials was not sufficient to ensure the rigorous enforcement of conformity in a manner similar to a strategically important English county.[4]

The institutional weakness of the church and state in Ireland meant that the Irish educational system also lacked central direction. In England the extensive system of parish and grammar schools, leading up to the universities of Oxford and Cambridge, was officially supervised by the state and the church, thus providing Henry VIII and his bishops with an important means of social control. In Ireland little central direction was exercised over the schools; and the country had no university. The attempt by the reformation parliament in

2 C. Mooney, 'The church in Gaelic Ireland: 13th to 15th centuries', in P.J. Corish (ed.), *A history of Irish Catholicism*, ii (1969), fascicle 5, 1–10; J.A. Watt, *The church and the two nations in mediaeval Ireland* (Cambridge 1970).
3 G.R. Elton, *Policy and police. The enforcement of the reformation in the age of Thomas Cromwell* (Cambridge 1972).
4 D.B. Quinn, 'Anglo-Irish local government, 1485–1534', *Irish Historical Studies*, i (1939), 354f., T.W. Moody, F.X. Martin, F.J. Byrne (eds.), *A new history of Ireland* (Oxford 1976), iii, 1–27.

1537 to establish a system of parochial schools bore little fruit. Provision for education as the sixteenth century progressed came increasingly into Catholic rather than officially approved protestant hands.[5]

Though some of these problems were not unfamiliar in some of the remoter areas of England, the scale and size of the difficulties faced by the reformation in Ireland was far greater than in England.[6] Indeed, such was their extent that progress in many areas during the sixteenth century was simply impossible. Furthermore the reformation in Ireland was faced with an additional challenge peculiar to the island – its ever present racial and cultural divisions. The mere existence of a distinct church *inter Hibernicos*, together with the presence of large numbers of Gaelic speaking parishioners in the Pale dioceses, constituted a major problem for a centrally directed, state sponsored reformation derived from England.

There were marked differences in the way the leaders of the Irish reformation approached this problem in the sixteenth century. Some, anxious to impose the English reformation model as quickly as possible, concentrated their attention upon the Pale, and the largely anglicized church there where the authority of the Dublin government was strongest. The first protestant Archbishop of Dublin, George Browne, from his arrival in 1536, urged that the English model, based upon discipline and civil power, be followed. The royal supremacy and subsequent changes must be imposed by the combined efforts of government and church: disobedience and hostility must be punished. Others, aware of the peculiar problems faced by the church, and looking towards the areas bordering and outside the Pale, took a more cautious approach. Bishop Edward Staples of Meath, more experienced than Browne in Irish conditions, stressed consent above coercion, and argued that Browne's emphasis upon discipline would merely create obedience through fear. Instead he advocated greater emphasis upon education and instruction, with a view to creating genuine popular support and enthusism for the changes.[7]

In any case, for much of the sixteenth century, both the scale of the problems faced by the church, and the practical constraints under which the Dublin

---

5 J. Simon, *Education and society in Tudor England* (Cambridge 1966), part II; T. Corcoran (ed.), *State policy in Irish education A.D. 1536 to 1816* (Dublin 1916), 45; Moody, Martin, Byrne (ed.), *New history of Ireland*, iii, 137f.; B.I. Bradshaw, *The dissolution of the religious orders in Ireland under Henry* (Cambridge 1974), 223–6.

6 Many of the problems encountered by the reformation in Lancashire are also familiar to the Irish religious historian: see C. Haigh, *Reformation and resistance in Tudor Lancashire* (Cambridge 1975).

7 B.I. Bradshaw, *The Irish constitutional revolution of the sixteenth century* (Cambridge 1979), 156f.; *id.*, 'Sword, word and strategy in the reformation in Ireland', *Historical Journal*, xxi (1978), 478f.; id., 'George Browne, first reformation Archbishop of Dublin, 1536–1554', *Journal of Ecclesiastical History*, xxi (1970).

government operated dictated a cautious approach towards spreading the reformation in Ireland. Neither church nor state was in any position to insist upon
conformity throughout the whole island. Instead, the authorities concentrated
upon making real those claims to jurisdiction embodied in the reformation
legislation where it was practicable to do so. Thus the dissolution of the monasteries took place in those areas where the government possessed some influence.[8] Similarly, Sir Anthony St Leger as Lord Deputy 1540–48 was successful
in winning over many Irish bishops to accept the royal supremacy, even in areas
not under direct government control. Like Staples, St Leger was committed
to creating an indigenous reformation through teaching and instruction. Even
during his second deputyship, 1550–51, when he was faced with the task of
putting into effect the liturgical innovations of Edward VI, he sought to use
argument rather than force.[9] Some were, therefore, prepared to adapt the reformation to Irish conditions. In Elizabeth's reign this approach lived on, with
bishops such as Hugh Brady in Meath (1563–84), Nicholas Walsh in Ossory
(1578–85), and John Long in Armagh (1584–8) seeking to create an indigenous
protestant church, preaching and instructing, and building upon the pre-
reformation inheritance.[10]

Though constrained by practical difficulties, the strength of the alternative,
more coercive approach to reformation policy, advocated by such as Archbishop
Browne, ought not to be underestimated. Such a policy gained support amongst
English church leaders and civil officials because of the way in which it was
associated with the assumption that the reformation would go hand in hand
with the anglicization of the Irish inhabitants. In this approach, rather than
changing the nature of the English reformation to suit its Irish context, the
Irish setting was to be transformed to meet English requirements. The classic
example of such thinking was the *Act for the English order, habit and language*,
28 Henry VIII, *c*.15. According to the Act, it was the diversity of language and
customs in Ireland which kept the people so wild and savage. In order to bring
such 'rude and ignorant' people to the knowledge of God and obedience to
their sovereign, they must conform in 'language, tongue, in manners, order
and apparel, with them that be civil people, and do profess and acknowledge
Christ's religion ... as ... the English Pale doth'. In pursuit of this anglicized
ideal, the Act ordered that only those who could speak English were to be
appointed to benefices, though where no such person was available, it allowed
that an Irish speaker could be presented.[11] At the time of its passing, the Act

8 Bradshaw, *Dissolution of the religious orders*, pp. ix, 206.
9 B.I. Bradshaw, 'The Edwardian reformation in Ireland', *Archivium Hibernicum*,
   xxxiv (1976–7), 87–92; Bradshaw, *Irish constitutional revolution*, 245–51; Bradshaw,
   'Sword, word and strategy', 479f.
10 See Bradshaw, 'Sword, word and strategy'.
11 *Statutes passed in Ireland*, i, 119–27.

was little more than a defensive measure, designed to protect the Pale from 'degenerate' Irish influences, and was largely ineffectual in that aim. Nevertheless, subsequently it assumed considerable practical and symbolic significance in the eyes of some civil and ecclesiastical leaders, being seen as the original and definitive statement of the necessary link between anglicization and reformation.[12]

The growing importance of this link can be seen during Edward VI's reign, during the deputyship of Sir James Crofts, 1551–2. Crofts insisted that the conformist bishops accept the liturgical innovations of the Edwardian prayer book: as a result several bishops withdrew from the established church. To fill vacancies in Irish sees, the authorities looked to English clergy, such as Hugh Goodacre and John Bale.[13] In the long term this was to prove an important development. By the simple expedient of importing suitably trained, firmly protestant clergy from England, and giving them the support of the state in enforcing conformity, it was hoped to create a protestant church and people, without the necessity for fostering an indigenous reformation. This implied that the purpose of the reformation in Ireland was not to take over the existing church and slowly transform it into a protestant one, but to create a protestant church *de novo*, not merely on the English model, but actually using English clergy. Naturally, at first such clergy would not be well placed to preach to and proselytize the Irish people, but that hardly mattered, for two reasons. First, they were the vanguard of an anglicizing movement which would, it was assumed, reform and transform Irish society; and second, they could rely upon the civil arm to ensure that people attended their services and sermons. But such ambitions could not be realized in sixteenth century Ireland. Neither church nor state in the sixteenth century were in any position either to enforce conformity throughout Ireland with the help of English preachers, or to spread the gospel to the Irish population with the help of native protestant clergy. The consequent stalemate ensured that the policy debate over how to implement the reformation in Ireland had a certain air of unreality. Both the persuasive and coercive strategists were advocating a policy without having the means to put it into effect.

Towards the end of the sixteenth century, however, there were substantial changes in the balance of forces, both within and outside the established church. Within the established church, efforts were made in the 1590s to reform the ministry, the vital first step towards creating a truly protestant church in

12 See, for instance, the interpretation of the Act in the 1594 Ecclesiastical Commission: C. McNeill (ed.), 'Harris: Collectanea de rebus Hibernicis', *Analecta Hibernica*, vi (1934), 426; or in the papers of Lord Cornwallis: B.L.Add. MS 39,853, fol. 6v.
13 Bradshaw, 'Edwardian reformation', 89f., 93–6.

Ireland. At the same time, it became apparent that the ties, religious, social, cultural and political which bound the Irish people to Catholicism were not just still close, but were in fact growing yet closer. Though this book is concerned with the history of the reform of the established church from the 1590s onwards, it is evident that the latter development was of primary importance in defining the religious context within which the established church would have to operate, and deserves brief consideration.

The nature of religious allegiance and commitment in sixteenth century Ireland is complex and, as yet, not wholly clear. The main difficulty in assessing such matters lies in the diverse and amorphous nature of Catholicism in the early modern period, and the near impossibility of judging the precise extent of popular religious awareness and commitment. The obvious distinction in Irish Catholicism was between survivalist and counter-reformation Catholicism. Even the former, however, was far from being a neatly defined entity. Rather, it differed according to its location. In the remoter, wholly Gaelic areas of Ireland the traditional church and priesthood carried on in its distinctive fashion undisturbed throughout the sixteenth century. In the Anglo-Irish and government controlled areas, though the Catholic faith survived, it was in a more informal and complicated fashion, depending upon three sorts of ministry: regular clergy, particularly observant friars; secular priests, often maintained by prominent families; and crypto-Catholic clergy who held benefices in, and were nominally members of, the established church, but who followed closely the traditional pattern of pre-reformation worship. The second strand of Irish Catholicism was the counter-reformation mission and, later, church. During the latter years of the sixteenth century a number of seminary trained, Tridentine-inspired clergy came to Ireland, seeking to create a clearly defined, doctrinally aware, separate Catholic church which would establish in Ireland counter-reformation norms of morality and discipline. Though their impact can be traced in both Gaelic and Anglo-Irish areas, it was amongst the Anglo-Irish and the urban elite that they wielded the most influence.[14]

---

14 The most important modern works on the diverse nature of Catholicism in the reformation period are: R.D. Edwards, 'Ireland, Elizabeth I and the counter-reformation', in S.T. Bindoff, J. Hurstfield, C.H. Williams (eds.), *Elizabethan government and society* (London 1961); P.J. Corish, 'The origins of Catholic nationalism', in Corish (ed.), *History of Irish Catholicism*, iii (1968), fascicle 8; P.J. Corish, *The Catholic community in the seventeenth and eighteenth centuries* (Dublin 1981); J. Bossy, 'The counter-reformation and the people of Catholic Ireland, 1596–1641', *Historical Studies*, viii (1971); Bradshaw, *Dissolution of the monasteries*, 206–16; A. Clarke, 'Colonial identity in early seventeenth century Ireland', *Historical Studies*, xi (1978); Aidan Clarke, 'Ireland 1534–1660', in J. Lee (ed.), *Irish historiography* (Cork 1981), 42f.; N.P. Canny, *The formation of the Old English elite in Ireland* (Dublin 1975).

The extent to which the people of Ireland were committed to these various types of Catholicism is open to interpretation. It has been argued that, as early as the end of Mary's reign, Catholicism in Ireland was secure, fortified by the official restoration of the religion by Mary, which allowed the counter-reformation to consolidate the work of the survivalist clergy. The anglicizing and aggressive colonial policy followed by subsequent governments further alienated the native population from state and church.[15] On the other hand, it can be claimed that this anticipates considerably the effective impact of the counter-reformation upon Ireland, and that in fact by the end of the century and even later the issue was still far from decided between protestantism and Catholicism.[16]

In speaking of religious commitment, it is clear that there was a large section of the population, especially in rural areas, who can hardly be said to be either protestant or Catholic. In their case it was not religious commitment, but other factors, such as the attitude of their landlord, or social or cultural ties, which bound them to the Catholic church. Yet even with the Anglo-Irish elite of the Pale area who were by the early seventeenth century clearly in the counter-reformation camp, it is difficult to say precisely why or when they abandoned their earlier nominal acceptance of the religious changes of the Henrician reformation. Various chronologies and aetiologies have been suggested.[17] It is sufficient here to note the close interaction between religious and secular causes. Political policies which can broadly be summed up under the heads anglicization and colonization led increasingly to the alienation of the Anglo-Irish in the later sixteenth century as they began to be excluded from office and political influence. At the same time there were significant changes in the pattern of Anglo-Irish higher education, as the Anglo-Irish gentry and merchants sent their sons to the continental Catholic academies, rather than Oxford and Cambridge. This opened up another channel for the spread of Tridentine ideas to Ireland, and was linked to the growth of open recusancy amongst the Anglo-Irish.

By the end of the sixteenth century it was increasingly evident that the established church was in need of a thorough overhaul. Internally, vigorous reform was needed in many areas – church fabric, finances, quality of the ministry – if it was effectively to preach the reformation, and translate the constitutional theory of the reformation legislation into doctrinal and pastoral reality. This task was given added urgency in late Elizabethan Ireland by the

15 Bradshaw, 'Edwardian reformation', 96; Bradshaw, 'Fr Wolfe's description of Limerick City, 1574', *North Munster Antiquarian Journal*, xvii (1975), 50.
16 N.P. Canny, 'Why the reformation failed in Ireland: *Une question mal posée*', *Journal of Ecclesiastical History*, xxx (1979), 431–4.
17 For a useful summary see Canny, 'Why the reformation failed'.

changes in religious and political allegiance amongst the Irish population. Thus, the internal logic of the reformation process, and the ineluctable pressure of external forces, both led the Church of Ireland leaders in the 1590s and early seventeenth century to set about, as a matter of urgency, the task of reforming the established church and transforming it into a genuinely protestant church. It is with this 'second reformation', its birth, implementation, and impact, that this book is concerned.

CHAPTER 2

The native ministry and the reformation

The Church of Ireland towards the end of the sixteenth century was still staffed by native clergy. Time and again in the visitations familiar local native Irish or Anglo-Irish names appear, little different from those that had served in the church in previous generations.[1] Their qualifications and religious outlook also differed little from their forefathers. Few of the clergy had university degrees. Nearly all were reading ministers, who could not preach but simply read the service. Their approach to worship and piety were likewise rooted in tradition. Though the Book of Common Prayer was the prescribed liturgical norm, it was used and misused in careless fashion: sometimes it was simply ignored, sometimes it was read in Latin, often it was freely adapted to accommodate the time-honoured methods of pre-reformation worship with which the people were familiar.[2] Indeed, the links with the pre-reformation Catholic church were close. Both at the start of the Henrician reformation, and again after the death of Mary, the Church of Ireland had perforce to accept those existing benefice holders who were willing even nominally to conform. The problem was that, in the decades after 1558, little progress was made in instructing these semi-Catholic clergy in reformed doctrine, or in replacing them with protestant ministers. Thus, as late as 1587, it was noted in the diocese of Ferns that many of the clergy serving the established church had been ordained according to the Roman rite.[3]

It was obvious by the 1590s that reform was necessary. The major question was, what form would it take? One of the most influential figures in answering this question was Adam Loftus, Archbishop of Dublin. He had come to Ireland as a young cleric early in Elizabeth's reign, being appointed Archbishop of Armagh in 1562, and then translated to the richer and more central see of Dublin in 1567. As Archbishop and, from 1581, Lord Chancellor, Loftus was the effective leader of the Church of Ireland, well placed to direct the

1 Visitations cited below, p. 34, n.17.
2 E. Spenser, *A view of the present state of Ireland* (ed.) W.L. Renwick (Oxford 1970), 87; S.P. 63/144/35 (1588–92, 182f.); S.P. 63/131/64 (1586–8, 428); T. Haynes, 'Certain principal matters concerning the state of Ireland', Armagh Public Library, fol. 11r; N.L.I. MS 1620, p. 8; Canny, 'Why the reformation failed in Ireland', 433f.; R.D. Edwards, *Church and state in Tudor Ireland* (Dublin 1935), 266–8.
3 T.C.D. MS 566, fol. 116r.

reformation along the lines he desired.[4] The lines which he favoured were similar to those mapped out by his predecessor, George Browne: he looked towards the creation of an *Ecclesia Anglicana* in Ireland, committed to a policy of anglicization, and relying upon the secular arm to enforce conformity. In relation to the specific task of reforming the clergy, Loftus shared the general concern of leaders of the protestant reformation with the pastoral capacity of the ministry. The clergy's function was to preach the gospel, teaching their flocks the 'true religion', and guarding against the dangers of heterodoxy or recusancy. Consequent upon this view of the clergy was a greater stress upon the abilities of individual ministers than before the reformation, when the church had tended to stress the sacramental function of the clergy. In England during the reign of Elizabeth, considerable efforts were made by the bishops to improve the standard of the ministry replacing reading ministers by preachers, and seeking to attract university graduates to serve in the church. By the early seventeenth century, the standard of pastoral care, measured in terms of the number of preachers and graduate clergy, had improved markedly in many English dioceses.[5]

When such standards were applied to Ireland, nearly all the clergy of the established church failed to meet them. The view which Loftus and other English prelates in Ireland took of the native ministry was almost universally negative, justified complaints about their incapacity often being subtly married to racial antipathy or distaste at the low social status of Irish ministers. Marmaduke Middleton, Bishop of Waterford 1579–82, reported that the clergy he found in his diocese were 'little better than kern'.[6] Thomas Jones, a close ally of Loftus as Bishop of Meath, dismissed the native clergy whom he found in the dioceses of Cashel and Emly in 1607 as 'fitter to keep hogs than serve in the church'.[7] Even more significantly, Loftus also dismissed the native prelates, even those who were capable exponents of persuasion, because of their lack of protestant zeal. To Nicholas White, an Anglo-Irish protestant, a churchman such as John Garvey, Bishop of Kilmore, appeared an excellent candidate for the vacant see of Armagh in 1589, since White stressed, not

4 H.H.W. Robinson-Hammerstein, 'Erzbischof Adam Loftus und die elisabethanische Reformationspolitik in Irland', Marburg Univ., Dr. Phil Thesis, 1976.

5 D.M. Barratt, 'Conditions of the parish clergy from the reformation to 1660 in the dioceses of Oxford, Worcester and Gloucester', Oxford Univ., D.Phil Thesis, 1950, chaps 2, 3; M.R. O'Day, 'The reformation of the ministry, 1558–1642', in M.R. O'Day, F. Heal (eds.), *Continuity and change. Personnel and administration of the church in England 1500–1642* (Leicester 1976); M.R. O'Day, 'Clerical patronage and recruitment in England during the Elizabethan and early Stuart periods', London Univ., Ph.D. Thesis, 1972, chaps 1, 6.

6 S.P. 63/73/70 (1574–85, 229).

7 S.P. 63/222/111/iii (1606–8, 242).

religious forwardness, but personal abilities and persuasive commitment. According to White, Garvey was 'expert in the language of this country, by which with his own good example of life and conversation he doth edify more than many that be apter for the pulpit'.[8] To Loftus, however, Garvey and other persuasive strategists appeared, because of their distaste for the imme- diate imposition of conformity through forceful means, to be little more than time-serving neuters. According to Loftus, Garvey was 'now very aged ... no preacher, and scarcely well thought of for religion, as one justly suspected to incline to papistry, if he have any religion at all'.[9] The candidate whom Loftus recommended instead of Garvey in 1586 was an English university graduate, Richard Thompson, who was Treasurer of St Patrick's Cathedral in Dublin. The dignities and prebends of that cathedral were used by Loftus in the 1570s and 1580s as a means of supporting protestant English graduate clergy, around whom he sought to build up a reformation movement in Dublin.[10] As a result, in 1597, he could claim that the chapter contained 'as many learned graduates as belong to any one church that I know of in England'.[11]

St Patrick's, however, was merely a microcosm. In the 1590s the task of reforming the ministry in the wider Irish church was begun. Given the unreliability of episcopal leadership in Ireland, reliance was placed instead upon centralized reform, based on two institutions, the Ecclesiastical High Commission, and the Court of Faculties. The former had general responsi- bility for ecclesiastical policy, and the enforcement of conformity among the populace; the latter dealt with abuses in the ministry.[12] Both were closely con- nected with Loftus and his reformation strategy. The Ecclesiastical Commission had always been strongly supported by Loftus, and its reissue in 1594 was at least partly the result of his pressure.[13] The reason for his enthusiasm was the extensive power which the 1594 Commission granted to him and his fellow commissioners to enforce conformity and root out recusancy, thus bypassing unwilling or ineffective bishops. The Commission also had a second area of competence – to reform the established church, by making visitations, inves- tigating lay encroachment upon church lands, seeing that curates received ade- quate stipends, and taking order for the repair of churches.[14] The activity of

8 S.P. 63/141/4 (1588–92, 118).
9 S.P. 63/12/1 (1586–8, 35); Loftus's comment upon Garvey was made three years before White's, when Garvey was a candidate for the see of Ossory.
10 Robinson-Hammerstein, 'Erzbischof Adam Loftus', 195–7, 255–9.
11 J. Strype, *Annals of the reformation and establishment of religion ... during Queen Elizabeth's happy reign*, 4 vols (Oxford 1824), iv, 429f..
12 Robinson-Hammerstein,'Erzbischof Adam Loftus', 98–148 deals comprehensively with the history of these two bodies in Ireland.
13 S.P. 63/157/35 (1588–92, 387).
14 J. Morrin (ed.), *Calendar of the patent and close rolls of chancery in Ireland*, 3 vols

the Commission was placed firmly within the context of anglicization, by
harking back to the 'Act for English order' of Henry VIII as the model for the
reformation in Ireland. Consistent failure to enforce this act was seen as the
cause of the 'great forwardness, perverseness, and dangerous diversity amongst
our people in Ireland, and especially in the clergy'.[15]

The main vehicle for implementing reform among the parochial clergy,
however, was the Court of Faculties, which dealt with appeals from clergy to
hold benefices despite legal disabilities, and also had the power to make
visitations throughout all Irish dioceses. It was not free from criticism: in
the 1570s, when its activities had been extended considerably under the layman Robert Garvey, it had been accused of merely legalizing current abuses,
and granting dispensations for profit without seeking to institute improvements.
Subsequently, however, the Commission for Faculties was granted to Loftus,
whose power in the 1590s was delegated to two English judges, Ambrose Forth
and Justinian Johnson. Though still the subject of criticism, the Court was,
under Loftus's oversight, wielded into an instrument of reform.[16]

Forth and Johnson extended their activities in the 1590s to cover at least 15
dioceses throughout the three southern provinces.[17] Detailed information was
gained about benefices and their incumbents, and the extensive abuses and
irregularities amongst the clergy. The main weapons which the judges possessed were deprivation, and sequestration of fruits. In all, records survive of
114 sentences of deprivation in the early 1590s, usually upon one or more of
three grounds: 'manifest contumacy' – this applied to those who were clearly
unwilling to conform to the established church, such as apostate benefice
holders; pluralism or non-residence; defect of orders.[18] Deprivation was not
necessarily always effective – some ministers retained their livings by paying
for a dispensation, or because no other candidates could be found willing to
serve them. Nevertheless, the efforts of the two judges marked the beginning
of the first serious attempt to reform the ministry of the Church of Ireland,
and did result in changes being made in the parochial ministry.[19] The char-

(Dublin 1861–3), ii, 291–5; McNeill (ed.), 'Harris: Collectanea', 424–8; local commissions were issued for Cork, Cloyne and Ross in 1594, Ardfert and Aghadoe in
1595, and the provinces of Connacht and Thomond in 1597: *Report of the Deputy
Keeper of the public records in Ireland*, xvi (1884), 250, 264f. ibid, xvii (1885), 53.

15 Morrin, *Patent rolls*, ii, 293; McNeill (ed.), 'Harris: Collectanea', 426.
16 Robinson-Hammerstein, 'Erzbischof Adam Loftus', 114–25, 136–9; T.C.D. MS
    566, fol. 194r; S.P. 63/168/18 (1592–6, 74).
17 The surviving records of the Court are in T.C.D. MS 566; for details of visitations
    in this manuscript and their dates see, H.J. Lawlor, 'Two collections of visitation
    reports in the library of Trinity College', *Hermathena*, xxxi (1905).
18 T.C.D. MS 566, fols 194r–199r.
19 The impact of the court's activities in the 1590s upon the parochial ministry can

acter of these changes was important: most of the new clergy appointed by the state to vacant benefices were native Irish or Anglo-Irish, but a significant proportion were of English origin.[20] Since the proportion of English ministers amongst the state appointees was much higher than the proportion of such clergy amongst those deprived by the Court of Faculties, the thrust of the reform movement was to replace unsuitable native clergy where possible with English protestant ministers.

Despite the evidence of official determination to tackle the problem of the reform of the ministry, it would nevertheless be a mistake to assume that the activities of the 1590s were wholly the result of Loftus's determination to impose on the Irish church from above his ideal of a protestant preaching ministry. To a far greater extent, the official moves were a response to pressures from below, both within and outside the established church, which could not be ignored, and forced its leaders into action. Within the church, the ministry was simply crumbling away in many areas by the 1590s: progressive impoverishment, the ravages of war and disorder, the dilapidated churches, and, above all, the demise of the final generation of conformist Marian clergy, all meant that the ministry of the Church of Ireland was no longer in a position to fulfil even its limited function of serving the traditional religious needs of the people. The visitations of the late 1580s and early 1590s, and the records of the Court of Faculties, with their consistent account of irregularities, abuses, vacant benefices, lay incumbents, ill-educated and crypto-Catholic clergy, bore witness to the extent of the crisis, and the urgent necessity for official action.

be seen from the record of clergy appointed to benefices by the state by means of letters patent. After a peak of 125 in the decade following Elizabeth's accession, the decennial figures for such appointments are as follows:

Years		Presentations
1570–9	–	6
1580–9	–	3
1590–9	–	44

Not all the presentations by letters patent are the direct result of the Judges' actions. Presentation fell to the Lord Deputy in several ways: (i) when the crown still possessed the advowson; (ii) through lapse; (iii) when the see was vacant; (iv) through deprivation of the incumbent. Only in the case of deprivation would the Judges' actions directly result in the filling of a living by letters patent. But the correlation between presentations and the Court's activities is such as to suggest that the information about lapsed and vacant benefices discovered by Forth and Johnson provided the Lord Deputy with more accurate information about livings which were in his presentation. Sources: Morrin, *Patent rolls*, i, ii; R. Lascelles, *Liber munerum publicorum Hiberniae* 2 vols (London 1824), ii, pt 5, 97 ff.

20 John Allbright, Anthony Sharpe, Thomas Tedder, William Whitrede, John Charden, Christopher Hewetson, Robert Grave, Luke Challoner, Meredith Hanmer (Welsh).

The greatest pressure for change in the ministry of the Church of Ireland came, however, not from inside, but outside the established church, from the other side of the religious divide. As survivalist Catholicism was reinforced by the new wave of seminarist clergy and missionaries in the later sixteenth century, a distinct and separate Catholic church structure emerged, parallel to, and in direct competition with the established church. The impact upon the ministry of the Church of Ireland was particularly severe in three respects. Firstly, its conservative-minded clergy were made superfluous. From the protestant point of view, the native clergy were insufficiently committed to the reformation; from the counter-reformation point of view, they were equally unsatisfactory, little better than church papists. Secondly, religiously committed local ordinands were increasingly attracted to the Catholic church, at the expense of the established ministry. The latter, as a consequence, was left with those who were motivated more by secular or material motives in their calling – hence the excessive pluralism, poor pastoral care, worldly concerns, and lack of commitment of many native clergy.[21] Finally, as the seminarist clergy established a distinct and separate system of worship, people who had previously attended the Church of Ireland withdrew. This withdrawal, together with the urgings of the Catholic missionaries and their kinsmen, put considerable pressure upon the native clergy to abandon their calling.

Scattered evidence of such withdrawal exists in the Pale dioceses – in Ossory, for example, two clerics were recorded in 1591 as having recently apostatized.[22] But the most striking and dramatic example comes from the church in Munster, in the dioceses of Cork, Cloyne and Ross. During the period 1587–1617 these sees were held by the hard-working and able William Lyon.[23] Though English himself, his clergy were without exception almost all local. Some were native Irish; others were connected with the Anglo Irish and merchant families of Cork and the surrounding areas.[24] Like most native ministers

---

21 On the superior quality of Catholic clergy, see Spenser, *View of the present state of Ireland*, 162; S.P.63/218/53 (1603–6, 476); S.P. 63/219/105 (1603–6, 562).

22 T.C.D. MS 566, fol. 114r.

23 Lyon was born in Cheshire and educated at Oxford. He came to Ireland as chaplain to Lord Grey in the 1570s. He was made Bishop of Ross in 1582, held Cork *in commendam* from 1583, and had the sees of Cork and Cloyne annexed to Ross from 1587; Ware, *Bishops*, 565; A. Wood, *Athenae Oxoniensis* (ed.) P. Bliss, 4 vols (London 1815–20), ii, 859.

24 Two sets of visitations survive for the three dioceses. The earlier set is in T.C.D. MS 566, fols 146r–169v, which is dated 9 Aug. 1591 (fols 146r, 154r, 168r), and was made by the Court of Faculties. The second set was made by Bishop Lyon and is in Bodleian Library, MS Carte 55, fols 580v–586r. They probably date from about a year later than T.C.D. MS 566, since one church is described as vacant for the past year through the deprivation of the incumbent by Dr Forth (fol. 582r).

of the time, none were graduates or preachers.[25] By the 1590s, however, this ministry was in a poor condition. Visitations of his three dioceses by Lyon *c.*1592 revealed the extent to which resources were stretched:[26]

Diocese	Parishes	Clergy	Benefices vacant
Cork	75	25	16 [27]
Cloyne	125	30	55
Ross	26	13	5

The most revealing aspect of this table is the number of vacant benefices.[28] From the beginning of his episcopate, Lyon had encountered difficulties in filling vacancies – the majority of vacant benefices were collative and had remained unfilled since his arrival. However, a significant proportion (26 per cent) of the 76 void benefices had fallen vacant within the past three years, through deprivation by the judge of the Court of Faculties, or the death or resignation of the previous incumbent, thus suggesting that the problem had become more acute by the early 1590s.[29]

Even where benefices possessed ordained incumbents, cures were not always served. Some clergy were non-resident or pluralist; others held their livings only in title, the incomes really being taken up by a layman.[30] However, despite these problems, according to Bishop Lyon the existing ministry had managed to attract local parishioners to established church services. But such conformity as existed disappeared suddenly in the early 1590s. In 1595 Lyon wrote that 'within these two years ... where I have had a thousand or more at church or sermon, I now have not five.'[31]

Three elements contributed to the defection. One was the attempt by Lyon to introduce protestantism into his dioceses, a difficult endeavour, given the inability of his clergy to preach or teach protestant doctrine. He sought to accomplish this through educating the children, and distributing the new testament and prayer book in English and Latin amongst the parochial clergy. Such was the hostility to innovation, however, that the school books were vandalised.[32] A second reason for the popular desertion may have been the impact of the Munster plantation which, paradoxically, may have helped to

25 S.P. 63/183/47 (1592–6, 396).
26 Bodleian Library, MS Carte 55, fols 580v–585r.
27 A further 22 benefices were in the hands of a layman, Dermot Long: ibid., fol. 581v.
28 Since, in some parishes, two livings were endowed, the number of benefices is greater than the number of parishes.
29 Benefices vacated in the past three years: Cork – 8; Cloyne – 9; Ross – 3.
30 Bodleian Library, MS Carte 55, fol. 579r.
31 S.P. 63/183/47 (1592–6, 396).
32 S.P. 63/191/8 & 8/1 (1596–7, 15–17).

strengthen counter-reformation Catholicism in Munster.[33] Though, in the long run, the English settlers in Munster were to form the basis of the protestant church in that province, in the 1580s the religious impact of the early settlement was more ambiguous, apparently helping to stiffen Catholic resistance through the introduction of experienced English recusants.[34] This leads directly to the third element in the popular disaffection, the change in the nature and cohesiveness of Catholicism. Through the plantation, Munster had links with English Catholicism, through trade and education the province was close to the continent, especially to Spain. Such connections help to explain the growth of a separate, Tridentine-inspired Catholic church in Munster during the last decades of the sixteenth century. The parallel with the history of English Catholicism may be quite close here. In England, for a long time after the Act of Uniformity in 1559, little obstinate recusancy was encountered: rather, half-hearted attendance at church was the norm. After the Bull of Excommunication in 1570 however, recusancy increased substantially. Though in its early years the growth of recusancy may have had purely native origins, it undoubtedly gained in strength and resolution as the seminary priests began to arrive in England from Europe in the years after 1574. It was the continentally trained priests who insisted that it was totally wrong for Catholics to attend what was an heretical service, and sought to rule out the kind of compromise made by church papists.[35] In Ireland, a similar transition from half-hearted conformity to active and determined recusancy can also be noted. In the Pale area, Archbishop Loftus in 1590 claimed that the widespread recusancy then prevalent had only developed in the previous six years. Before then, they had, he claimed, been restrained by the Ecclesiastical High Commission 'and – however they were affected inwardly in their consciences – yet outwardly they showed great duty and obedience, in resorting to service, sermons and in receiving the communion.'[36] Loftus may have been slanting the evidence against his enemy Sir John Perrot, by tracing the origins of recusancy to his Lord Deputyship, since evidence of recusancy in the Pale exists for much earlier.[37] In Munster, however, the change from conformity to recusancy can be dated with some precision, from several contemporaries' accounts. As Sir John

33 S.P. 63/183/47 (1592–6, 396); S.P. 63/164/47 (1588–92, 494); B. Rich, 'The anothomy of Irelande' (ed.) E.M. Hinton, *Publications of the Modern Language Association*, IV (1940), 84; *idem*, *A new description of Ireland* (London 1610), 54, 93; 'Suggestions for the government of Ireland', printed in F.M. Jones, *Mountjoy, 1563–1606: the last Elizabethan deputy* (Dublin 1958), 190.
34 On the role of the settlers in the seventeenth century, see below, Chap. 5.
35 F.X. Walker, 'The implementation of the Elizabethan statutes against recusants', London Univ., Ph.D. Thesis, 1961, 13.
36 S.P. 63/154/37 (1588–92, 365).
37 Edwards, *Church and state*, 194f.; 235–40.

Dowdall, governor of the fort of Duncannon in Waterford, summed up, the transition from 'indifference' to recusancy was 'about the year 1593 or a little before'.[38]

The effects of popular recusancy soon became apparent. The priests worked upon the people to withdraw from the protestant church, getting them to swear on oath that they would not attend its services. Local civic officials in Cork, who previously had co-operated with Lyon in enforcing attendance at church on Sundays, now refused such help, and themselves stopped going to church.[39] Most importantly, the native clergy started to abandon their ministry. Such a move was hardly surprising when one examines the leading recusant families in Cork – Tirry, Coppinger, Marshall, Miagh – all names that were represented amongst the clergy serving the Church of Ireland in the late 1580s and 1590s.[40] As Lyon reported in 1595,

> the priests of this country forsake their benefices to become massing priests because they are so well entreated and so much made of amongst the people; many have forsaken their benefices by the persuasion of those seminaries that come from beyond the seas ... [41]

The trend towards recusancy was strengthened considerably by the *de facto* toleration extended to Catholicism in Munster during the Nine Years War, and reached a peak at the end of Elizabeth's reign, when many ministers abandoned the Church of Ireland thinking that the new monarch would legalise the wartime toleration.[42]

By the time James came to the throne, therefore, the indigenous ministry of the established church in Cork, Cloyne and Ross had been effectively destroyed. Of course it may be doubted if, even before the crisis of the 1590s,

38 B.L. Royal MS A lvi, fol. 4v; Sir Henry Brouncker, President of Munster, claimed in 1606 that there had been no recusants there 16 years before: S.P. 63/219/134 (1606–8, 25); a similar claim was made by John Hull, a Cork cleric: *An exposition upon a part of the Lamentations of Jeremy* (London 1618), 293; in Limerick, the first bailiffs to absent themselves from church were those of 1596: N.L.I. MS 16,085, p. 52.

39 S.P. 63/183/47 (1592–6, 396); Bodleian Library, MS Carte 55 fol. 577r.

40 See visitations cited above, p. 36; and W.M. Brady, *Clerical and parochial records of Cork, Cloyne and Ross*, 3 vols (Dublin 1863–4), i, 48, 208, 280, 281, 294; ibid, ii, 144, 387.

41 S.P. 63/183/47 (1592–6, 396); and see also Bodleian Library, MS Carte 55, fol. 577r.

42 Edwards, *Church and state*, 294f.; H. Fitzsimon, *Words of comfort* (ed.) E. Hogan (Dublin 1881), 113; in 1603 Loftus, and his close ally, Bishop Jones, complained of the 'dangerous effects' wrought by the 'former connivency' in Munster: S.P. 63/215/68 (1603–6, 60).

it provided a particularly effective pastorate: but at least it had clergy holding benefices who were able to communicate with their parishioners – this, as shall be demonstrated, was not to be the case in the seventeenth century, however doctrinally committed the ministers then were.[43] With the creation of a separate Catholic church, and the insistence of the seminarists that the people refrained from attending the Church of Ireland, the *raison d'être* of the indigenous ministry was lost. In late 1604 Lyon recounted the state of his dioceses 'overwhelmed with the palpable darkness of idolatry', the 'few incumbents that are' being unable to execute their functions because of the activities of Catholic clergy. Consequently, no marriages, christenings, etc., had been celebrated by any except Catholic priests in the three dioceses for the past 11 years – i.e. since 1593, the year which Dowdall had denoted as the beginning of widespread recusancy in Munster. Furthermore, it was the Catholic priests who took up the tithes – a startling indication of the extent to which the separate Catholic church had taken over the functions of the established church.[44]

The clarity of the divide between the two churches, and the extent of the withdrawal from the established church was not always as marked, or as easily datable as in Cork, Cloyne and Ross. Nevertheless, the implications of the withdrawal applied generally throughout Ireland. As the religious divide between the two churches hardened, the middle ground crumbled. Previously, indigenous clergy could conform to the established church whilst at the same time continuing to worship and conduct their ministry in the traditional, pre-reformation manner. Thanks to the activities of Loftus and the Ecclesiastical High Commission and Court of Faculties, on the one hand, and, even more importantly, because of the growth of a separate Catholic church on the other hand, the indigenous clergy were faced increasingly with an unavoidable choice between a clearly protestant and a clearly Catholic church. Given their lack of enthusiasm for protestantism, and the anglicizing tenor of Loftus's reformation policy, there was a natural tendency for traditionally minded clergy to identify with the Catholic church and their fellow countrymen.

There remains, however, another type of native minister – the Irish cleric who was genuinely committed to protestantism. For, despite Loftus's jaundiced opinion, not all indigenous clergy were time-serving neuters. The interest of these native protestants for the historian lies less in their overall impact – they were for the most part isolated individuals – than in the way in which

43 See below, Chap. 5.
44 S.P. 63/221/35A (1606–8, 131). This is misplaced in the *Calendar*, under 1607. The document can be dated from internal evidence to 1604: firstly, it is evidently a response to the request from the English Privy Council for information about the state of Irish dioceses, made in Jan. 1604 (see below, p. 64); secondly, the reference to plague dates it to the latter part of 1604, since the plague broke out in Cork on 13 Oct. 1604 (N.L.I. MS 16,085, p. 58).

their religious allegiance developed and interacted with their cultural and racial loyalties. In particular, by examining the way their protestantism grew and waned, the inherent contradictions and difficulties of the indigenous reformation can be demonstrated. The defection of the indigenous reading minister was a serious blow to the hopes of the persuasive strategists, but, in the short term, such clergy could hardly have provided the basis for an indigenous *protestant* church. However, if those Irish who were committed protestants did not remain within the established church, then neither the persuasive strategy, nor indigenous protestantism, had much future in Ireland.

In the case of several native-born bishops who served in the west of Ireland in the later sixteenth century, it is possible to show that they were committed protestants, and to trace the generally similar pattern which their careers took, as they attempted to create an indigenous reformation. The remote west seems at first sight inhospitable ground for such an endeavour: it was under loose government control, almost wholly Irish speaking, and largely without protestant, though not without conformist, bishops and clergy. Yet it was the very fact of its isolation, and its consequent unattractiveness for English clergy, which made it necessary to rely upon native talent, and follow a more persuasive policy there. In particular, the state sought in the second half of the sixteenth century to encourage the emergence of a native church through the provision of protestant education for promising or socially important children from the area. Resources did not allow this to be provided *in situ*. Instead those children selected were encouraged to go to England, usually to Cambridge, the more protestant of the two universities.

There were two promising areas for such protestant nurseries in the west in the later sixteenth century: the lordship of Thomond, and the town of Galway. The Lordship of Thomond comprised two dioceses, Killaloe and Kilfenora, both of which in the early decades of Elizabeth's reign had papally provided bishops, recognized perforce by the crown. An established church nominally existed in Thomond – the Archdeacon, John Neylan, had been presented by royal grant. However, he had difficulty securing the fruits of his dignity because of the presence of a papally provided rival.[45] Nevertheless, some members of the Neylan family conformed, and it was one of these who provided a detailed account of the state of the church in Killaloe and Kilfenora, dating from the 1560s.[46] The church was in poor condition, lacking suitable

45 Bodleian Library, MS Carte 55, fol. 589r.
46 Bodleian Library, MS Carte 55, fols 588r–596v. Though undated, the document can be assigned to the 1560s through the references to Terence O'Brien as Bishop of Killaloe (fol. 596v) 1554–69, and Conor O'Mulryan as Dean, who was appointed in 1559, see H. Cotton, *Fasti ecclesiae Hibernicae*, 6 vols (Dublin 1845–78). The only clue as to authorship is the endorsement (fol. 589v), 'A book put by Nelan'.

clergy, and suffering very badly from lay encroachment. Bishop Terence O'Brien of Killaloe led a dissolute life 'of small effect to edify the people'.[47] The Bishop of Kilfenora was at least accounted a 'poor old honest man', but he had no more of his bishopric than the name.[48] Only one other cleric was mentioned, Archdeacon Neylan, who was judged to be 'a grave ... man'.[49] The Treasurership of Killaloe was in the hands of Conor, the third Earl of Thomond, and the two sons of the first Earl held chantorships.[50] As Neylan commented, 'there is no manner of benefice in Thomond from the bishopric to the sextonship but in the hands of lay people, of which fault I cannot excuse either spiritual or temporal.'[51]

Neylan's account of Thomond made it quite clear that great power rested in the hands of the O'Brien dynasty in general, and the Earl of Thomond in particular. Hence, the success of the authorities in procuring the English education and upbringing of Conor's son Donogh was extremely important for the future of Thomond.[52] Whereas Conor had proved an unreliable ally for the crown, going into rebellion in 1570, Donogh, who succeeded as fourth Earl in 1581, remained a staunch supporter of both the crown and protestantism until his death in 1624.[53] Another member of the ruling family, Sir Turlough O'Brien of Ennistymon, the grandson of the second Earl, who was made seneschal of the baronies of Corcomroe and Burren in 1575, was likewise both loyal and protestant.[54] Scattered lay conformity was to little purpose without a satisfactory ministry, however, and here the authorities again looked to the O'Briens, in particular to the O'Briens of Arra. Murtagh, second son of the chief of this sept, was in 1570 entrusted with the revenues of

The Neylan family of Clare was one of the first to conform to the established church, and produced a bishop of Kildare, Daniel Neylan, and several other clergy: B.L. Harleian MS 6842, fol. 103r; Ware, *Bishops*, 392; J. Frost, *The history and topography of the county of Clare* (Dublin 1893), 277; P.R.O.I., Chancery pleadings, Parcel E 136; P. Dwyer, *The diocese of Killaloe from the reformation to the close of the eighteenth century* (Dublin 1878), 99.

47 Bodleian Library, MS Carte 55, fol. 596v.
48 Ibid., fol. 589r.
49 Ibid.
50 Ibid.
51 Ibid.
52 Vicary Gibbs, *Complete peerage*, xii, 702ff.; S.P. 63/58/5/ii; S.P. 63/70/11; *Carew Cal.*, 1575–88, 115.
53 On the O'Brien family see, J. O'Donoghue, *Historical memoirs of the O'Briens* (Dublin 1860); D. O'Brien, *History of the O'Briens from Brian Boroimhe* (London 1949).
54 O'Brien, *History of the O'Briens*, 103f.; S.P. 63/161/52 (1588–92, 449f.) – more fully summarised in Phillips (ed.), *History of the Church of Ireland*, ii, 617–21; Canny, 'Why the reformation failed', 441f.

the see of Killaloe, and allowed to enjoy them whilst a student at Magdalene College, Cambridge.[55] At Cambridge, Murtagh professed protestantism, and was reported to be a satisfactory student of the scriptures. He returned to Ireland, and *c.*1576 was consecrated Bishop of Killaloe 'in view of his learning and loyalty'.[56] Thus, by the 1580s, when Donogh became Earl, both church and state in Thomond were headed by an English educated protestant.

The other western area where an attempt was made to foster a protestant church was Galway city. Here the mainstay of the reformed religion was Francis Martin, a member of one of the city's oldest families. It was he who brought up Galway born Roland Lynch, and instructed him in protestantism. Through the means of the Dublin government, Lynch was trained in divinity at Cambridge, and on his return to Ireland was made bishop of Kilmacduagh, a see which he held from 1587 to 1625.[57] Sir Turlough O'Brien, in a uniquely informative personal analysis of the native church in Thomond and Clanrickard in 1591, described Lynch as 'indeed a right religious man, for sincere profession and private life'.[58] Another Galway man, John Lynch, was made Bishop of Elphin in 1583, and held the see until 1611. He had been educated as a lawyer at Oxford during Mary's reign, and had served first as a friar, and then as Vicar of the College of Galway, a College of eight vicars endowed by the corporation.[59] Such origins and education, together with the complaints made by his successor about the impoverishment of the see, could lead one to categorise him as one of the time-serving native prelates of dubious religious convictions so criticised by Loftus. Yet, if Turlough O'Brien is to be believed, Lynch's conversion was genuine, the result of doctrinal conviction, coming through his reading of Calvin's *Institutes*.[60] A third Galway protestant bishop was Nehemiah Donellan. Like Roland Lynch and Murtagh O'Brien, rather than following the usual Irish trail to Oxford, he received a protestant education at Cambridge, graduating from St Catherine's in 1582.

55 W.B. Steele, 'The sept of the Mac-I-Brien Arra', *Journal of the Cork Historical and Archaeological Society*, 2nd ser., iii (1897), 18; T.C.D. MSS 2770–2774/1041; Ware, *Bishops*, 595; J. Strype, *The life and acts of Archbishop Matthew Parker*, 3 vols (Oxford 1821), iii, 265ff.

56 B.L. Cottonian MS, Titus B XII, fol. 213r; Ware, *Bishops*, 595; S.P. 63/161/52, fol. 117v.

57 P.R.O.I., T.2925; S.P. 63/122/45; Ware, *Bishops*, 643.

58 S.P. 63/161/52, fol. 118v.

59 Wood, *Athenae Oxoniensis*, ii, 850; Ware, *Bishops*, 634.

60 S.P. 63/161/52, fol. 119r. The genuineness of Lynch's commitment is confirmed by Sir Henry Sidney who, whilst on circuit in Connacht in 1583, stayed at Galway and heard Lynch preach, characterizing him as 'a reformed man, a good divine and preacher in three tongues, Irish, English and Latin': *Carew Cal.*, 1575–88, 353.

On his return to Ireland he served first under one of the foremost native bishops, Nicholas Walsh in Ossory, then he was appointed as coadjutor to the Archbishop of Tuam, and finally in 1595 succeeded him as Archbishop.[61] He also prepared a translation of the new testament into Irish, which formed the basis of the edition eventually published in 1602.[62]

Galway's role as a centre for native protestantism is confirmed by contemporary reports. In 1574, according to the Jesuit missionary David Wolfe, 15 young men in the town had accepted the reformed doctrines.[63] Another Catholic source, though not, in this case, first hand, referred to Galway in 1577 as the town 'where dwell the greatest heretics of that realm'.[64] The government naturally sought to encourage this growth in heresy. The endowment of the College of Vicars Choral was supplemented. A government official appointed to serve in Galway was chosen because of his concern with religious reform.[65] In 1586, Sir Richard Bingham, governor of Connacht, reported to Walsingham that the people of Galway were, for the most part, 'very well affected in religion ... and more given to embrace the doctrines of the gospel generally than any people in Ireland'.[66] This verdict was confirmed by Sir Turlough O'Brien, who said in 1591 that Galway had been 'the paradise of Ireland in number and zeal of professors of the gospel'.[67]

Nevertheless, despite these signs of protestant vitality, the strength of survivalist Catholicism, and the difficulties which any indigenous reformation faced in the west, ought not to be underestimated. Mass was still celebrated in the 1570s and 1580s.[68] Bingham recognised the essential problem facing the reformation in Connacht, where there were no protestant educational facilities or parish clergy. He accepted that the chief aim must be to reform the native Irish, 'howbeit, it is a rare thing to find an Irishman meet for that purpose.'[69] Even more importantly, O'Brien's use of the past tense in his reference to Galway must be noted. By the time he was writing, 1591, the conformists in Galway, as in Munster, had defected from the established church, due, he thought, to the efforts of 'certain Romish flatterers', and the remissness of the magistrates.[70]

61 Ware, *Bishops*, 615f.; S.P. 63/161/52, fol. 119v; *Al. Cantab.*
62 See below, p. 107f.
63 *Calendar of state papers relating to English affairs, preserved principally at Rome, in the Vatican archives and library* (London 1916–26) 2 vols, ii, 161.
64 *Calendar of state papers, preserved at Rome*, ii, 337.
65 M.D. O'Sullivan, *Old Galway* (Cambridge 1942), 111.
66 S.P. 63/122/45 (1586–8, 10).
67 S.P. 63/161/52, fol. 119r–v.
68 S.P. 63/38/52; *Cal. Carew.*, 1575–88, 253f.
69 S.P. 63/122/45 (1586–8, 10).
70 S.P. 63/161/52, fol. 119r–v.

It was apparent by the end of the century that the native prelates such as Donellan and the Lynches were not able to counter this withdrawal, or attract any substantial number of new converts to the protestant church. For this generation of native prelates, early protestant zeal and reformist drive were generally soon dissipated by the local difficulties of proselytization. Thus, according to Turlough O'Brien, John Lynch had, after his conversion, set about 'preaching the reformation according to the truth of the gospel'. On being appointed bishop, however, his pastoral zeal waned, and he abandoned his diocese to live in Galway and provide for his wife and children.[71] In the case of Murtagh O'Brien, Bishop of Killaloe, the failure of early promise was soon evident. After his consecration he paid little attention to his spiritual duties, and when he succeeded as chief of the sept on the death of his elder brother, he led a secular life. According to Sir Turlough, Murtagh, as a member of a chiefly family, felt that the office of bishop was below him, and saw it merely as a source of revenue, buying and selling benefices, and behaving 'in all ungodly and indecent manner', eschewing the gospel of Christ.[72]

The consistency of the pattern points to the serious difficulties under which the indigenous reformation laboured in the west. Where even committed, theologically trained prelates failed in their pastoral duties, little could be expected from ordinary reading ministers. Part of the problem was that though the bishops themselves were protestant, they were working in a wholly Catholic environment; not just their fellow countrymen, but their kinsmen and family were often Catholic. Murtagh O'Brien was criticised by Turlough O'Brien for his failure to bring up his children as protestants.[73] In 1615 the wife and family of Bishop Roland Lynch were reported to be all Catholics.[74] Similarly, in 1611, it was reported that the wife and children of Archbishop Magrath of Cashel and Emly refused to accompany him to church.[75] Recusancy was also common amongst the families of the native clergy who continued to serve the Church of Ireland in the early seventeenth century.[76] Familial pressure could be accentuated by the lack of support, or active discouragement, of local lords and chiefs. While the Earl of Clanrickard, an extremely powerful figure in Connacht, was loyal to the government, this allegiance did not extend to reli-

71 Ibid, fol. 119r; Lynch was subsequently severely criticised for alienating the endowments of his see: Ware, *Bishops*, 634; P.R. 277.
72 S.P. 63/161/52, fol. 117v.
73 Ibid.
74 B.L. Add. MS 19,836, fol. 104v.
75 S.P. 63/231/56 (1611–14, 81).
76 Hull, *Lamentations*, 280; B. Rich, *The Irish hubbub* (London 1617), 54; H.M.C., *Report on the manuscripts of the late Reginald Rawdon Hastings*, 4 vols (1928–47), iv, 59; W. Scott, J. Bliss (ed.), *The works of Archbishop Laud*, 7 vols (Oxford 1847–60), vii, 65.

gious matters, as evidenced by Turlough O'Brien's suspicion that Bishop Roland Lynch's lack of courage 'freely to preach the word' sprang from his fear of the 'secret frownings' of the Earl.[77]

The protestantism of the native prelates therefore created an inner tension between religious conviction and familial and racial loyalty. The activities of the Catholic friars and seminary priests on the one hand, and the anglicizing thrust of the Ecclesiastical Commission and Court of Faculties on the other, merely accentuated this dilemma. In the long term, the families and children of the native clergy tended to abandon the established church and commit themselves fully to Catholicism.[78] Hence the Elizabethan bishops were for the most part the last generation of native prelates: at the end of Elizabeth's reign, ten out of the sixteen Irish bishops were either native Irish or Anglo-Irish.[79] In all but one case, however, they were succeeded by either a Scot or an Englishman; by the end of the following reign, only three out of the twenty-three Irish bishops were native born.[80]

Amongst the ordinary reading ministers the change of allegiance was not always as dramatic as it had been in Munster: in the Pale the withdrawal of the native clergy was a much slower process, and a few became protestant;[81] in Connacht, in some of the remoter dioceses, remnants of the traditionally minded ministry survived until the late 1620s.[82] Nevertheless, whatever the vagaries of chronology, the general trend was clear. The character of the ministry was changing, as the older generation of conformist clergy died, and their children turned to Catholicism. For those who advocated an anglicizing reformation, the withdrawal, whilst it posed initial problems of shortage of personnel, in the longer term offered a welcome opportunity to reconstruct

---

77 S.P. 63/161/52, fols 118v–119r.
78 Thus Archbishop Magrath's son became a monk: B.L. Add. MS 19,836, fol. 115r; an exception to this tendency for the second generation to join the Catholic church was the family of Nehemiah Donellan. This case can be seen as demonstrating the importance of education: all his sons went to Trinity College Dublin and subsequently served in the church or the government service. However, even here it should be noted that the youngest son, even though he was ordained a Church of Ireland minister, later became a Catholic in 1641: A.D.
79 They were:

John Crosby	– Ardfert	John Lynch	– Elphin
Nehemiah Donellan	– Tuam	Daniel Neylan	– Kildare
Nicholas Stafford	– Ferns	Miler Magrath	– Cashel
Murtagh O'Brien	– Killaloe	Henry Ussher	– Armagh
Owen O'Connor	– Killala & Achonry	Roland Lynch	– Kilmacduagh

80 They were: William Daniel – Tuam; James Ussher – Armagh; and Roland Lynch – Kilmacduagh.
81 See below, Chap. 5.
82 See below, Chap. 6.

the ministry of the Church of Ireland closer to their model of an English–style, graduate, preaching church. For those who advocated a persuasive, indigenous strategy as the best means of fostering protestantism, the defection of the native clergy destroyed one of the essential elements in their strategy – the reservoir of conformist, Irish speaking, though not protestant, ministers, upon whom the second generation of a doctrinally aware ministry could be built. Consequently, by the end of Elizabeth's reign, the earlier ambivalence over religious policy, within the established church at least, was less in evidence. The trend of official church policy was towards an anglicizing reformation, relying upon coercion and civilly enforced conformity. As yet, this policy had not yet been fully spelt out, since the outbreak of the Nine Years War cut short any efforts to extend the reforms which had been begun. However, in the aftermath of the war, with the Dublin government for the first time being able to claim that it governed the whole island, there appeared to be an ideal opportunity to the leaders of the Irish church of resuming, defining and extending the reform programme.

CHAPTER 3

Reformation policy

In April 1603, as he neared the end of his highly successful term as chief governor of Ireland, Lord Mountjoy wrote to Robert Cecil that the country was 'now made capable of what form the King shall give it'.[1] The new monarch was known to have a particular interest in religious matters, which gave rise to the hope that a coherent reformation policy for Ireland might not only be formulated, but even implemented. Many of the constraints which military and political expediency had placed upon religious policy were removed after the defeat of O'Neill. For the first time the government could claim with some justification that its power extended throughout the whole island; it could therefore begin to think in terms of thorough-going reform backed by the full authority of the state. In the typology which Edmund Spenser had outlined in his *View*, the initial stage of conquest and subjugation had been completed; there remained the secondary process of planting civility, obedience and religion.

The task of planting religion was, however, considerably more complicated after 1603. Previously religious policy had largely been concerned with the heartland of the established church, the Pale and Munster, where the power of the government was strongest. The familiar problems of this region continued to trouble the government and church in the early seventeenth century. However, added to this were the challenges posed by other regions of Ireland, which now, with the extension of government power, came within the church's ambit. In the west the problem of how to spread protestantism in a wholly Gaelic society remained to be tackled. In Ulster, the reformation had made hardly any impact in the sixteenth century. The plantation of the six counties after the flight of O'Neill thus offered the church a chance to work hand in hand with the settlers in planting protestantism, and creating a church *de novo*.

Before examining the progress of the reformation in each of these areas in any detail, however,[2] it is necessary to investigate official policy in relation to two central issues which affected every province and diocese of the established church: the provision of an adequately trained and qualified protestant

1 S.P. 63/215/38 (1603–6, 24). A similar opinion was expressed by another official, Geoffrey Fenton: S.P. 63/217/75 (1603–6, 335).
2 See below, Chaps 5, 6, 7.

ministry;[3] and the strategy which these clergy were to employ in their pastorate – the familiar question of reformation policy. Though within the leadership of the Church of Ireland a consensus was emerging towards the end of the sixteenth century in favour of an anglicizing, coercive strategy, the formulation of religious policy for Ireland did not rest with Loftus or the Irish bishops, but was determined through a decision making hierarchy which, though simple in theory, could be complex in practice. In theory the King made policy, which was expanded and expounded by the English Privy Council and put into effect by the Lord Deputy and the Irish government. In practice, however, matters were somewhat different. James had, firstly, no personal knowledge of Ireland and its problems – he relied upon information supplied by the Irish government and took note of their recommendations about policy. Secondly, he depended heavily upon his advisers in England, both prominent officers of state, such as Robert Cecil, Earl of Salisbury, and courtiers with experience of Ireland, like Lord Mountjoy, the Earl of Devonshire. Thirdly, he was subject to political pressures both in England, and from Ireland, which limited his freedom of action. Finally, the sheer distance at which the Dublin government operated from the central power in England ensured that, in the implementation of policy, the inclinations of officials in the Irish administration could be allowed considerable latitude in 'interpreting' royal commands.

Nevertheless, the personal views of the King remained important, especially in relation to the formulation of religious policy. For on this subject James had firmly held and well reasoned views. Quite early in his reign, in dealing with the contentious religious issues which he had inherited on his succession, James showed that he was committed to a strategy which, in Irish terms, placed him on the side of the persuasive strategists. Thus, whilst he was unwilling to grant toleration to Catholics, at the same time he had no innate desire to enforce severe measures against them. As one contemporary summed up his approach, James sought 'to establish that one and only religion which is here preferred, persecution forborne.'[4] He therefore believed that it was not possible to 'force' consciences, and, when not obscured by political pressures, his fundamental intellectual position remained opposed to the 'hard' reformation strategy.[5]

James's attitude was shared by his two most influential advisers on Irish matters at the start of his reign, Robert Cecil and Lord Mountjoy. Cecil, like his master, emphasised reform of the church and the ministry as the priority,

3 See below, Chap. 4.
4 S.P. Dom. 14/15/26.
5 F.H. Shriver, 'The ecclesiastical policy of James I: two aspects: the puritans (1603–1605) – the Arminians (1611–25)', Cambridge Univ., Ph.D. Thesis, 1968, 110.

rather than the enforcement of severe measures against Catholics.[6] Mountjoy, probably the most influential figure in formulating Irish reformation policy, likewise favoured a moderate, gentle approach.[7] His religious outlook, like that of the indigenous bishops in the sixteenth century, reflected his background. Whilst he was a thoroughly conformist member of the established church, he had been brought up in a Catholic environment, had Catholic friends and relations, and therefore, like the Irish bishops, lacked that aggressively protestant attitude towards Catholicism which Loftus exhibited. As Fynes Moryson, his secretary and companion in Ireland, remarked: 'In his innated temper he was not factious against the papists but was gentle towards them'.[8] Thus·it had not merely been the exigencies of the military and political situation which had led Mountjoy to follow a policy of *de facto* toleration for Catholicism during his time as Lord Deputy. This was proved once the Spanish threat was removed in 1602. With the Nine Years War effectively over, the Dublin government, led by Loftus, assumed that it was finally time to put into effect the coercive measures against Catholics they had been forced to abjure in the 1590s because of the war. Accordingly, during Mountjoy's absence in Connacht, they had proceeded to enforce conformity in Dublin.[9] On his return, Mountjoy angrily reversed the policy. He saw it not merely as impolitic at such a confused time, but as fundamentally misconceived. He told Cecil in January 1603: 'I am of opinion that all religions do grow under persecution. It is truly good doctrine and example that must prevail.'[10] Mountjoy's reformation strategy was most cogently expounded in his 'Suggestions' for reducing Ireland to 'civility and justice'.[11] Composed in the last year of Elizabeth's reign, these represented his blueprint for official policy in the wake of victory over O'Neill. With regard to religion, he saw the crucial issue as being whether consciences could be 'forced'. His belief that they could not gave intellectual, as well as

6 Shriver, 'Ecclesiastical policy of James I', 46f.; J.L. Hurstfield, 'Church and state, 1558–1612: the task of the Cecils', in *Freedom, corruption and government* (London 1973), 97f, 102f.
7 Jones, *Mountjoy*, 168ff.
8 F. Moryson, *An itinerary* (London 1617), ii, 266.
9 Jones, *Mountjoy*, 169f.; Phillips (ed.), *History of the Church of Ireland*, ii, 491f.
10 S.P. 63/212/118 (1601-3, 556); Mountjoy did not, of course, rule out the use of force against those who proved disloyal to the state on account of their religion: McNeill (ed.), 'Harris: Collectanea', 372f.
11 Salisbury MS 139/136, printed Jones, *Mountjoy*, 188–92. I have accepted Jones's attribution of this anonymous document to Mountjoy, ibid, 221f., but it must be noted that the treatise also appears among Francis Bacon's papers, conforms with Bacon's other known views on Ireland, and is printed as part of Bacon's works: J.S. Spedding (ed.), *The letters and life of Francis Bacon*, 7 vols (London 1861–74), iii, 45ff.; see also C. McNeill (ed.), *The Tanner letters* (Dublin 1943), 31.

pragmatic, justification to his plea for the 'absolute necessity' of a provision-
al toleration of religion in Ireland. During this time, persuasive preachers could
be sent over, good bishops provided, care taken to translate the bible and works
of instruction into Irish, and the long process of reforming the abuses in the
Church of Ireland begun. He realised that this would take a long time: it was
all the more essential therefore that, during this period, the authorities should
not risk the people's 'alienation of mind from the government' by instituting
harsh or repressive measures against Catholics. When Mountjoy returned to
England in May 1603 as Lord Lieutenant of Ireland, it meant that the three
leading figures who directed Irish policy in England, the King, Cecil and
Mountjoy, were united in their general approach to reformation strategy.

However, there remained the Irish dimension to the policy making process,
consisting of the secular officials of the Dublin government and the leaders of
the church of Ireland. These too were united in their strategy, but united to
a different strategy. Lord Deputy Sir George Cary (1603–5) and his successor,
Sir Arthur Chichester (1605–15), together with the other leading official, Sir
John Davies (Solicitor-General 1603–6, Attorney-General 1606–9), strongly
supported the demands for the expulsion of Catholic priests and the civil
enforcement of conformity made by the ecclesiastical leaders.[12] The chief
spokesmen for the latter were Archbishop Loftus and his protégé, Thomas
Jones, Bishop of Meath, who, on Loftus's death in 1605, succeeded him as
both Archbishop and Lord Chancellor.[13] Thus, after Mountjoy's departure,
both the ecclesiastical and the secular leaders in Ireland were agreed upon a
religious policy markedly at variance with that favoured on the other side of
the Irish Sea.

Loftus and Jones lost no time in impressing upon the King the need for a
firm religious policy, writing to James in June 1603 to outline their proposals. Though gently phrased, their letter clearly restated their commitment
to coercion as an essential concomitant to their anglicizing reformation. They
urged that preachers be sent from England to make up for the lack of indigenous clergy; then the people could be forced 'by some moderate coactions'
to come to church; if the latter step were not taken, they warned, then 'the
preachers shall but lose their labours (few or none will come to hear them)'.[14]

---

12 Cary had been closely associated with Loftus's abortive campaign to enforce con-
    formity in 1602: see above, p. 50; for Chichester's and Davies's views see below,
    pp. 52, 55, 60.
13 Jones was born in Lancashire *c*.1550, and came to Ireland in the 1570s as a min-
    ister. He married the sister of Loftus's wife, was made Dean of St Patrick's in
    1581, and served as Bishop of Meath 1584–1605: D.N.B.; T.C.D. MS 1065, p. 175.
14 S.P. 63/215/68 (1603–6, 60).

At the same time, they urged that all Catholic priests be expelled, a demand which was supported by members of the Dublin administration.[15]

In March 1604 the two prelates returned to the question of reformation policy. Having the previous January been informed by the English Privy Council of James's conviction that 'true religion is better planted by the word than the sword', Loftus and Jones on this occasion opened with a tactful reference to their distaste for coercion: 'for our parts we neither do wish any violence or extremity to be used'.[16] Their difficulty was that 'knowing the wilfulness of this people, and the induration of their hearts against the true religion', they were unable to see 'how, without some moderate course of coaction, they can be reclaimed from their idolatry to come to hear the glad tidings of the truth'.[17] Both the assumptions which lay behind this approach, and the implications it had for the scope and method of enforcement of the reformation need to be examined in some detail.[18]

The strategy assumed that Irish religion was for the most part a stubborn traditionalism and ignorant superstition, which long experience had shown to be inimical to persuasion. Sir Arthur Chichester, writing to Salisbury in 1611, argued: 'how mild and favourable soever they be dealt withall, I think there is little assurance of their obedience longer than they are kept down by force'.[19] The Munster settler and official, Sir Parr Lane, was equally insistent upon the failure of moderation. In his poem 'News from the holy isle' – highly informative about official attitudes, though written in execrable verse – he warned of the danger of giving the Irish people 'too much heart by giving way'.[20] His recipe for religious policy was to

> Win faith by law, and rather lead than draw,
> And where need is, bestow the lash of law.[21]

Indeed, in Ireland, Lane thought, the state should be prepared to go beyond the law where necessary:

> When some at first did but on Ireland look,
> They swore they should by Littleton and Coke
> Rule without soldiers or their envying swords,
> As if the kern were adders charmed with words.[22]

15 Ibid.; S.P. 63/215/77 (1603–6, 67f.); S.P. 63/215/90 (1603–6, 78).
16 P.R.O. 31/8/199/6 (1603–6, 590); A.P.C., 1601–4, 508; S.P. 63/216/8 (1603–6, 152f.).
17 S.P. 63/216/8 (1603–6, 152f.).
18 The theological and intellectual basis for the policy is examined below, Chap. 8.
19 S.P. 63/231/92 (1611–14, 166).
20 T.C.D. MS 786, fol. 144v.
21 Ibid., fol. 148r.
22 Ibid., fol. 145r.

Persuasion and moderation, however, had in the past been proven useless – ultimately, the sword 'must cut the knot none can untie'.[23]

> Religion must be squared by the word,
> And that must be maintained by the sword.[24]

Parr's preference for compulsion reflected the ingrained response of contemporary magistrates towards rebelliousness or religious contumacy. But the traditional Tudor concern with the role of law and social discipline was in this case combined with an acute sense of the obduracy of the people which reinforced his belief that only compulsion could bring the ordinary people to the established church.

Underpinning such a belief was the conviction that the mass of Irish people were not firmly attached to Catholicism. As the Irish Privy Council claimed in 1606, 'for the most part they are not so affected to matters of religion but that due punishment and coercion of law may in some part reclaim them.'[25] Sir Henry Brouncker, President of Munster, and one of the strongest supporters of coercion, similarly thought that 'the Irish make generally no great conscience of any religion': it was only the example and influence of the social and educational elite which ensured that the people withdrew from the established church. If conformity were rigorously enforced, he argued, many would gladly come to church.[26] In this hierarchical view of religious allegiance, the English officials were groping towards some distinction between conservatism bred of ignorance and stubbornness, on the one hand, and genuine doctrinal commitment, inspired by the counter-reformation, on the other. Davies in particular felt that the upper classes and especially the urban patriciate were firm in their Catholicism, and contrasted this with the lower classes, whom he saw as far more manageable and malleable. A sufficiently firm policy would, he was convinced, succeed in detaching the mass of the people from the recusant leaders, and bring the former to church. Furthermore, the continued conformity of the commonality would, in the long run, put pressure upon the elite to follow suit.[27]

The strategy of Loftus and Jones also assumed a limitation of the scope of the reformation in Ireland, in that official efforts were to be concentrated upon the cities and towns in the anglicized region – in effect the urban areas of the

23 Ibid.
24 Ibid., fol. 168r.
25 S.P. 63/219/145 (1606–8, 41).
26 S.P. 63/219/102A (1603–6, 544); on the authorship of this document, see below, p. 56 n 40.
27 S.P. 63/218/53 (1603–6, 463ff.); and see also S.P. 63/231/82 (1611–14, 153).

Pale and Munster, together, perhaps, with Galway city.[28] Thus, when asking
for preachers from England, Loftus and Jones had specified that they should
be placed in 'the several cities and port towns (which are the fittest places for
them)'.[29] This geographical focus reflected two of the basic assumptions upon
which the coercive strategy rested: that the reformation was inextricably linked
to anglicization; and that it had to be enforced by the state. For it was in the
towns of the Pale and Munster that the population was most anglicized, and
therefore capable of understanding the English preachers; and it was here too
that the power of the Dublin government was traditionally strongest. The concentration upon the towns also arose from the way in which the reformation
was perceived to have spread in other countries, where it had generally relied
heavily upon princely power, and grown from an urban base. Sir Henry
Brouncker, and his friend Parr Lane, who co-operated in implementing the
coercive strategy in Munster, both felt that civility and religion were dissemin-
ated from the towns – 'the flame of true religion breaking out in the towns,
the sparks will fly abroad and kindle a fire in the country'.[30] Such a strategy
conveniently avoided the problems caused by the defection of the native ministers, and their inability to preach protestantism. The rural areas would be
left until later, while the English clergy set about establishing protestantism
in the towns. Brouncker, indeed, was quite explicit about this, admitting that
he ignored the countryside in Munster, because the church had no way of
communicating with the Irish speaking rural inhabitants.[31] Nevertheless, the
urban emphasis had one serious drawback. In the early years of the reformation, it may well have made sense to concentrate upon the towns. But by the
early seventeenth century such a policy merely directed the energies of the
church and state to the very areas where the seminarists and missionaries had
gained their firmest hold – where 'jesuited papistry' was strongest.

Despite such drawbacks, Loftus and the Dublin authorities were united in
urging their proposals on the King. They had, moreover, chosen an oppor-
tune moment to do so. Despite the personal preferences of James and his advisers, there was growing pressure in England for a firmer line against recusancy,
especially following the meeting of parliament in 1604. This was even more
accentuated in the next year, in the hysteria after the discovery of the gunpowder plot.[32] At the same time, the influence of the Earl of Devonshire over

28 See also below, p. 108.
29 S.P. 63/216/8 (1603–6, 153); and see the Irish Privy Council's intention to concentrate its reformation policy upon the 'English Pale and civil counties': S.P.
   63/216/20 (1603–6, 169).
30 S.P. 63/219/102A (1603–6, 543); T.C.D. MS 786, fol. 159v.
31 S.P. 63/219/102A (1603–6, 543).
32 P. Magrath, *Papists and puritans under Elizabeth I* (London 1967), 365–73; A.J.

the conduct of Irish affairs was waning throughout 1605, and was terminated at the end of the year as a result of his irregular marriage to Lady Penelope Rich.[33] Thus Loftus and Jones got what they had demanded. On 5 July 1605 a royal proclamation was issued banishing priests from Ireland, and ordering people to attend service or suffer a 12*d* fine.[34] From October onwards the Dublin government put this into effect.[35] Already in Munster, Brouncker, exploiting the President's considerable freedom of action, had, since August 1604, been enforcing a similar proclamation.[36]

The scene was set for the first major test of the coercive reformation strategy in practice.[37] It soon became clear that the distinction between the elite of recusant leaders and the ordinary people was an accurate one. The former, apart from a few isolated examples, proved steadfast in their recusancy, preferring to go to gaol rather than conform. With the commonality in the towns, however, the government had more success, a considerable number being forced to attend protestant services.[38] Success at this level, however, was hardly a major achievement. As one Irish Jesuit put it: 'It was, indeed, a great feat to compel ignorant people, who were without advice or judgement, to stain their consciences, and then to boast that the poor creatures had done so of their own free will.'[39] There was an obvious danger that such nominal conformity would prove ephemeral, if coercion ceased. The officials in Ireland were acutely aware of this. In the long run, they hoped, even the recalcitrant burghers would be forced to conform, whilst the nominal adherence of the commonality could, with time, be turned into something more permanent. Officials repeatedly stressed in their letters to England that there must be no 'U-turn': Davies emphasised the need for a 'round and constant course'; Fenton and Jones both pleaded that compulsion should not be suspended merely because of Catholic complaints to England; Brouncker despatched Parr Lane to England with a wide-ranging defence of the coercive strategy and its

Loomie, 'Toleration and diplomacy. The religious issue in Anglo-Spanish relations, 1603–1605', *Transactions of the American Philosophical Society*, new ser., liii (1963).

33 Jones, *Mountjoy*, 179f.
34 S.P. 63/217/79 (1603–6, 343); McNeill (ed.), 'Harris: Collectanea', 373ff.
35 S.P. 63/217/67 (1603–6, 325f.); S.P. 63/217/79 (1603–6, 343).
36 B.L. Harleian MS 697, fol. 180v.
37 For a detailed chronological treatment of the enforcement of the penal legislation, see R.D. Edwards, 'The history of the penal laws against Catholics in Ireland from 1534 to ... 1691', London Univ., Ph.D. Thesis, 1933, 427ff.
38 McNeill (ed.), 'Harris: Collectanea', 373–6; S.P. 63/217/85 (1603–6, 354); S.P. 63/218/17 (1603–6, 405); S.P. 63/218/53 (1603–6, 463ff.); S.P. 63/219/135 (1606–8, 25 – not calendared fully); S.P. 63/219/102A (1603–6, 543ff.).
39 H. Fitzsimon, *Words of comfort* (ed.) E. Hogan (Dublin 1881), 154.

assumptions.[40] Behind this pleading, and behind the optimistic reports about the policy's success which officials regularly despatched to England, was the very real fear that support for the policy in England was only lukewarm, a product of circumstance – in particular the fear following the gunpowder plot – rather than conviction.

That doubts did indeed exist in England first became apparent in relation to Munster, where Brouncker's firmness aroused fierce Catholic protests. Twice, first in 1604, and again in 1606, Cecil personally warned Brouncker to be more discreet.[41] Finally in January 1606, the English Privy Council (not without some internal wrangling) gave its Irish counterpart explicit orders to abandon the rigorous enforcement of conformity, a message which was reinforced by new royal instructions in June 1606, and further letters from the English Privy Council to its Irish counterpart and to Brouncker in April 1607.[42] These various letters represented a comprehensive rebuttal of both the assumptions and methods of Loftus's reformation policy, showing the English authorities to be the true heirs of St Leger and Mountjoy. Their central conviction was that to enter upon a 'compulsory course' at the present time would hinder rather than help the reformation. This belief arose both from considerations of expediency, and from deep-seated conviction about the religious situation in Ireland and the nature of religious conversion. The pragmatic reason for a milder policy was quite simple – the fear that the harsh measures against Catholics might cause disaffection and threaten the hard won security of the Dublin government. The English Privy Council were anxious about 'how lately these people have been reduced from a general revolt', and concerned about 'how apt they may be to a relapse'.[43] The fears of the English Privy Council were fuelled by complaints from leaders of the Catholic community about the harshness of the policy, and its disruptive impact upon the social and economic life of the towns, especially in Munster. To the Dublin authorities, this

40 S.P. 63/217/94 (1603–6, 371); S.P. 63/217/78 (1603–6, 338); S.P. 63/217/85 (1603–6, 354); S.P. 63/219/102A (1603–6, 543ff.) – though unattributed this latter document is clearly a product of Brouncker's efforts to put his case to the English Privy Council, being brought to England by Lane in 1606 (see the endorsement on S.P. 63/219/102B). See also S.P. 63/219/145; where Chichester attributes Brouncker's success in Munster to the fact that complaints against him have been given 'a deaf ear' in Dublin and 'referred back again to him'.

41 H.M.C. *Calendar of the manuscripts of the ... Marquis of Salisbury ... preserved at Hatfield House*, xvi, 419f.: though undated the letter is clearly in response to Brouncker's of 23 Aug. 1604: S.P. 63/216/37 (1603–6, 193); S.P. 63/218/21 (1603–6, 412).

42 P.R.O. 31/8/199/36 (1603–6, 390); S.P. 63/240A, fols 204 *et seq.*; P.R.O. 31/8/202/70 (1603–6, 496ff.); P.R.O. 31/8/199/86 (1606–8, 137); P.R.O. 31/8/199/85 (1606–8, 138).

43 P.R.O. 31/8/199/36 (1603–6, 390).

was exaggerated special pleading, but in London more credence was given to Catholic complaints. The contrasting attitudes of Dublin and London can be seen in the treatment of Sir Patrick Barnwall. He had been despatched to England by the Irish authorities as the leader of the recusant opposition for, as they thought, condign punishment. While in London, however, he was treated less as a prisoner and more as a Catholic spokesman and emissary, putting their case against coercion.[44] The concern with putting the Catholic case against coercion remained a major preoccupation with Anglo-Irish writers in the early seventeenth century, who sought to establish two essential facts: that the Irish people of all classes were deeply and inalienably attached to Catholicism; and that their religion was perfectly compatible with political loyalty to the crown, and enforcement of conformity would only serve to alienate them from their sovereign.[45]

Though this latter point was never wholly accepted by James, in practice the Catholic complaints about the harshness of religious policy received a favourable response in England. The strain that such a policy placed upon the machinery of government and law enforcement in Ireland, its alienating effect upon the previously loyal urban leaders, and its economic impact, were not, in the judgement of the King and his advisers, outweighed by the possibility of success in the long term, whatever optimistic reports Irish officials might make. As James later explained, religious policy in Ireland had to be founded upon the principle that it should not occasion 'any disturbance among the people'.[46]

Mere expediency, however, does not sufficiently explain the English rejection of Loftus's and Jones's policy. James also subsequently restated his intellectual commitment to the principle that 'instructio precedat correctionem', and this commitment, which implied a fundamentally different analysis of the religious situation in Ireland, also lay behind the rejection of 1606–7.[47] The preference of the King and English Privy Council for persuasion and gentle means was made quite explicit in their instructions:

> if there be not a care and diligence used to plant knowledge and religion by preaching the word, the authority temporal shall rather harden than

---

44 S.P. 63/219/145 (1606–8, 41); S.P. 63/218/63A (1603–6, 488).
45 See J. Coppinger, *A mnemosynum or memoriall to the afflicted Catholickes in Irelande* (?Bordeaux 1606); D. Rothe, *Analecta sacra*, 3 pts (Cologne 1616–9). On the protestant side, two replies were dedicated to disproving Catholic claims, and defending the policy of enforcing conformity: Parr Lane, T.C.D. MS 786; T. Ryves, *Regiminis Anglicani in Hibernia defensio* (London 1624).
46 P.R.O. 31/8/202/261 (1611–4, 246); and see A.P.C., 1613–4, 159.
47 T.C.D. MS 582, fol. 135r.

attract their hearts to that conformity which is and ought to be so much desired ... [48]

The emphasis the Dublin government placed upon the towns and the anglicized part of Ireland was likewise rejected. Instead, they were urged to:

> take special pains to plant religion where the people have been least civil, because commonly they are the more easily brought to any impression than where already by notorious precedent negligence or contrary opinion is rooted, which time must remove and not sudden violent compulsion.[49]

Rather than concentrating official efforts on enforcing conformity, more attention should be paid to the reform of the church, to equip it with a preaching ministry, capable of bringing the gospel to the people.[50]

   The major difference in the way in which London and Dublin saw the religious situation in Ireland was, fundamentally, about timing and the evaluation of the dynamic of Irish religious commitment. The English Privy Council stressed that 'a main alteration in religion is not suddenly to be obtained by forcing against the current and stream, but by gaining it little by little as opportunities may be taken'.[51] In other words, to the persuasive strategists, time was essential, since their policies could not work overnight. As Sir Francis Bacon succinctly argued in 1616, the crucial question was:

> whether time will make more for the cause of religion in Ireland, and be still more and more propitious; or whether deferring remedies will not make the case more difficult. For if time will give his Majesty the advantage, what needeth precipitation to extreme remedies? But if time will make the case more desperate, then his Majesty cannot begin too soon.[52]

Loftus, Jones, and the officials in Dublin all agreed with the latter proposition – hence the urgency of their requests to implement their preferred reformation strategy. To their eyes, the time within which the persuasive strategy might have worked had run out. Bacon, however, like the King and his advisers, did not agree: 'In my opinion, time will open and facilitate things for reformation of religion there, and not shut up or block the same'.[53]

48 P.R.O. 31/8/199/86 (1606–8, 137).
49 P.R.O. 31/8/199/36 (1603–6, 390).
50 P.R.O. 31/8/199/86 (1606–8, 137).
51 P.R.O. 31/8/199/36 (1603–6, 390).
52 Spedding (ed.), *Letters and life of Bacon*, v, 378f.
53 Ibid., 379.

In the event, then, 1603 did not prove to be the dramatic turning point in religious policy which either Mountjoy or Loftus had hoped. Far from being decisively settled, the debate over religious policy continued along familiar lines, but with a significant change in the protagonists. Now it was no longer a matter of internal debate between different factions of the Church of Ireland, but a conflict between the approaches of church and secular leaders in Dublin, and the King and his advisers in London. The importance of this shift was that, though policy was in theory ultimately decided in England, in practice the government in Dublin had a considerable degree of latitude in the way in which it actually implemented its instructions. At the same time, the Church of Ireland, though it too acknowledged the King as its supreme governor, was nevertheless proud of its independence, and unwilling to accept that its analysis of the religious situation in Ireland could be wrong, even though it conflicted with that of the King and his advisers in England. Moreover, in the eyes of those who had originally initiated the policy of enforced conformity, it had been a success – all that had been lacking was the nerve on the part of the King to implement it over a sufficiently long period for it to take effect. The King's verdict on Brouncker's presidency in July 1607, that he had erred in 'being over quick and harsh in matters of religion', was not accepted in Ireland.[54] Parr Lane wrote his 'News from the holy isle' largely to defend Brouncker's memory from such aspersions.[55] The Dublin authorities, when they investigated the state of Munster after Brouncker's death in June 1607, claimed that the disruption caused by the President's policy had been exaggerated by the Catholic complainants – 'the severity intended was more verbal than actual'.[56] The Dublin government also pointed to the effects of the change in policy as proof of the correctness of their interpretation of the situation in Ireland. Richard Moryson reported that the people of Munster confidently expected toleration, and in September 1607, the earl of Thomond said that priests were flocking back to Munster from England and Europe.[57] The effects of the leniency imposed from England was to undo all the good which the severe measures had achieved. According to the Irish Privy Council, writing in October 1607 about the activities of the newly returned priests, 'They withdraw many from the church that had previously conformed themselves; and others, of whom good hope had been conceived, they have made altogether obstinate'.[58]

Subsequently, people looking back upon the beginning of James's reign would view it as a lost opportunity. Sir Robert Jacob, the Solicitor-General,

54 P.R.O. 31/8/201, pp. 202f. (1606–8, 222).
55 T.C.D. MS 786, fols 140v, 143v.
56 S.P. 63/222/112 (1606–8, 245); S.P. 63/221/87 (1606–8, 198f.).
57 S.P. 63/221/87 (1606–8, 198); S.P. 63/222/125 (1606–8, 258).
58 S.P. 63/222/159 (1606–8, 310).

wrote in 1613: 'When his Majesty first came to the throne they had the whole nation so much under their power, that with the severe execution of the laws they might have wrought the people to what conformity they list.'[59] In the same year, Sir Charles Cornwallis came to Ireland as a commissioner to investigate complaints arising out of the elections for parliament, and he afterwards recorded his opinion that the cause of religion in Ireland had been too much neglected, not just during Elizabeth's reign, but also when James had first come to the throne. In particular, if, after the gunpowder plot, the King had 'taken advantage of the opportunity' and 'executed the extremity of his indignation' upon the Irish Catholics, 'then (before they would have gotten a settled resolution) it would have been a matter of no difficulty to have brought all the recusants to church.'[60] Chichester too remained convinced, even in 1612, that a course of 'severe justice' would win the people to the protestant church. However, he lamented, 'in that course governors here have not been sufficiently supported'.[61]

The conflict between London and Dublin should, in theory, have been resolved by the instructions from the King and Privy Council of 1606–7. Yet, though they paid lip-service to the ideal of persuasion, the Dublin officials and church leaders did not in practice wholeheartedly espouse it. Their conviction that coercion was the correct approach underpinned the religious policy that was actually followed in Ireland, and surfaced, whenever political circumstances were favourable, in demands that London sanction greater severity. Though the Irish authorities had been ordered to suspend the wholesale rigour with which conformity had been enforced in the period 1604–6, they had been allowed a certain degree of latitude by the English Privy Council to maintain a mild form of coercion, lest they should give the impression of a sudden change in policy or a *de facto* toleration for Catholics. This latitude was exploited to continue the campaign against the commonality in the anglicized areas.[62] The Church of Ireland also sought to enforce conformity through the use of excommunication.[63] Furthermore, the latitude of the Dublin government in this respect was greatly increased in 1613 when the King's displeasure was aroused by the behaviour of the recusant party in parliament.[64]

Thus, until the whole policy came under reconsideration in the early 1620s, a cautious *modus vivendi* had been achieved between a formal commitment to

59 Bodleian Library, MS Carte 63, fol. 96r.
60 B.L. Add. MS 39, 853, fol. 9r.
61 S.P. 63/232/22 (1611–4, 268).
62 S.P. 63/232/15 (1611–4, 380).
63 S.P. 63/222/112 (1606–8, 247); S.P. 63/231/72A (1611–4, 109); B.L.Add. MS 34,253, fol. 3r; T.C.D. MS 1066, p. 135; P.R., 471.
64 B.L.Add. MS 4819, fol. 281r; B.L.Add. MS 4763, fol. 168r; S.P. 63/232/7 (1611–4, 482).

persuasion, and a practical reliance upon a modified, less socially disruptive, form of coercion. This could, of course, only be a kind of holding operation, since the King consistently refused to sanction any return to the thorough-going severity of the early part of the reign. The underlying commitment to coercion remained strong however, particularly amongst the church leaders, and surfaced again in the 1620s, when coercion was effectively suspended.[65] Reformation policy during the first two decades of the seventeenth century was therefore rather confused, with neither the persuasive nor the coercive strategies being tested thoroughly and effectively in practice. It is therefore rather difficult to evaluate which of the two approaches was more likely to succeed in furthering the reformation in Ireland. It is always possible, how-ever, that the underlying premise behind this question, that success was indeed possible, was invalid – that the reformation had already failed by the early seventeenth century. As has been noted, this was what Catholic writers were particularly anxious to demonstrate in the first two decades of the century, and what their protestant opponents sought with equal fervour to deny.

Indubitably, both the persuasive and the coercive strategies faced consider-able difficulties. Some of these difficulties were common to both: for each the impoverished state of benefices, extensive lay encroachment, ruined churches, popular hostility, and an ill-qualified ministry were severe handicaps. Others applied more particularly to one strategy. The persuasive approach, on the one hand, failed signally to appreciate the growing strength of Catholicism in Ireland, particularly the process which began in the late sixteenth century, and which led to the creation of a distinct and independent national Catholic church. The appeal of this church to the Irish population, and the with-drawal of the Irish from the established church, was a severe blow for the persuasive strategists. The proposition that time would favour the reformation had been patently disproved by the 1620s, when a comprehensive alternative ecclesiastical structure had been erected by the papacy in Ireland, collecting tithes, performing marriages, and exercising ecclesiastical discipline.[66] The persuasive policy also suffered from the way in which the behaviour of English officials and settlers tended to alienate the native population from what was seen as a new English church and state. It can also be criticized for the ide-alistic view it took of the reformation, conversion, and faith – assuming that preaching and persuasion, rather than coercion and princely power, had originally spread protestantism in Europe. Finally, at the other extreme, the persuasive approach also provided a cloak for those *politiques* who sought to postpone the task of reform indefinitely for fear of its disruptive social and political impact.

65 See below, pp. 205ff.
66 Moody, Martin, Byrne (eds.), *New History of Ireland*, iii, 226f.

On the other hand, the rigorous policy of Loftus and Jones was not without its limitations either. The primary emphasis upon the enforcement of conformity focused attention outwards, upon the Catholic population, rather than inwards, upon the serious abuses within the established church which prevented it from fulfilling its mission in Ireland. Even some of the more enthusiastic lay supporters of the policy recognized this danger: Davies, for instance, criticised Loftus and Jones for their failure to reform their own dioceses.[67] The English Privy Council were naturally even more emphatic on this point, insisting that the Irish prelates direct their energies towards internal reform, as the necessary preparation for a campaign of proselytization.[68] A second difficulty with the rigorous policy was its political and economic impact. Though the degree of disruption caused during 1604–6 was disputed, there can be little doubt that a considerable strain was placed upon the machinery of government, particularly at local level, where the recusant elite still played an important role. Thirdly, the close association between the coercive strategy and anglicization meant that a considerable amount depended upon the speed with which the Irish people could be anglicized, and the extent to which the processes of anglicization and protestantization were indeed indissolubly linked. Finally, if the persuasive strategy took too idealist a view of the nature of conversion and religious faith, equally, the coercive strategists can be accused of taking an excessively reductionist and pragmatic attitude towards the same issues.

The question remains, however, of whether these drawbacks could be overcome, or whether they were sufficiently serious effectively to spancel the protestant reformation. It is not possible to answer this question simply by examining the policy debate between coercive and persuasive strategists. Rather, it is necessary to investigate the condition of the Church of Ireland, the kind of clergy it attracted, and the way in which these clergy approached their pastorate in Ireland.

67 S.P. 63/216/4 (1603–6, 143).
68 P.R.O. 31/8/199/86 (1606–8, 137).

CHAPTER 4

The creation of a protestant ministry

However it was thought the ministers of the church of Ireland should set about the task of spreading the reformation, it was generally agreed between London and Dublin that an essential first step was to ensure that the church had clergy who were well-trained, clearly protestant, and capable of preaching to and teaching the people. The returns of the Court of Faculties had revealed how very far the church was from attaining such an objective, and though an attempt was made to initiate reform in the 1590s, it was cut short by the Nine Years War. The ravages of war further weakened the church, already badly hit by the defection of native clergy in Munster, leaving the ministry at the beginning of the seventeenth century in a parlous state, devoid of preachers, financial support, and even, in many areas, churches.

The need to tackle these problems was recognized in official circles in Ireland at the beginning of James's reign.[1] As Chichester put it, 'it is the clergy itself that hath marred the people ... in which there must be a reformation'.[2] Even more importantly, the extent of the problem was appreciated in England by the King and his advisers. In a sermon preached before James, one of his chaplains lamented the state of the Irish church:

> Divers hold reverend places in that church that are unworthy of the meanest rooms, blind guides, that were never acquainted with the things of God; others like Isachar, a strong ass couching down between two burdens, finding rest good and the land pleasant. So that the fountains of living water ... [are] dried up ... How many churches in that kingdom without either prayer or the reading of the scripture? How many heaps of rubbish where churches stood?[3]

At the Hampton Court conference in 1604 James himself raised the question of how to provide 'fit and able' clergy for the Irish church, the matter being referred to the English Privy Council, which entered into correspondence with

1 S.P. 63/216/4 (1603–6, 143f.); S.P. 63/216/15 (1603–6, 161f.); S.P. 63/216/1 (1603–6, 134); S.P. 63/216/59 (1603–6, 217ff.); S.P. 63/219/76 (1603–6, 510); S.P. 63/222/117 (1606–8, 250).
2 S.P. 63/219/76 (1603–6, 510).
3 J. Hopkins, *A sermon preached before the king's majesty* (London 1604), sig. C5v.

the Dublin government, asking for detailed information about the clergy and their livings in Irish dioceses.[4]

But good intentions proved difficult to translate into actual improvements in the ministry. Two basic difficulties hindered progress: shortage of suitable clergy, especially graduate ministers; and lack of livings capable of supporting such clergy. The history of the reform of the ministry in Ireland is largely the history of the attempt to solve these two problems. For much of James's reign the shortage of preaching clergy persisted. Initially, Loftus and Jones had hoped that it could be surmounted through 'importing' English preachers, and they had asked that one hundred be sent to Ireland.[5] Though, late in 1605, it was reported that the King was sending to Ireland 'the best preachers to advocate protestantism', this was not on the scale envisaged by the Irish bishops.[6] It amounted merely to 'several of their best preachers', probably destined for the province of Ulster.[7] In fact, the plans of the English and Irish Privy Councils of 1604, after the matter was raised at Hampton Court, did not result in any immediate improvement in the ministry – as Sir George Fenton commented in 1607: 'of this little hath ensued'.[8]

The second decade of the seventeenth century therefore began with the same problem. In 1611, Andrew Knox, a Scottish bishop, newly appointed to the see of Raphoe, complained with pardonable exaggeration that there were no more than four preachers in Ireland who had 'knowledge and a care to propagate the evangel'.[9] The Commissioners of 1613 formed a similar impression, remarking on the 'small number, less sufficiency and little residence of ministers', and summarising the problem thus: 'The defect of ministers and preachers grows out of the want of livings wherewith to sustain them, the reason whereof is the multitude of impropriations and want of endowments.'[10]

One difficulty which any reforming efforts faced was the shortage of adequate and accurate information about the livings and clergy of the established church throughout Ireland. Officials in Dublin had long been calling for a general royal visitation of the whole church in order to supply the want, and, in 1615, the King ordered that it be done.[11] This regal visitation only covered

4 W. Barlow, *The summe and substance of the conference ... at Hampton Court* (London 1604), 7, 94f.; P.R.O. 31/8/199/6 (1603–6, 590); A.P.C. 1601–4, 508f.; S.P. 63/216/8 (1603–6, 151ff.); P.R.O. 31/8/199/11 (1603–6, 241f.); S.P. 63/216/20 (1603–6, 168).
5 S.P. 63/216/8 (1603–6, 151f.).
6 *Calendar of state papers and manuscripts relating to English affairs ... in the archives ... of Venice*, 1603–7, 281.
7 Ibid., 300; probably a reference to the clergy Bishop Montgomery brought with him to Ulster: see below, p. 134.
8 S.P. 63/221/8 (1606–8, 88).
9 S.P. 63/231/56 (1611–14, 81).
10 P.R., 399.
11 S.P. 63/216/4 (1603–6, 142f.); S.P. 63/219/76 (1603–6, 510); S.P. 63/221/8 (1606–8,

the three southern ecclesiastical provinces (together with the dioceses of Meath and Ardagh), since there was little point in including the as yet inchoate Ulster church.[12] The three main visitors, Archbishops Jones of Dublin, Hampton of Armagh, and Bishop Montgomery of Meath, confirmed that there was a severe shortage of suitably qualified clergy, speaking of the 'great and general defect of fit and worthy persons to supply the service of the several churches in this kingdom'.[13] The figures for the number of clergy which can be derived from the visitation returns support the judgement of the visitors.[14] In all, 24 dioceses were covered: they were served by 525 clergy – of these 364 were reading ministers, and only 161 preachers. Even allowing for the small size of Irish dioceses, such a ministry was clearly inadequate if the Church of Ireland was to be seen as a national church. 525 clergy were expected to serve almost three times as many parishes; even more seriously, the church possessed only as many preachers as a well-endowed, medium sized contemporary English diocese. It is true that in the Pale and Munster some dioceses had particularly heavy concentrations of preachers – 31 were resident in Meath, for example – but this served only to highlight the paucity in remoter dioceses, or in the whole province of Tuam, where only 11 resident ministers could preach.[15]

The details of the kind of clergy, and their distribution, will be discussed more fully in later chapters. Here, the main concern is with tracing the way in which the supply of clergy developed after 1615, through comparison with, subsequent visitations. The first of these was in 1622, when the Commissioners despatched from England to enquire into the state of Ireland demanded from every bishop a thorough account of his clergy and their livings: the returns constitute, in effect if not in name, another regal visitation.[16] Unfortunately

88); B.L. Cottonian MS, Titus B XII, fol. 186r; P.R.O.I. Acta regia, R.C. 2/5 (1615–25, 74ff.); T.C.D. MS 1066, loose leaves inside front cover; M.V. Ronan (ed.), 'Royal visitation of Dublin, 1615', *Archivium Hibernicum*, viii (1941), 1–5.

12 S.P. 63/233/29 (1615–25, 70); Meath and Ardagh, though in the ecclesiastical province of Armagh, were not in the secular province of Ulster.

13 T.C.D. MS 566, fol. 93v; B.L. Add. MS 19,836, fol. 135r.

14 The original returns of the visitors were destroyed in the bombardment of the Irish Public Record Office. I have relied for the most part on Bishop Reeves's transcription, T.C.D. MS 1066, and a contemporary copy, B.L. Add. MS 19,836. For further details of the sources for the visitation see Note to Table 1, pp. 81f., below; and P.B. Phair, 'Seventeenth century regal visitations', *Analecta Hibernica* xxviii (1979).

15 See Table 1, below, pp. 81f.

16 The only original returns which survive are those for Kildare – N.L.I. MS 8013, ix – and Ossory – Lambeth Palace MS 2013. The fullest of the other surviving sources are two near contemporary copies: T.C.D. MS 550 – all the Ulster returns, apart from Dromore; and Armagh Public Library, 'The returnes of the bishops of Ireland to his Majesties Commissioners in May, June and July 1622' – this

comparison with 1615 is not easy. Firstly, in the case of several dioceses, though the bishops are known to have made returns, these have not survived.[17] Secondly, even where returns exist, comparison with 1615 is sometimes made difficult by the paucity of information given, most particularly by the failure to indicate which clergy were actually resident in the diocese.

A way round the difficulties is possible. In their final report, the Commissioners gave their own total for the number of preachers in Ireland – 380. This is not immediately comparable with the 1615 figure; one first has to subtract the number of preachers recorded as serving in the Ulster dioceses not covered in the previous visitation, *c.*136 in all. When this is done, a figure of 244 preachers is arrived at for the 24 dioceses which were also visited in 1615.[18] Yet even this total may be inaccurate. It is possible that the commissioners simply counted the number of preachers returned for each diocese, and then added up the totals, which would have considerably inflated the number of preachers, through the repeated inclusion of ministers beneficed in more than one diocese. In this case, the figure of 244 could best be compared with the total number of preachers beneficed in the southern dioceses, without regard to pluralists being counted more than once – 229. Such a comparison would suggest that the number of preachers had increased only slightly since 1615 – a perfectly reasonable conclusion, on first sight. However, in the case of those dioceses where comparisons can be made, either of the number of preachers resident, or of the number beneficed, in both 1615 and 1622, it is found that generally there had been a substantial increase in the total of preachers, thus making it seem unlikely that the total overall had remained virtually static.[19] The increase in those dioceses where comparisons can be made is indeed commensurate with an overall growth in the number of preachers from 161 to the figure originally derived from the commissioners report – 244. If the total of 244 is accurate, then a remarkable improvement in the quality of the clergy in the three southern provinces had taken place in

contains not the originals (as Phair, 'Regal visitations, 101, claimed), but copies, occasionally merely summaries, made for Sir James Ware. The original of the Killaloe return was destroyed in the Irish Public Record Office, but a full transcript survives in the usually reliable Dwyer, *Killaloe*, 98ff.

17 Exeter College, Oxford, MS 85, p. 36; the most notable loss is the return for Dublin diocese.

18 Preachers in Ulster dioceses: Kilmore – 16; Raphoe – 17; Clogher – 9; Down and Connor – 28; Armagh – 38; Derry – 24; Dromore – 5. The total might be a slight underestimate, since it is not always clear which clergy were preachers.

19 In Killaloe, the number of resident preachers increased from 5 to 15 in the period 1615–1622; in Meath 31 to 32. In Ardfert, the number of preachers beneficed rose from 2 to 5; in Kildare from 8 to 15; in Tuam from 4 to 8; Ferns from 11 to 18; Ossory from 9 to 12; Clonfert from 1 to 4.

the seven years since the regal visitation – the number of preachers had grown by almost 52 per cent.

Was this rate of growth sustained between 1622 and the second regal visitation of 1633–4? A confident conclusion about the trend 1622–34 is not possible, because of the intractability of the sources.[20] It can tentatively be suggested, however, through comparing the number of clergy beneficed overall (without respect to whether they were resident) in each diocese, that the ministry in Ulster continued to grow, most especially in the eastern dioceses of Down, Connor and Dromore, and in Clogher. In all four dioceses this growth was reflected in a marked increase in the number of preachers. Those southern dioceses where comparison is possible suggest that outside the well endowed Ulster church, growth was less rapid; nor can any conclusion be drawn about the trend in the number of preachers.[21] A more accurate picture of the changes in the ministry of the Church of Ireland in the south can be gained from comparing the two regal visitations. Between 1615 and 1634 the number of beneficed clergy rose by almost 30 per cent, and this was almost certainly linked to a rise in the number of resident clergy.[22] Within the ministry, the balance between preaching and reading ministers changed substantially 1615–34. The rapid rise in the number of preachers 1615–22 ensured that, whereas in 1615 the reading ministers outnumbered the preachers by almost two-to-one, by 1634 there was at least 20 per cent more preachers than reading ministers. There were, therefore, two long term trends: on the one hand, the number of clergy was rising overall; on the other hand, within the ministry, reading ministers were being replaced by preachers. However, the growth in the number of preachers and clergy was not even throughout the church. The number of clergy and preachers grew substantially in the richer northern dioceses. But in the Pale, the two dioceses for which comparison is possible show that there was little growth overall in the number of clergy 1615–34: thus the increase in the number of preachers was almost wholly at the expense of reading ministers. In the settled dioceses of Munster, however, and in the two exceptional western dioceses of Killaloe and Elphin, the size of the ministry overall increased substantially.[23]

What was the relationship between the increase in the number of preachers and the financial resources of the Church of Ireland? Was it the richness of Irish livings which attracted ministers, or was it, on the other hand, more a matter of the Irish church encountering problems in providing for the new

20 See note 1 to Table 2, below, pp. 83f.
21 Table 2.
22 Table 3, below, p. 85. Even with the underestimation of the number of resident clergy, the second column of the 1634 visitation returns in Table 3 shows a slight rise in the number of resident clergy since 1615.
23 See Table 3.

ministers? Certainly in the early years of James's reign the financial restrictions under which the Church of Ireland laboured were considerable. The regal visitation of 1615 showed that a large proportion of the church's resources and income was in the hands of laymen, either illegally, through the sometimes blatant use of force, legally through impropriate rectories and vicarages, or quasi-legally, under 'colour of law', by exploiting the confused state of Irish landholding. The power that was thereby conferred upon the gentry was considerable, since they had in their possession, not merely considerable amounts of church income, but often also substantial powers of patronage. Even the scale of legal impropriation was sufficient severely to reduce the resources available to support preachers. The proportion of impropriate livings in Ireland was far higher than in England, 60 per cent compared to roughly 40 per cent.[24] It varied from province to province: in Dublin over 62 per cent of rectories were impropriate; in Cashel, generally only a half; whilst in Tuam, where the bishops were weak, local lords rapacious, and respect for the Church of Ireland minimal, it increased remarkably, to 94 per cent in Clonfert, and 98 per cent in Elphin, amounting to almost 80 per cent overall in the province.[25] Often such impropriations could deprive parishes not just of their endowed income, but also of their ministers, since many impropriators refused to pay for curates to serve the cure. Thus in Cashel, 25 out of the 60 rectories impropriate had no curate provided by the farmer.[26]

The church had little chance of winning back such legally held impropriations. Indeed, the problem got worse during the reign of James. It is true that the 1622 Commissioners claimed that only 1,289 out of 2,492 parishes in Ireland were impropriate – 51.7 per cent: apparently a drop on the 1615 figure of 60 per cent.[27] However, the fall was only apparent, brought about by the inclusion of the Ulster dioceses, relatively free from the burden of impropriations, in the commissioners' survey. The regal visitation of 1634 confirmed that the scale and the extent of the practice had if anything grown. In those southern dioceses for which details are available, just under 62 per cent of the parishes were impropriate.[28] It was not until the determined efforts of Wentworth and Bramhall in the second half of the 1630s that substantial progress was made in recovering legally held impropriations, by buying out the holders.[29]

24 J.E.C. Hill, *Economic problems of the church. From Archbishop Whitgift to the Long Parliament*, repr. (London 1971), 144f.; and see Table 4, below, p. 88.
25 Table 4.
26 B.L. Add. MS 19,836, fols 51r–54v; T.C.D. MS 1066, pp. 192–9.
27 B.L. Add. MS 4756, fol. 19r.
28 Table 4.
29 E.P. Shirley (ed.), *Papers relating to the Church of Ireland (1631–9)* (London [1874]), 1–24; *Report of her Majesty's commissioners on the revenues and condition of the estab-*

A more promising means of improving ecclesiastical income during the early decades of the century was through the recovery of alienated or illegally detained lands and endowments. The legacy of the sixteenth century in this respect was little short of catastrophic, leaving many Irish seas severely impoverished. The major difficulty was the lack of regulation of ecclesiastical leasing. In England leases of capitular and episcopal lands were limited to 21 years by the statute of 1571, but in Ireland no statutory provision was made until 1635.[30] In the mean time, see endowments declined dramatically. Part of the problem lay in the unrest and strife of the sixteenth century, which left many bishops in severe financial straits. In order to procure current income they leased future profits from their lands, by granting the land in long leases, or even in fee farm, at very low rents, in return for a sizeable entry fine. Native bishops also came under increasing pressure to alienate their lands. Their kinsmen sought favourable leases; similarly they were in no position to resist the importunity of the local chiefs.[31] Finally, the destruction of the ecclesiastical registers and other records in the sixteenth century wars made it extremely troublesome for later bishops to discover precisely which lands belonged to the church, and prove legally their claim to them.[32]

Much effort was devoted during James's reign to trying to repair the damage suffered by the church in previous decades. The first step was a proclamation in 1609 which limited and defined the powers of bishops and other clergy to alienate and lease lands.[33] Though naturally it did not immediately eliminate ill-judges leasing by churchmen, it at least succeeded in laying down standards which could be enforced over the next two decades.[34] The second step was to seek to recover what had been lost. The lead in this was taken by the Ulster bishops, who took advantage of the reallocation of land in the plantation to ensure that previous losses were rectified, and the church generously re-endowed. The fact that the land was escheated to the

lished Church of Ireland (Dublin 1868), Appendices 28, 29, 167; H.F. Kearney, *Strafford in Ireland 1633–41. A study in absolutism* (Manchester 1959), 120–5.

30 *Statutes passed in Ireland*, ii, 92f.
31 S.P. 63/125/11 (1586–8, 99); S.P. 63/161/52; Dwyer, *History of Killaloe*, 131; James Hardiman, *History of the town and county of Galway* Dublin 1820), 242; *Report of the commissioners on revenues of the Church of Ireland*, 166f.; P.R.O. 31/8/200, p. 7 (1608–10, 439f.); B.L. Add. MS 1449, fol. 167r; Phillips (ed.), *History of the Church of Ireland*, ii, 499; K.W. Nicholls (ed.), 'The episcopal rentals of Clonfert and Kilmacduagh', *Analecta Hibernica*, xxvi (1970), 130–4.
32 G. O'Brien (ed.), *Advertisements for Ireland* (Dublin 1923), 53.
33 P.R.O. 31/8/202 (unpaginated) (1608–10, 238f.); B.L. Harleian MS 697, fol. 191r; a bill was prepared for the 1613 parliament to regulate ecclesiastical leases, but it was never passed: S.P. 63/231/72A (1611–14, 108); S.P. 63/232/12 (1611–14, 249).
34 P.R.O. 31/8/200/120 (1611–14, 300f.); P.R.O. 31/8/202/91 (1611–14, 478f.); A.P.C. 1621–3, 389; S.P. 63/237/6 (1615–25, 401f.).

state made the process infinitely simpler, since complicated legal proceedings were thereby avoided: all that was needed was a royal grant. Bishops newly appointed to Ulster sees early in James's reign were regularly granted assistance in any suits they had 'for recovery of rights wrongfully alienated'.[35] James's most important act of generosity to the Ulster church was his grant of the extensive termon lands to the bishops, despite the fact that the prelates were found to have no legal claim to them.[36]

Subsequently, bishops in the southern provinces pressed for similarly favourable treatment. Several prelates sought and obtained commissions to find and return detained property.[37] From 1617 onwards, the letters patent appointing southern bishops regularly included special provisions to help them regain alienated lands.[38] In 1618–9 the efforts reached a head, with the despatch of a petition to England, entrusted to the experienced Bishop Montgomery of Meath, who had been largely responsible for securing such good terms for the Ulster church in the plantation. The petition requested the extension to the rest of the country of the summary methods which had been used to find land for the church at the start of the Ulster plantation. However, though the King was willing to grant commissions for individual sees, legal opinion in England was against the use of summary methods.[39] A comprehensive statement of royal policy in 1620 merely stated that the Irish bishops were to be given all assistance possible in the pursuit of their claims through legal means.[40] Consequently, bishops and clergy had to rely upon the time-consuming, expensive, and often ultimately unsatisfactory legal processes.[41] Again, it was not till the 1630s, when Wentworth ordered that ecclesiastical suits be dealt with at Council Table, and together with Bramhall

35 Bodleian Library, MS Tanner 75, fol. 1v; T.W. Moody, J.G. Simms (eds.), *The bishopric of Derry and the Irish Society of London 1602–1705* (Dublin 1968), 83; P.R., 307; P.R.O.I., Acta regia, R.C. 2/5 (1615–25, 129).
36 S.P. 63/227/122 (1608–10, 280f.); S.P. 63/227/125 (1608–10, 283); S.P. 63/227/133 (1608–10, 292); S.P. 63/227/148 (1608–10, 303); S.P. 63/ 228/69 (1608–10, 415f.); S.P. 63/228/70 (1608–10, 417); B.L. Add. MS 4792, fols 157r–158r; S.P. 63/228/59 (1608–10, 409ff.).
37 A.P.C. 1613–14, 45f.; P.R.O.I., Acta regia, R.C. 5/2 (1615–25, 129f.); P.R., 307, 329.
38 P.R., 329; Bodleian Library, MS Tanner 75, fols 1v–2r.
39 S.P. 63/234/27 (1615–25, 212); S.P. 63/235/1 (1615–25, 235); S.P. 63/235/2 (1615–25, 236).
40 P.R., 470f.; see also, S.P. 63/237/35, fol. 73r–v.
41 See, for example, the long and fruitless struggle of Bishop Lyon to recover the see land of Cloyne, leased by a predecessor for 5 marks *p.a.*: T.C.D. MS 1066, p. 432; S.P. 63/221/82 (1606–8, 196); Bodleian Library, MS Carte 62, fol. 269r; T.O. Ranger, 'The career of Richard Boyle, first earl of Cork, in Ireland, 1588–1643', Oxford Univ., D. Phil. Thesis, 1959, 177ff.

ensured that obstructive secular interests could be overcome, that really substantial progress was made in winning back fraudulently or illegally detained
church possessions.[42]

The recovery of church property, whether impropriations or lands illegally
alienated, was never during the first decades of the century sufficient to
provide for the increase in the number of preachers in the southern provinces.
Only in relation to Ulster can one resort to economic determinism to explain
the rise in the number of preachers: there the benefices were endowed with
considerably more income and lands than in the rest of Ireland, and were
therefore capable of supporting the growth in the number of clergy that
occurred from the second decade of the seventeenth century. Another
important element in the prosperity of the Ulster church was the buoyancy
of clerical income during the first three decades of the century. In the wake
of the depredations of the Nine Years War, the value of church livings had
in many places both in Ulster and the rest of Ireland been severely reduced.[43]
But just as income from benefices, linked as it was with the prosperity of the
land and the economy, through glebe lands, tithes in kind, and other dues,
suffered in times of recession, so it benefited from the years of peace and prosperity which followed the end of the war. This was particularly so in Ulster,
where income from land rose substantially as a result of the plantation, further
swelling the already rich livings in the province.[44] Elsewhere in Ireland, however, the growth in clerical income was uneven, and generally on a smaller
scale. In Meath, the value of livings rose moderately during the period 1604–
34.[45] In Kildare, the increase was larger: during the seven years 1615–22, when
there was a rapid rise in the number of preachers, the value of livings likewise grew, especially in the planted deanery of Killahye.[46] However, such an
increase was not general: in Ossory over the same period, only a slight rise in
value occurred: tantalizingly, the increase in the number of preachers in the
diocese was much less than in Kildare.[47] The correlation between the growth

42 Sheffield City Library, Strafford MSS, vol. 6, p. 204; Kearney. *Strafford*, 126–8;
    Phillips (ed.), *History of the Church of Ireland*, iii, 36–46; and see above, p. 68 n. 29.
43 J. Healy, *History of the diocese of Meath*, 2 vols (Dublin 1908), i, 210–2; see the
    lower values of benefices in Ferns and Leighlin as a result of the Nine Years War:
    T.C.D. MS 1066, pp. 144–55.
44 R.J. Hunter, 'The Ulster plantation in the counties of Armagh and Cavan', M.Litt.
    Thesis, Dublin Univ., 1969, 400ff.
45 S.P. 63/216/20/ii (1603–6, 172–5); B.L. Add. MS 19,836, fols 122r–133v; T.C.D.
    MS 1066, pp. 25–48.
46 B.L.Add. MS 19,836, fols 15r–19v; T.C.D. MS 1066, pp. 25–37; N.L.I. MS
    8013/ix. In Killahye, the value of benefices, where comparison is feasible, increased
    from a total of £217 in 1615 to £344 in 1622.
47 B.L. Add. MS 19,836, fols 33r–39r; T.C.D. MS 1066, pp. 53–73; Lambeth Palace,
    MS 2013.

in the number of preachers and an increase in the value of benefices is supported by the example of the diocese of Elphin, one of the few western dioceses where the ministry improved in both quantity and quality 1615–34.[48]

However, for the most part, in default of significant improvement in the value of livings, the church had to resort to juggling with its existing resources. In practice, this meant the judicious use of pluralism, gathering together several livings, contiguous where possible, in order to support one preacher. Thus in Cork, when in the early seventeenth century Bishop Lyon sought to rebuild his shattered ministry by importing English clergy, he was forced to unite five or six benefices in order to provide them with adequate income.[49] Other bishops followed his example, and most preachers in the three southern dioceses possessed more than one living, some many more. In dioceses where parishes were small, this rationalization could be seen as beneficial; some of the parishes bequeathed to the reformed church from the middle ages were uneconomically small.[50] Nevertheless, in the majority of cases it was justified more by financial necessity than financial prudence or pastoral convenience: hence the large number of examples where preachers held parishes so far apart that they could not possibly serve both. James Ussher, in his return to the 1622 Commissioners as Bishop of Meath, pointed to the conflict between financial necessity and pastoral care:

> If the smallness of the means which cometh to the incumbents be regard-ed, then many of the livings in this diocese are fit to be united to make up a competent means for the minister. But if the spaciousness of the parishes (which are large and consist of ... many inhabitants ...), and the difference of patrons ... [be regarded] I think none of them fit to be united ... [51]

The solution to one problem – how to support preaching clergy – merely created another: pluralism. Hence, paradoxically, whilst the quality of the clergy improved the extent of the parochial pastorate could actually decline, especially in the Pale dioceses where the increase in the number of preachers was at the expense of reading ministers, and was not associated with any over-all rise in the number of clergy.[52]

48 See below, pp. 119f.
49 S.P. 63/221/35A (1606–8, 131).
50 S.A. Millsop, 'The state of the church in the diocese of Down and Connor during the episcopate of Robert Echlin 1613–35', Queen's Univ. Belfast, M.A. Thesis, 1979, 37–41, 6of.
51 U.W., i, App. V, p. cxxv.
52 See Table 3, below, p. 85.

Only in Ulster can it be said that rich livings were sufficiently attractive to encourage preachers to come to Ireland. The generous endowment of the church in the escheated counties set it apart from the remainder of the Irish church in its ability to support an expanding ministry from *c.*1610 to the 1630s. Elsewhere in the country it was less a matter of attracting preachers with the offer of rich livings, than of trying to cope with the increase in the supply of preachers by making existing resources go as far as possible.

In these parts of Ireland, and even to a certain extent in Ulster, the essential motive force behind the increase in the number of preachers and clergy was less economic forces, than the coincidence of demand and supply of trained ministers. At the very time when the Church of Ireland, devoid of indigenous preachers and protestant clergy, was most in need of graduate ministers, the supply of such clergy was expanding notably, both within Ireland, and in Scotland and England. The sole source of protestant graduate clergy within Ireland was Trinity College Dublin, the first Irish university. For the first two decades after its foundation in 1591, however, its contribution to the Irish church was on a small scale, since it was only one struggling College.[53] Consequently, Loftus and those concerned with creating a protestant ministry in Ireland in the early part of the century had to look for suitably qualified clergy from overseas. In effect, this meant the universities of England and Scotland.

As early as 1603–4 Loftus and Jones had sought to solve the manpower shortage in the Irish church by bringing over large numbers of English preachers. However official action on the scale they hoped for was not forthcoming.[54] In fact, instead of an officially organized immigration, the influx of Scottish and English ministers proceeded piecemeal, a product of private and occasionally public enterprise, slow at first, but increasing rapidly in the second and third decades. Some of the earliest arrivals were brought over by English officials serving in Ireland, often as chaplains, and subsequently decided to remain and make their careers in the Irish church.[55] English and Scottish bishops played a major role in attracting their kinfolk and countrymen to seek preferment in their dioceses. The correlation was most notable in relation to Scottish bishops, who, even where Scottish settlement was not heavy, brought with them Scots ministers.[56] By far the most important cause of the influx of English

---

53 On Trinity's contribution see below, pp. 95–7.
54 See above, p. 64.
55 See, for instance the career of Thomas Ram, Bishop of Ferns and Leighlin 1605–34, who initially came to Ireland with the Earl of Essex in 1599: Ware, *Bishops*, 447f.; D.N.B.; or the case of Mathias Holmes, who came to Ireland with Sir Richard Bingham, and remained as a preacher in Dublin and founding fellow of Trinity: see below, p. 161.
56 As in Cashel and Emly in the 1620s: T.C.D. MS 1067, pp. 219–39.

and Scottish clergy after *c.*1610, however, was the policy of plantation. Not just in Ulster, where the links between the settlement and the church were extremely close, but also in other areas, such as Munster and even Leinster, settlers either brought ministers with them, or subsequently encouraged them to emigrate from England or Scotland.[57]

Why, suddenly, was there such a large supply of ministers available, when previously in the sixteenth century, it had proved difficult to get any English or Scots clergy to come to serve in Ireland? The answer lies both in the changing conditions in England and Scotland in the seventeenth century, and in the opportunities which the Irish church offered. One important development in late sixteenth century and early seventeenth century England was the growth in the supply of graduate and university educated clergy. Whilst it would be crass to speak of a surplus of suitably qualified graduate clergy, it is definitely true that preferment in England was more difficult to procure in James's reign than it had been early in Elizabeth's, when bishops were crying out for graduate preachers.[58] Ireland, therefore, offered one of several career options open to those graduate ministers in England who did not find it easy to procure a benefice.[59] Furthermore, it also offered a welcome to those less well qualified clergy, especially reading ministers, who, faced with increasing competition from graduates, found preferment blocked in England.[60] To those who were prepared to look to Ireland, the prospect was made more attractive by the possibility of rapid promotion and, in the case of Ulster, a reasonably valuable living. For, given the shortage of suitably qualified ministers in Ireland, promotion to a dignity or a deanery could come at a much younger age than in England.[61]

This was but one of several aspects of the Irish church which proved attractive to a variety of people from England and Scotland. One basic element in the influx in James's reign, of course, was the peace and prosperity of the island, fully recovered from the ravages of war and strife in the previous reign. Another more particular inducement to serve in Ireland arose from the great urgency of the Irish church's demand for clergy. Just as in England at the beginning of Elizabeth's reign, the severe shortage of ministers had necessitated a lowering of standards for the admission of ordinands, so in Ireland, the sudden

57 See below, Chapters 5, 6.
58 O'Day, 'Reformation of the ministry', 57f.; M.H. Curtis, 'The alienated intellectuals in early Stuart England', *Past & Present*, xxiii (1962), 32ff.; but see also the important revision of Curtis's findings in I. Green, 'Career prospects and clerical conformity in the early Stuart church', ibid., xc (1981), 82ff.
59 Green, 'Career prospects and clerical conformity', 87.
60 O'Day, 'Clerical patronage and recruitment', 158, 259f.; H. Hajzyk, 'The church in Lincolnshire *c.*1595–*c.*1640', Cambridge Univ., Ph.D. Thesis, 1980, 176.
61 Bodleian Library, MS Sancroft 18, p. 11.

demand for clergy in James's reign meant that Irish bishops were in no position to impose rigorous standards either on ordinands, or on ministers who presented themselves for preferment.[62] As Archdeacon Higate of Clogher explained to the 1622 Commissioners, during the rapid expansion of his diocese's ministry over the past decade, three kinds of minister had been admitted: firstly, some were 'grave ancient preachers' with M.A.s; others were younger graduates, also able; but some were 'such as necessity of time did allow ... scarce endowed with a mediocrity of learning'.[63] Traditionally Ireland had been seen as a refuge by 'English runagates', and the lower standards in the church were exploited by clerical malefactors forced to flee from England, and appointed on trust by Irish bishops.[64] One minister was accused of leaving his wife in England, having told her that he was going to France, taking a benefice in the Church of Ireland, and committing bigamy by marrying again.[65] Another English émigré, John Aston, was discovered to be a dabbler in spiritualism.[66] These were not merely isolated examples. As Jones, Hampton and Montgomery put it in their report on the 1615 visitation, because of the great want of 'fit and worthy persons', 'we have been hitherto driven to accept of, and to employ, such as come out of England unto us being admitted unto orders there, whom we have at first taken on trust, but in trial have found many of them very offensive and scandalous.'[67] Or, as a less restrained lay observer put it, Irish ministers 'ought to be no vomited persons out of England'.[68]

Other English and Scottish clergy sought refuge in Ireland, not because they were guilty of some misdemeanour, or had some defect of character, but because they found in Ireland a much more tolerant attitude towards their precisian views. The tolerance which the Irish church extended towards puritan and presbyterian practices was, to a certain extent, the product of its desperate need for clergy, which led bishops to turn a blind eye to the pre-cisian ideals of ministers who were often first rate pastors and preachers. However, it also arose from the markedly Calvinist stance of the Irish church,

---

62 In a great many cases in Ireland, candidates for ordination were admitted to both the diaconate and the priesthood within a few days, rather than with an interval of a year as prescribed in England: see details of ordinations given in T.C.D. MS 1067, *passim*.

63 B.L. Harleian MS 2138, fol. 16v.

64 B. Rich, *The Irish hubbub or, the English hue and crie* (London 1617), 51.

65 N.L.I. MS 643, pp. 112f.; but see also Ryves, *Regiminis Anglicani defensio*, 35f.; the problem persisted in the 1620s: T.C.D. MS 1188.

66 S.P. 63/223/66 (1606–8, 460); S.P. 63/223/68 (1606–8, 461f.); S.P. 63/224/103 (1606–8, 521); S.P. 63/224/110 (1606–8, 537): Aston's employer accused him of being a bigamist and a liar to boot.

67 B.L.Add. MS 19,836, fol. 135v; T.C.D. MS 566, fols 92r, 93v.

68 Huntingdon Library, San Marino, MS 335, fol. 24v.

which had always possessed a puritan wing which had arrived at a satisfactory *modus vivendi* with the Irish bishops, based upon common opposition to and distaste for Roman catholicism.[69] The practical symbol of this tolerance was the lack of ecclesiastical canons, like those of 1604 in England, in the Irish church, which ensured that ministers were not faced with the same necessity of subscribing to the Thirty-Nine Articles or the Prayer Book as they were in England.[70] The results of the liberal attitude towards puritanism were most evident in the Ulster church. As Daniel Neal saw it in his *History of puritans*, since conformist clergy in England were unwilling to emigrate to Ireland to meet the great demand for ministers in the early days of the plantation, 'it fell therefore to the lot of the Scots, and English puritans ... who being persecuted at home, were willing to go anywhere within the King's dominions for the liberty of their consciences'.[71]

Certainly, this is true of the Scots presbyterians, who provided a substantial proportion of the ministers for the rapidly growing ministry in the eastern dioceses of Ulster, and proved to be effective and enthusiastic pastors.[72] This points to the final motive for coming to Ireland which, though difficult to quantify, must also be considered along with the more mundane and materialist reasons – a genuine spiritual call to evangelise in Ireland. For some clergy and writers Ireland was viewed as a mission field, in the same light, say, as the Americas, calling out for preaching and proselytization.[73]

Though their capacity, honesty and motives for coming to Ireland may have varied, the immigrant clergy shared two essential characteristics which had crucial implications for the development of the reformation: they were protestant; and they were not Irish. Their protestantism helped to ensure that by the 1630s the Church of Ireland's ministry was no longer doctrinally ambivalent, as it had been in the sixteenth century. To that extent, therefore, a significant first step had been taken along the road to a doctrinal reformation. Yet, it was possible that this achievement might be at the expense of the essential second step – of bringing the Irish people to accept protestantism. The very foreignness of the preachers carried with it the danger that the ministry, whilst

69 On the origins of puritanism in Ireland, see Robinson-Hammerstein, 'Erzbischof Adam Loftus', 70–92; J.S. Reid, *History of the presbyterian church in Ireland* (ed.) W. Killen, 3 vols (Belfast 1867), i, chap. 1.

70 See the opposition in the lower house of Convocation in 1634 to the imposition of the 1604 canons: T.C.D. MS 1038, fols 112v–117r.

71 D. Neal, *The history of the puritans or protestant non-conformists*, 2nd ed., 2 vols. (London 1754), i, 474.

72 Reid, *History of the presbyterian church*, i, 93ff.; W.D. Baillie, *The Six Mile Water revival of 1625* (Newcastle, Co. Down 1976).

73 G.S., *Sacrae heptades, or seaven problems concerning Antichrist* (s.l. 1625), sig. **4–**4v; S.P. 63/217/67 (1603–6, 326); McNeill (ed.), *Tanner letters*, 74f.

protestant, would be unable to communicate its reformed gospel to the mass of the people. Unless the exhortations of James and the English Privy Council to teach and evangelize the people were enthusiastically carried out, the protestantization of the ministry would have been achieved at the expense of distancing it still further from the people.

To those who viewed the reformation as Jones or Loftus had done, the anglicizing influence of the immigrant protestant preachers was to be welcomed: it was exactly what they had hoped for as part of their reformation strategy. English clergy were to preach in the anglicized areas, in English, and the congregations were to be provided through the enforcement of conformity by the civil authorities. To those who advocated a more persuasive strategy as necessary for the creation of indigenous protestantism, however, it was extremely important that there should be some counterweight to the anglicizing influence of the immigrant clergy, some means of producing native protestant ministers capable of communicating the gospel to their fellow countrymen. The obvious way to achieve a better balance between foreign and native clergy was to train Irish students for the ministry in a native seminary. Thus the foundation of Trinity College in 1591 was seen by Elizabeth as a means of providing education for the uncivil and barbarous Irish youth, so that they could better serve the church and state.[74] James, who generously re-endowed the university, saw its function in a similar light: it should, he thought, attract and educated dedicated native Irish students, who could subsequently be sent out to convert the Irish to protestantism.[75]

Given the context in which Trinity was founded, the fulfilment of these aims was difficult. Rather than itself shaping Irish educational development, the new university, when it was finally established, was to a large extent a belated reaction to the already changing pattern of Irish higher education. During the second half of the sixteenth century, the usual pattern of Irish students who wished to pursue their studies going to England, generally to Oxford, began to change. Instead, closer ties developed with the counter-reformation centres of learning on the continent.[76] The implications of this switch for the Church of Ireland were considerable. Firstly, the only source of indigenous graduate clergy was drying up. Secondly, higher education now had a clearly Catholic, indeed counter-reformation context and content for Irish students. Thus, by the time that Trinity was founded it was apparent

---

74 H.L. Murphy, *A history of Trinity College Dublin* (Dublin 1951), 8–14; W. Urwick, *The early history of Trinity College, Dublin 1591–1660* (London 1891), 5–8; Morrin, *Patent rolls*, ii, 227.

75 See below, pp. 96f.

76 H.H.W. Robinson-Hammerstein, 'Aspects of the continental education of Irish students in the reign of Queen Elizabeth I', *Historical Studies*, viii (1971).

that its secular role – spreading civility amongst the Irish people – and its religious purpose – acting as a protestant bulwark – could not easily be combined. If it desired to attract a broad range of Irish students, it would have to play down its religious exclusiveness. Naturally, no question of doing so arose: Archbishop Loftus played a large part in the foundation of Trinity, and explained his view of its purpose in a series of speeches early in the 1590s. His chief concern was that all students received a firmly protestant education, and he also stressed the need for the College to cater for the demand of the church for graduate preachers.[77] To this end, Trinity was modelled upon the Cambridge puritan college Emmanuel whose purpose had been primarily, even solely, to provide ministers for the English church.[78] Hence the provision in Trinity's charter that fellows should only remain in the college for seven years: after that they were expected to go forth and use their clerical talents in the church.[79] Hence the choice as second provost of Walter Travers, the prominent English puritan, whose ideal of a university was that it should be 'the seed and fry of the holy ministry throughout the realm'.[80]

At first, however, Trinity's contribution was on a small scale. The College suffered severely during the Nine Years War, losing the rents from its outlying estates, and even by 1615 only 23 graduates were serving in the 24 dioceses covered by the regal visitation.[81] However, the potential which Trinity had for supplying future needs was indicated by the number of students, usually unordained, but intended for the ministry, who were supported at Trinity by benefices without cure in their native dioceses. Used carefully, this was a means whereby a far-sighted bishop could educate a new generation of native protestant clergy. As Thomas Ram, Bishop of Ferns and Leighlin, explained in relation to the several students he sent to Trinity, he was anxious 'serere altere saeculo'.[82] In all 27 such students were at Trinity in 1615.[83]

The decennial figures for the number of Trinity graduates who can be traced in the Church of Ireland show that the College's contribution did indeed

---

77 W. Stubbs (ed.), *Archbishop Adam Loftus and the foundation of Trinity College, Dublin: speeches delivered by him on various occasions* (Dublin 1892); on the importance of Loftus in the foundation of Trinity, see Robinson-Hammerstein, 'Erzbischof Adam Loftus', 215–20.

78 E.S. Shuckburgh, *Emmanuel College* (London 1904); S.E. Morison, *The founding of Harvard College* (Cambridge, Mass. 1935), 92ff.

79 H.H.G. MacDonnell, *Chartae et statuta Collegii sacrosanctae et individuae Trinitatis reginae Elizabethae, juxta Dublin* (Dublin 1844), 7.

80 W. Travers, *A full and plain declaration of ecclesiastical discipline* ([Heidelberg] 1574), 144; J.P. Morgan, 'Godly learning: puritan theories of the religious utility of education 1560–1640', Cambridge Univ., Ph.D. Thesis, 1977, 113.

81 T.C.D. MS 1066; B.L.Add. MS 19,836.

82 T.C.D. MS 1066, p. 156.

83 T.C.D. MS 1066; B.L.Add. MS 19,836.

increase substantially during the first thirty years of the seventeenth century. In all, roughly one half of the graduates in this period are known to have entered the ministry in Ireland. Only for the graduates of the 1630s does this proportion fall, perhaps as a result of the lack of career opportunities in the Irish church in the 1640s and 1650s.[84] Nevertheless, even during its most productive years, Trinity was sending forth on average less than five graduate clergy a year. If the College was to serve the whole Irish church, as its founders had envisaged, its productivity would have to improve. In fact, however, Trinity never aspired to the role of national university. Originally, it is true, some had seen it as such. The university was viewed as a means of transforming Irish society. Thus, it had featured in the plans to plant Ulster. According to one proposal, Trinity was to be granted six advowsons in each of the six counties 'for the encouragement and advancement of the scholars of the college ... and to furnish the churches of Ulster with sufficient incumbents.'[85] Though the College was eventually granted 19 advowsons, the grant did not have the desired effect.[86] The hoped for symbiosis – the plantation supplying students, the College providing graduate ministers – did not take place. Trinity failed to attract students from Ulster, nor did it supply the Ulster church with a significant number of clergy. Even in relation to the College advowsons, of the 21 presentations listed 1612–26, only six were Trinity men.[87] The failure of Trinity in this respect was reflected in the 1622 visitation of the Ulster church: in the eight Ulster dioceses there were just 13 Trinity graduates, the same total as served the single diocese of Meath.[88] By 1634 the situation had hardly changed – just 9 Trinity educated ministers in the seven Ulster dioceses for which returns have survived, compared to 21 in Meath.[89] The concentration of Trinity *alumni* in Meath pointed to the area with which Trinity had by far the closest association – the Pale. Between them Meath and Kildare dioceses in 1634 had 37 Trinity educated clergy; 23 other dioceses between them yielded just 47 such clergy.[90] Returns for other dioceses in the Dublin province do not survive, but the figure of 16 Trinity graduates derived from the 1630 survey of the diocese of Dublin suggests that the number of Trinity graduates was considerably higher than 37 in 1634.[91]

---

84 See my T.C.D. Moderatorship dissertation, 'The religious role of Trinity College Dublin 1590–1630', 28f.
85 *Cal. Carew*, 1603–24, 22.
86 T.C.D. Muniments P/33/3; P.B., 183a; T.C.D. Muniments P/33/26.
87 P.B., 185b, 186a.
88 Sources, see above, p. 65 n. 16.
89 T.C.D. MS 1067.
90 T.C.D. MS 1067.
91 T.C.D. MS 843, pp. 321–369.

Trinity developed, therefore, not as a national university, but as a Pale based institution. In this area its contribution to the protestant ministry was significant – roughly half the graduate clergy by the 1630s. But outside the Pale it was still, even in the early 1630s, the English and Scottish universities that provided the vast majority of the Irish church's graduate preachers.

The reformation of the clergy, so tentatively begun in the 1590s, had by the 1630s achieved a considerable amount. The old doctrinally ambivalent reading ministry had been transformed into a protestant preaching ministry. Problems of course remained. Some new ministers were not an ornament to the Church of Ireland. William Lithgow, a seasoned traveller, reporting on his journey around Ireland in the early 1620s, claimed that many unsuited men, such as soldiers and mechanics, were admitted to the ministry in Ireland. The evil example of their 'lewd lives' had, he thought, been 'the greatest hindrance to that land's conversion'.[92] Similarly, Archbishop Ussher lamented in 1630 in a letter to Laud that the scandalous life of the 'many unworthy ministers gives exceeding much hindrance to the progress of the gospel amongst us'.[93] The effectiveness of the ministry was further hampered by financial restraints. In the southern provinces, pluralism was frequently resorted to as the only way to support preachers, given the lay stranglehold on church resources. Simple comparison between the number of clergy beneficed, and the total number of parishes suggests that even in the 1630s a substantial number of parishes were served at best occasionally.

Perhaps the greatest problem facing the established church was that of its mission. Having reformed the ministry, how did the Church of Ireland now set about bringing the protestant gospel to the people: in other words, having made the first step along the road to a doctrinal reformation, how was it to take the second? It has already been suggested that there were two possibilities. On the one hand, the influx of English and Scottish ministers seemed to point towards the goal of anglicization, and to the reformation strategy of Loftus and Jones. On the other hand, the foundation of Trinity raised the possibility that a native seminary might be able to counterbalance the influence of the immigrant clergy, by providing trained native preachers dedicated to the evangelization of their fellow countrymen. The first approach was tested in Munster and the Pale; the second in the Gaelic areas of Ireland.

92 W. Lithgow, *The totall discourse of the rare adventures, and painefull peregrinations of long nineteene yeares travells* (ed.) G. Phelps (London 1974), 255; though he does note that the church also possessed 'many sound and religious preachers of both kingdoms'.
93 Bodleian Library, MS Sancroft 18, p. 9.

TABLE I: THE MINISTRY OF THE CHURCH OF IRELAND IN THE 1615
VISITATION

Diocese	Clergy[1]	Resident[2]	Resident preachers[3]	Resident reading ministers[4]
Dublin	77	56	21	35
Kildare	35	28[5]	4	24
Ossory	39	31	4	27
Ferns	43	41	10	31
Leighlin	36	34	10	24
Total: Dublin province	230	190	49	141
Cashel	10	4	1	3
Emly	14	13	1	12
Waterford	8	6	3	3
Lismore	35	25	10	15
Cork	32	24[6,7]	13	11
Cloyne (& Youghal Coll.)	53	35[6]	15	20
Ross	16	14[7]	10	4
Limerick	36	29	8	21
Ardfert	22	20	1	19
Killaloe	32	26	5	21
Kilfenora	7	6	1	5
Total: Cashel province	265	202	68	134
Tuam	34	31	3	28
Kilmacduagh	7	4	1	3
Clonfert	10	6	0	6
Killala and Achonry	6	5	0	5
Elphin	19	18	7	11
Total: Tuam province	76	64	11	53
Meath	76	65[5]	31	34
Ardagh	8	4	2	2
Total: Armagh province	84	69	33	36

TABLE I: THE MINISTRY OF THE CHURCH OF IRELAND IN THE
1615 VISITATION
SUMMARY

	Clergy	Resident	Resident preachers	Resident reading ministers
Dublin province	230	190	49	141
Cashel province	265	202	68	134
Tuam province	76	64	11	53
Armagh province	84	69	33	36
Total	655	525	161	364

Notes to Table 1

1 Prelates holding livings *in commendam* or otherwise have not been included; nor have unordained students holding benefices.
2 Where no details of residence are given it has been assumed, where the minister is not recorded in another diocese, that he was resident. Resident, or course, means merely resident in the diocese, not resident on the living.
3 Where clergy have degrees, they are assumed to have been preachers, with one or two exceptions, where they were specifically returned as reading ministers: e.g., Thady Dowling in Leighlin: T.C.D. MS 1066, p. 159; B.L.Add. MS 19,836, fol. 20r.
4 Where a minister is not returned as a preacher, and does not possess a degree, he is assumed to have been a reading minister.
5 John During, returned as resident in both Meath and Kildare, has been included only in the total for the latter.
6 Four clergy – Manasses Marshall, Thomas Westmore, Richard Allen, and John Twinbrook – were returned as resident in both Cork and Cloyne. The first two have been included in the Cork return, the latter two in that for Cloyne.
7 One cleric, Robert Snowsell, is recorded as non-resident in both Cork and Ross, yet appeared before the visitors there: B.L.Add. MS 19,836, fol. 66v. He has been assumed to have been resident in Cork.

Note on sources

Generally, T.C.D. MS 1066 has been relied upon, in conjunction with B.L.Add. MS 19,836, in compiling the above Table. The two are often complementary, giving rise to the possibility that they represent different drafts of the visitors' report, the T.C.D. MS generally being closer to the bishops' returns to the visitors, and the B.L. being the final summary sent to England. Certainly, there is little doubt that the B.L. MS is a fair copy, since the copyist has omitted part of the Ossory visitation recorded in T.C.D. MS 1066, pp. 58f.

In relation to two dioceses T.C.D. MS 566, Archbishop Jones's own rough copy of the visitation, has been used: Meath (fols 2r–17v); and Dublin (fols 72r–92r). In the latter case, T.C.D. MS 566 is considerably fuller and more reliable than the transcriptions in T.C.D. MS 1066 or B.L.Add. MS 19,836.

TABLE 2: COMPARISON OF NUMBER OF CLERGY IN 1622 AND
1634 VISITATIONS

	1622			1634[1]		
Diocese	Clergy	Res.	Resident preachers	Clergy	Appeared	Preachers
Armagh	47	46	37	49	26	15
Clogher	23	19	9	34	21	20
Down & Connor	37	36	28	71	50	47
Dromore	8	8	5	24	17	9
Kilmore	25	23	16	26[2]	22	8
Raphoe	27	26	17	23	10	10
Total	167	158	112	227	146	109
Kildare	35			37	23	14
Meath	71	64	30	73	50	29
Cashel	17			23	13	10
Ardfert	28			29	21	10
Killaloe	48	36	15	52	31	13
Total	199			214	138	76

Notes to Table 2

1 The 1634 visitation returns for each diocese consist of two parts: the first is a straightforward list of benefices, together with the clergy holding them, as in the 1615 visitations, but with the significant difference that only rarely are details given of whether clergy are preachers or reading minister, resident or non-resident, graduate or non-graduate; the second list contains the names of some, but only some, of the clergy from the first list, with details of their educational qualifications, ordination, and the date(s) upon which they were appointed to their benefice(s). Through assuming that graduates were preachers, and by checking previous visitations in which the clergy also appeared, some indication can be gained about which clergy were preachers. But it should be noted that since it has been assumed, where there is no definite evidence that a minister is a preacher, that he is a reading minister, the number of preachers given in this table for 1634 is almost certainly an underestimate. The degree of underestimation varies from diocese to diocese, depending upon the extent to which alternative sources are available to indicate whether clergy are preachers or not.

However, there remains the problem of ascertaining which clergy were resident. It could be suggested that the second list consists of those clergy resident in the diocese. At first sight this hypothesis is plausible. Generally, the criterion for inclu-

sion in the second list was an appearance before the visitors by the minister concerned, though where a cleric was ill, he could be excused from appearing in person [see, for example, Alexander Montgomery in Achonry (T.C.D. MS 1067, pp.
160, 165ff.)]. For the correlation between appearance and inclusion see the lists for
the dioceses of Killala and Achonry, and Kildare (T.C.D. MS 1067, pp. 146–68,
193–214) – where, uncharacteristically, details of whether clergy appeared before
the visitors or not are recorded. Providing all clergy appeared before the visitors,
and that non-resident ministers did not flock back to their livings just before the
visitation, the second list should give a reasonable indication of the extent of
residence. Unfortunately, however, the first proviso does not hold: not all resident
clergy appeared before the visitors. For it is very unlikely that non-residence was
on a sufficient scale to explain the absence of almost half the diocesan clergy from
the second list in dioceses such as Armagh and Raphoe; all the more unlikely because
most of the clergy omitted were curates, the least likely clergy to hold livings in
other dioceses.

The only totally reliable figures which can be derived from the 1634 visitation,
therefore, are those for the total number of clergy beneficed: these can usefully be
compared with 1622 (Table 2) and 1615 (Table 3). The total in the second column
can best be seen as a minimum for the number of resident clergy. Sometimes, as
in Kilmore, Ardfert, Elphin, or Limerick, it almost certainly comes quite close to the
actual figure. In the case of most dioceses, however, it would seem to be a considerable underestimate. The total in the third column can similarly be seen as a minimum, probably a considerable underestimate in most cases. Occasionally, however,
as in the case of Down and Connor, the fullness of the information provided about
degrees, and the indications from other sources, enable reliable and useful conclusions to be drawn about the relative growth of the preaching ministry since 1615
or 1622.

2   The figure for the total number of clergy in Kilmore might be a slight underestimate, since the first folio of the visitation from which Reeves was copying in
MS 1067 was missing.

Note on sources
The originals of the 1634 visitation were destroyed in the Irish Public Record Office.
Again, Bishop Reeves's transcript, T.C.D. MS 1067, has been relied upon. Given the
lack of any surviving contemporary copies, and the reliability of Reeves's transcriptions generally, there are, by default, few problems with the sources for the 1634
visitation.

TABLE 3: COMPARISON OF NUMBER OF CLERGY IN 1615 AND
1634 VISITATIONS

	1615				1634[1]			
Diocese	Clergy	Res.	Pr.ers	Reading min.s	Clergy	App-eared	Preachers	Reading min.s
Kildare	35	28	4	24	37	23	14	9
Meath	76	65	31	34	73	50	29	21
Cashel	10	4	1	3	23	13	7	6
Emly	14	13	1	12	11	9	5	4
Waterford	8	6	3	3	7	5	4	1
Lismore	35	25	10	15	40	24	10	14
Cork	33	24	13	11	39	23	19	4
Cloyne	44	35	15	20	52	28	16	12
Ross	16	14	10	4	20	15	9	6
Limerick	36	29	8	21	46	37	13	24
Ardfert	22	20	1	19	29	21	12	9
Killaloe	32	26	5	21	52	31	13	18
Kilfenora	7	6	1	5	9	6	4	2
Killala	} 6	5	0	5	8	5	4	1
Achonry					9	5	3	2
Elphin	19	18	7	11	31	27	17	10
Total	393	318	110	208	486	322	179	143

Note to Table 3

1 The number who appeared was probably less than the number resident; the number of preachers is also an underestimate. See note 1 to Table 2, above, pp. 83f.

TABLE 4: IMPROPRIATE RECTORIES IN 1615 AND 1634 VISITATIONS

Diocese	1615			1634		
	Rect-ories	Improp-riate	%	Rect-ories	Improp-riate	%
Kildare	72	43	59.7	64	49	76.6
Ferns	89	53	59.6			
Leighlin	76	45	59.2			
Ossory	119	69	57.9			
Meath	188	133	70.7	194	138	71.1
Cork	73	22	30.1	77	29	37.7
Cloyne	101	62	61.4	112	77	68.8
Ross	28	10	35.7	39	19	48.7
Waterford	29	15	51.7	31	16	51.6
Lismore	60	48	80.0	57	46	80.7
Cashel	79	60	76.0	66	51	77.3
Emly	36	15	41.7	35	26	74.3
Limerick	82	21	25.6	77	21	27.3
Ardfert				65	46	70.8
Killaloe	113	48	42.5	115	51	44.4
Tuam	77	42	54.6			
Clonfert	51	48	94.1			
Achonry	20	17	85.0			
Killala	22	19	86.4	27	25	92.6
Elphin	49	48	98.0			

SUMMARY

Dublin province[1]	544	343	63.1	258	187	70.1
Cashel province	601	301	50.1	674	382	56.7
Tuam province	219	174	79.4	27	25	92.6
Total	1364	818	60.0	959	594	61.9

DIOCESES FOR WHICH FIGURES ARE AVAILABLE IN BOTH 1615
AND 1634: SUMMARY

Dublin province[1]	260	176	68.0	258	187	70.1
Cashel province	601	301	50.1	609	336	55.2
Tuam province	22	19	86.4	27	25	92.6
Total	883	496	56.2	894	548	61.3

Note to Table 4

1 Dublin province plus the diocese of Meath. Although a part of the province of Armagh, Meath was traditionally and geographically more closely linked to the Dublin province.

CHAPTER 5

Protestant preachers in Munster and the Pale

Though the end result was similar, the creation of a protestant ministry in Munster followed a somewhat different course from that in the Pale. In the latter at the start of James's reign the bishops had two resources at their disposal from which they could create a protestant preaching ministry. The considerable degree of continuity in the parochial ministry 1590–1615 ensured that a body of native clergy still existed which, with the help of the educational facilities of Trinity, could possibly be turned into protestant pastors. Secondly, they could also resort to the familiar expedient of 'importing' English graduate clergy. In Munster, on the other hand, the withdrawal of the native population from the established church around the turn of the century, and the tenuous influence of Trinity in the province, left Bishop Lyon with very little alternative other than importing English ministers.

The process began as early as 1604 when Lyon began to rebuild the ministry in his three dioceses Cork, Cloyne and Ross.[1] In procuring clergy Lyon was greatly helped by the close links which the rejuvenated Munster plantation had with England, particularly with the south-west of England.[2] In 1607 Archbishop Jones led a visitation of the diocese of Lismore which, together with Cashel, Emly and Waterford, was held by the native Irish prelate, Miler Magrath.[3] In Lismore, the visitors found seven or eight unbeneficed English preachers 'which are lately come over with the undertakers and are not otherwise provided for', and appointed them to serve some of the many vacant livings in the diocese.[4] By 1615 Bishop Lyon's three dioceses had 73 resident clergy, 38 of them preachers.[5] The composition of the ministry was strikingly different from the 1590s. Only one cleric from the 1590s visitations was still

---

1 S.P. 63/221/35A (1606–8, 131); and see also Fitzsimons, *Words of comfort* (ed.) Hogan, 156.
2 Clarke, 'Ireland 1534–1660', 46.
3 Original visitation in Armagh Public Library, 'Returns of the bishops ... 1622', fols 116r–137r; further contemporary papers in T.C.D. MS 566, fols 120v–130r; see also T.C.D. MS 1066, pp. 212–24; summary of visitation, sent to England along with Jones's comments: S.P. 63/222/111 (1608–8, 235–44).
4 S.P. 63/222/111/iii (1606–8, 243); Armagh Public Library, 'Returns of the bishops', fols 130v–134v, gives the names of these clergy.
5 See Table 1, above, p. 81.

serving in 1615.[6] With one exception, all the prominent urban and merchant families were unrepresented in 1615.[7] Finally, only seven native Irish ministers were returned for the three dioceses.[8] The predominantly English origin of the clergy was reflected in the fact that, of the 27 graduate clergy, only three had been to Trinity.[9] By 1634, the number of Trinity graduates had increased to seven, but the overall composition of the ministry had changed little.[10] Only two native Irish were recorded as having been ordained since the last regal visitation,[11] otherwise the clergy were overwhelmingly English – all of the remaining eighteen graduate clergy who can be traced had been to either Oxford or Cambridge.[12]

The way in which Cork, Cloyne and Ross were seen as a source of preferment and employment by English graduates represented, in fact, a wider trend in the relationship of the Irish church to its English counterpart. Increasingly it came to be included within the English patronage network, which extended down from the court to the local gentry who held advowsons. Certainly, the focus of power in relation to the appointment of bishops shifted from Dublin to London during James's reign.[13] When Lyon died in 1617, John Boyle, a prebendary of Lichfield Cathedral, and elder brother to the earl of Cork, had to go to considerable expense in London to procure the support of the duke of Buckingham for his appointment.[14] At a somewhat lower level, the church in Munster provided for English clergy an opportunity for advancement or preferment which was perhaps unavailable in England. Thus Edward Byam,

---

6 Donogh O'Heneghan: Bodleian Library, MS Carte 55, fol. 581v; T.C.D. MS 1066, p. 391; B.L.Add. MS 19,836, fol. 64v.

7 The one exception: John Gold: T.C.D. MS 1066, p. 380; B.L.Add. MS 19,836, fol. 61v.

8 Donogh O'Heneghan, Teig McDonnell O'Sullivan, Conor Farshine, Thady McDaniell, Ulick Bourke, Teig O'Donovan, Patrick Coyne.

9 George Lee, Patrick Coyne, Randal Holland: A.D.

10 Mark Paget, Helkiah Hussey, Randal Holland, Joseph Travers, John Johnson, David Thomas, Patrick Coyne: T.C.D. MS 1067, pp. 369–402.

11 Murtagh Hagherin, Dermot O'Coghlan: T.C.D. MS 1067, pp. 409f., 437f.

12 One minister, the chancellor of Cloyne, John Temple, was Scottish: Armagh Public Library, 'Returnes of the bishops', fol. 132v; T.C.D. MS 1067, p. 427. The identifiable graduates are: *Cambridge:* Richard Ashe (T.C.D. MS 1067, p. 438); Thomas Blackwell (p. 419); Edward Clarke (p. 416); Joseph Fowle (p. 414); Anthony Kingsmill (pp. 419f.); Augustine Kingsmill (pp. 439f.); Hugo Scampe (p. 436); Israel Taylor (pp. 424f.); *Oxford:* Edward Byam (p. 406f.); Richard German (pp. 407f.); Francis Pratt (p. 435); Thomas Scott (p. 434); Ludovic Vigors (p. 434f.).

13 As also took place in relation to secular patronage: Ranger, 'Career of Richard Boyle in Ireland', 198.

14 Grosart, *Lismore papers*, 2nd ser., ii, 105–7; N.L.I. MS 13,236/13; Ranger, 'Career of Richard Boyle in Ireland', 191, 205.

born in Somerset in 1585, the third son of a minister, was educated at Exeter College, Oxford, where he graduated M.A. in 1607. In 1612 he was ordained and presented to a rectory in Somerset, which he held until 1625. In that year, his elder brother succeeded him, and Edward turned his attention to Ireland, emigrating to Cloyne, where he was elevated to the precentorship in 1627, subsequently holding the dignity along with two other livings in the diocese.[15]

Immigrant clergy also played an important role in ensuring that the Pale had a protestant ministry, especially in the early years of James's reign, when Trinity's contribution was minimal. In a survey of the main livings in Meath and Dublin of 1604, only four of the 23 graduate clergy were from Trinity.[16] Though there was a sprinkling of Scots clergy, particularly in Meath, where George Montgomery was bishop from 1612 to 1621, generally the Pale émigré clergy were from England or Wales, the closest links being with the western coast of Britain – Cheshire, Wales, Devon and Cornwall.[17] Had these immigrant clergy been the sole incumbents of the Pale dioceses, the ministry would have been little different from that in Cork, Cloyne and Ross. However, since the Pale had not experienced the same sudden withdrawal from the established church which had taken place in Munster, a significant number of the old local clergy continued to serve throughout the period 1590–1615.[18] But these old

15 *Al. Oxon.*; T.C.D. MS 1067, pp. 406f.; E.S. Byam, *Chronological memoir of the three clerical brothers ... Byam*, 2nd ed. (Tenby 1862).
16 S.P. 63/216/20 (1603–6, 168–74: transcription inaccurate). *Trinity graduates:* Luke Ussher, John Richardson, Michael Bellarby, Nicholas Smith. A further three clergy had been to Trinity without graduating: Thomas Tedder, Simon Bolger, John Carie. The clergy from other universities who can be traced are: *Cambridge:* Barnabas Bolger (see below, pp. 93f.); William Daniel (see below, pp. 106ff.); William Pratt (S.P. 63/118/45/i); Luke Challoner (see above, p. 35); Christopher Hewetson: John Albright; Apollo Waller; Thomas Ram; Edward Hubersty; *Oxford:* Jonas Wheeler (B.L. Add. MS 19,836, fol. 33r; Wood, *Athenae Oxoniensis*, ii, 890f.); Meredith Hanmer; John Rider; William Pilsworth.
17 See, for example, W.C. Trevelyan, C.E.Trevelyan (ed.), 'Trevelyan papers', part III, *Camden Society*, cv (1872), pp. xiv, 149f.; and the origins of students attending Trinity in 1620: T.C.D. Muniments P/1/27. Ossory had a particularly high concentration of Welsh clergy: Lambeth Palace MS 2013; and see U.W., xvi, 350f.
18 *Kildare:* 7 clergy served from 1591 through to 1615: John Dorren, Donald Byrne, John Tracy, Bernard Kelly, William Man, Richard Malone; Robert Pearse. Sources: 1591 visitation – T.C.D MS 566, fols 107r–111r; visitation from c.1610 – T.C.D. MS 1066, pp. 39–50; 1615 visitation – T.C.D. MS 1066, pp. 25–37; B.L. Add. MS 19,836, fols 15r–19v. *Ossory:* 11 clergy served the church 1591–1615: Thomas Wale, Barnabas Bolger, Robert Joyce, Andrew Archer, Melchior Shea, Walter Barry, John Butler, William Daniel, Patrick Fitzgerald, James Laughlin, George Dodd. Sources: 1591 – T.C.D. MS 566, fols 111v–115r; 1615 – T.C.D. MS 1066, pp. 53–73; B.L. Add. Ms 19,836, fols 33r–39r. *Ferns:* 12 clergy served from 1587 through to 1612–15: James Bussher, David Brown, William Campion, Richard

reading ministers could hardly be described as a vital, forward-looking force in the reformed church. At best they could read the prayer book and new testament in Irish, and thereby maintain contact with ordinary people forced by the state to attend Sunday services.[19] Even in the Pale they were to a large extent the last representatives of their kind, under pressure from both sides of the religious divide, like their counterparts in Munster in the late sixteenth century. On the one hand, bishops were looking to England not just for protestant preachers, but even for reading ministers – as early as 1604 the eastern part of the diocese of Meath was served largely by English reading ministers.[20] On the other side, the strength of recusancy and the depth of antipathy to the state church meant that few of the younger generation of native Palesmen looked towards the established church for a clerical career. Bishops found it increasingly difficult to get new native ordinands to take over as the previous generation of conformist clergy died. Bishop Ram, when first appointed to Ferns and Leighlin, did, it is true, encounter two or three local men anxious to serve in the established church, and these he ordained. But, as Ram himself lamented in 1612, such men were rare.[21] Similarly, in 1615 Archbishop Jones, commenting upon the visitation of his own diocese, Dublin, felt called upon to explain the many unserved and impoverished parishes in the two native Irish deaneries of Athy and Wicklow. Ostensibly, their condition could be explained by the refusal of the impropriators to give curates adequate stipends. In fact, there were deeper reasons. Even if the financial support had been available, Jones could not have found the clergy to serve the cures. English émigrés would hardly have been prepared to serve in such remote, Irish speaking areas, whilst the supply of ordinands from the indigenous population had simply dried up, 'for the natives of that kingdom being generally addicted to popery do train their children up in superstition and idolatry.'[22]

Jones had pointed to a major defect in the Irish reformation: the failure to establish an effective, state-controlled educational system. Chichester had perceived the vital necessity, following the suspension of the rigorous enforcement of conformity, of shaping the minds of the younger generation: 'our better hopes must be in the next age, by the good and careful education of the children'.[23] In theory, of course, provision had already been made. Statutes

Devoreux, Robert Dreighan, Walter French, Patrick Kelly, John Lacy, Denis Quilty, Richard Raw, James Stafford, James Synott. Sources: 1587 – T.C.D. MS 566, fols 115v–118v; 1612 – T.C.D. MS 1066, pp. 144–55; 1615 – T.C.D. MS 1066, pp. 93–132; B.L. Add. Ms 19,836, fols 26r–32r.

19 See below, p. 118.
20 S.P. 63/216/20/ii (1603–6, 175).
21 T.C.D. MS 1066, p. 156.
22 T.C.D. MS 566, fol. 92r; B.L. Add. MS 19,836, fol. 14v.
23 S.P. 63/218/65 (1603–6, 490); and see also S.P. 63/219/145 (1606–8, 41).

of 1537 and 1570 had provided for the establishment of parochial and diocesan schools.[24] The foundation of Trinity in 1591 completed the three tier structure. But, as so often in Ireland, there was a substantial difference between passing and actually implementing statutory reforms. Even by 1615 schools had still not been established in several dioceses according to 12 Elizabeth c.1. And where they had been, as in the Pale dioceses, the alternative system of Catholic schooling and teaching ensured that it was almost impossible to attract large numbers of native Irish or Anglo-Irish pupils.[25] The returns of the 1615 visitors, who had been specifically instructed to examine schoolteachers, amply bear this out. The dioceses of Kildare and Ossory both possessed satisfactory teachers, but in neither case were there many pupils, because of what the visitors termed the people's 'backwardness in religion'.[26] Bishop Ram recorded that the reason why Catholics were so loth to attend the diocesan schools in Ferns and Leighlin was that they had been told by a Catholic priest that it was a deadly sin to attend an heretical school.[27] The success of one of his schools, at Maryborough in Leighlin, in attracting 'a good number of scholars' was not due to any appeal to the indigenous population, but to the fact that Maryborough was a garrison town and plantation centre with a substantial English population.[28] Only when they were lax in enforcing religious conformity amongst their pupils could free schools hope to attract large numbers of Catholic pupils. The Dublin free school, according to the 1622 Commissioners, had 122 pupils, of whom 43 did not attend church. In the previous dozen years or so, the school had indeed sent 100 scholars to Trinity; it had also, however, sent 160 overseas, several of whom subsequently returned as priests.[29]

Archbishop Ussher is said to have affirmed that the persistence and widespread appeal of Catholic schools made the reformation hopeless.[30] Leonard Shortall, a Trinity graduate, and himself a teacher, shared such pessimism. He accepted that the best means of spreading the reformation was through persuasion, which would be most successful with young people, caught before the 'infection' of popery set in. Yet, by the 1620s he recognised that it was the Catholic, not the protestant schools that were shaping the minds of the younger generation. Hence he pressed for the complete extirpation of Catholic pedagogy by the civil arm.[31] In default of such a comprehensive panacea, the protestant church and the state was left with an enduring problem. In particular,

24 See above, p. 24f; *Statutes passed in Ireland*, i, 322–38.
25 Ronan ed., 'Visitation of Dublin, 1615', 4.
26 B.L. Add. MS 19,836, fols 19v, 39v; T.C.D. MS 1066, pp. 37, 73.
27 T.C.D. MS 1066, pp. 141f.
28 Ibid, p. 172; B.L. Add. MS 19,836, fol. 25r.
29 N.L.I. MS 8014, iv, 1; MS 8014, v, 8.
30 U.W., xvi, 448.
31 Ibid, 447–9.

the failure of the protestant educational system to attract native pupils restricted the character of Trinity's intake of students, and made it difficult for the College to fulfil its role as a native seminary. Attempts were made, both by the state and the college, to circumvent the difficulties caused by the lack of an educational infrastructure. The Court of Wards, in grants of wardship regularly specified that suitable charges should be educated in 'English habit and religion' at Trinity.[32] On the assumption that this was enforced, a large number of wards from Catholic families have been assumed to have been educated at Trinity, thereby giving a very misleading picture of the composition of the early student body.[33] In fact, of the 110 grants which specified that wards attend Trinity, hardly more than half a dozen were carried out. In 1618 the Commissioners of the Court of Wards admitted that they were unable to enforce the educational provisions in grants of wardship.[34] The 1622 Commissioners confirmed that not a single ward was then studying in Trinity.[35]

A second method of attracting native students was through the provision of financial support. As a result of the re-endowment by James, Trinity was able, in the second decade of the seventeenth century, to increase the number of students supported on the foundation.[36] From 1617 an extra allowance of £3 *per annum* was granted to 'native scholars'.[37] Since these scholars sometimes entered Trinity at an early age, the College provided a schoolmaster-fellow to bring them up to matriculation standard: in effect the College provided a small free school of its own in an effort to surmount the inadequacy of the official educational system.[38]

The role of Trinity in relation to native students was rather similar to that which persuasive strategists had envisaged for Cambridge in the later sixteenth century – as a protestant seminary for the indigenous Irish church. Indeed, a degree of continuity existed, as Trinity assumed the role previously played by Cambridge. The Bolger family from Kilkenny demonstrate this neatly. Barnabas Bolger in 1591 was beneficed in Ossory as an unordained student.[39] He came from a prominent Ossory clerical family – another Barnabas, perhaps his father,

32 V. Treadwell, 'The Irish court of wards under James I', *Irish Historical studies*, xii (1960), 8.

33 H.F. Berry, 'Probably early students of Trinity College, Dublin (being wards of the crown), 1599–1616', *Hermathena*, xvi (1911); these were included in A.D.

34 S.P. 63/234/17 (1615–25, 203).

35 N.L.I. MS 8014, iv, 9; B.L. Add. MS 4756, fol. 69r.

36 T.C.D. Muniments, P/1/79, P/1/151; Mahaffy, *Epoch in Irish history*.

37 Though Provost Temple had originally suggested that there be 30 such scholars (T.C.D. Muniments P/1/79), and some money was paid from 1617 (P.B., 170b), the accounts for 1623 give the number in receipt as only 20: P/1/151; P.B., 239.

38 P.B., 206b.

39 T.C.D. M5 566, fol. 111v.

had in the late 1550s been one of the leading opponents of the vigorously
protestant bishop, John Bale.[40] The second Barnabas, however, proved to be
more sympathetic to protestantism. This was almost certainly a product in
part at least of his education: not only did he go to go to Cambridge, he chose
the puritan seminary of Emmanuel, graduating M.A. in 1598.[41] Bolger then
came back to Ireland, attending the newly founded Trinity for a while, and
serving in the church in Dublin, before returning in 1612 to his native Ossory
as Dean.[42] There he married Elizabeth Deane, daughter of the English Bishop
of Ossory, Richard Deane.[43] His brother Simon was also loyal to the protestant
church. Like Barnabas he was supported whilst at university by a benefice
without cure in Ossory. He chose, however, to go to Trinity as a scholar.[44]
Though he never graduated, he went on to serve the church in Ossory like
his brother.[45] Perhaps the most significant fact of all about the Bolger family
was that Barnabas's son, a third Barnabas, also went to Trinity and thence to
the ministry as a preacher, thereby reversing the trend amongst the families
and children of many Irish conformist native clergy.[46]

Another example of the way in which early native conformity could, through
the education of the second generation at a protestant university, subsequently
be turned into doctrinal commitment, was the Wall, or Wale, family of Kilkenny.
Originally Hiberno-Norman, most branches of the family remained Catholic
throughout the early modern period.[47] However, some of the Kilkenny branch
conformed to the established church in the early years of the reformation.
William Wale held the precentorship of Ossory from 1543, through the religious changes of two reigns, probably until that of Elizabeth.[48] Thomas
Wale held the treasurership of Ossory 1585–*c*.1609, and sent his son, Robert,
to Trinity. Robert was a scholar who, like Simon Bolger, did not graduate but

---

40 Leslie, *Ossory clergy*, 130; J. Graves, J.G. Primm, *The history, architecture and antiquities of the cathedral of St Canice* (Dublin 1857), 284.
41 *Al. Cantab.*.
42 Leslie, *Ossory clergy*, 59; T.C.D. MS 2640, p. 5: the reference here to Sir Bolger
   would suggest that he returned for a short while in 1595 to Trinity after he had
   proceeded B.A. in Cambridge: A.D. claims Bolger as Sch. 1595, but without any
   evidence: P.B., 197b merely has Bolger as a student, Muniments P/1/73 claims
   him as one of the 'able men' produced by Trinity.
43 Leslie, *Ossory clergy*, 59.
44 Ibid., 130; A.D.; T.C.D. Muniments P/1/73.
45 B.L. Add. MS 19,836, fol. 33v.
46 A.D.; Leslie, *Ossory clergy*, 273.
47 H. Gallwey, *The Wall family in Ireland* (Dublin 1970); Graves, Primm, *Cathedral
   of St Canice*, 159ff.
48 Leslie, *Ossory clergy*, 74.

returned to the church in Ossory, and eventually succeeded his father as treasurer.[49] Yet another generation of Wales also went to university in Dublin – another Robert Wale was a scholar there in 1623.[50] Though Trinity performed a useful service in educating reading ministers like Simon Bolger and Robert Wale, ideally, the persuasive strategists desired that it should produce native preachers – men like Neal Malloy, for instance. Born in King's County, the second son of Cosny Malloy, Neal entered Trinity as a scholar in 1612, holding at the same time a rectory without cure in his native diocese of Kildare. In 1616 he graduated with a B.A., and the following year he was ordained by Bishop Pilsworth of Kildare, and presented by the Lord Deputy to the vicarage of Fercall in the diocese of Meath, where he was resident in 1622, and returned as a good preacher.[51] By 1634 he had acquired both the precentorship of Kildare and a wife, the daughter of Bishop Pilsworth.[52]

The crucial question about these native clergy is whether they were indeed representative of the ministers which Trinity was producing for the Church of Ireland, or whether they were merely isolated examples. If the former were the case, then the Irish university could have exercised a considerable influence upon the development of the ministry in Ireland. In fact, Trinity did produce some native ministers, but never in such numbers as to significantly alter the composition of the ministry of the Church of Ireland. By the end of the second decade of the seventeenth century unease was growing in official circles in England that Trinity was failing to fulfil its role in regard to native students as the King and his predecessor had hoped. Complaints were made that 'foreigners were entertained' in the College, at the expense of 'the natives'.[53] From the very figures proffered by Provost Temple to rebut the allegation, it can be demonstrated that the charge had some foundation. Temple claimed in 1620 that 78 of the 97 students in the College were Irish. This was, firstly, an over-estimate of the number of students, since Temple included 15 fellows in their number. Secondly, Temple's definition of 'Irish' was flexible, to say the least. The 70 'Irish students' remaining after the elimination of the fellows were composed of: 13 'Irish by habitation' – i.e. the sons of planters and English officials who had settled in Ireland; 18 'Irish fellow commoners and pensioners' – these included many obviously new English sons of clergy and administrators, such as Thomas Ram, Samuel Downham, and Anthony and Arthur Stoughton; and 39 'Irish by birth' – a loose

---

49 Ibid.; P.B., 197b; T.C.D. Muniments P/1/54/i
50 A.D.; Leslie, *Ossory clergy*, 92.
51 A.D.; B.L. Add. MS 19,836, fol. 19r; T.C.D. MS 1067, p. 71; U.W., i, App. V, p. cxv.
52 T.C.D. MS 1067; p. 213; A.D
53 T.C.D. Muniments, P/1/99, P/1/101, P/1/102, P/1/103, P/1/104.

description, which lumped together native Irish, Anglo-Irish and the offspring of the new English who had been born in Ireland.[54] Thus, of the 70 'Irish students' only about thirty were of native or Anglo Irish extraction. Furthermore, the extent to which the College sought to equip these students as Irish speaking evangelists can be doubted. The predominantly anglicizing ethos, instilled from the foundation by Loftus, was reflected in the way in which the teaching of Irish was neglected. Initially, in the 1590s, thanks to the efforts of one Irish speaking fellow, William Daniel, Trinity had been closely involved with the project to translate into Irish and print the new testament, an essential tool for the indigenous reformation.[55] Upon his departure, however, interest in Irish as a means of proselytization seems to have lapsed. Even the native scholars' places were misused. According to the statutes framed by Provost Bedell in 1628, these scholars were to 'cultivate the Irish language, or learn it and present religious exercises in it'.[56] But before Bedell arrived as Provost in 1627 the teaching of Irish was neglected, whilst the term 'native' merely restricted the scholarships to those born in Ireland of what-ever race.[57]

English official concern with Trinity's failure in this regard came to a head in 1620, when the King gave the Lord Deputy a comprehensive account of his view of Trinity's role in Ireland, which, as an exposition of James's preference for a persuasive strategy, deserves to be quoted in detail:

> And because we understand that the simple natives of that our kingdom, who by experience we hear are found to be far more tractable amongst the rude Irish than amongst the unconformable English, are still kept in darkness, and are ready thereby to be misled into error, superstition and disobedience by the popish priests, who abuse their simplicity and ignorance, which proceedeth through want of ministers who could speak their own language ... because our College of Dublin was first founded ... principally for breeding up the natives of that kingdom in civility, learning and religion, we have reason to expect that in all this long time ... some good numbers of the natives should have been trained up in that College, and might have been employed in teaching and reducing those that are ignorant among that people, and to think that the government of that house have not performed the trust reposed in them, if the revenues thereof have been otherwise employed; and therefore we do require that henceforth special care be had ... and for the supplying of the present want, that choice be made of some competent number of

54 T.C.D. Muniments P/1/127; and see also P/1/126.
55 See below, pp. 108f.
56 Translated from Mahaffy, *Epoch in Irish history*, 364.
57 Ibid., 203.

towardly young men already fitted with the knowledge of the Irish tongue, and be placed in the university ... for two or three years till they have learned the grounds of religion and be able to catechize the simple natives and deliver unto them so much as themselves have learned, and when any livings that are not of any great value fall void among the mere Irish, these men to be thought upon before others, or to be placed with other able ministers that possess livings among the mere Irish, where for defect of the language they are able to do little good, to be interpreters unto them ... ; and that you consider with our primate ... for this or some other good course to be taken for supplying this defect, which we think will be a principal means to reclaim the poor ignorant people ... [58]

Temple rejected the idea of placing native Irish speakers in the College for two or three years on the grounds that it would jeopardise the chances of the existing students of preferment in the church.[59] But there were deeper reasons why the King's proposals were unrealistic – above all, as Temple pointed out, it was difficult to see how Trinity could attract significant numbers of native students, given the defects of the official educational system, and the solidarity of the Catholic population.[60]

Whatever the causes, the results were fairly clear cut by the time of the 1634 regal visitation. Though Trinity was producing about half the graduate clergy for the Pale region, the majority of Trinity ministers were little different in background and capabilities from the immigrant clergy serving in the same area. In the diocese of Meath in 1634, out of a total of 38 clergy who had been at university (33 of whom had graduated), Trinity supplied 19 (16 graduates). Only six of the Trinity men were clearly native Irish or Anglo-Irish; five more can be confidently identified as new English. Though no details of the origin of the remaining eight can be traced, their surnames would strongly suggest that they were of new English stock.[61]

The failure of the Church of Ireland to prefer native Irish and Anglo-Irish clergy, for which both contemporaries and later historians have criticised it,

---

58 P.R., 471; P.R.O.I., *Acta regia*, R.C. 2/6 (1615–25, 276f.).
59 T.C.D. Muniments P/1/126.
60 Ibid., P/1/99.
61 *Native Irish or Anglo-Irish*: Thady Lysaght, Nicholas Smith, Neal Malloy, Joseph Ware, Josselin Ussher, Walter Fitzsimon. *New English:* Roger Puttock (T.C.D. Muniments P/1/127), John Goldsmith (ibid.), Randal Adams (ibid.; Wood, *Athenae Oxoniensis*, iv 604), Robert Cook (U.W., i, App. V, p. lxxi), Lancelot Lowther (B.Nightingale, *The ejected of 1662 in Cumberland and Westmorland*, 2 vols (Manchester 1911), ii, 1165). *Not known:* Samuel Clarke, Henry Bolton, Thomas Fleetwood, Richard Mathewson, William Meots, Myles Pemberton, William Smith, Nicholas Tedder.

was therefore only partially the fault of the church itself.[62] The fundamentally anglicizing assumptions behind the reformation sought to eliminate rather than encourage the use of the Irish language, and made it difficult to attract native ordinands. Ultimately, however, the shortage of suitable candidates for preferment was the result of the hold which Catholicism had upon the people and especially upon the educational system. The persuasive strategy was consequently caught in a vicious circle: in order to convert the native Irish, it needed native ministers; but the supply of native ministers was meagre because the native Irish were unconverted.

This brings us to the final aspect of this chapter – an assessment of the pastoral impact and effectiveness of the ministry in the Pale and Munster during the first part of the seventeenth century. From the above discussion of the composition of the ministry, and the earlier treatment of the preference of Irish churchmen for a coercive, anglicizing strategy, it is evident that the persuasive, indigenous approach was not, in James's reign, the context within which the pastorate of the church of Ireland is best examined. The church in both the Pale and Munster relied upon the secular arm to enforce conformity and provide pastors with native auditors. During the first two decades of the century, whilst the common people were forced to attend service by the 12*d.* fine, the Church of Ireland's clergy had to minister to two different kinds of congregation. On the one hand, there was a nucleus of English parishioners, often quite numerous in plantation areas, who were protestant; on the other hand there was the native population, forced into conformity by the civil arm, but certainly not protestant. While the former were regular churchgoers, the latter were merely occasional.

In the parish of Youghal, the graduate preacher, Thomas Wilson, had a nucleus of English church goers, comprising one hundred souls in all.[63] To this core of protestants Brouncker's coercion campaign added peripheral groups of conformist Irish inhabitants. Davis, in his circuit of Munster in 1606, reported that some Irish families were beginning to attend church in Youghal, and that more would follow suit.[64] More did, thanks to the exercise of 'some moderate coercion' by Brouncker, so that by November some 600 people were attending church.[65] According to Wilson, only two male recusants remained in the town.[66] However, it was plain that when pressure was relaxed, as it was after Brouncker's death in 1607, Wilson would be left with a rump of English parishioners.

62 B.L. Add. MS 4756, fol. 64r.; Canny, 'Why the reformation failed', 439.
63 S.P. 63/218/53 (1603–6, 468).
64 Ibid.
65 S.P. 63/219/134 (1606–8, 24f.); S.P. 63/219/135 (1606–8, 25); S.P. 63/219/137 (1606–8, 26)
66 N.L.I. MS 12,813, vol. 2/49.

Even where people were forced to attend protestant services for longer periods, the extent to which they developed any lasting commitment to protestantism can be doubted. In Munster little was achieved with those forced to attend service, since the ministers for the most part were unable to communicate with them. Bishop Lyon, at the start of Brouncker's campaign, had sought to provide for Irish services, but, as has been seen, by the second decade of the century, the ministry was largely composed of English clergy.[67] In 1618 the earl of Thomond appealed to the English Privy Council to order that the churches in Munster be provided with 'readers and interpreters' who could communicate with the common people who were forced to attend church.[68] But little happened: by 1634 the character of the ministry had changed little. Its priorities were, perhaps, best indicated by the parishes in which the pluralist graduate preachers chose to reside – those with the greatest number of English residents. Israel Taylor, for example, a Lincolnshire born cleric, who was appointed to the precentorship of Cork in 1613, and held it with many other benefices in Cork and neighbouring dioceses, chose to live in the parish of Clonfert (Cloyne), because of the presence there of 'a plantation of English'.[69]

In the Pale, however, more provision was able to be made for the local population who were unable to understand English. The native reading ministers who continued to serve the church were supplied with Irish translations of the new testament and the prayer book, to read to their parishioners. Only in the Pale dioceses did the 1615 visitors record any such provision for the Irish speaking population.[70] Nevertheless, even in the Pale there is little evidence to suggest that the conformity brought about by coercion was anything other than ephemeral. As one submission to the 1622 Commissioners concluded, when considering the question of whether the prosecution of the 'meaner sort' had wrought 'any reformation or no':

> experience hath manifested it hath not in any remarkable manner; some few have conformed when they have been attached, being not able to pay their fines, and having no other choice but to lie perpetually in prison

67 S.P. 63/219/134 (1606–8, 25).

68 *Carew Cal.*, 1603–24, 376f.

69 Taylor (M.A. Christ's Cambridge) served first as a minister in Lincolnshire, before he was recommended to Ussher by a mutual clerical friend, and came to Ireland c.1610: J. Peile, *Biographical register of Christ's College Cambridge*, 2 vols (Cambridge 1910), i, 209; U.W., xvi, 363; J.I. Dredge, *The writings of Richard Bernard. A bibliography* (Horncastle 1890), 25; Armagh Public Library, 'Returns of the bishops', fol. 61r.

70 Parishes with the Book of Common Prayer in Irish: Dublin diocese – 10; Kildare – 22; Ferns – 5; Leighlin – 15; Ossory – 17. In Ossory a further 11 parishes had 'Irish books', presumably both the new testament and prayer book: T.C.D. MS 1066; B.L. Add. MS 19,836.

> or go to church, which they commonly perform once or twice, and return
> to their vomit.[71]

The suspension of the enforcement of the 12*d.* fine in 1621 therefore marked
the end of conformity amongst the ordinary people. As Lord Chancellor Loftus
(the son of the Archbishop) told the 1622 Commissioners, in the sixteen or
eighteen parishes near his home (Rathfarnham) where previously 100–140
people had come to church, 'there were not now eight'.[72]

Though the bishops complained vociferously that as a result of the suspension of the 12*d.* fine their churches were deprived of congregations, the
way forward now lay with the rump of English protestant parishioners. Like
Israel Taylor in Cloyne, protestant preachers in the Pale concentrated their
efforts on the richer parishes where the English settlers and officials lived,
abandoning the outlying Irish parishes to poor native reading ministers, where
these could be had, or simply leaving the cures unserved, where they could
not. A survey of the diocese of Dublin in 1630 confirms this pattern.[73] On the
one hand were the English speaking university educated preachers, often
dignitaries of one of the cathedrals, who held the most valuable livings, and
served the parishes in the centre of the city, and the chief towns such as Athy
and Wicklow, where substantial numbers of English lived. On the other hand
were the poor reading ministers, usually local men, almost always pluralists.
The various livings which they held were worth little, their parishes had few
or no conformists, their churches were often ruined. Generally a Catholic priest
was recorded as active in the parish, supported by prominent local gentry.
The parish of Baldoyle affords a typical example:

> the church is altogether ruinous; there is nothing but bare walls. It is an
> impropriation. Mr Thomas Fitzsimons ... is farmer to it. The tithes
> thereof is worth xl *libri per annum.* One Richard Kelly, clerk, is curate,
> and hath but xxxiiii s. *per annum* for his pains. There is mass common-
> ly said upon Sundays in the said Mr Fitzsimon's house, where the parish-
> ioners commonly resort. There are no protestants in the parish.[74]

The preaching ministry in Dublin, then, was only for the English population,
for the group of confirmed protestants. The improvement in the quality of
the ministry had not been associated with any greater appeal to the Catholic
population, or any extensive evangelical success amongst them. Nor was the

71 N.L.I. MS 8014, i; and see also B.L.Add. MS 4756, fol. 62v.
72 N.L.I. MS 8014, ii.
73 T.C.D. MS 843, pp. 321–69; reliably transcribed in M.V. Ronan (ed.), 'Archbishop
    Bulkeley's visitation of Dublin, 1630', *Analecta Hibernica* viii (1941), 57–98.
74 T.C.D. MS 843, p. 330; Ronan (ed.), 'Visitation of Dublin, 1630', 65.

limited number of native clergy able to attract any significant number of their fellow countrymen to church.

The symbol of pastoral failure in the protestant church as a national church was the decay of the church fabric. The Dublin government under Chichester had made strenuous efforts to repair the damage caused to church buildings by the neglect of the sixteenth century and the devastation of the Nine Years War.[75] The Chancery Court under Archbishop Jones launched a campaign in March 1609 to secure the repair of churches in the counties of Dublin, Wicklow, Carlow and Kildare, by taking recognizances from prominent local people to undertake the task of repair.[76] In all, 100 recognizances were entered into, and 71 were performed.[77] The fruits of these official efforts would seem to be reflected in the 1615 regal visitation, when the province of Dublin, where the activities of the court of Chancery were concentrated, had a markedly higher percentage of churches in repair (almost 55 per cent) than the province of Cashel (30.4 per cent).[78]

Comparison of the visitations of Meath, Ossory, and Kildare in 1615 and 1622 reveals, however, that the success was probably more apparent than real, since the figures for 1615 do not appear to have been accurate. The overall contrast between the two visitations is quite startling: in 1615, 50.8 per cent of the churches were fully repaired in the three dioceses; by 1622 only 33.3 per cent were in good condition.[79] Two explanations are possible: a sudden and dramatic deterioration in the church fabric within the space of seven years; or an inaccuracy in either the 1615 or the 1622 returns. The former seems unlikely. On the balance of evidence, the 1615 visitors seem to have been at fault, giving an over-sanguine account (to put it politely) of the state of the church fabric in the Pale dioceses.[80] Dilapidation was endemic: in 1621 it was reported that the parish churches 'are generally ruined and defaced'.[81] One year later, the notes of the 1622 Commissioners contained a succinct summary of the reason for this: 'Churches and altars of churches demolished especially where Pope reigns most.'[82]

75 J. Perrot, *The chronicle of Ireland 1584–1608* (ed.), H. Wood (Dublin 1933), 183; W. Farmer, 'Chronicles of Ireland from 1594 to 1613' (ed.) W.L. Falkiner, *English Historical Review*, xxii (1907), 535; S.P. 63/271/7 (Add. 1625–60, 188).

76 B.L.Add. MS 19,838, fols 128v *et seq.*; see also S.P. 63/228/22 (1608–10, 375f.).

77 It seems that the bonds for those recognizances that were not performed were never collected. In 1624 the government belatedly noted this fact, and in 1629 set about trying to collect the forfeited bonds. By this stage, however, it was less an attempt to repair churches, than a means of raising revenue: B.L.Add. MS 19,828, fols 155v *et seq.*; S.P. 63/269/96 (Add. 1625–60, 155); Signet Office 1/503 (1625–32, 487).

78 See Table 5, p. 113.

79 See Table 6, p. 114.

80 See note to Table 6, pp. 114f.

81 S.P. 63/236/9–12 (1615–25, 326).

82 N.L.I. MS 8014, ii.

As a result of the Commissioners report, the King issued 38 'Orders and directions' for the Church of Ireland in 1623, one of which commanded bishops to see that churches were repaired.[83] Prominent parishioners were to be called together and, as in 1609, recognizances taken for the reparation: and, in the diocese of Meath, this was done.[84] However, official action could not by itself cope either with the scale of the problem or the immense practical difficulties. By 1630, the state of church fabric in the Pale was considerably worse. In Dublin only 23 per cent of the churches were fully repaired, 12.5 per cent were partly repaired, and 64.5 per cent were ruined.[85] In the same year, Archbishop Ussher recorded the condition of the churches in the part of his diocese which fell within the Pale: only 18 per cent were fully repaired, whilst 75.8 per cent were totally ruined.[86] These statistics represent the virtual cession by the established church of large numbers of parishes to the Catholic clergy. With the parishes in the hands of non-resident pluralists, and devoid of conformist parishioners, the church had neither the incentive to restore ruined buildings, nor the local financial or material support to effect such a restoration.

It has already been suggested that the way in which the expansion of the number of preaching ministers was financed in some southern dioceses – through pluralism – carried with it the danger that the extent of the pastoral care of the established church would be diminished. It is now clear that in the Pale and Munster this did indeed take place. The preachers concentrated upon the richer parishes where English settlers provided a regular congregation, and left the remoter, Irish-inhabited parishes, to ill-paid curates, where these could be found, or even to the Catholic priests. The limitation of the pastorate of the ministry arose partly from financial considerations – in order to support themselves, preachers needed several benefices, often more than they could serve themselves. It also sprang from the origin and training of the ministers of the established church. In the Pale the majority, in Munster nearly all the preachers were of English origin, committed to an anglicizing reformation, trained in English-style universities, and ill equipped to cope with or even to contemplate the proselytization of the native parishioners. Even in the Pale, the survival of native reading ministers from the previous century, and the education of native protestant clergy by Trinity, served little pastoral purpose, since by the 1630s it was evident that such conformity did not lead to any similar adherence to protestantism on the part of their countrymen. In other words, by the 1630s, despite the significant improvement in the quality of the clergy of the established church, neither the persuasive nor the coercive reformation

83 S.P. 63/237/34, fols 72v–73r (1615–25, 417).
84 Armagh Public Library, 'Orders of Council and other documents relative to the diocese of Meath', Items 19–24.
85 T.C.O. MS 843, Ronan (ed.), 'Visitation of Dublin'.
86 S.P. 63/250/63 (1625–32, 529).

strategy had much chance of success in the Pale or in Munster in the forsee-able future. Whether through official reluctance and incompetence or recusant resilience, the Pale and Munster seemed safe for Catholicism.

TABLE 5: CONDITION OF CHURCH FABRIC: 1615

Diocese	Churches	Repaired or in repair	Church up, chancel down	Chancel up, ch. down	Unrepaired	No ch.	No information
Dublin	117	53 (45%)	7	0	11	0	46
Kildare	68	33 (49%)	6	3	5	1	20
Ferns	99	77 (78%)	5	1	2	3	11
Leighlin	72	41 (57%)	5	1	5	0	20
Ossory	113	53 (47%)	10	14	13	3	20
Meath	234	102 (44%)	20	2	40	0	70
Cashel	84	18 (21%)	0	0	24	14	28
Emly	34	6 (18%)	3	1	13	0	11
Waterford	29	4 (18%)	1	0	18	3	3
Lismore	63	29 (46%)	5	1	21	1	6
Cork	87	31 (36%)	10	0	25	5	16
Cloyne	122	36 (30%)	14	5	56	3	8
Ross	27	13 (48%)	2	0	8	0	4
Limerick*	45	10 (22%)	2	0	7	0	26
Ardfert	42	17 (41%)	1	0	5	1	18
Killaloe	117	39 (33%)	0	6	43	3	26
Kilfenora	18	0	0	0	15	0	3
Kilmacduagh	21	14 (67%)	0	2	1	0	4
Killala	22	13 (59%)	0	0	2	0	7
Achonry	20	11 (55%)	0	0	0	0	9
Elphin	49	25 (51%)	0	0	6	0	18
Ardagh	29	9 (31%)	0	0	4	0	16

Totals: provinces:

Dublin	469	257 (54.8%)
Cashel	668	203 (30.4%)
Tuam	112	63 (56.3%)

Total: all dioceses:

22 dioceses	1512	634 (42.8%)

* two deaneries only

TABLE 6: COMPARISON OF CHURCH FABRIC: 1615–22

Diocese	Date	Rep-aired	Ch. up chancel down	Chan. up church down	Unrep-aired	No church	No inform-ation
Kildare	1615	33	6	3	5	1	20
	1622	16	10	0	37	4	1
Meath	1615	102	20	2	40	–	70
	1622	54	21	13	119	4	2
Ossory	1615	53	10	14	13	3	20
	1622	62	1	9	33	–	8

Note to Table 6

The 1622 surveys give a far fuller record of the state of the churches in those dioceses where the returns can be compared with those of 1615. Considerably more churches were returned as unrepaired or decayed by the 1622 visitors than had been done by the 1615 visitors. There are two reasons for this: the progressive deterioration in church fabric during the period; and the inadequacy and inaccuracy of the returns made by the regal visitors.

Certainly, the trend in church fabric seems to have been towards decay, rather than improvement: only in Ossory did the number of churches in repair grow. The more normal pattern was that observed in Meath, where 14 churches which had been partly ruined (i.e., church or chancel in decay) in 1615 were by 1622 wholly unrepaired; similarly 22 churches which were in a satisfactory condition in 1615 were by 1622 partly ruined or decayed. By contrast, only 2 churches partly ruined in 1615 were wholly repaired by 1622, and only 6 completely ruined in 1615 were partially repaired seven years later. However, so substantial was the apparent decay of church fabric, as measured by the increase in the number of wholly unrepaired churches in all three dioceses, that it seems highly unlikely that the increase can solely be attributed to natural causes during the short space of seven years uninterrupted by war or natural disaster. Rather, much of the increase is attributable to the inadequacy of the 1615 visitation returns, in particular to the large number of churches for which no details were given by the visitors. In Meath, of the 70 churches for which no details were given in 1615, in 1622 47 were returned as ruined, and only 7 as wholly in repair. Similarly in Kildare, of the 20 churches of which no details are given in the regal visitation, 15 were ruined and only 2 fully repaired seven years later. In addition, some of the returns for either 1615 or 1622 must be inaccurate, since they appear contradictory: the stark contrast between the state of 42 churches in Meath in 1615 which were returned as being in good repair, and their condition in 1622 when they were wholly unrepaired or ruined, can only partly be explained by natural deterioration. Similarly in Kildare, returns such as that for the parish church of Killadory reveal a fundamental inconsistency: in 1615 the church was said to be 'bene' (B.L.Add. MS 19,836, fol. 19r), but in 1622 it was returned as follows: 'pulled down in time of rebellion and never since rebuilt' (N.L.I. MS 8013, fol. 4r).

On balance, there is more reason for accepting the 1622 returns as accurate. Firstly, they are fuller and more circumstantial. Secondly, they accord with other accounts of the appalling state of church fabric in the Pale area. Finally, the visitors in 1615 admitted that they had left insufficient time in their circuit of Ireland to check on all the abuses in the church (B.L.Add. MS 19,836, fol. 136v; T.C.D. MS 566, fol. 95v). It would appear that one of the problems which they failed adequately to examine was the state of repair of parish churches.

CHAPTER 6

Protestantism in Gaelic Ireland

The Gaelic west of Ireland was one of the areas which the King and the English Privy Council were especially anxious should be evangelized by the Irish church. For in Connacht the people were, according to James's analysis, 'least civil', and therefore most amenable to conversion through preaching and instruction. Yet the Dublin officials and the leaders of the Irish church did not see the west as an area deserving of immediate attention: their priority was the Pale and Munster. Even when ordered by the English Privy Council in 1606 to alter their priorities, the Irish Privy Council claimed that no reforming activity could take place in the west 'before the erection of citadels in the places of greatest moment, and preparing of the minds of the inhabitants to hear the gospel preached and taught.'[1] In other words, the establishment of civil order and 'civility' were essential preconditions for reformation.

Nevertheless, it was not possible simply to ignore the challenge posed by the west of Ireland until the process of anglicization was complete. A few clergy in the Church of Ireland demonstrated a willingness to meet this challenge. They differed from their sixteenth century predecessors in their polemical aversion to Catholicism, and in their support for coercion, but in other respects a strong element of continuity can be discerned with the earlier efforts of native evangelists such as Bishops Brady, Walsh and Donellan. Indeed, the mainstay of the new evangelism, William Daniel, owed much to all three prelates in the early part of his career.

Daniel's early career followed a similar pattern to that of his fellow Kilkenny-man Barnabas Bolger, being collated to a prebend in Ossory by Walsh, which he held without cure whilst he studied at Cambridge.[2] Like Bolger, he chose the puritan seminary of Emmanuel as his college, and subsequently returned to the newly founded university in Dublin.[3] There became a fellow, and sought to develop the College's potential as a centre for the propagation of the gospel through Irish.[4] The essential basis for such evangelism was the provision of

---

1 S.P. 63/221/42 (1606–8, 142).
2 T.C.D. MS 566, fol. 111v; Leslie, *Ossory clergy*, 144; Grosart (ed.), *Lismore Papers*, 2nd ser., i, 39.
3 *Al. Cantab.*: B.A. 1590, M.A. 1593.
4 As with Bolger, the nature of Daniel's relationship with Trinity has been somewhat unclear. A.D.'s claim that Daniel was a scholar of Trinity in 1592 is based on the list of foundation scholars in the charter (McDonnell (ed.), *Charta*, 3) but this was little more than a formality, since the College did not admit students until

protestant texts in Irish. There were three main priorities: a vernacular bible; an Irish version of the Book of Common Prayer, which would avoid the ridiculous compromise of service being read in Latin to Irish-speaking congregations; finally, simple protestant devotional and instructive works, such as catechisms.

In England and many other continental countries, the translation of the bible had been an essential first step in the spread of the reformation. In Ireland, however, no native equivalent of Tyndale emerged in the early years of the reformation, nor could the country boast a native printing press with Gaelic type. It was not until Elizabeth's reign that progress was made in either of these respects.[5] In 1567 the Queen ordered that 100 marks be allocated 'for the making of a character to print the new testament in Irish'.[6] With this type a catechism was printed in 1571, translated into Irish by the Cambridge educated treasurer of St Patrick's, John Kearney.[7] Again through Kearney, this time with the help of that other Cambridge man, Nicholas Walsh, a start was made upon what was to prove the long and difficult task of translating the bible into Irish.[8] Lack of a printer and the death of the two collaborators delayed the project, until in the 1580s it was taken up by Nehemiah Donellan, yet another Cambridge graduate, and the printer William Kearney.[9] The latter, a kinsman of the Treasurer of St Patrick's, had plied his trade for many years in England, before being encouraged to return to Ireland in 1587 by the English Privy Council.[10] When Daniel came back to Ireland from Cambridge, he joined with Donellan in seeking to complete the translation begun by Kearney (John) and Walsh. Together with Maoilín Óg Mac Bruaideadha, a member of a Thomond family who were hereditary poets to the O'Brien dynasty, they worked in Trinity College.[11]

1593. In fact, Daniel's first appearance in the College records after the Charter is as a fellow *c.*1594 (P.B., 2a; Marsh's Library, MS Z4.2.7, p. 467).

5 J. Quigley, 'The history of the Irish bible', *The Irish Church Quarterly*, x (1917); S.C. Greenslade (ed.), *The Cambridge history of the bible*, 3 vols (Cambridge 1963), iii, 172f.; B. Dickens, 'The Irish broadside of 1571 and Queen Elizabeth's types', *Transactions of the Cambridge Bibliographical Society*, i (1949); E.W. Lynam, 'The Irish character in print, 1571–1923', *The Library*, 4th ser., iv (1924); E.R. McC.Dix, *The earliest Dublin printing* (Dublin 1901).

6 S.P. 63/22/70 (1509–73, 356); 'Fitzwilliam muniments at Milton, England', *Analecta Hibernica*, iv (1932), 299f.; J. Ware, *The antiquities and history of Ireland* (Dublin 1705), 15; D.B. Quinn, 'Information about Dublin printers, 1556–1573, in English financial records', *Irish Book Lover*, xxviii (1942), 113.

7 Dickens, 'Irish broadside', 48f.; 'Fitzwilliam muniments', 300.

8 A.P.C., 1587–88, 201; H.O Domhnuill [Uilliam Ó Domhnaill or William Daniel], *Tiomna nuadh* (Dublin 1602), fols 1v, 3v.

9 A.P.C., 1587–88, 201; B.L.Add. MS 4792, fol. 126r; T.C.D. Muniments.

10 A.P.C., 1587–88, 201; B.L.Add. MS 4792, fol. 126r; T.C.D. Muniments P/1/14.

11 Daniel, *Tiomna nuadh*, fol. 3v; Moody, Martin, Byrne (ed.), *New History of Ireland*, iii, 512, 524.

Trinity sought further to enhance its potential as a centre for Gaelic proselytization by offering support for William Kearney to set up his press in the College, and it was there that the Irish translation was set in print, up to the sixth chapter of Luke. Though a dispute led to Kearney's departure at that stage, the College negotiated new terms with him in 1596, which showed the extent of Trinity's involvement in the project. Kearney was to be supported as a fellow, and to be advanced sufficient money to print 1000 copies of the new testament. Upon his death, his press was to be left to Trinity 'for the continuance of that trade in the College'.[12] However, the hopes that Trinity might develop as a centre of Gaelic printing and evangelism were soon quashed by the financial difficulties of the 1590s. The printing project was left uncompleted, the University never inherited Kearney's press, and Daniel abandoned his fellowship to serve the church as a preacher, leaving Trinity without the services of any notable Irish speaking fellow.[13] Daniel therefore carried the project to completion outside Trinity, the New Testament being published in Dublin in 1602 with the financial support of William Ussher, Clerk to the Council, and the assistance of John Frankton, who was in 1604 appointed official printer to the Irish state.[14] With the first project partially completed, Daniel turned his efforts to the Prayer Book. Inspired by the encouragement of the Dublin administration, most especially Sir James Ley and Lord Deputy Chichester, and with the help of native speakers in Connacht, Daniel published his second translation in 1608.[15]

In view of the difficulties which he faced, Daniel's work as a translator was a considerable achievement. The practical difficulties, of finance, printing, and production were especially onerous, as Daniel himself recorded.[16] The scholarly task, too, was considerable. In his translation of the new testament, though he had the work of Kearney and Walsh, and the assistance of Donellan to draw upon in the early stages, after 1596 the responsibility was Daniel's alone, with the help of just one Irish scribe, Domhnall Óg Ó hUiginn.[17] Daniel was probably one of the few clergy in the Church of Ireland capable of carrying

12 Daniel, *Tiomna nuadh*, fol. 3v; T.C.D. Muniments, P/1/25.
13 Daniel, *Tiomna nuadh*, fol. 2r; S.P. 63/193/38 (1596–7, 121); see below, p. 110; for the fate of the Irish type see T.C. Barnard, *Cromwellian Ireland. English government and reform in Ireland 1649–1660* (Oxford 1975), 179.
14 Daniel, *Tiomna nuadh*, fols 2r, 3v; Bodleian, MS Carte 61, fol. 174r; B.L.Add. MS 4756, fol. 28v.
15 S.P. 63/227/142 (1608–10, 300); S.P. 63/217/95 (1603–6, 357f.); J. Perrott, *The chronicle of Ireland 1584–1608* (ed.) H. Wood (Dublin 1933), 184; Chichester was the dedicatee – Daniel, *Leabhar nurnaightheadh gcoimhchoidchiond agus mheinisdraldacha* (Dublin 1608).
16 Daniel, *Tiomna nuadh*, fol. 1v.
17 Ibid.

out such a task.[18] His difficulties were accentuated by the lack of any lengthy scholarly tradition of Gaelic biblical translation. Nor had he a reliable English translation. Hence he felt obliged to use the original Greek for the new testament.[19] In his second translation, Daniel naturally used his earlier work for the new testament epistles. For the old testament ones he had access to at least part of the new authorized version of the bible which was then in preparation.[20] For the remainder of the Prayer Book, he used the new English edition of 1604.[21]

Daniel outlined the purpose of his translations in the prefaces to his two works. His analysis of the religious situation in Ireland had much in common with that of Loftus and Jones, emphasising the deleterious effect which the Antichristian papacy had had upon an island which had once been a beacon of Christian light. Now, he proclaimed, Ireland 'doth generally sit in darkness', for 'yet hath Satan hitherto prevailed ... through the ignorance of our ministers, the carelessness of our magistrates, and the subtlety of Antichrist and his vassals, the filthy fry of Romish seducers, the hellish firebrands of all our troubles'.[22] However, he combined this familiar analysis with an assertion of the necessity of paying particular attention to the Gaelic Irish. They had 'been hitherto deprived of this heavenly comfort and means of their salvation' because the liturgy came to them 'in the cloud of an unknown tongue'. Not only did they live under this fruitless gospel, but they had also been led to believe by their 'blind malicious guides' that 'our divine service is nothing else but the service of the Devil.'[23] Sent into the 'mere Irish churches', Daniel's translations would, he hoped, serve to lighten this darkness and allay misconceptions.[24]

He thus combined the harsh anti-Catholicism of English protestantism with a genuine commitment to spreading the gospel through Irish. In the former attitude he was, of course, different from his native protestant predecessors. But Daniel was of a new generation. He had been educated at the puritan

18 Grosart ed., *Lismore papers*, 2nd ser., i, 39.
19 Daniel, *Tiomna nuadh*, fol. 1v.
20 William Eyre, who had been with Daniel at Emmanuel, was one of the Cambridge scholars who prepared the old testament part of the Authorized Version. In 1608 Eyre came to Trinity Dublin on the recommendation of Ussher's friend, Sam Ward, and whilst in Ireland he lent Daniel a copy of the translation then being made. Bodleian, MS Rawlinson C 849, fols 262v–263r; C. McNeill (ed.), 'Reports on the Rawlinson collection of manuscripts preserved in the Bodleian Library, Oxford, Classes A–D', *Analecta Hibernica*, ii (1931), 32f.
21 The desire for speedy publication caused Daniel to omit the Psalms from his translation: S.P. 63/217/95. However, it is wrong to claim that he omitted all the old testament epistles for a similar reason, as does H.R. McAdoo, 'The Irish translations of the Book of Common Prayer', *Éigse*, ii (1940), 250.
22 Daniel, *Tiomna nuadh*, fol. 1v.
23 Daniel, *Leabhar*, [fol. 3r].
24 Ibid.

seminary of Emmanuel, and had had early and first hand experience of the growing depth of the religious divide in Ireland, on his first venture into the pastoral ministry. This had begun with an attempt to revivify the moribund protestant reformation in Galway. In 1595 Lord Deputy Russell had visited Galway, and both his chaplain and Bishop Roland Lynch had preached to the inhabitants. As a result, the mayor requested the Dublin authorities to make some provision for more regular preaching in the city.[25] The administration turned to Daniel, recently installed as a fellow at Trinity, and he left his post there and set out early in 1596 'with cheerfulness to fulfil the work of the ministry'.[26] In September 1596 he described to Burghley how he had spent his time there 'most painfully in instructing this people both in the English and Irish tongue with great hope to prosper'. He had successfully rooted out 'their famous idols', but at the cost of considerable local hostility – some of the townspeople had stoned his residence. Indeed, he reported that the people generally 'dare not hear the word preached, nor baptise, nor marry publicly, nor bury their dead, but according to the Roman superstition'. Daniel's response was familiar. He demanded the banishment of the 'traiterous seminaries', those 'filthy frogs of the synagogue of Antichrist', since they were 'the smoking firebrands of all these troubles'.[27] Daniel persevered in Galway: in 1597 he was appointed to the Ecclesiastical Commission for Connacht, and he remained in the city until 1601.[28] When he left to see his new testament through the press in Dublin, he was succeeded in Galway by another protestant preacher and Trinity fellow, Abel Walsh, the son of Daniel's erstwhile patron, and an ex-student of Daniel's at Trinity.[29]

That Daniel had indeed made some impact in Galway is confirmed by one of those 'seminaries', Eugene Bernard, who arrived in the city in 1606. According to Bernard, Daniel and Walsh, whom he styled 'the most famous of the heretical preachers of this kingdom', had 'unfortunately succeeded in inducing many to attend their meetings and services.' Furthermore, they had won over some of the traditionalist native priests who 'allowed themselves first to communicate with, and afterwards be deceived by, the heretics, who told them that they could enjoy their benefices and say mass.' If Bernard's account is accurate, then the established church had made some progress in Galway.

25 *Carew Cal.*, 1603–24, 239.
26 S.P. 63/193/38 (1596–7, 121); he was granted a *concordatum* of £20 a year by the state for his services as a preacher in Galway: B.L. Add. MS 4792, fol. 126r.
27 S.P. 63/193/38 (1596–7, 121).
28 Fiant 6090, *Report of the Deputy Keeper of the Public Records of Ireland*, xv (1884); S.P. 63/206/126 (1599–1600, 360); S.P. 63/208 pt i/68 (1600–1, 208).
29 Walsh was resident in Galway by June 1602: Bodleian, MS Rawlinson C 919, p. 83; Leslie, *Ossory clergy*, 153; Walsh spent the remainder of his career in Tuam diocese, becoming Dean in 1610: T.C.D. Muniments P/1/73.

On the other hand, if one accepts Bernard's veracity, then it appears that protestant success was short-lived. Through preaching and lecturing – this in the face of repeated official efforts to arrest him – Bernard managed 'to effect a great improvement in this city'.[30] As a result, he claimed, few would associate with the protestant preachers.[31]

Even if it had not been for the efforts of Bernard and other seminarists, it is quite possible that the overwhelming practical and internal problems facing the reformed church in Connacht would have severely limited its evangelical effectiveness. The church's main problem was the shortage of protestant preachers. As the earl of Thomond remarked, when recommending Daniel for the archiepiscopal see, 'Would to God there were many of his sort, so able and willing ... '[32] Not even the elevation of Daniel to the archbishopric in 1609 led to any improvement. The problem and its main cause were explained by Sir Oliver St John in 1611, after he had visited Connacht. Apart from Daniel and his aged and retired predecessor, Donellan,

> there is indeed no ministry at all, nor churches standing, and very few places where those that are well affected in religion can assemble; and which is worst of all, the livings left so small as scarcely in the province, out of the chief towns, any other benefice can be found worth £10 *per annum*; and no possible means, as the country now stands, to make them better.[33]

St John's verdict was confirmed four years later by the regal visitors in their report on the state of the church in the province of Tuam. In Galway it appeared as if Martin, Lynch, Daniel and Walsh had never preached. The corporation by 1615 was firmly recusant, and little effort had been made to provide the city's churches with reformed clergy.[34] The College of Vicars had only two of its statutory complement of nine clergy. Of these two, the visitors found that one, the warden, who had been appointed by the corporation just before their arrival, was 'home lesae famae et vix probate vitae'; whilst the other minister was a pluralist, 'vagus undequique cursitans'. In conclusion, the visitors opined 'quod in eadem civitate vixissent pro maiore parte sine servitio divino et pene absque deo in terris'.[35]

30 E. Hogan (ed.), *Hibernia Ignatiana sue Ibernorum Societas Iesu patrum monumenta* (Dublin 1880), 206; Fitzsimons, *Words of comfort*, ed. E. Hogan, 161.

31 Hogan (ed.), *Ibernia Ignatiana*, 206; Daniel had, in late 1605, returned to Galway, and was still there in July 1606: Bodleian, MS Rawlinson C 849, fol. 6r.

32 S.P. 63/226/63 (1608–10, 186).

33 S.P. 63/231/31 (1611–14, 47).

34 J. Hardiman, *History of the town and county of Galway* (Dublin 1820), 218; O'Sullivan, *Old Galway*, 111, *Carew Cal.*, 1603–24, 145.

35 B.L.Add. MS 19,836, fol. 97r.

If such was the condition of the city which once had been described as the paradise of the reformed gospel, then the state of the surrounding dioceses which had never been as forward, could only be worse. As indeed it was. Tuam diocese, where Daniel was Archbishop, was, it is true, superficially well staffed. But only two (or possibly three) of the clergy were resident preachers. The remaining 31 were reading ministers, all clearly local men, existing on miserable livings, and presumably little different from those traditionalist clergy who had nominally conformed, and who earned the scorn of both protestant and Catholic commentators.[36]

In Tuam a vestigial protestant presence at least existed: in other dioceses even this was absent. One example will suffice. The see of Achonry, had been held by Archbishop Magrath since 1608.[37] By 1615 the diocese could boast five clergy. The Dean, William O'Flanegan, was non-resident, though he served the cure after a fashion, being also Dean of the neighbouring diocese of Killala.[38] The precentorship was held by Andrew Magrath, collated by his father, the Archbishop. He was returned by the visitors as 'by profession a monk', and possessed, despite his non-residence, 11 out of the 34 livings in the diocese.[39] The Archdeacon, Dermot Ultagh, was likewise non-resident: in addition the visitors declared him to be illiterate.[40] In all, just two clergy were resident in the diocese, which seems to have been used by Magrath to support those clergy whom the visitors of 1607 had thrown out of his other dioceses, Cashel and Emly.[41]

The church's difficulties were both caused and accentuated by its impoverishment. As it was put in 1621, the clergy 'are as ignorant as poor'.[42] Whatever financial problems other Irish provinces had appeared minor when compared with the near destitution of the church in Tuam. Most of the benefices were valued not in pounds but in shillings; vacancies were frequent; the scale of impropriation was massive – almost 80 per cent of rectories in Tuam province.[43] To a certain extent, as Daniel observed, such destitution was a reflection of

---

36 B.L.Add. MS 19,836, fols 97r–103r; T.C.D. MS 1066, pp. 435–51. The uncertainty over the number of preachers arises from the fact that John Shaw B.A. was included as a curate in Galway in T.C.D. MS 1066, but omitted in B.L.Add. MS 19,836. For Bernard's comment on the quality of the traditionalist clergy in Tuam, see Hogan ed., *Ibernia Ignatiana*, 206.

37 He had been granted Killala and Achonry in 1608 as 'compensation' for his enforced surrender of Waterford and Lismore: S.P. 63/223/29 (1606–8, 421f.).

38 B.L.Add. MS 19,836, fols 118r, 115r.

39 Ibid.

40 Ibid., fol. 118r.

41 Such as Ultagh, Magrath and O'Flanegan: see above, pp. 32, 88.

42 S.P. 63/236/9–12 (1615–25, 328ff.).

43 See above, Table 4, p. 87.

the poverty of the region itself.[44] However, the main reasons for the financial difficulties were two: the strength of the local lay landholders; and the inability or unwillingness of the bishops and clergy to oppose them. Magnates such as the earl of Clanrickard could ride roughshod over the rights of the clergy, especially since neither felt any particular loyalty to the established church.

The sees of Clonfert and Kilmacduagh, held by Roland Lynch till 1622, showed how a native prelate could, whether through necessity or cupidity, alienate considerable amounts of church land. In 1615 the visitors found that the value of the sees had declined remarkably during Lynch's episcopate. In 1602 Clonfert had been worth £160, in 1615, £40; in 1587 Kilmacduagh had been valued at £100, by 1615, only £24.[45] Two explanations were advanced. On the one hand the decline could be seen as a pragmatic and natural reaction of the bishop to a difficult financial and political situation. Lynch claimed that his sees had suffered severely during the recent rebellion, leaving him desperately short of revenue to repair the ruined cathedral of Kilmacduagh, and to pay off arrears of first fruits and twentieths owed to the exchequer. Furthermore, due to the action of Sir John King in the Presidency Court of Connacht, the monastery of Portu Puro, with which the see had been endowed, had been lost.[46] In order to procure money Lynch said that he had been forced to lease land to local laymen who were willing to pay sizeable entry fines in return for favourable leasing terms. On the other hand, the visitors rejected Lynch's explanation – 'admirandam relationem censemus'. Instead they ascribed the fall in value of the sees to negligence and fraud on Lynch's part, casting him as a lukewarm, time-serving Irish prelate, concerned more with feathering his own nest than protecting the rights of the church.[47]

One apparently promising feature of the Tuam visitation was the provision for educational facilities in the archiepiscopal diocese. Not only did Tuam possess a school, but it was run by a protestant preacher, Isaac Lally, born in Connacht but educated at Trinity, and attracted native pupils, some of whom were supported at school by livings without cure in Tuam diocese.[48] However, the fact that the school had a protestant teacher, and attracted native pupils, even the fact that some of the pupils were beneficed in the established church, did not mean that the institution was an effective instrument of protestant proselytization, or even a reliable means of providing a new generation of

44 Armagh Public Library, 'Returns of the bishops ... 1622', fol. 44v.
45 B.L.Add. MS 19,836, fol. 104r.
46 The impact of the rebellion was certainly serious: see Shirley ed., *Papers relating to the Church of Ireland*, 69; however, the history of Portu Puro was more complicated than Lynch made out: see J.C. Erck, *An account of the ecclesiastical establishment in Ireland: as also, an ecclesiastical register* (Dublin 1830), 244f.
47 B.L.Add. MS 19,836, fol. 104r.
48 A.D.; B.L.Add. MS 19,836, fol. 103r; N.L.I., MS 16,058, pp. 62f.

protestant preachers. Of the 26 students studying in Lally's school in 1615 and also possessing benefices, only six served in Tuam as clergy in 1622.[49] In fact, Lally's school was a source of Catholic, as well as protestant clergy: three of his students went on to become Jesuits at Salamanca.[50] Not even those few who pursued their studies at Trinity subsequently used their talents to foster the reformation in their native province: of the three students beneficed in Tuam in 1615 who went on to Trinity, all subsequently made their clerical careers in the richer eastern dioceses, one subsequently becoming Catholic.[51] Aeneas Callanan, one of the few native Irish graduates of Trinity beneficed in the Tuam province in 1615, was returned by the visitors as 'studiosus in Collegio, nunc apostata', and subsequently probably departed for Spain.[52]

And Lally's school in Tuam was by far the best in the province. In other dioceses a protestant educational system simply did not exist. Neither Achonry, Killala, Clonfert or Elphin possessed a diocesan schoolmaster.[53] In Kilmacduagh, it is true, a school operated in the cathedral, and attracted over 300 pupils. It was, however, conducted by a Catholic school master, which earned Bishop Lynch a serious reprimand from the visitors.[54] As this example suggests, the education of the youth of Connacht was firmly in the hands of Catholic teachers, the most notable of whom, Alexander Lynch, ran a school in Galway.[55] Lynch, trained as a Jesuit, ran a successful school, according to the 1615 visitors, attracting pupils from as far away as the Pale, and maintaining a high academic standard. The visitors summoned Lynch before them, and ordered him to conform: upon his refusal, they took a recognizance of £400 binding him to forbear teaching until he should conform. To replace Lynch they ordered that Lally should move his school from Tuam to Galway.[56] However, the protestant church could not abolish the Catholic educational system in Tuam by *Diktat*, and by the early years of Charles I's reign, the Catholic school was again operating in Galway.[57]

49 B.L.Add. MS 19,836, fols 97r–103r; Armagh Public Library, 'Returns of the bishops ... 1622', fols 37v–44v: Mathew Darcy, David MacGriavoy, Murtagh O'Kelly, Mark Lynch, John Bermingham, David O'Mulavoyle.

50 D.J. O'Doherty, 'Students at the Irish College, Salamanca (1595–1619)', *Archivium Hibernicum*, ii (1913), 31f.

51 A.D. s.v. Thady, Murtagh and William Donnellan.

52 A.D.; B.L.Add. MS 19,836, fol. 105v; T.C.D. MS 1066, p. 250; S.P. 63/239/56 (1615–25, 496).

53 B.L.Add. MS 19,836, fols 116v, 119r, 106r, 114v.

54 Ibid, fol. 109r–v.

55 O'Doherty, 'Students at Salamanca', 13; J. Rabbitte, 'Alexander Lynch, schoolmaster', *Journal of the Galway Archaeological Society*, xvii (1936), 34ff.; O'Sullivan, *Old Galway*, 462, doubts this identification, however.

56 B.L.Add. MS 19,836, fol. 103r.

57 O'Sullivan, *Old Galway*, 464f.

Daniel's efforts in Tuam, therefore, bore little fruit. As Sir James Ware would have it, Daniel in his later years took to drink and tobacco, and died in 1628 disillusioned, having never fulfilled the promise of his youth.[58] Certainly, his position as an evangelist in Connacht was difficult, faced with dilapidated churches, impoverished benefices, inadequate clergy and local hostility. For the most part, similar conditions prevailed throughout the west, with similar effects. There were, however, two exceptions, deserving of closer study: Killaloe and Elphin.

The main asset which the reformation possessed in Killaloe was the support of the earl of Thomond and some members of his family.[59] However, during the sixteenth century, any advantage which this might have offered protestantism was vitiated by the lack of any similar commitment on the part of Murtagh O'Brien, entrusted with ecclesiastical leadership in Killaloe.[60] It was not until Murtagh was finally induced to resign in 1611 that the annals of the reformation in Thomond can be truly said to begin.[61] Murtagh O'Brien was replaced by an Englishman, John Rider.[62] Educated at Oxford, Rider had been beneficed in the Church of England before coming to Ireland in the late 1590s, where he served initially as Dean of St Patrick's and Archdeacon of Meath.[63] His approach to religious policy was similar in most respects to that of other émigré clergy. His attitude towards Catholicism was that of a hostile protestant controversialist, denying that the Church of Rome was a true church, and arguing that Catholicism and political loyalty were incompatible. Like Loftus and Jones, he thought that recusancy legislation was the necessary basis for the protestantization of Ireland. Unlike them, however, he demonstrated a willingness to employ indigenous, Irish-speaking clergy and encourage their education at university.[64]

When he arrived in Killaloe, Rider was met by two problems familiar to all his fellow Church of Ireland prelates: shortage of clergy; and lack of resources to support them. The previous bishop had bequeathed him, he claimed, only seven clergy. His first priority therefore was to expand the ministry.[65] This

---

58 T.C.D. MS 6404, fols 67r, 105v.

59 See above, pp. 42f.

60 See above, pp. 45.

61 Ware, *Bishops*, 595.

62 R.D. Edwards (ed.), 'Letter book of Sir Arthur Chichester 1612–1614', *Analecta Hibernica*, viii (1938), 28f.

63 Ware, *Bishops*, 595f.; Wood, *Athenae Oxoniensis*, i, 577; B.L. Lansdowne MS 984, fol. 119r. For much of his early career in Ireland, Rider was supported by the Rectory of Winwick in Chester, to which he had been presented in 1597 by the Earl of Derby; he retained it in commendam with his bishopric for three years before resigning it in 1615: Wood, *Athenae Oxoniensis*, i, 548.

64 For Rider's views see below, pp. 181f., and sources there cited.

65 Dwyer, *Killaloe*, 145, 148; in addition to the seven listed by Rider in his return to the 1622 visitors, another three ministers at least are known to have been inducted

he achieved with remarkable rapidity, exploiting the considerable amount of patronage which rested in the bishop's hands, and regaining impropriate vicarages as benefices with cure.[66] By 1615, 31 clergy were beneficed in Killaloe, 26 of them resident.[67] These clergy were for the most part little different from those appointed elsewhere in the province of Cashel by English bishops: English immigrants and other non-local clergy; only nine ministers in 1615 bore local names.[68] The hope for the indigenous ministry in Killaloe lay with the eleven native scholars who held benefices without cure.[69] As has been seen in Tuam, such studiousness did not always redound to the benefit of the church. In Killaloe, however, the close links which Rider had with Trinity ensured that the native students had a clearly protestant education. Eight of the eleven students in 1615 attended Trinity, and all of these were subsequently ordained.[70] Amongst them were the Lysaght brothers, Daniel and Andrew, born in Tenemolis, Co. Clare. Daniel was granted the rectory and vicarage of Rath in 1612, to hold whilst studying at Trinity where he proceeded B.A. in 1613 and M.A. in 1616. He then returned to Killaloe, where he served Rath until 1620, when he moved to the archdeaconry of the neighbouring diocese of Kilfenora. In his place at Rath, Rider collated his brother, Andrew who had been a scholar at Trinity at the same time as Daniel, but who had never graduated. Though not a preacher, he could, nevertheless, read the service in Irish to his parishioners.[71]

Though Rider could procure native reading ministers, he had less success in attracting, and retaining the services of, native preachers. Thus the increase in the number of resident preachers from five in 1615 to 15 in 1622 was accomplished almost wholly through the appointment of English ministers; only one of the preachers in 1622 was local – Richard Hogan, a Trinity graduate.[72] At

to Killaloe benefices before Rider's episcopate, and to have served during the second decade of the century: Hugh O'Hogan, Daniel O'Kennedy, Patrick O'Hogan: Ibid, 102.

66 Ibid 141f.
67 T.C.D. MS 1066, pp. 235–56.
68 Peter Butler, Walter Fitzsimon, Cornelius McConsidine, Cornelius Mc Mahon, Hugh O'Hogan, Patrick O'Hogan, Cornelius O'Sherin, Daniel O'Kennedy, Bartholomew White (see O'Dwyer, *Killaloe*, 112). For details of local family names see R.C. Simington ed., *Books of survey and distribution* (Dublin 1967), iv.
69 Daniel Lysaght, Andrew Lysaght, James Darcy, Mark Lynch, Donogh O'Kennedy, John Hogan, Gerald Fitzgerald, Brian O'Hogan, Stephen Stephens, Nicholas Nelly, Thady Donnellan.
70 T.C.D. Muniments P/1/54; A.D.; Daniel and Andrew Lysaght, Thady and William Donellan, Mark Lynch, John Hogan, Gerald Fitzgerald, Nicholas Nelly.
71 P.R., 230, 506; A.D. Dwyer, *Killaloe*, 112.
72 Dwyer, *Killaloe*, 120. The other resident preachers in 1622 were: John Blanrave, Nicholas Booth, Nicholas Bright, William Capell, Andrew Chaplain, Marmaduke

the lower level, that of the reading ministry, Killaloe was, however, provided with an Irish speaking ministry. There were at least twelve native reading ministers in 1622, six of whom were returned as reading the Irish Book of Common Prayer to their parishioners.[73] Rider was fully aware of the importance of this stratum, and suggested to the 1622 Commissioners that special provision be made for those who read the 'service in the Irish tongue unto the parishioners, that others by their example may be encouraged to practice the reading of the Irish language, for the gaining of many of the natives'.[74]

The vital question was: were the native clergy successful in winning over 'many of the natives'? Rider gave conflicting answers. On the one hand, he stated that the natives 'hitherto will not hear us'.[75] Yet, on the other hand, some pages later in the same report, when complaining of the strength of Catholicism and the large number of priests active in his diocese, he claimed that the Catholic clergy were 'drawing back those whom the minister had formerly gained'.[76]

What seems to have happened in Killaloe was somewhat similar to that which had happened in the Pale and elsewhere in Munster. Rider, like other English bishops in these provinces, was fully committed to the legal enforcement of conformity, and was granted help by the earl of Thomond in this regard. By the statutory fine, and by excommunication, Rider in the early years of his episcopate constrained many of the local population of Thomond to attend protestant services. However, by 1622 this policy had run into difficulties, both locally and nationally. In Killaloe, Rider had discovered that Catholic juries were understandably reluctant to present recusants under 2 Eliz., and sheriffs unwilling to force them to do so. Sheriffs also proved unco-operative when it came to executing Rider's writs *de excommunicato capiendo*.[77] Finally, on a national level the enforcement of conformity against the ordinary people had been effectively suspended in 1621.[78] The consequence, Rider complained, was that 'the natives that come to church in the several parishes are all gone hack again'.[79]

Clapham, Thomas Edens, Peter Ellis, Edmund Phillips, Thomas Prichard, Marmaduke Taylor, Thomas Tunstead, Richard Walker, William Wevill.
73 Dwyer, *Killaloe*, 101–49: Peter Butler, John Hogan, Richard Hogan, William Kennedy, Andrew Lysaght*, Teig McKnavin, Brian O'Brian*, Murtogh McConsidin*, Dermot O'Harney, Daniel O'Meara, Brian O'Molahna*, Cornelius O'Sherin*, Bartholomew White: those marked with an asterisk read the service in Irish. One John Corbet, not obviously of local origin, was also recorded as doing so.
74 Dwyer, *Killaloe*, 130.
75 Ibid.
76 Ibid., 143.
77 Ibid., 139, 143.
78 Ibid., 144f.; and see below, p. 206.
79 Ibid., 145.

The role of the native reading ministers in Killaloe is now clearer. They were not inspired protestant evangelists, going out amongst their countrymen and convincing them of the truth of the protestant gospel. Rather, as described by the earl of Thomond, their purpose was to ensure that the church could communicate with 'the inferior sort and far greater number of inhabitants ... by civil or ecclesiastical censures enforced to repair to their churches, [who] are for the most part ignorant of the English tongue ... '[80] The danger, of course, was that when conformity was no longer enforced, as after 1621, they would have little purpose as ministers in the established church.

By the 1620s it was becoming apparent that the roots of native protestantism in Thomond were shallow, and that those who had conformed were coming under increasing pressure from their Catholic countymen. By 1622, though the High Sheriff of Clare was usually (though not always) conformist, the Under-Sheriff and other officials were recusants.[81] Though the Earl and Sir Turlough remained protestant, they could not offset the growing strength of Catholicism, even amongst the O'Brien family, as was illustrated by the last moments of Turlough, who died in 1623:

> in his weak and languishing condition his near friends and papist kindred would not suffer him to have any protestant minister to come near him, and after his death they hurried and buried him in a friar's habit in a superstitious island near the River Shannon.[82]

Because of the decline in lay support, and the consequent lack of native ordinands, English ministers naturally came to dominate the church in Killaloe. By the regal visitation of 1634, the number of resident clergy, insofar as they can be counted, had fallen from 36 to 31.[83] Of these, only six were native Irish, the remainder being of English extraction.[84] Just as the church looked to English clergy to serve the cures, so it looked to English settlers to provide the parishioners. In Thomond itself, a gradual influx of planters, including some Dutch as well as English, was encouraged in this period by the Earl.[85] And in Ely O'Carroll, in the extreme east of the diocese, an official plantation was begun in 1619, which transformed the town of Birr into an English stronghold.[86]

80 *Carew Cal.*, 1603–24, 376f.
81 Dwyer, *Killaloe*, 143.
82 S.P. 63/276/89 (Add. 1625–60, 298f.).
83 T.C.D. MS 1067, pp. 261–76; but see above, p. 83 n. 1.
84 Edmund Hurley, William Flanegan, Daniel McBrodin, Murtagh McConsidin, Brian McDonogh, Cornelius O'Sherin.
85 B. Cunningham, 'Political and social change in the lordships of Clanrickard and Thomond, 1569–1641', University College Galway, M.A. Thesis, 1979, 149.
86 N.D. Atkinson, 'The plantation of Ely O'Carroll 1619–1693', Dublin University

Thus the attempt to marry the coercive reformation with a commitment to an indigenous, Irish-speaking ministry yet again failed. Unlike Daniel in Tuam, Rider to a certain extent surmounted the practical and financial difficulties which he encountered. However, this merely brought him face to face with the entrenched position of Catholicism, and its prior claim upon the people's loyalty. Like Daniel, Rider in his old age lost interest in the day-to-day running of his diocese, and he ceded it to his son-in-law, the English-born Dean of Limerick, George Andrews.[87]

The other western diocese which was an exception to the general poverty and inadequacy of the Church of Ireland in this region was Elphin. In many ways Elphin followed a similar pattern to Killaloe. It was granted to a native reformed bishop in the sixteenth century whose protestant zeal declined with age. As a result the effective beginning of the reformation dates from his replacement in 1611 by an Englishman, Edward King. King had been born in Huntingdonshire and educated at St John's College, Cambridge, under the presbyterian Alvey. When the latter came to Trinity (Dublin) as provost, he was probably accompanied by King, who became a fellow in the new College.[88] As Bishop, King faced severe economic constraints. The only benefice adequately endowed was the bishopric – worth £300 by 1615 thanks to King's success in recovering see lands.[89] The next most valuable benefice in 1615 was the deanery worth only 20 marks, whilst the remaining livings ranged from 20s. to £6.[90] The poverty was largely the result of the local lay stranglehold over church property. Of the 49 rectories, 46 were impropriate, and even the remaining three were detained by laymen illegally.[91] Most seriously from the

M.Litt Thesis, 1958; T.L. Cooke, *The early history of the town of Birr, or Parsonstown* (Dublin 1875).

87 Sheffield City Library, Strafford MSS, vol. 6, p. 100; according to Wentworth, Andrews undid much of the good Rider had done in restoring the sees finances.

88 There is some disagreement about King's career. He was certainly born in Huntingdonshire: Wood, *Athenae Oxoniensis*, ii, 850; Ware, *Bishops*, 634. A.D. claims him as M.A. T.C.D., 1596, fellow 1600, D.D. 1614; but Venn gives him as sizar St John's, matric. *c.*1594, B.A. 1598, M.A. 1601. It is Venn that is correct. King was indeed a graduate of T.C.D.: T.C.D. Muniments P/ 1/73. But the College only awarded him a D.D.: Ware, *Bishops*, 634. Ussher confirms that King studied at St John's College under Alvey for his other degrees: U.W., xvi, 35; McNeill ed., *Tanner Letters*, 116. A.D. has almost certainly confused Edward King with John King, a lay benefactor of the College, referred to in the College accounts of December 1595: P.B., 91a. Edward King does not appear in the college records until the arrival of Alvey in 1601, when his wages are recorded along with those of the other fellows: P.B., 24a.

89 T.C.D. MS 1066, p. 489; B.L.Add. MS 19,836, fol. 110r; P.R.O. 31/8/202/84 (1611–14, 346f.).

90 B.L.Add. MS 19,836, fols 110r–114v; T.C.D. MS 1066, pp. 489–501.

91 See Table 4, above, p. 86.

point of view of pastoral care, a large number of vicarages were likewise detained, supposedly as impropriate, without any provision being made for curates.[92]

Nevertheless, King managed to overcome these difficulties, and created a protestant ministry. As St John remarked in 1615, not only had the Bishop 'drawn divers preachers into his diocese', but, as a consequence, he 'begins to have congregations'.[93] The contrast with the remainder of Connacht was noted by St John, and confirmed by the 1615 visitors. In all, Elphin had 18 resident clergy in 1615: of these seven were preachers, well over half the total preachers in the province of Tuam.[94] King's links with Trinity were reflected in the presence of three Trinity men amongst the preachers. Generally, the ministry was evenly divided between those with Irish, and those with new English surnames.[95]

By 1634, however, the ministry in Elphin had changed markedly. It had, firstly, grown substantially. A total of at least 27 clergy were resident, of whom at least 17 were preachers.[96] Secondly, its character had altered: the ministry was now dominated by English names, with just a scattering of native Irish clergy. Even the five graduates from Trinity included William Newport, Miles Sumner, William Hollowell (from Cheshire), and John King (son of the Bishop, educated at Trinity (Dublin) and Christ's Cambridge).[97] This change was closely linked to the growth of English settlement in the diocese, and the growing attractiveness of Irish livings for English clerics. As the easternmost diocese of Tuam, in counties Sligo and Roscommon, Elphin attracted English settlers from quite an early date, an influx which was encouraged after 1618 by the plantation of the neighbouring counties of Leitrim and Longford.[98] Amongst the émigré clergy was Lionel Sharpe, who graduated from Balliol in 1619 and procured a benefice in Ireland through his uncle's influence with the Lord Deputy. He was ordained by Bishop King in 1623, and in 1634 was returned by King as 'a good divine, M.A. and a preacher'.[99] Such people as

---

92 B.L.Add. MS 19,836, fol. 113v.

93 S.P. 63/233/9 (1615–25, 17).

94 See Table 1, above, p. 81.

95 The Trinity ministers were: John Ankers, William Roycroft, Florence Nelly. Roycroft had been a scholar, but had not graduated. The Irish clergy were: Florence Nelly, Randal O'Dunmory, Hugh Brehon, Roger O'Scully, Hugh O'Greghan, Piers O'Skimin, Thady O'Rourke.

96 See Table 3, above, p. 85.

97 A.D.; Hollowell, though not listed in A.D., was at Trinity: T.C.D. Muniments P/1/127: for King see Peile, *Biographical register of Christ's*, i, 394.

98 Roscommon was one of the few areas of English settlement in Connacht in 1614: *Carew Cal.*, 1603–24, 292ff.; by 1641 there were an estimated 140 families of English and Scots protestants in Co. Sligo: T.C.D. MS 83Q, fol. 24r.

99 *Al. Cantab.*; B.L.Add. MS 3827, fol. 134r; T.C.D. MS 1066, p. 172.

Sharpe would not have been attracted to Elphin had not the financial rewards improved substantially since 1615. This was indeed the case. Between 1615 and 1634 the average value of a living rose from £2 13s.4d. to just over £5: by uniting benefices, the increase in the income of individual clergy could be even greater. Nor was the improvement confined to the lower clergy, since the bishopric too had grown in value under King. Through increasing rents on leases as they fell due, and by reducing fee farms to 60 year leases, King's see by 1638 was worth £1,340.[100] His efforts won the approval of Wentworth, who gave a revealing account of the kind of church which Elphin had created in Elphin:

> The town of Elphin where there was nothing but Irish cabins without a chimney, he hath in his time built very prettily so as you would take it for a handsome village in England, but shows for no less in these parts than a godly city, a handsome little church raised forth out of the ground at his own charge, and a very pretty little but strong castle close by ... [101]

As Daniel and other native Irish bishops in Tuam province died in the 1620s, they were replaced by Englishmen and Scotsmen. These new prelates, like King in the town of Elphin, sought to create a church after the fashion of their native land. They sought to impose English norms in their sees, particularly in relation to episcopal finances, and brought with them their clerical fellow-countrymen to see that these norms were implemented and a truly protestant ministry established. Not for them any attempt to mediate between their foreign clergy and the local inhabitants by a stratum – even a subordinate stratum – of native, Irish speaking clergy. They found the local population hostile, and such native clergy as they inherited were generally found unfit for the ministry.

In Killala and Achonry, Miler Magrath was succeeded by two Scots, Archibald Hamilton and Archibald Adair. Under them, the diocesan clergy were transformed from a wholly native body in 1615 to a largely Scottish ministry in 1634.[102] The Scottish ministry's relations with the local inhabitants were difficult and troublesome. Ostensibly, the main cause of friction was the familiar problem of tithes and dues. In fact, however, the conflict went considerably deeper, having racial and religious overtones. For Bishop Hamilton had brought in Scottish clergy to replace the local native ministers, and with

---

100 Ware, *Bishops*, 634; Shirley (ed.), *Papers relating to the Church of Ireland*, 56f.; S.P. 63/256/95 (1633–47, 189f.).
101 Sheffield City Library, Strafford MSS, vol. 6, p. 209.
102 B.L.Add. US 19,836, fols 115r–119r; T.C.D. MS 1066, pp. 503–12; T.C.D. MS 1067, pp. 146–63.

them had set about exacting tithes and dues according to English, rather than Gaelic custom. Since these foreign clergy did not actually minister to the local people from whom they demanded support, and were frequently non-resident, friction was hardly surprising.[103]

The way in which race, religion and cultural tradition became intertwined in such disputes, and the extent of polarization, can be seen in the dioceses of Clonfert and Kilmacduagh. Bishop Roland Lynch, whose conduct had been so heavily criticised by the visitors in 1615, died in December 1625.[104] After an embarrassing vacancy of six months, during which no one could be persuaded to accept the two remote and impecunious sees, Robert Dawson, Dean of Down and Chaplain to Lord Deputy Falkland, took on the task.[105]

Dawson's analysis and evaluation of his predecessor's conduct was even less charitable than that of the 1615 visitors. According to Dawson, Lynch had been 'so favourable to his country', that he had let the Dean and Chapter of Kilmacduagh retain their places, though recusants. Together with Lynch's wife, this Dean and Chapter had, he claimed, persuaded Lynch to alienate all the revenues of the church 'as the surest way to prevent any of the British nation, or conformable to the Church of England, to succeed in his sees, least they might restrain the popish insolency or discover the nature of that country.' The most revealing aspect of Dawson's account are the terms which he claimed the local inhabitants presented to him upon his arrival:

> The present bishop being an Englishman and the first (of any quality) that there dwelt in these dioceses, is very unwelcome, and cannot obtain any correspondency with the inhabitants, but upon their terms, viz.:
> To permit them to hold all their lands as their own.
> Secondly to permit their vicar general from the Pope to exercise juris-diction and suffer his own power and authority to sleep.
> Thirdly to permit them to hold all the church livings as they formerly held by lease, and appoint such incumbents upon any vacancy as may bear the name and they have the profits; and to let them swallow up all the glebes that lie convenient to their own lands, and the other rectories and vicarages which are not in lease they will keep by colour of impropri-ations; and to give further way to any encroachments upon the church as occasion falls out.
> And lastly, to permit the free exercise of their Romish superstition in every church, and even in the town where the bishop resideth.

103 Signet Office, 1/1, pp. 463ff. (1625–32, 458).
104 See above, pp. 113.
105 S.P. 63/243/397 (1625–32, 143); S.P. 63/243/428 (1625–32, 153).

And because the present bishop seeks for redress in these particulars
the [inhabitants] do by all means prosecute him and his clergy ... [106]

Even if Dawson was exaggerating in order to improve his case to the Dublin
authorities, the general tenor of his relations with the local population is clear.
The English interloper was the focus of strong native animosity, since he was
viewed as a threat to the *modus vivendi* which had been achieved between the
local population and the established church which enabled the former to both
practice their Catholic religion and enjoy the established church's incomes.
Dawson saw the conflict in racial and religious terms, between Catholic Irish
and protestant English, as if the lines of demarcation were indissolubly drawn.
The Irish, he complained two years later, had plotted the dismemberment of
the see 'to prevent the coming of all English into these parts for reformation,
and to preserve for themselves the free exercise of their superstition.' Nor had
he at this later stage made any progress in breaking this impasse, since 'the
clergy (being natives) and laity as one man in a joint knot of faction ... oppose
and oppress me. I have in vain these four years (to my utter impoverishing)
struggled by course of law to untie that knot, which I now conceive cannot
be loosed, but must be cut.'[107]

One way of cutting the knot was by appealing to Bishop Laud for help in
his financial difficulties. By this means he managed to secure the return of the
monastery of Portu Puro to the see, but he was still struggling to recover the
remainder of his episcopal possessions in 1639.[108] In his efforts to overcome
the 'joint knot of faction' he was more successful, since the high proportion
of collative benefices enabled Dawson to alter the constitution of the ministry
as he wished. With few exceptions, upon the death, resignation or deprivation
of native incumbents, Dawson collated a minister who was clearly English.
From October 1627, up to 1639, a whole series of such appointments are
recorded in Clonfert and Kilmacduagh, transforming the ministry in a similar
manner to that of Bishops Hamilton and Adair in Killala and Achonry.[109]

Dawson's experiences demonstrate the extent to which religious and racial
antipathy had become bound up, dividing the Catholic Irish from the protestant English. The hostility of the local population was linked both to their

106 S.P. 63/250/116 (1625–32, 547f.).
107 S.P. 63/253/50 (1625–32, 668).
108 Sheffield City Library, Wentworth MSS, vol. 6, p. 80, vol. 20/129; Laud, *Works*,
    ed. Scott and Bliss, vii, 57; S.P. 63/257/8 (1633–47, 212): see also K.W. Nicholls,
    'The episcopal rents of Clonfert and Kilmacduagh', *Analecta Hibernica*, xxvi (1970),
    131–133; Shirley ed., *Papers relating to the Church of Ireland*, 69f.
109 Representative Church Body Library, Dublin, J. Leslie, Clonfert and Kilmacduagh
    clergy, pp. 416, 421, 431, 434, 436, 442, 448, 453, 457, 460, 465, 468, 477, 482,
    489, 496f., 505, 516, 523, 538, 540, 546, 551, 553.

determination to preserve the free exercise of their religion, and to their fears for the impact which an English interloper would have upon their enjoyment of church property. All this was far removed from the situation envisaged by the English Privy Council earlier in the century, when it had imagined that the rude and ignorant people of the west could be converted with relative ease if suitable preachers were sent to minister unto them. Whatever the possibility this policy had of success in the early seventeenth century, by the late 1620s and 1630s it was doomed, since, on both sides of the religious divide, opinion and allegiance were hardening.

One man, however, refused to accept the inevitability and irreversibility of the identification of the English with protestantism and the Irish with Catholicism. William Bedell, born in Essex in 1571, was educated at Emmanuel Cambridge, and served for many years as a pastor in the Church of England before in 1627 being appointed provost of Trinity College Dublin.[110] Upon taking up this position, Archbishop Abbot had instructed him to 'have a principal care of the bringing in of the natives of that country' into Trinity.[111] Bedell took this to heart, and his concern with educating, instructing and evangelizing the native people of Ireland remained with him throughout the remainder of his career, all of which was spent in Ireland. As provost he instilled new vitality into Trinity's religious life, and sought to remedy the College's previous neglect of the Irish language. He himself set about learning Irish, and ordered that the College's native scholars 'for the better conversion of their own countrymen should be exercised in the reading of the scriptures in the Irish language.'[112] He also instituted an Irish lecture in the College, and Irish prayers in the chapel on holy days.[113] The lecturer was a native speaker, who was also entrusted with the duty of ensuring that the Irish scholars pronounced the language correctly.[114] In short, Bedell's zeal in fostering the Irish language as an evangelical weapon contrasted markedly with the pious intent and effective indifference of the College authorities during the previous two decades.[115]

Bedell also tried to complete the programme of providing essential religious texts in Irish. Whilst at Trinity he began what would prove to be a lifelong task of translating the old testament, and in 1631 he published a catechism,

110 Bedell was well served by seventeenth century biographers: E.S. Shuckburgh, (ed.), *Two biographies of William Bedell* (Cambridge 1902); Nicholas Bernard, 'A character of Bishop Bedell', in *The judgement of the late Archbishop of Armagh*, 2nd ed. (London 1659); G. Burnett, *The life of William Bedell* (London 1685).
111 T.C.D. Muniments P/1/181.
112 Shuckburgh ed., *Two biographies of Bedell*, 41.
113 T.C.D. Muniments, Registry, p. 15.
114 McNeill ed., *Tanner letters*, 87.
115 See the treatment of this topic in H.J. Monck Mason, *The life of William Bedell, D.D. Lord Bishop of Kilmore* (London 1843), 95–151.

together with basic religious texts in parallel English and Irish versions.[116] By this time he had left Trinity, having been made Bishop of Kilmore and Ardagh in 1630. In these largely Gaelic dioceses, straddling the border between the Ulster plantation and Connacht, he set about putting into practice the pastoral concerns, and openness to Irish culture and people, which he had attempted to instil into his Trinity students. Through his gentle demeanour and his persuasive efforts he did, at the least, succeed in making himself acceptable to the local population, and avoided any open religious polarization and racial hostility which Dawson had aroused in Clonfert and Kilmacduagh. Consequently, Bedell, almost alone amongst the protestant clergy in Ireland, was spared the hatred and mistrust of the native Irish in the rising of 1641.[117]

Bedell was significant, however, less for his achievements in converting native Irish – which were as yet unclear when his ministry was cut short by the rising – than for the way in which he pointed the contrast between his approach and that of other Irish prelates and churchmen. For he differed fundamentally from the vast majority of protestant clergy in Ireland in his theology, his reformation policy, and his cultural and religious tolerance. Indeed, his affectation of Irish language and manners was mocked by his fellow churchmen as inappropriate to an English bishop in Ireland.[118] It was with this firm commitment to anglicization that the future path of the Church of Ireland lay. Despite Bedell's efforts, and despite the fact that the province was almost wholly Irish speaking, the established church in the 1630s sought to create an anglicized church in Connacht, relying upon English-speaking clergy, and concentrating in their ministry upon those areas where English or Scots had settled.

The challenge which the Gaelic west had posed to the protestant church at the start of the seventeenth century had therefore largely been ignored. With the exception of Daniel and Rider in the early years of their episcopates, little effort was made to bring the protestant gospel to the native population. The failure was a product of a complex nexus of causes. Firstly there were the immense practical difficulties of supplying suitably trained clergy and supporting them. Secondly, the strength of the Catholic church, and its close ties with the local population, ensured that the emasculated attempts which were finally made to evangelize the people had in any case little chance of success. Thirdly, the ideological and theological preconceptions of the established church, as shall be seen, reinforced the already inherently elitist nature of the anglicizing and coercive reformation strategy.

When proposals were made in the 1630s to plant parts of Connacht, they

116 Quigley, 'Irish bible', 54ff.; Maddison, 'Boyle and the Irish bible', 81–5; W. Bedell, *The A.B.C., or the instruction of a Christian* (Dublin 1631); Shuckburgh, *Two biographies of Bedell*, 55f.
117 Shuckburgh ed., *Two biographies of Bedell*, 74f., 205.
118 Ibid., 29; for Bedell's theological views, see below, pp. 216–8.

were therefore enthusiastically supported by the English and Scots bishops of the region. Not only did they hope to improve the financial position of the church as a result of the redistribution of land, but, as Bishop King argued, settlement was the natural way to forward the reformation.[119] The colonial mentality, and its religious assumptions, appeared clearly in two of the early plantation proposals, dating from 1630. The first concerned lands along the Shannon, including those of Arra in the diocese of Killaloe. The author argued bluntly that 'As there are not English in that country, neither is there the face of a church or any resident ministers. If there was a plantation churches would be endowed.'[120] The second suggested planting counties Roscommon, Sligo and Mayo. These, according to the author, were inhabited by a 'poor and indigent people, as barbarous in all respects as the Indians or the Moors.' The plantation would serve to civilize them, by bringing in English magistrates and ministers who 'may spread the protestant religion and rebuild the churches.'[121] Whether such optimism was justified may be gauged from an examination of the extent to which the major official plantation scheme of the early seventeenth century -- in Ulster -- helped to spread the reformation in that province.

119 Sheffield City Library, Strafford MSS, vol. 20/127, 20/144, 20/146, 20/166.
120 S.P. 63/269/89 (Add. 1625–60, 150–2).
121 S.P. 63/269/45 (Add. 1625–60, 128f.).

CHAPTER 7

Ulster: the colonial reformation

However uninspiring the condition of the established church in Connacht by the end of the sixteenth century, in Ulster it was still less impressive. In Connacht the fragmentary basis of an established church at least existed: the presidency enabled the Dublin government to exercise a certain degree of authority in the region; and the bishops at least formally acknowledged royal supremacy. In Ulster, however, not even this perfunctory foundation had been laid. The power of the O'Neills and other Irish chiefs ensured that the province remained outside the ambit of the Dublin government, and this was reflected in the way in which the Ulster clergy continued to owe their allegiance to the Pope. Consequently, the province was, with the exception of some few areas, such as the garrison at Carrickfergus, and the southern border regions, largely *terra incognita* for the Church of Ireland during the latter part of the sixteenth century.[1]

Such relative freedom was, of course, ended by the defeat of O'Neill and his allies in the Nine Years War: after 1603, the extension of the government's and the Church of Ireland's power and influence into Ulster went hand in hand. At first, given the nature of the province, it seemed as if the reformation would have to follow a similar course to that attempted initially in Connacht, since the province was almost wholly native Irish. Thus Irish-speaking bishops were appointed and encouraged to reside in their Ulster dioceses in an attempt to provide a protestant ministry for the indigenous inhabitants.[2] Given the shortage of such clergy in the Church of Ireland, the prospects for the reformation in Ulster did not appear particularly bright. However, the flight of the Earls in 1607, their attainder, and the subsequent plantation of

---

1 Most sees in the province were, as a result, simply left unfilled by the crown in the later sixteenth century: Clogher was without a royal nominee from 1571 to 1604; Derry *c.*1569–1603; Down and Connor 1582–93; Dromore *c.*1575–1607; Kilmore 1559–85 and 1589–1603; Raphoe 1561–1604. Carrickfergus was a protestant outpost because of the English garrison there.

2 Archbishop Ussher was ordered to spend the summers in that part of his diocese which was *inter hibernicos*: S.P. 63/217/63 (1603–6, 317). Denis Campbell was nominated to the sees of Derry and Raphoe in 1603, but died before he could be consecrated: Leslie, *Derry clergy*; S.P. 63/161/52 fol. 119v. Robert Draper, an Irish speaker, like Ussher and Campbell, was made bishop of Kilmore and Ardagh in December 1603: S.P. 63/215/92 (1603–6, 86).

the six escheated counties utterly altered the whole basis of the reformation in Ulster. Now it was part of a colonial strategy, part of the planned settlement of the province.

Precisely what the colonial context implied for the development of the reformation in Ulster was not abundantly clear from the previous history of settlement in Ireland. While the latter part of the sixteenth century had seen considerable colonial activity in Ireland, the religious impact of these ventures had not been particularly emphasised. Even the major official project, the Munster plantation, had been conceived largely in secular terms, with its religious impact in its first decade being decidedly ambiguous.[3] Yet, even in its purely secular implications, and still more in the wider context of European colonization, settlement had a decisive impact in shaping religious policy, especially with regard to relations with the native population.[4] For plantations obviously had a direct impact upon local inhabitants. Most particularly, the tensions and conflicts between settlers and natives could lead to the alienation of the latter, with obvious implications for efforts to spread settlers' religious beliefs. In the early modern period in Ireland and America, it has been suggested, the aggressive attitudes of the colonists towards the natives had precisely such an alienating effect. Nicholas Canny has argued that this aggression sprang from the English colonists' belief in their cultural superiority over the Irish or the Indians. This in turn was linked with the increasing awareness of primitive civilizations and the nature of historical and cultural development. Thus the Irish, like the American Indians, were categorized by the English as pagans, savages, and barbarians. By consigning the natives to a lower order of humanity, it is argued, the settlers could justify the 'indiscriminate slaying and expropriation' of the indigenous population.[5] This view of settler/native relations was, therefore, bleak – ruthless exploitation was the primary concern of the English, with little more than lip-service being paid to the civilizing or conversion of the natives. In Ireland, Canny claimed, the harshness of English

3 See above, p. 37f.
4 Robert Ricard, *The spiritual conquest of Mexico* transl. L.B. Simpson (Los Angeles 1966); C.R. Boxer, *The church militant and Iberian expansion 1440–1770* (Baltimore 1978); K.O. Kupperman, 'British attitudes towards the American Indian', Cambridge Univ. Ph.D. Thesis, 1977; R.H. Pearce, *The savages of America: a study of the Indian and the idea of civilization*, rev. ed. (Baltimore 1965); F. Jennings, *The invasion of America. Indians, colonialism and the cant of conquest* (Williamsburg 1979); B.W. Sheehan *Savagism and civility. Indians and Englishmen in colonial Virginia* (Cambridge 1980); H.C. Porter, *The inconstant savage: England and the North American Indian 1500–1660* (London 1979).
5 N.P. Canny, 'The ideology of English colonization: from Ireland to America', *William and Mary Quarterly*, xxx (1973); idem, *The Elizabethan conquest of Ireland: a pattern established* (Hassocks 1976).

settlers and officials during the Deputyship of Sidney led to a complete break-down in the relations between the English on the one hand, and the native and Anglo-Irish on the other.[6]

If this was indeed the situation in the 1570s, one might expect that the Ulster plantation, far from helping to win the native inhabitants over to the established church, might actually drive them away. However, colonial ideology cannot be easily defined and explained in so precise a manner. In such matters it has been noted that 'the evidence is ... scattered, and no individual writer stuck consistently to one point of view'.[7] Thus, while it is undoubtedly true that colonists in Ireland and America were at times aggressive and arrogant, and that this can be partially explained as a product of their sense of cultural superiority, other explanations for their behaviour must also be taken into account, in particular those relating to the legal and religious contexts.

English behaviour in Ireland, and also in America, can, firstly, be examined within the much more straightforward and familiar contemporary context – that of 'law and law determined processes'.[8] The persistent Tudor concern with the exercise of social control through the legal system, and the emphasis upon the common law as the basis of an ordered society, are especially helpful in explaining the excesses of the colonists. Where normal legal process was threatened by rebellion or violence, there was a natural tendency by those in authority to react harshly. In a colonial situation, such as Ireland or America, the danger often appeared great: hence the ferocity of the response. In particular, where the people seen as responsible for the threat were relatively powerless, they could be treated with great severity. As one historian of English colonization in America has put it,

> Europeans of the late sixteenth and early seventeenth centuries were capable of acting with barbarity towards those who were powerless, whether they were Indians or Europeans. The civilization of which they were so proud and confident was not fully internalized. When they were outside their normal society and its constraints, their deviations from standards of civilization could be enormous. This was especially true if, as in the case of colonization or service in war, the condition of being separated meant personal risk and the possibility of great power over other human beings. It was the effect of unrestricted power, not preconceived racism, which caused the English to treat the American Indians as they did.[9]

6 Canny, *Elizabethan conquest*, Chap. 7.
7 Ibid., 131.
8 H.H.W. Robinson-Hammerstein, review of Canny, *Elizabethan conquest*, in *Irish Historical Studies*, xxi (1978), 106–11.
9 Kupperman, 'British attitudes towards the American Indian', 352; see also *idem*, *Settling with the Indians. The meeting of English and Indian cultures in America*,

From this point of view, the aggressive behaviour of colonists in Ireland was the result of their anxiety about their safety, and their desire to establish their political and legal authority over the native population. Once this had been achieved, then it was possible to resort to more pacific relations with the local inhabitants. This was reflected in the two stages of colonization favoured by some theorists, such as Edmund Spenser and William Herbert. Thus the first stage of Spenser's plan for the reformation of Ireland envisaged the extensive use of force to 'pacify' the country and establish the rule of law. In the second stage, however, instruction and persuasion would be used, in order to win over the native population to 'civility' and religion.[10]

It should be noted that, just as this approach was double edged, so too was the weapon of cultural superiority. Whilst, on the one hand, the latter could be used to justify ruthless exploitation and extermination, it could also lead naturally to the acculturation of the native population by gentle means – one must lead the ignorant natives gently towards the delights of civility. Thus colonization was not *necessarily* associated with harsh methods. Much depended upon the individual psychology of the settlers, the degree of security they enjoyed, and the extent to which the natives proved amenable to acculturation.

The second context within which English colonization must be viewed is the religious one. It is true that in Ireland religious reform was not, in the late sixteenth century, a particularly prominent element in colonial motivation – simple economic and strategic considerations weighed more heavily with both the government and private venturers.[11] Similarly, in relation to America, though the missionary aim was more clearly expressed, many historians have dismissed it as a hypocritical cover for more mundane motives of personal and national profit.[12] But the idealism of European colonization, whose primary aim was frequently claimed to be the conversion of hitherto ignorant and savage people to Christianity, ought not to be doubted simply because it went hand in hand with more easily identifiable economic aims. As Cortez put it, 'the chief and principal cause of our coming into this country, was to set forth

1580–1640 (London 1980), 188. While Canny's interpretation is a possible means of explaining the massacres of the native Irish, it cannot be used similarly to elucidate the reason for the massacres of Spaniards at Smerwick, or after the Armada. Within the framework of legal process, however, both the Irish and the Spanish massacres are explicable.

10 Spenser, *View of the present state of Ireland*, 140ff.; W. Herbert, *Croftus sive de Hibernia liber*, ed. W.E. Buckley (London 1887), 18–22, 54.
11 See above, p. 37f.
12 Jennings, *Invasion of America*; L.E. Pennington, 'The Amerindian in English promotional literature 1575–1625', in K.R. Andrews, N.P. Canny, P.E.H. Hair (eds). *The westward enterprise: English activities in Ireland the Atlantic and America, 1450–1650* (Liverpool 1978), 175f. and references there cited.

the faith of Jesus Christ, and there withal doth follow honour and profit which seldom times do dwell together'.[13] The difficulty lay in the way in which, in practice, the religious and more pragmatic aims of colonization could become separated. This was all the easier, since, in colonial theory, it was generally accepted amongst English writers that, before evangelization could take place, the basis of order had to be established and the native population brought to civility. Rather than seeing 'religion' as a means whereby the people could be brought to 'civility', as the Spanish writers did, the protestant authors insisted that civility was a necessary prerequisite for conversion.[14] As one propagandist preacher stated in 1609, the Indians in Virginia must be brought 'to civility, and so to religion'.[15] Naturally, until such civility had been achieved, the church had little incentive for missionary endeavour: its main task was to preserve and strengthen the piety of the settlers. Hence the lack of evangelical zeal amongst the early colonists in America did not *necessarily* bear witness to the hypocrisy of their original intention of converting the natives: it can also be seen as a product of their view of the relationship between conversion and civility.

In Ireland, even though the formal commitment to a missionary aim was not present during the sixteenth century, a similar approach to the religious dimension of colonization can be discerned. Both Herbert and Spenser consigned evangelization to the second stage of their programme. In addition, the necessity of establishing civility and order as a prerequisite to conversion fitted neatly with the preferred reformation strategy of protestant clergy in Ireland, which stressed the need for the way to be prepared for the reformation by the exercise of the legal power of the state. Another explanation for the savagery of the colonists in Ireland during Sidney's time could therefore be two essential elements in contemporary theology: 'the natural wilfulness of man which yields only to fear, and ... punishment perpetrated upon the unruly as the execution of God's justice'.[16] Like the stress upon legal process, this approach initially emphasised the necessity of coercion. However, where the former only had the limited aim of imposing magisterial authority and social order, the latter looked beyond, to the use of the newly ordained legal powers to establish protestantism. Whereas the settlers might rest content with the first stage, once their safety and economic prosperity had been secured, the church was

13 F. Lopez de Gomara, *The pleasant historie of the conquest of the weast India, atchieved by H. Cortes*, transl. T. Nicholas (London 1578), 299.

14 Thus protestant writers were hostile to the Spanish 'conversion' of American natives by means of mass baptism: Porter, *Inconstant savage*, 134; Bodelian Library, MS Rawlinson C 919, p. 989.

15 Quoted in Porter, *Inconstant savage*, 374; see also Kupperman, 'British attitudes towards the American Indian', 337; and S.H. Rooy, *The theology of missions in the puritan tradition* (Delft 1965), 284.

16 B.I. Bradshaw, review of Canny, *Elizabethan conquest*, in *Studies*, lxvi (1977), 47.

concerned that the whole process should be carried through – that the religious and the more pragmatic aims of colonization should not become separated.

In the planning and official activity which prepared the way for the Ulster plantation, 1608–10, the aims of the settlement were generally phrased in broad terms – to spread 'civility and true religion', and to secure the province for the King. As one typical treatise put it, the plantation 'will bring wealth, civility and the form of true religion into that province; which though it be an ancient inheritance of his Majesty ... yet hath it been suffered to lie in the hands of barbarous and irreligious people for hundreds of years past'.[17] James, who took a personal hand in planning the project, likewise viewed it in an idealistic light: as he subsequently explained, even if pragmatic considerations and *raison d'état* had not led him to favour it, he would still have undertaken the project as a moral and religious enterprise, good in itself.[18] Such idealism flourished because of the optimistic assumptions which the English officials made about the beneficial impact of the plantation upon the province and its inhabitants. James and the English Privy Council had already, in 1606–7, expressed their conviction that the 'least civil' people in the remoter areas of Ireland would prove to be the easiest to win over to English government civility and religion.[19] Davies, after a detailed examination of the province, confirmed that, in his view, Ulster was just such an area. Though as yet wild and unreformed, he wrote in 1606, with the churches destroyed and all the livings held by Catholic priests, nevertheless, conformity would, he thought easily be established once the 'work of reformation' were undertaken, since 'all the people of that province, at least the multitude, are apt to receive any faith'.[20]

However, it remained to be seen whether such optimism was borne out by the experience of plantation. In particular, the implementation of the plantation plans have to be examined to seek the answer to two vital questions: how, in a colonial context, would the work of reformation be set about; and how would the local inhabitants react to it? The man entrusted with the task of shaping the nascent protestant church in Ulster was George Montgomery, and it is in his approach and experiences that the answers to these questions can be found. Montgomery was appointed to the sees of Derry, Clogher and Raphoe in February 1605. Unlike other Irish bishops he had not been recommended initially to the King by the Dublin authorities, but owed his appointment to his personal favour with James. Both George and his brother Hugh had made

17 B.L., Cottonian MSS, Titus B X, fol. 408v.
18 P.R.O. 31/8/202/40 (1611–14, 309f.); on James's personal involvement, see P.R.O. 31/8/201, p. 426 (not calendared).
19 See above, p. 58.
20 Morley ed., *Ireland under Elizabeth and James*, 361, 378; S.P. 63/218/53 (1603–6, 468).

themselves useful to the King before his accession to the English throne, and were subsequently rewarded for their services, the former with a bishopric, the latter with lands in Ulster.[21] George's influence at the English court ensured that he was the dominant prelate in the Ulster church, cutting a considerable political, as well as religious, figure.

A survey of his three dioceses taken soon after his arrival showed that Montgomery had inherited a church which was overwhelmingly Gaelic, both in its personnel and its structure.[22] In formulating his reformation policy, his first task was to decide two points: to what extent would he accept and adapt the existing ecclesiastical structure; and, even more importantly for the reform- ation, how easy would it be, and what methods would he use, to win over the native clergy? Montgomery accepted that he had initially to build upon the existing structure – after all, this was before the plantation offered an altern- ative framework within which a new church could be constructed. In Clogher and Derry he effectively took over the structure of the church which he had inherited, helped, perhaps, by the lack of a rival Catholic bishop.[23] In Raphoe, on the other hand, where a Catholic prelate still lived, Montgomery had not, by the time of the survey, managed to gain possession of either the episcopal register or the see finances.[24] With regard to the native clergy, Montgomery

21 D.N.B.; Trevelyan and Trevelyan (eds.), 'Trevelyan papers', iii; *Calendar of state papers domestic, 1603–10*, 199; M. Perceval Maxwell, *The Scottish migration to Ulster in the reign of James I* (London 1973), 49f., 68–74.
22 Printed in 'O'Kane papers', *Analecta Hibernica*, xii (1943), 79–123. Neither the authorship of the date of the survey are stated, though both can be inferred. Denis Campbell is described as the last Bishop of Derry (ibid., 89), which would imply that the survey was drawn up by, or possibly for, his successor, Montgomery. Montgomery quotes most of the survey in a later paper he wrote for the King (below, n. 38. The terminal date for the survey is September 1607 when the Earls of Tyrone and Tirconnell, included in the survey (ibid., 88f.), left Ireland. The earliest date is either that of Montgomery's appointment in June 1605, or, more probably, that of his arrival in Ireland. Precisely when he arrived, however, is unclear: Davies complained about his absence in a letter of *c*.September 1606 (Morley ed., *Ireland under Elizabeth and James*, 361; on the dating of this letter see G.A. Hayes McCoy, 'Sir John Davies in Cavan in 1606 and 1610', *Breifne*, i (1960)). The 'Trevelyan papers', iii, 101f. show that Montgomery was in Derry by October 1606. The survey may well date from between September 1606 and September 1607.
23 'O'Kane papers', 89, 91 show that in Derry the five '*custodes*' – the laymen who traditionally collected the episcopal revenues – were all settlers. In Clogher the last papally appointed bishop had died *c*.1592; in Derry the Catholic bishop had been killed by the English in 1601.
24 Ibid, 90; all the *custodes* were native Irish, two of them being sons of the former Catholic bishop; the register was in the hands of the current Catholic bishop, Niall O'Boyle.

had only isolated success in winning them over. The Dean of Derry, deprived because of his Catholicism, subsequently conformed, though whether this happened in Montgomery's episcopate is not known.[25] One 'quick-witted erenagh', Eugene (Owen) McCawell, Montgomery thought should be won over by the offer of a position, on the grounds that 'malo enim canem blandientem quam latrantem', but it was Montgomery's successor who actually secured his conformity.[26] Another cleric mentioned in the survey was judged to be of 'a good nature' – possibly an indication of his religious disposition.[27] However, the only concrete evidence of Montgomery gaining a native minister for the established church was in Raphoe, where a native convert from Catholicism was appointed Dean in 1609.[28] Overall, however, Montgomery, rather than seeking to convert native clergy, preferred to rely upon English and Scottish ministers. Even before he came over to Ireland, he gained special licence from the King to bring with him 19 preachers who were let retain their English or Scots benefices to support them whilst in Ireland.[29] Apart from the livings held by these ministers, most of the benefices in Derry at the end of Montgomery's episcopate were held by unconforming Catholic priests.[30]

Such was Montgomery's ecclesiastical policy: what of his success in gaining the conformity of the local lay inhabitants, and what of their reaction to Montgomery and the established church? Here too, he had little notable success. In July 1607 he wrote to Salisbury from Dublin, 'having spent almost a whole year in the north and most barbarous parts of Ulster not without some hope of doing good'. His experience there, however, had taught him 'the great difficulty of reducing this people to civility'.[31] Two explanations for Montgomery's lack of success can be advanced. One, favoured by Montgomery himself, lay the blame upon the barbarity and obduracy of the people, misled by their chiefs and priests. In March 1607 he referred to organized resistance to his efforts to win over clergy: 'Some courses have been used here to discourage and draw back the priests'; and he blamed his failure in Raphoe upon the malign influence of the Earl of Tyrconnell.[32] In Montgomery's opinion, therefore, Davies's evaluation of the people's malleability was far too optimistic. Davies and Chichester, however, refused to accept this: they ascribed

25   Ibid., 88; W.A. Reynell (ed.), ' "The estate of the diocese of Derry" compiled by Dr. George Downham', *Ulster Journal of Archaeology*, i–ii (1895–96), 254; T.C.D. MS 550, p. 204.
26   'O'Kane papers', 88; see below, p. 139.
27   'O'Kane papers', 89.
28   Phelim O'Dogherty: P.R. 142. See below, p. 144f.
29   S.P. 63/223/35 (1606–8, 427); Sign manual X/II (1615–25, 253).
30   S.P. 63/231/4 (1611–14, 3f.).
31   S.P. 63/222/96 (1606–8, 214).
32   Bodleian, MS Carte 61, fol. 344r.

Montgomery's failure to his misconceived reformation policy. Rather than concentrating upon winning over the native inhabitants 'like a new St Patrick', as Davies had hoped, and reforming the native clergy, as Chichester thought he should, Montgomery devoted his energies to improving the financial position of the church, and building up a secure material base for the established ministry.[33]

It is certainly true that Montgomery's first concern was not evangelization, or a gentle missionary approach to winning over local clergy and people. In his view conformity was established through legal and, if necessary, coercive measures. Thus he reported how he had dealt with Friar O'Lunn, who had been imprisoned for a time, but was released by Montgomery who had, according to his own account,

> thus far prevailed with him that he is contented afterward to forbear saying of masses upon pain to be hanged ... I have caused him to peruse our service book in Latin, which he well liketh of ... but [he] hath no benefice, nor will undertake any charge in the church, but is desirous to live privately ... Further I have no hope to work him into.[34]

Tyrconnell also complained before his flight in 1607 of the means used to gain people for the established church in his territory (which basically comprised the diocese of Raphoe). Priests were daily persecuted, he claimed, and he himself had been told that he must go to church 'or else he could be forced to go thereto'.[35] Montgomery's emphasis upon coercion, and his lack of missionary endeavour make sense, however, when considered in the context of colonization. Even before the Ulster plantation, he had been closely involved with settling Scots in Derry, and, after 1607, he was one of the earliest advocates of planting the lands of the attainted earls.[36] Above all, his dedication to colonization can be seen in the zeal with which he participated in the implementation of the plantation project. For over two years he fought to ensure that the Ulster church got the maximum benefit out of the escheated lands.[37] As a plantation commissioner, in the forefront of Irish politics, Montgomery naturally had little time for missionary or pastoral work in his dioceses. However, such activity was not, it has been suggested, of primary concern in the initial

33 S.P. 63/218/53 (1603–6, 468); S.P. 63/227/103 (1608–10, 253).
34 Bodleian, MS Carte 61, fol. 344r.
35 S.P. 63/222/200 (1606–8, 374).
36 Trevelyan and Trevelyan (eds.), 'Trevelyan papers', iii, 101f., 149f.; S.P. 63/222/97 (1606–8, 217f.).
37 Perceval-Maxwell, *Scottish migration*, 68–74; Carew Cal., 1603–24, 13–22; S.P. 63/228/37 (1608–10, 390); G. Hill, *An historical account of the plantation in Ulster* (Shannon 1970), 120f., 209–12.

stages of colonization. The major priority was to erect secure foundations –
to create a strong, well-endowed, state supported church, along anglicized
lines, served by protestant ministers, who could serve the settlers and would be
in a position to preach to the natives when, civilized by the planters, they were
forced to come to church.

Hints of such an approach had appeared before the plantation, in
Montgomery's decision to bring English and Scots clergy with him, and in his
preference for a coercive strategy. Within the framework of the plantation,
Montgomery's commitment to a 'colonial reformation' was much more explicit. His major statement of policy was probably presented to James when he
went to court in early 1610.[38] It consists of two linked sections, the first of
which dealt with the condition of the Gaelic church which Montgomery had
encountered upon his arrival – effectively summarising the points arising from
the earlier survey of the three dioceses. The second part detailed Montgomery's
plan for the transformation of this Gaelic church in the escheated counties
(the five dioceses of Derry, Clogher, Raphoe, Armagh and Kilmore). He sought
to create a new church, almost *ab initio*. The plantation, with its transformation
of traditional landholding patterns, and alteration of the whole social and political structure, provided the ideal opportunity for replacing the Gaelic inheritance with an anglicized structure. Even at the parochial level Montgomery's
proposals – most of which were carried out – were concerned with abolishing
traditional Gaelic ways. Parishes were to be endowed with glebes, not as before
with termon land. This latter was to be granted to the bishops as demesne, to
restore their diminished finances.[39] Tithes were to be paid in kind by both
natives and planters, 'without challenging [i.e. challenging the new method

38 B.L., Cottonian MS, Titus B XII, fols 669r–675v; partly printed in T.F. Colby
    ed., *Ordnance survey of the county of Londonderry ... parish of Templemore* (Dublin
    1837), 49–54; and fully printed in Shirley (ed.), *Papers relating to the Church of
    Ireland*, 25–38. The first half, which deals only with Montgomery's three sees, is
    clearly related to the earlier survey (fols 669r–670v). The second half, though deal-
    ing with all the planted dioceses, refers to the experience of the 'present bishop'
    (674r). That this is Montgomery is indicated by the fact that the document was
    clearly written in England ('this kingdom' – 673v) with reference to Ireland ('that
    kingdom' – 674r), and Montgomery is the only prominent Ulster bishop known
    to have gone over from Ireland to England at this time. In Nov. 1609 he was
    preparing to go to England on official business concerning the plantation (Bodleian,
    MS Tanner 75, fol. 328r), and in Feb. 1610 Chichester referred to him as return-
    ing to England on official business (S.P. 63/228/36 (1608–10, 389f.)). It was pre-
    sumably when he was in England that Montgomery presented the document to
    the King, since it can be approximately dated from internal evidence to after 1
    May 1608 (the death of Sir George Paulett – 671v), and before March 1610, when
    the King granted the termon lands to the bishops as requested in the document.
39 B.L., Cottonian MSS, Titus B XII, fol. 673r.

with] any Irish customs formerly used in those places, seeing this is a new plantation and erection of churches ... '[40] Rather than the traditional Gaelic rector and vicar in each parish, Montgomery wanted the King to unite the livings into a single parsonage or rectory.[41] The final element in the plan for the new church was to procure new clergy. Montgomery naturally envisaged that these should come from England, and asked James to send over ministers 'of worth and approved government'.[42]

This constituted the first stage of colonization – quickly creating civilized settlements by importing English settlers, English institutions and English law. There remained the second stage – the much longer process of acculturation of the native population and establishing conformity amongst them. While some scope existed here for missionary endeavour, Montgomery placed it firmly within the context of legal process and the establishment of social order and control. His only reference to evangelism in the paper he presented to the King came in relation to the greater need for strong bishops and firm ecclesiastical discipline in Ulster

> where the people is not yet reduced to order and obedience, than in other places already reformed. For, howsoever the ministers in their particular charges may labour diligently by instruction and persuasion to reform the people, yet if there be not a superior ecclesiastical magistrate, that shall have power to countenance the ministry ... and by authority of ecclesiastical censure to punish the obstinate, and draw the people to conformity, hardly will any good be done among the natives of that kingdom; and for this purpose the bishop must be very well countenanced by authority, and assisted by concurrence of the civil magistrate, whereof the present bishop hath had sufficient proof and experience.[43]

In his submission to the King, Montgomery also indicated the way in which he hoped the plantation would further the cause of the reformation. As a result of his own experience, he held out little hope that the native adults would be won over, 'because people once nursled up in superstitious and barbarous courses are with exceeding great difficulty brought either to true religion or any civil behaviour.'[44] Instead, the younger generation would have to be 'civilized', a task which Montgomery hoped could be accomplished in two ways. Firstly, he urged that a comprehensive educational system be set up, with grammar schools, and a college in Derry so that those youths who had not sufficient

40 Ibid., fol. 673r.
41 Ibid.
42 Ibid., fol. 673v.
43 Ibid., fol. 674r.
44 Ibid.; S.P. 63/222/96 (1606–8, 214).

means to attend Trinity could nevertheless be 'civilly brought up ... in the knowledge of true religion and the liberal arts'.[45] The second means was through the influence which the settlers and the civil authorities exerted upon the indigenous population. The mixture of settlers and native Irish upon the church's termon lands, Montgomery suggested, would be 'a great means of bringing the natives to civility, loyalty and religion'.[46]

In relation to this latter means, there was some disagreement amongst those involved in the plantation about the precise form of settlement which would best further the assimilation of the native population. Some advocated that the native Irish be 'mixed with the English so they may be better civilized', whilst, on the other hand, the plantation articles of 1610 prescribed distinct and concentrated settlements, in order to maintain the cultural purity of the colonists.[47] All were agreed, however, that the spreading of civility was one of the prime aims of the plantation. Hence the official concern to regulate the conditions upon which native Irish would be allowed to reside in the areas designated for English or Scottish settlement:

> The condition of those that shall be received as tenants shall be, that those that be conformable in religion, and come to church, and that shall wear English apparel, use their ploughing after the English manner. With a caution to bring up their children in learning, or some trade ... [48]

In the mean time, until the process of acculturation was complete, the church was left with the problem of what policy it should follow towards the unconformable native Irish. As has been seen, Montgomery took a pessimistic view of the chances of missionary success amongst the Irish adults. However, his successor as bishop of Derry, Brutus Babington, did not, and his optimistic, missionary approach to the native inhabitants, if his own account is to be believed, had some success.

Babington, born in Cheshire and educated at Cambridge, unfortunately had only a short episcopate – he was active in Derry from late 1610 until his death on 10 September 1611.[49] Unfortunately, as he was one of the few advocates

---

45 B.L., Cottonian MSS, Titus B XII, fol. 673.
46 *Carew Cal.*, 1603–24, 39ff.
47 N.L.I. MS 8014, iii, 12; T.W. Moody (ed.), 'The revised articles of the Ulster plantation 1610', *Bulletin of the Institute of Historical Research*, xii (1935), 181f.; *idem*, 'The treatment of the native population under the scheme for the plantation of Ulster', *Irish Historical Studies*, ii (1938–9); N.P. Canny, 'Dominant minorities: English settlers in Ireland and Virginia, 1550–1650', in A.C. Hepburn (ed.), *Minorities in history* (London 1978), 54ff.
48 B.L. Add. MS 4756, fol. 118v.
49 *Al. Cantab.; Al. Oxon.*; Peile, *Biographical register of Christ's College*, i, 121; C.H.

of a persuasive missionary approach to the native Irish, and it would have been of great interest to examine how his policy developed when the plantation got fully under way. Unlike Montgomery, Babington's first priority upon his arrival was to win over the native clergy. And, as he explained in January 1611, even in the short time at his disposal, he had done more to reclaim 'the better part of my clergy than any of my predecessors'.[50] When he arrived in Derry, he had found the leading priests, upon whom the 'unlearned multitude' depended, to be hostile and refractory. Unlike Montgomery, however, he did not counter recalcitrance with coercion: 'notwithstanding this their stubbornness I did not violently go to work with them nor urge them by authority, but endeavoured rather to persuade their consciences by arguments and reasons'.[51] By 'dealing with them lovingly and kindly', he overcame the hostility of the leading priests, and persuaded the most important of them, Owen McCawell, publicly to accompany him to church. At a subsequent meeting of the Irish priests, well over half agreed to submit and accept several 'points of very good consequence'.[52]

It was therefore, possible to persuade some of the native clergy to serve in the established church. However, a major problem remained: how to accommodate them within an intrinsically colonial church committed both to anglicization and a coercive disciplinary framework. Babington had perceived this difficulty, and had sought through the judicious moderation of anglicizing trends, and the temperate exercise of his disciplinary powers, to limit the alienating impact of this foreign, draconic church upon the people of Derry. He provided for those clergy who conformed to read in their churches 'such scriptures as are translated in to the vulgar tongue', and likewise to use the Irish translation of the prayer book. Similarly, he was cautious in his enforcement of discipline. Though, like Montgomery, he found his diocese 'rude and barbarous' and demanded the same coercive authority as his predecessor, Babington, according to his own version, was sensitive in the way in which he used such power. He sat personally in his court every week (an unusual step for an Irish bishop), where he punished offenders,

> *cum moderamine*, in such a sort, as that albeit it seemed very harsh to them at the first ... the people nevertheless is now a little begun to fear to transgress, and not to distaste government. And I nothing doubt, but

and T. Cooper, *Athenae Cantabrigienses*, 3 vols. (Cambridge 1853–1913), iii, 44; D.N.B.; P.R. 182f.; date of his death given in P.R.O.I., Calendar of Exchequer Inquisitions, 1A.48.73, p. 323.

50 S.P. 63/231/4 (1611–14, 3).
51 Ibid.
52 Ibid.; McCawell had previously been singled out by Montgomery: 'O'Kane papers', 88; in 1612 he was appointed Archdeacon of Derry: P.R., 226.

by due mixture of *poenae cum premio* ... I shall in short time bring this
rude and uncivilized people to some good conformity ... [53]

Though the shortness of his episcopate makes it difficult to evaluate his likely
long term success, his experience did point to one inherent difficulty facing
reformation policy in Ulster – the conflict between missionary endeavour and
the claims of ecclesiastical discipline. Whereas the former called for gentle
means, taking into account the contrasting mores and culture of the local inhabitants, the latter implied an essentially coercive framework. Put another way,
the dilemma was how to restrain the obdurate Catholic clergy and laity without
at the same time driving away the less committed Irish – how to combine
social control by legal means with religious evangelism.

Andrew Knox, Montgomery's successor not only as bishop of Raphoe, but
also as *de facto* leader of the Ulster church, was the man who tried to tackle
this and other problems facing the plantation church. Knox had several things
in common with Montgomery: he was a Scot, who began his career serving
in his native church, was advanced due to his favour with James, and was fully
committed to a coercive reformation policy.[54] In one important respect, however, he differed from Montgomery, in having extensive experience, as Bishop
of the Isles from 1605 to 1619, of reforming a wholly Gaelic diocese in the
remote Scottish highlands. His success in the Isles, accomplished to a large
extent at the head of an army, was confirmed by the Statutes of Iona in 1609,
and the following year James appointed him to Raphoe to perform a similar
task – to reclaim 'the ignorant multitude ... from their superstitious and popish
opinions' as the Scottish Privy Council put it.[55] Knox was optimistic about
the possibility of success. Though he thought that the Church of Ireland suffered from a dire shortage of preachers, if this were remedied, and the Catholic
priests banished, he was 'in good hope ... within very short time to reform all
Ulster'.[56] Knox set vigorously to work immediately upon his arrival in Ireland,
both at the local level, in reforming his own diocese, and nationally, in getting
the bishops to agree to a comprehensive reformation strategy.

He produced two sets of proposals, one in 1611 for the Ulster bishops,
though in fact subscribed to by all the Irish prelates, and another in 1612, this

53 S.P. 63/231/4 (1611–14, 3).
54 D.N.B.; Percevall-Maxwell, *Scottish migration*, 257.
55 *Register of the Privy Council of Scotland*, ix, 15, 24ff., 569f.; W.C. Mackenzie, *The
    highlands and isles of Scotland* (Edinburgh 1937), 216f.; D. Gregory, *The history of
    the western highlands and isles of Scotland* 2nd ed. (Edinburgh 1881), 329ff.; [D.
    Laing ed.], *Original letters relating to the ecclesiastical affairs of Scotland*, Bannatyne
    Club, 2 vols (Edinburgh 1851), i, 427*f.
56 S.P. 63/231/56 (1611–14, 81).

time for the whole Irish church, but with special reference to Ulster.[57] A dominant theme in Knox's proposals was the need for firm measures against priests and recusants: 'There must be a uniform order set down for the suppressing of papistry'.[58] Even before he came to Ireland, as commissioner in charge of apprehending priests in Scotland, and as bishop of the Isles, he had clearly indicated his belief in the reformative value of coercion. The hostility and 'deadly hatred' which he encountered from the native Irish in Raphoe, merely strengthened his belief that the civil power was an essential adjunct to religious reformation, and led to a toughening of his demands for the 'suppression of papistry' in the second set of proposals in 1612. Bishops were to be allowed to excommunicate recusants; a new and stricter penal statute against Catholics was demanded in the forthcoming Irish parliament; and the ecclesiastical high commission, so favoured by Loftus and Jones, was to be restored.[59]

Yet, at the same time, Knox tried to direct the church's energies towards evangelization, and adapt its pastorate to the conditions in Ulster: he advocated reform in conjunction with suppression, rather than after it. The contrast with Montgomery was noted by Chichester, who characterized Knox as a zealous reformer of priests and people who 'has done more good in his church government in the short time of his being among them than his predecessor in all his time'.[60] In his two sets of proposals, Knox stressed the pastoral role of bishops. They were to go through their dioceses 'teaching and catechizing the gentry and citizens', and rebuilding churches and appointing fit pastors. Whilst Knox insisted that all Catholic priests holding benefices should be deprived, he urged that those willing to accept the Book of Common Prayer should be allowed to retain their livings. In addition, where better qualified clergy were unavailable, he was prepared to accept as ministers 'such as can read the service of the Church of England to the common people in a language which they understand.'[61]

In Raphoe Knox put his precepts into practice. When he first arrived he found that there were no conformist native ministers.[62] To serve the vacant

---

57 *Knox's draft of the 1611 articles*: P.R.O. 31/8/203/228 (1611–14, 31f.); Sheffield City Library, Strafford MSS, vol. 20/140; articles actually agreed by Irish bishops in 1611: S.P. 63/271/7 (Add. 1625–60, 188f. – wrongly titled); *Archivium Hibernicum*, ii (1913), 164f. (partial version). *Knox's draft of 1612 articles*: S.P. 63/231/26B (1611–14, 26f.); version referred to Lord Deputy and bishops: P.R.O. 31/8/200/96a (1611–14, 242ff.); further comments by the King and Irish bishops on these articles: T.C.D. MS 582, fols 134r–136v.
58 P.R.O. 31/8/203/228 (1611–14, 31).
59 S.P. 63/232/30 (1611–14, 315); S.P. 63/231/26B (1611–14, 26f.).
60 S.P. 63/231/79 (1611–14, 149).
61 P.R.O. 31/8/203/228 (1611–14, 31f.).
62 S.P. 63/270/11 (Add. 1625–60, 168).

cures, he imported fellow Scots and, exercising his extensive powers of patronage, appointed them to parishes.[63] From 1611 onwards, as settlers began to
arrive in Ulster in significant numbers, so too Scottish clergy were appointed
to serve the areas of settlement in Raphoe.[64] In addition, however, two native
Irishmen was appointed, both converts from Catholicism.[65] Knox, for all his
commitment to plantation, took a positive attitude towards indigenous clergy.
Although by 1622 the number of settler clergy in Raphoe had grown to around
20, the number of native ministers had also increased – to seven, two of whom
were identified as converted priests.[66] Knox had also procured the services of

63 In 1622, of the 27 benefices in Raphoe, 17 were collative (T.C.D. MS 550, p. 222).
   In the formative years of the protestant church in Raphoe, during the second
   decade of the century, Knox had even greater control over patronage in his diocese,
   for two reasons. First, the King allowed him to present to all void benefices, even
   where they had been vacant for more than 18 months, and were therefore techni-
   cally in the Crown's presentation; second, Trinity College, Dublin, which had 7
   advowsons in Raphoe, showed little interest in presenting its students to them,
   allowing Knox in effect to choose incumbents as he pleased for the seven livings
   (P.R.O. 31/8/202/131 (1615–25, 3); T.C.D. Muniments P/33/21; P.B., 185b).
64 Settler clergy: date of first recorded appearance in Raphoe:

Name	Date	Sources
Archibald Adaire	April 1611	Leslie, *Raphoe clergy*, 14; S.P. 63/231/26A (1611–14, 80; P.R. 339).
Alex. Conyngham	1611	*Raphoe clergy*, 27; Lodge, *Peerage of Ireland*, vii, 178.
Dugald Cambell	1 Sept 1611	*Raphoe clergy*, 55; T.C.D. MS 1067, p. 142; T.C.D. Mun. P/33/ 21; P.B., 185b.
John Vaux	7 Feb 1613	*Raphoe clergy*, 97, 107; T.C.D. MS 1067, p. 142; P.B., 185b.
Robert Bennett	c.1615	1611–14, 525; Laing ed., *Original letters*, ii, 395.
William Paton	6 July 1613	*Raphoe clergy*, 50, 114, 134; T.C.D. MS 1067, p. 143; P.B., 185b.
William Atkin	16 May 1615	*Raphoe clergy*, 33; P.B., 185b.
Claud Knox	16 May 1615	*Raphoe clergy*, 42, 68, 73; T.C.D. MS 1067, p. 141; P.B., 185b.
Arch. Anderson	April 1618	*Raphoe clergy*, 66; *Al. Cantab.*.
Wm Conningham	26 Mar 1618	*Raphoe clergy*, 66; T.C.D. MS 1067, pp. 140, 142.
John Knox	6 Jan 1620	*Raphoe clergy*, 25, 78, 133; T.C.D. MS 1067, pp. 142f.

65 Phelim O'Dogherty and Brian O'Deveny: T.C.D. MS 550, pp. 218f.; P.B., 185b.,
   T.C.D. Muniments P/33/21; Leslie, *Raphoe clergy*, 13f. 134.
66 T.C.D. MS 550, pp. 212–222; Torlough O'Kelly, Owen O'Doweny, Owen Congal,
   Brian McNelus, Brian O'Doweny,* Owen O'Mulmock,* Richard Melyn. Those
   noted with an asterisk were converted priests.

an Irish schoolmaster, described as 'an Irish native who is conformable in religion and who is a very good humanist.'[67] Between him and the seven native clergy, who, according to Knox, endeavoured 'by all means the conversion of their country people', Raphoe had at least the basis (or perhaps the remnants) of an indigenous church capable of ministering to the native population.

In two other dioceses a similar balance had been struck between native and settler clergy, giving rise to the hope that the established church might provide a ministry for both sections of the Ulster population. In Derry, the legacy of Babington was the conformity of two native Irish rectors, and seven curates.[68] In Kilmore the pattern was somewhat similar to Raphoe, with benefices initially remaining vacant until the arrival of English or Scots clergy, though in Kilmore, one conformist family, the O'Gowans did provide two clergy for the established church.[69] By 1615 the planted portion of the diocese (that part which was in Cavan) had a total of six native Irish clergy.[70] Nevertheless, the vast majority of the clergy in Raphoe, Derry and Kilmore were of English or Scottish origin, having arrived with the settlers in the years after 1610. And in the two remaining dioceses in the escheated counties, Clogher and Armagh, the disparity between native and 'settler' clergy was even greater: in Armagh none of the ministers in 1622 was obviously of Irish origin – all those who antecedents can be traced were either English or Scottish, usually the former.[71] Clogher was little different: it boasted one native curate, a 'reformed Irish papist'.[72]

It was, in fact, Clogher and Armagh that represented the future of the Ulster ministry: in the end the delicate balancing act between suppressing Catholicism by the use of the civil power, and at the same time attracting native converts to the protestant church, failed. Even in Raphoe, where Knox took a positive attitude towards the native clergy, the seeds of this failure can be discerned. Though there were Irish clergy in Raphoe, they were all, as Knox put it, 'curates ... under British ministers' – in other words, they formed an inferior stratum of subservient reading ministers, as in Killaloe.[73] A bishop such as George Downham, the Cambridge educated, English bishop of Derry

---

67 T.C.D. MS 550, p. 223; P.R., 394.
68 T.C.D. MS 550, pp. 190–204: William McTaggart, Patrick McTally; and seven unnamed curates. In all there were 39 resident clergy in Derry.
69 P.R.O.I., Calendar of Exchequer Inquisitions, 1A.48.73, p. 103; A.D. s.v. Nicholas Smith; T.C.D. MS 550, pp. 144f., 148f.; Hunter, 'Ulster plantation in the counties of Armagh and Cavan', 52.
70 T.C.D. MS 550, pp. 144–51: Hugh McConyne, Philip O'Siredock, Nicholas Smith [alias O'Gowan]; Shane O'Gowan, Thomas Brady. In all, twenty clergy were resident in the Cavan portion of Kilmore.
71 T.C.D. MS 865, 26–48.
72 T.C.D. MS 550, pp. 184f.; N.L.I., MS 8014, x.
73 T.C.D. MS 550, p. 229; see above, p. 118.

from 1616 to 1634, with little sympathy for the native Irish clergy, could thus categorise them as inferior and unsuitable for important benefices.[74] The career of Phelim O'Dogherty in Raphoe further illustrates the fate of native ministers. Originally appointed dean of Raphoe in 1609 after his conversion from Catholicism, he held his dignity together with the valuable rectories of Conwall and Taughboyne.[75] But when Knox arrived, he brought with him another Scot, Archibald Adaire, for whom he immediately secured the Deanery.[76] Another émigré Scots cleric, Thomas Bruce, was appointed to Taughboyne before 1614; and in May 1615 another Scot was presented to Conwall.[77] O'Dogherty instead became rector of Tullyferna, but he soon left the ministry, reportedly dying a recusant c.1618.[78] A similar tendency for native clergy to be displaced by 'settler' clergy can be observed in Derry.[79]

74 See Downham's judgement of Patrick McTally: 'an Irish man of mean gifts, having little Latin and no English, but thought by my predecessor sufficient for a parish consisting wholly of Irish.' T.C.D. MS 550, p. 191.

75 P.R., 142; P.B., 185b; Leslie, *Raphoe clergy*, 13f.

76 S.P. 63/231/26A (1611–14, 25); S.P. 63/231/56 (1611–14, 80).

77 S.P.Dom. 31/8/202/120 (1611–14, 525); P.B., 135b; T.C.D. Muniments P/33/21.

78 P.B., 135b; T.C.D. Muniments P/33/21; T.C.D. MS 550, p. 227; Sheffield City Library, Strafford MSS, vol. 20/162.

79 See the parishes of Balteagh and Donogheady. In the former parish, Brian McConnogher was presented to the rectory by the crown *sede vacante* in December 1615. The following December, just three months after Downham's appointment to the see of Derry, Edmund Harrison, Downham's brother-in-law and a fellow graduate of Christ's College Cambridge, was presented to the rectory. In the report on the diocese of Derry dating from c.1606–7, Denis O'Farren is recorded as rector of the parish of Donogheady: at that time he was also a student at Trinity, according to the same source. Ardstraw was one of the advowsons granted to Trinity College Dublin by James: yet the first recorded Trinity presentation, in May 1615, is of a Scot, one Mr Young (P.R., 294; N.L.I. MS 4489, p. 47; Venn, *Al. Cantab.*; 'O'Kane papers', 102; P.B., 185b). William Mc Taggart, the former Catholic dean of Derry who had conformed, held two rectories in 1622, both in small parishes, the cures of which were according to Downham discharged by the incumbent 'after a fashion'. In 1624 McTaggart exchanged one rectory with an Oliver Mather. In 1628, perhaps after his death, he was replaced in his two parishes by one Valentine Gonnes. Patrick McTally, of whom Downham had been so critical, was likewise replaced by a non-Irish cleric: in 1624 the crown presented George Perinchief to the vacant rectory of Donogh, formerly held by McTally. (Leslie, *Derry clergy*, 31, 238, 299; Moody, Simms (eds.), *Bishopric of Derry and the Irish Society*, 144; T.C.D. MS 550, p. 191, p. 254; P.R., 584).
    In the return for the diocese of Derry made by Bishop Downham in 1622, the pattern observed in Raphoe, where native clergy generally held subordinate posts, can also be seen. Apart from the two native Irish rectors, the indigenous clergy generally either served as curates under an English rector, or had the cure of a small native Irish parish.

The reasons for the subordinate and inferior status of the native clergy were fairly obvious. They simply failed to meet the criteria which the English and Scottish bishops established for protestant ministers. This was partly a result of the nature of the criteria – the bishops were after all committed to an anglicizing, coercive reformation, and the indigenous clergy did not fit satisfactorily into such a context. The shortage of suitably qualified ordinands was also, of course, a product of the strength of Catholicism in Ulster: most young scholars and aspiring clerics would naturally have turned to the Catholic church, pursuing their studies if necessary in the European seminaries and universities, rather than resorting to the protestant seminary of Trinity College. Thus, the hope expressed by Montgomery when bishop of Derry that a comprehensive educational system be set up in order to ensure that the younger generation of native Irish be brought up in 'religion and civility' was never fully realised.

There had been in the plantation scheme provision for an educational infrastructure in Ulster. A free school was endowed for each of the escheated counties, and special provision was made for Trinity College, with the grant of advowsons.[80] Initially, many difficulties were encountered before the schools could be established – the lands which they had been assigned were frequently misappropriated to private use.[81] Consequently, educational provision developed in rather a haphazard fashion – in Derry, for instance, it was only thanks to a generous bequest from a London planter, Mathias Springham, that a school could be built in 1617.[82] By the middle of the seventeenth century, however, the free schools, together with some private and parochial schools, were generally functioning.[83] But the extent to which, as Montgomery had envisaged, they led the native population to 'civility and religion' is unclear, since little is known about whether the schools attracted many pupils from outside the settler community.[84] Only in the case of Fermanagh free school has any information survived: in 1630 it was reported that the school had *c.*60

---

80 See above, p. 79; also, Hill, *Plantation in Ulster*, 216; Hunter, 'Ulster plantation in the counties of Armagh and Cavan', 629; P.R., 255; T.C.D. MS 1134, pp. 112f.; *Carew Cal.*, 1603–24, 4–8; T.W. Moody (ed.), 'Ulster plantation papers, 1608–13', *Analecta Hibernica*, viii (1938), 243ff.; M. Quane, 'Cavan Royal School', *Journal of the Royal Society of Antiquaries of Ireland*, c.(1970).

81 S.P. 63/233/51 (1615–25, 101ff.); S.P. 63/234/16 (1615–25, 200f.); S.P. 63/247/12 (1625–32, 363f.); T.C.D. MS 1134, pp. 112f.; T.W. Moody, *The Londonderry plantation* (Belfast 1939), 172, 186–90, 205, 219; A.B. (ed.), *A breefe memoriall of the lyfe and death of Doctor James Spottiswood, Bishop of Clogher in Ireland* (Edinburgh 1811), 12f.; Colby ed., *Ordnance survey of Londonderry*, 139f.

82 Colby (ed.), *Ordnance survey of Londonderry*, 140.

83 Barnard, *Cromwellian Ireland*, 184; T.C.D. MS 550, p. 196; N.L.I. MS 8013, i; P.R.O.N.I., D 683/35.

84 According to the letters patent for one school, its purpose was 'for teaching the youth of the said county both good literature and principles of true religion': P.R., 577.

pupils, of whom all except three were 'Irish natives'.[85] The school was run by
Richard Bourke, educated at Trinity, probably originally from Killaloe, and a
minister of the Church of Ireland.[86] Raphoe also, of course, possessed a native
schoolmaster, one Brian Moryson, but apart from the fact that one of his pupils
subsequently went to Salamanca to become a Jesuit, nothing is known about
whom he taught.[87] Nevertheless, had the schools attracted many native students
and confirmed them in protestantism, it might have been expected that a significant proportion would have gone on to higher education or to serve in the
established church. Yet neither amongst the students at Trinity, nor in the
ministry of the Church of Ireland do many such persons appear. The failure
of Trinity to attract such students was all the more notable since Chichester
had made a special effort to foster closer links in the early seventeenth century. In his circuit of Ulster in 1605, he had tried to encourage promising
young native Irish benefice holders and students to come to Trinity: about ten
were admitted to Trinity as scholars, supported both by the state and by Sir
Hugh Montgomery.[88] But their subsequent careers, with one exception, left
no trace at or after Trinity. The only one about whom any details survive did
indeed enter the church subsequently: Hugh (Eugene) Maguire served as a
minister in his native Clogher: but by 1628 he had left the protestant ministry, and was installed as Catholic Dean of Clogher.[89]

The failure of Trinity to provide for native Irish students from Ulster was
paralleled by the inability of the plantation church to attract native Irish ordinands. Far from being the basis of a broadly based, multi-racial protestant
church, the native clergy in Raphoe and Derry in 1622 were, as seen from the
perspective of the regal visitation of 1634, merely an ephemeral, anachronistic
remnant of the pre-plantation ministry. For, by 1634, the native ministers had
generally been replaced by 'settler' clergy in nearly all of the Ulster dioceses:
in Raphoe, for instance, even the curates were Scottish and English.[90] Though
partly a product of the strength of Catholicism, this state of affairs was also
brought about by the preferences of the bishops concerned. This was evident
in Kilmore, where that unique Irish bishop, William Bedell, presided. Thanks
to his interest in Gaelic evangelism, there was, in 1633, a significant native
element still present in the Kilmore ministry.[91]

Given the decline in the number of native clergy, two other aspects of the
plantation church assume greater importance: the pastoral and evangelical

85 T.C.D. MS 1134, p. 113.
86 A.D.; Dwyer, *Killaloe*, 121; T.C.D. MS 1134, p. 113.
87 O'Dogherty, 'Students at Salamanca (1595–1619)', 95.
88 Berry, 'Early students of Trinity College', 25–7; 'O'Kane papers', 88, 91.
89 H.M.C., *The manuscripts of the Earl of Cowper ... calendar of Coke MSS*, i (1888), 367.
90 T.C.D. MS 1067, pp. 137f.
91 Ibid., pp. 117ff.

capacity of the 'settler' clergy; and the overall success of the plantation in bringing the natives to conform to English standards of 'civility and religion'. With regard to the former, the attention of the émigré clergy, in their daily ministry, was firmly focused upon the planters. This hardly startling fact is abundantly evident in the returns of the Ulster bishops in 1622. Firstly, as in the Pale dioceses, the repair of churches reflected the way in which the established church concentrated its ministry upon areas of settlement. Churches were repaired and refurbished where the Scots and English lived.[92] Thus the Haberdashers, one of the London companies involved in the colonization of Derry, ordered their agent to repair churches on their lands on the grounds that 'it will be a good inducement to draw over English inhabitants if they may have a church near them furnished with a good minister'.[93] When new churches had to be built, the traditional location was often changed to reflect the new pattern of settlement.[94] In Raphoe, for instance, Knox recommended in 1622 that, since the old church in Conwall parish was ruined and 'in a remote place', it should be transferred to Letterkenny, a market town, 'where there is [sic] 80 families of British inhabitants.'[95]

Secondly, settler clergy tended to be resident in the richer, lowland parishes where settlement was densest. By contrast the poorer, upland parishes, almost wholly populated by Irish, were generally either held by pluralist settler clergy, resident in a richer more settled benefice, or left in the care of Irish curates, where these could be found.[96] The pastoral care which the latter parishes

92 As can be seen by examining the parishes of the two deaneries of Mohey and Derry in the diocese of Derry. Since they were outside the Londoners' plantation, the condition of the churches in both these deaneries was poor in 1622. Yet, in Mohey, a significant number of Scots, English and servitors were planted, and this was reflected in the fact that although all 12 churches were ruined, in seven cases provision had been made, either for an alternative place of worship, or for a new church to be built; and in three of the five parishes where no provision was made, the cure was left to be served by an Irish curate – implying that there was little settlement there anyway. By contrast, in the deanery of Derry, comprising the Inishowen peninsula, and hardly settled at all, six of the seven churches were ruined, and in only one case was alternative provision made:– in the parish of Movill, one of the few settled parishes, where a chapel was built 'in a place most commodious for such Englishmen as do inhabit the said parish'. T.C.D. MS 550, pp. 168–95.

93 Adrian Moore to Tristram Beresford: Register House Edinburgh, MS N2/3 (unfoliated).

94 T.C.D. MS 550, pp. 196 (for 'Stationers' read 'Salters'), 197, 199, 201; *Carew Cal.*, 1603–24, 364ff., 415; B.L. Add. MS 4780, fol. 47v.

95 T.C.D MS 550, p. 215.

96 On the contrast between upland and lowland areas, see P.S. Robinson, 'The plantation of County Tyrone in the seventeenth century', Queen's University, Belfast, P.D. Thesis, 1974, 339–44.

received was often minimal: in Killelagh, in Derry diocese, the non-resident rector, Oliver Mather, lived in a neighbouring parish, two miles away, whence 'sometimes (as once in three weeks) he resorteth to the church, where no man cometh at him, the whole parish consisting of Irish recusants'.[97] A similar example came from the parish of Magheracloone in Clogher. William Moore, the vicar, was non-resident in 1622 'because there is no British plantation yet'.[98] Instead he kept an Irish curate (the sole native cleric in Clogher), but as there was no minister's house in the parish, and the church was unfurnished, it may be doubted whether any services were conducted.[99] Finally, it must be noted that only four of the settler clergy were reported in 1622 as being able to speak Irish – three of them serving in Raphoe.[100] The implications of these various facts for the pastorate of the Church of Ireland are obvious: areas of heavy settlement were provided with an adequate ministry, usually by graduate Scottish or English clergy; but the poorer, upland parishes, largely populated by native Irish, were for the most part simply abandoned.

Consequently, relations between the settler clergy and their parishioners in the wholly Irish parishes can hardly be described as pastoral: their reluctance to reside, inability to communicate, lack of enthusiasm for evangelism and commitment to anglicization, all served to distance them from their parishioners. In 1622 Sir William Parsons commented upon the problem of non-residence:

> for although each church has an incumbent yet there are few residents, for in all Irish countries, having neither congregation, society, or safe abiding, no man of learning would reside, besides the Irish let the churches lie down or extremely ruined.[101]

The relations of the settler clergy with the Irish were dominated not by evangelical, but monetary considerations. Though non-resident ministers made little provision for preaching to Irish parishioners whom they did not believe they could convert, they did not neglect to employ proctors or to use their servants to collect tithes and other dues.[102] The alienating effect of such exactions was exacerbated by the failure of the authorities in Ulster to regulate

---

97 T.C.D. MS 550, p. 203.
98 Ibid., pp. 184f.
99 Ibid.; N.L.I. MS 8014, x.
100 T.C.D. MS 550, p. 216; T.C.D. MS 865, pp. 34f.
101 B.L. Harleian MS 3292, fol. 28b; Parson's treatise was composed just two days before a major debate by the 1622 Commissioners on the plantation: ibid., 26r.; N.L.I. MS 8014, iii, 12.
102 For a detailed record of the relations between two ministers and their native Irish parishioners, as seen by the latter, see N.L.I., MS 8014, x.

the scale and nature of payments. Tithes in particular proved troublesome. Tithes had, of course, always been a source of friction between priests and people, not just in Ireland, but throughout Europe. In Ulster, however, the system proved especially burdensome for the native Irish, on several counts. Firstly, the plantation church imposed a new system of tithes and dues, based upon the English model, which differed markedly from the traditional Gaelic one with which the population were familiar. Secondly, the English and Scottish clergy were often 'more zealous and sharp than moderate and cautious' in exacting the innovatory tithes.[103] Francis Blundell, writing in 1614, thought that the ministers in Ulster were 'much to blame for exacting their duties so strictly of such men as never knew what it was to pay tithes until within these few years'.[104] This only served further to alienate the local population. As Chichester complained, the ministers were non-resident, the churches ruined, and no service was provided,

> yet nevertheless, intending their profits most among the Irish ... they did farm their said tithe milk to certain kern, bailiff errants, and such like extortious people, who ... did ... take away the same rudely, to the extreme displeasure of the poor people ... and with like envy to the ministers of the gospel and their profession.[105]

Thirdly, the church and the civil authorities in Ulster whilst they committed themselves to an anglicized system of financial support, failed at the same time either to codify and regulate the new dues, or to ban the old Gaelic exactions. This was not achieved finally till 1629.[106] In the mean time, unscrupulous ministers could, and did, not only exact the new English dues at exorbitant rates, but also continued to demand the traditional Irish duties as well.[107]

The predominance of financial over evangelical considerations was most vividly illustrated in relation to recusant fines, where parishioners could be fined for failing to attend a church which not only might not be served, but also might not be standing. As the inhabitants of Tyrone complained to the 1622 Commissioners:

103 P.R.O. 31/8/200, pp. 176ff. (1615–25, 22f.).
104 S.P. 63/232/58 (1611–14, 538).
105 P.R.O. 31/8/200, pp. 176ff. (1615–25, 22f.).
106 B.L. Add. MS 4756, fol. 22r; G. Hand and V.H. Treadwell (ed.), 'His Majesty's direction for ordering and settling the courts within his kingdom of Ireland, 1622', *Analecta Hibernica*, xxvi (1970), 211f.; Grosart (ed.), Lismore papers, 2nd ser., iii, 118f.; S.P. 63/250/10 (1625–32, 507); Morrin (ed.), *Calendar of patent rolls*, iii, 550–2; S.P. 269/1443 (1625–32, 472); S.P. 249/1485 (1625–32, 481).
107 N.L.I. MS 8014, viii, and x; Hand and Treadwell (ed.), 'Direction for the courts within Ireland', 211f.

Another grievance is the taxing of every poor man with 9*d* ster. for every Sunday and holyday that will not come to church, when as for the most part there is no church to come unto. And if there be, there is commonly none but an English or Scottish minister, whom the common people understand not; neither do they know, or were ever taught, what difference is in religion.[108]

From the point of view of the established church, the difficulties posed by remote Irish parishes were almost insuperable, since the inhabitants remained largely untouched by the plantation. In Tyrone, for instance, in the less fertile and mountainous parishes, the native Irish made few concessions to the colonial culture, language, or religion – indeed, they remained unassimilated in many respects up to the end of the nineteenth century.[109] However, there remained the native Irish who lived in the more fertile and densely settled lowland parishes. For even in the most heavily colonized areas, a considerable number of Irish remained. Given the shortage of English and Scottish undertakers and labourers, the Irish could never, as the plantation articles had originally envisaged, be totally removed from the settled areas. Instead, the authorities stressed the importance of enforcing conformity of dress, manners, customs, language and religion among those Irish that remained. As James reminded the settlers early in the plantation, they had been granted their estates to plant British families on them

> to give example of civility and good manners to the unreformed Irish, and reduce such of the Irish as live under them to conformity of religion and manners, and not to countenance or encourage them to the continuance of their former incivility ... [110]

The official approach to assimilation was twofold: by precept – enforced through the usual administrative and judicial machinery of the state; and by example – offered to the Irish by the colonists. Through these means it was hoped that they would be 'civilized' and brought into line with the values and culture of the settlers. In the lowland parishes some assimilation did occur, since the Irish were involved in the market economy, being permitted, for instance, to reside in plantation towns as artificers.[111] However, it remained to be seen to what extent economic assimilation was, as some of the planners of the plantation had seemed to assume, necessarily linked with religious confor-

108 T.C.D. MS 808, fol. 49r.
109 Robinson, 'Plantation of Tyrone', 346.
110 Bodleian, MS Clarendon 2/112, fol. 86r.
111 Robinson, 'Plantation of Tyrone', 346.

mity. The detailed examination of the plantation by the 1622 Commissioners suggested that Irish involvement with the settlers had led only to a limited degree of religious conformity.

Amongst the leaseholders on planted lands Irish names occurred frequently, and many were noted as conformist: thus on Lord Ridgeway's proportion in Clogher, two of the freeholders were described as 'an Irishman but goes to church'.[112] The 'but' however, was significant, since among the lower strata of natives, sub-tenants, labourers and servants, conformity was far rarer. On Sir Piers Crosby's proportion in Omagh, Co. Tyrone, the only two Irish leaseholders went to church, but these were more than balanced by the 120 other Irish families on the proportion who did not.[113] In the towns some evidence of assimilation exists. The provost and burgesses of Dungannon returned 31 English and Scots adult male inhabitants, 35 male 'Irish protestants', and 40 households of recusants.[114] In Co. Donegal, the fiant of incorporation of Rathmullan in November 1612 included amongst the burgesses Walter McSwyne and Mortagh O'Kelly.[115] The most informative return to the 1622 Commissioners, unfortunately unique, was that of the Rector of Tawnatalee (Ballymore), an English graduate cleric, Nathaniel Drayton.[116] The parish was in a planted area of Armagh, the chief landholder being Lord Deputy Grandison, who had helped to build the church in 1620 and had also provided for its furnishing. On Grandison's land 29 English households and a further 5 English adult males came to church; amongst the Irish 5 households and 8 adult males conformed. On the other proportions within the parish, a further 14 Scottish and English families were recorded, but no more native conformists. The very limited extent of native conformity is apparent when one contrasts the five households and eight adult males who did attend church with the 200 Irish families whom Drayton said failed to do so.[117]

It is evident, therefore, that the optimism of those involved in planning the plantation that the native population could with relative ease and speed be brought to accept English standards of 'civility and religion' was unfounded. The natives were far from being ignorant savages, their minds *tabulae rasae* ready to receive the impression of the superior civilization: they proved, as Montgomery had claimed, to be rather attached to their own culture and

112 N.L.I. MS 8014, viii.
113 Ibid.
114 Ibid.
115 C.S.P.I., 1611–14, 302; this was Sir Walter McSweeny of Rye: E. Maguire, *A history of the diocese of Raphoe* (Dublin 1920) ii 161. In the 1650s some members of the McSweeny family were still protestant: Simington ed., *Civil survey*, iii, 103, 106, 107.
116 Leslie, *Armagh clergy*, 65; N.L.I. MS 18,646.
117 N.L.I. MS 18,646.

customs. The process of acculturation and assimilation, insofar as it took place, was a matter of centuries, not decades, and was in the end as much a product of modernization as of plantation. Furthermore, it is now evident that there was no necessary and inevitable link between secular and religious assimilation, a fact which had serious implications for the church's reformation policy. Since the church thought that the 'civilizing' of the native population was a necessary precondition for their conversion, even the secular aspects of acculturation were essential for reformation strategy. Thus, sheer pragmatism demanded that the Irish should first learn English, since until they did, the settler clergy would be unable to preach to them. Yet considerable numbers of Irish monoglots remained in Ulster until well into the nineteenth century.[118] Despite this the protestant church remained committed fully to the essential link between secular acculturation and religious reformation, and continued to uphold its policy of anglicization within a firm disciplinary framework. As a result, until assimilation took place, the pastoral and missionary endeavour of the protestant ministry was stifled: in effect, missionary activity was postponed for the whole of our period and beyond. The church's commitment to an anglicizing reformation was, therefore, a liability, both distancing it from the native population, and alienating that population further from the established church.

The failure of the church, imprisoned in its reformation policy, to bridge the gap between it and the native inhabitants was recognized by some dispassionate lay observers. Davies and Chichester had, early in the course of the Ulster reformation, criticized Montgomery for his mistaken priorities.[119] The 1622 Commissioners similarly noted the failure of the ministry to cater for the native Irish in Ulster, and ascribed it to a lack of missionary zeal and pastoral concern. If the Ulster clergy, the Commissioners claimed,

> would diligently instruct their charge, and according to their abilities relieve such poor as duly frequent the church, we doubt not, but that in a short time their churches which are now almost empty would be filled with auditors.[120]

The church itself, however, signally failed to see the problem in such terms. Rather than stressing its own missionary failure, the church instead pointed to the lack of progress in establishing the necessary preconditions of civility, obedience and discipline: until this was done pastoral activity was of little use. And, in the remoter upland Irish parishes in particular, these conditions simply did not prevail. The reason for the failure to spread the reformation

118 G.B. Adams, 'Aspects of monoglottism in Ulster', *Ulster Folklife*, xxii (1976).
119 See above, pp. 134, 141.
120 B.L. Add. MS 4756, fol. 19v.

therefore lay, as the church saw it, with the planters and the civil authorities who had patently failed to carry out the original intentions of James. In this respect, the church's explanation for its failure to spread the reformation in Ulster paralleled the church's analysis of its lack of success elsewhere in Ireland: insufficient secular support and the reluctance of the civil authorities to enforce conformity. Bishop Downham's account of his difficulties in Derry in 1622 thus makes familiar reading. The Catholic priests, placed in every parish, 'carry the natives after them generally', and, so long as they remained, he saw no hope of reformation.[121] His major complaint was that he could not get the necessary co-operation from local sheriffs to remove the priests. When he excommunicated priests and procured a writ *de excommunicato capiendo*, the sheriffs of Derry, Donegal and Tyrone 'cannot be got to apprehend them and bring them to prison'. Even where he succeeded in having the priests convicted and committed, 'they have by corruption been set at liberty to follow their former courses.'[122]

In fact, it was simply not in the planters' or local officials' interests to co-operate with the crusade against Catholicism which Downham demanded, since much of the settlers' prosperity depended upon reaching a *modus vivendi* with the native Irish. The result was that local officials tolerated Catholicism *de facto*. Indeed, Sir Thomas Phillips claimed that one of the sheriffs of Londonderry, Richard Kirby, had actually permitted a Catholic priest to sue one of his parishioners for non-payment of dues.[123] In brief, the settlers were far from being a tightly knit community of evangelically and missionary minded protestants:

> The protestantism of the dominant class on the City's plantation [Londonderry] was not militant. A policy of *laissez faire* best suited those who had vested interests in Londonderry. They were no more anxious to unsettle the natives by enforcing the law against religion than to deprive themselves of profitable tenants by observing the articles of plantation.[124]

The difficulty to which Downham was pointing was that which has already been alluded to in discussing the ideology of colonization – that of ensuring that the religious and pragmatic aims of colonization did not become separated. The primary concern of the planters was simply to establish order and secular control, and once this had been achieved, the settlers were content to settle down to work their land. The church, on the other hand, was insistent

121 T.C.D. MS 550, p. 206.
122 Ibid.
123 Moody, *Londonderry plantation*, 286f.
124 Ibid., 287.

that once order had been established the power of the government, with the co-operation of the settlers, should be used to enforce civility and conformity amongst the native population.[125] Thus the attempt by the Irish and English governments in the articles of plantation to ensure that those Irish who remained on lands assigned to the English and Scots conformed to English custom, manners and religion was continuously resisted by the pragmatic settlers.[126] Consequently, when the matter was finally settled in 1625, the conditions for Irish settlement on undertakers' lands, whilst they retained the commitment to secular conformity, had dropped the earlier insistence upon religious conformity.[127] There was, in short, a conflict between private and public interest in relation to the plantation's aims which became increasingly evident as the settlers began to arrive in Ulster and develop their holdings, and which culminated in the major confrontation between the Crown and the City of London in the 1630s.[128]

The reluctance of the settlers to fulfil the role originally envisaged for them was one of Downham's main complaints. In 1629 he complained vigorously to the Lords Justices about the recusancy of two of the Scottish settlers in Strabane, Sir George and Claud Hamilton. Not only were they not spreading protestantism, they were encouraging Catholicism, directly contrary to the original intention of King James –

> his intention was the reducing of the country then idolatrous and barbarous to the true reformed religion, and to civility of manners. But by the blind zeal of some in those parts it is come to pass, that not only the natives have been continued and confirmed in their superstition and rudeness, but also among the British there hath been made a plantation of popery ... to the perdition of the reduced people ... [129]

The comment which the Earl of Cork made upon Downham's letter when forwarding it to the English Privy Council was an apposite verdict upon the success of the colonial reformation as a whole: James's policy of 'planting civility and protestantism in ... Tyrone hath not had the good effect which was expected of it.'[130]

125 See above, p. 131.
126 See above, p. 150f.
127 A.P.C., 1623–5, 454ff.; ibid., 1625–6, 154ff.
128 Moody, *Londonderry plantation*, Chaps 14, 15.
129 Bodleian, MS Chatsworth 78, p. 55; see also Perceval-Maxwell, *Scottish migration*, 345.
130 S.P. 63/250/22 (1625–32, 509f.).

CHAPTER 8

The theology of the church of Ireland

By the 1630s, the character of the Church of Ireland had begun to emerge clearly: an elitist, anglicized church, whose commitment to a state-aided reformation remained despite, or perhaps because of, the lack of progress in spreading the reformation. The practical measures and historical forces which created and shaped the church in this manner have already been examined: the reform of the ministry, the importing of graduate clergy, the role of plantation, the failure to win significant native support. But there remains one vital, over-arching element which bound together the protestant church, and had, despite its somewhat abstract and abstruse appearance, considerable practical importance: theology.

Generally, historians of the Irish reformation have tended to neglect theology, a pardonable omission during the early part of the reformation, but much less so after the 1590s. For, as a result of the new emphasis which was then placed upon the need for a doctrinally aware ministry, the Irish church began to develop for the first time an identifiable theological consciousness and character, which had a marked influence upon the way in which the church viewed itself and its mission in Ireland. The importance of this development, and the relevance of Irish theology, has been minimised by historians for two reasons. Firstly, amongst those who have alluded to it, Irish theology has been dismissed as little more than a pale reflection of English theological concerns.[1] There is some truth in this, in so far as it goes. The influx of English clergy after the 1590s, together with the anglicized ethos of Trinity, modelled as it was upon a Cambridge college, ensured that the theological training of Irish clergy was little different from that of their counterparts in England. However, that the theological concerns of Irish clergy were shared with those of England is hardly surprising, since both were part of the wider European reformation. What is essential, and what Irish historians have so far failed to do, is to investigate the way in which this common European heritage was applied to the Irish context – to see how apparently recondite subjects, such as predestination or eschatology, took on a vital practical importance in the particular context of the Church of Ireland. The second reason for the neglect of Irish theology

---

1 P. Kilroy, 'Division and consent in the Irish reformed church, 1615–34', University College Dublin M.A. Thesis, 1973; Moody, Martin Byrne (eds.), New History of Ireland, iii, 229; R.B. Knox, *James Ussher Archbishop of Armagh* (Cardiff 1967).

has been insufficient knowledge of the extent of the sources. Only the works of James Ussher, collected and published by Elrington and Todd in the mid-nineteenth century, and the Irish Articles of faith of 1615 have been widely known.[2] Even these have obscured as much as illuminated, with Ussher's writings and the Articles being taken as a single corpus, and considered solely within the context of English theological concerns, without any attempt to investigate how such concerns were related to the Irish context. Apart from these, the investigation of the published theological writings of Irish churchmen has only begun, whilst manuscript sources have received still less attention.[3] What needs to be done, therefore, is to explore the true nature of Irish theology, both as formulated in the church's confession of faith and as applied and expounded by Irish clergy.

THE IRISH ARTICLES OF 1615

The Irish Articles were a product of Convocation which met in tandem with the parliament of 1613–15.[4] Previously, the Irish church had not had a confession of faith, but merely a brief summary of beliefs, the Twelve Articles of 1566, deriving from the 'Eleven articles of religion' compiled early in Elizabeth's reign for the Church of England.[5] By contrast the 1615 Irish Articles represented a much fuller treatment of matters of faith, passed by both the bishops and lower clergy, and authorized by the Lord Deputy.[6]

2 U.W.; the Irish Articles were printed in U.W., i, App. IV; in W.D. Killen, *The ecclesiastical history of Ireland*, 2 vols. (London 1875), i, App. III; C. Hardwick, *A history of the articles of religion*, 3rd ed. (London 1895), App. VI; P. Schaff, *The creeds of the evangelical protestant churches* (London 1877), 526–44.
3 P. Kilroy, 'Sermon and pamphlet literature in the Irish reformed church, 1613–34', *Archivium Hibernicum*, xxxiii (1975); to the works mentioned by Kilroy should be added those by added those by R. Daborn, J. Hoyle, W. Ince, R. Puttock, J. Rider, C. Sibthorp, A. Spicer, J. Hill, J. Hull, G. Synge, noted below in the bibliography. The most important manuscript sources for the theology of the Church of Ireland are the two volumes of Ussher *collectanea* in the Bodleian: MS Barlow 13, MS Rawlinson C 849; various manuscripts in T.C.D. relating to the early intellectual history of the college, especially MSS 180, 221, 295, 285–8, 1210; and the MSS of William Daniel in Armagh Public Library.
4 See Reeve's 'History of Irish Convocation', T.C.D. MS 1062, pp. 47–58; U.W., i, 39–44.
5 *A brefe declaration of certein principall articles of religion* (Dublin 1567).
6 *Articles of religion agreed upon by the archbishops and bishops, and the rest of the cleargie of Ireland, in the convocation holden at Dublin in the yeare of our lord God 1615: for the avoidance of diver sities of opinions: and the establishing of consent touching true religion* (Dublin 1615). According to Archbishop King, James granted a

Assessment of the theological content and tenor of confessions of faith is not without its problems. The basic difficulty is the extent to which confessions can be interpreted as coherent statements of a complete systematic theology. The inner consistency of a confession drawn up by a clerical assembly, subject to various influences and divisions, may be difficult to isolate and define. In the case of the Irish Articles, this problem has so far been side-stepped by a simple expedient: attributing the composition of the Articles to one man, James Ussher.

Historiographical treatment of the Articles has therefore been reduced to evaluation of Ussher's own doctrinal opinions. Generally, in the evaluation of Ussher, two distinct schools of thought can be distinguished amongst historians. For a long time, the Articles were seen as a result of puritan influence upon the Church of Ireland exercised by Ussher. This interpretation can be traced back to Peter Heylin, its most vigorous exponent. Heylin saw post reformation church history in the British isles as essentially a conspiracy to subvert the anglican church. The Irish Articles, reflecting the puritan views of Ussher, seemed to Heylin specifically to demonstrate the baleful influence of the puritans upon the nascent protestant church in Ireland.[7] Though not always so trenchantly expressed, subsequent treatments of the Articles echoed Heylin's basic point. Neal, in his *History of the Puritans*, thus arrogated the Irish articles to the puritan tradition.[8] Similarly, several nineteenth century historians pointed to the predominant influence exercised by the precisian element within the Church of Ireland over the Articles.[9]

More recent scholarship has reacted against the assumption that because the Irish Articles were Calvinist, they were also puritan. Rather, it has been pointed out that the puritans took their place on one wing of a broad Calvinist consensus which had widespread acceptance in the churches of both England and Ireland in the early seventeenth century.[10] R.B. Knox, in his biography

license to Convocation in 1614 to frame articles of religion: T.C.D. MS 1062, p. 56; according to Nicholas Bernard, they were confirmed by Lord Deputy Chichester and Lord Chancellor Jones: *The life and death of ... Dr James Ussher* (Dublin 1656), 50; see also U.W., i, 49.

7 P. Heylin, *Aerius redivivus* (Oxford 1670), 394f.

8 Neal, *History of the puritans*, i 475.

9 J. Collier, *An ecclesiastical history of Great Britain* (London 1840), vii, 380f.; U.W., i, 48; Hardwick, *Articles of religion*, 179f.; Killen, *Ecclesiastical history of Ireland*, i, 452f.; Phillips (ed.), *History of the Church of Ireland*, ii, 548f.

10 R.B. Knox, 'The ecclesiastical policy of James Ussher, Archbishop of Armagh', London Univ., Ph.D. Thesis, 1956, 57ff.; *idem, James Ussher*, 16ff.; see also N.R.N. Tyacke, 'Arminianism in England, in religion and politics, 1604 to 1640', Oxford Univ., D.Phil. Thesis, 1968, chap. 1; *idem*, 'Puritanism, Arminianism and counter-revolution', in C. Russell ed., *The origins of the English Civil War* (London 1973).

of Ussher, went to considerable lengths to demonstrate that Ussher was far
from being a puritan, and that the Irish Articles were, therefore, the product,
not of a firm precisian, but of a moderate anglican.[11] Whilst Knox abandoned
Heylin's extreme assumption that the Articles were the product of a puritan
plot, and correctly placed them in the context of the Calvinist consensus,
certain difficulties remain about such an interpretation. In his efforts to rebut
Heylin's stance, he has strayed too far in the opposite direction. His resolute
insistence that the Articles contain nothing that is puritan-inspired, while consistent with the position of James Ussher, conflicts as shall be seen with the
Articles themselves. The fundamental flaw in Knox's argument can best be
described in logical terms. Knox's interpretation is based upon a syllogism:
Ussher wrote the Irish Articles; Ussher was a moderate Calvinist; therefore the
Irish Articles are to be placed firmly within the moderate Calvinist tradition.

The description of Ussher as a moderate Calvinist is apt: though he had
many puritan friends (a fact which misled earlier historians), and may even
have been willing on occasions to cater for their tastes on less important issues,
on important matters, such as episcopacy, for instance, Ussher's surviving theological works, and his correspondence, betray no trace of precisian scruples.
Where the syllogism falls down is in its first premise. There is in contemporary
sources a resounding silence about the composition and internal politics of
Convocation in general, and the drawing up of the confession in particular.
Faced with such a vacuum, historians have seized upon the one source which
referred to the composition of the Articles – Nicholas Bernard's account of
Ussher's life, published in 1656. Bernard had served as Ussher's secretary,
though he was not a witness of the events of 1615, having first met Ussher in
1624.[12] It is possible, though, that he heard from Ussher that he had written
the 1615 Articles. Against this, however, two telling points can be made. First,
Ussher himself, in his voluminous correspondence, and in the even larger
corpus of theological writings and miscellaneous papers which he left behind,
never mentions his own authorship of the Articles. Second, Bernard's ascription of the Articles to Ussher is somewhat equivocal: Bernard states simply: 'he,
being a member of the synod, was appointed to draw them up'.[13] Historians
have blithely assumed that this implies authorship – Ussher sitting down and
composing the confession. Yet, it is also open to another interpretation which
is, on the balance of evidence, much more plausible: that Ussher acted simply
as a kind of draughtsman, or even as a scribe – putting into final form the
results of the doctrinal deliberations of Convocation. It is highly unlikely that
he, a member of the lower house, would have been entrusted with the composition of the Articles *ab initio*, as if, as Ussher's grandson pointed out, he

11 Knox, 'Ecclesiastical policy of Ussher', 57ff.; *idem*, James Ussher, 16ff.
12 Bernard, *Life of Ussher*, 40, 57.
13 Ibid., 49.

could have had such a great influence upon it, as to be able to govern the church at his pleasure; or that the scribe of any synod or council should make it pass what acts or articles he pleases; or that one private divine should be able to manage the whole church of Ireland ... [14]

Once one lays aside the *canard* of Ussher's authorship, then the Irish Articles can be viewed in their proper context. The strained efforts to prove that even the most puritan sounding elements are perfectly compatible with Ussher's moderate stance become irrelevant. Instead, the composite nature of the Articles can be examined, and they can be seen for what they were – a product of the disparate concerns of Irish Convocation and the differing theological emphases within that gathering.

Lacking information about the composition or internal politics of Convocation, it is to the Irish Articles themselves that one must look for evidence about the various influences upon their composition. Their greatest debt was to the English confession of 1562: all but one of the Thirty-Nine Articles were included in one form or the other.[15] Many other Irish Articles were derived from the two sets of Homilies referred to in E.A. 35.[16] However, the dependence upon the English formulary did not mean that the Irish Articles were wholly derived from their English counterpart. There were, firstly, significant changes and omissions made in some of the incorporated English Articles. Secondly, the Irish Articles numbered 104, and therefore contained a considerable amount of new material, some of which marked a clear departure from the English Articles. In these additions, emendations and omissions lies the originality of the Irish church's confession. The three most important elements of this originality are its approach to predestination, concessions to puritan tastes, and the attitude towards Catholicism.

Undoubtedly the most notable addition to the Thirty-Nine Articles was the treatment of the doctrine of predestination. E.A. 17, which dealt with the topic, was open to varying interpretations. It did not state upon what basis God predestined some to everlasting life. The reference to God's promise as being

14 U.W., i, App. VIII, p. clxxxi; in 1634, according to Wentworth, Ussher disavowed the 1615 Articles in preference for the Thirty-Nine Articles: Sheffield City Library, Strafford MSS, vol. 6, pp. 56, 90; Scott, Bliss (eds.), *Works of Laud*, vii, 75.
15 See Knox, *James Ussher*, 17ff., and 'Ecclesiastical policy of Ussher', 69ff.; the latter contains a detailed comparison of the Irish and English Articles, which has been used as the basis for the following analysis. But it should be noted that it is not wholly accurate: Knox fails to note some small but significant differences, such as the phrasing of I.A. 23, compared with E.A. 9; he also mistakenly claims ('Ecclesiastical policy', 91, 76) that 'nothing is drawn' from E.A. 32, thereby ignoring the clear reliance of I.A. 64. He makes a similar error in relation to E.A. 39, which is used in I.A. 55.
16 Knox, 'Ecclesiastical policy', 73–83.

'generally set forth in holy scripture' was seen by some as implying a doctrine of universal redemption. And perhaps most importantly, it left out all reference to reprobation, thereby omitting the essential second element in the logically closed Calvinist system of double predestination.[17] Those English Calvinists who followed Beza and the Heidelberg theologians were especially troubled by the ambiguity of E.A. 17 when, in the 1580s and 1590s, it was exploited by Peter Baro and other Arminians *avant la lettre* at Cambridge. To counter this, Whitgift, along with the Cambridge Heads and other churchmen, drew up the Lambeth Articles in 1595, which defined the predestinarian question in a more rigidly Bezan manner.[18] However, though approved by Whitgift, the Queen refused to countenance them as the basis for public preaching or disputation – they were to be viewed only as the 'private judgements' of the compilers.[19]

Such a judicious *via media* was not to the liking of the Irish church in 1615, for the Irish Articles included a far more precise explication of the doctrine of predestination. Though based upon E.A. 17, the Irish Articles expounded it with the help of the Lambeth Articles.[20] In I.A. 15, for example, the reference of the English article. to effectual calling and the justification of the elect was included verbatim, but the fourth Lambeth Article was tacked on, thereby defining the fate of those not effectually called – the reprobate. In Irish Articles 32, 37, and 38, a far more detailed treatment was given to sanctification, largely omitted from the Thirty-Nine Articles, and to justification, again through the inclusion of the Lambeth Articles.[21] The more rigid approach to predestination in the Irish confession also resulted in a minor, though significant, alteration to the wording of E.A. 9, which dealt with the corruption of human nature due to original sin, 'whereby man is very far gone from original righteousness'. The Calvinist view of man as totally depraved led to I.A. 23 altering the clause to the much more negative view of manís sinfulness: 'whereby it commeth to pass that man is deprived of original righteousness'.[22]

---

17 E.J. Bicknell, *A theological introduction to the Thirty-Nine Articles of the Church of England*, 3rd ed. (London 1955), 220–8; H.C. Porter, *Reformation and reaction in Tudor Cambridge* (Cambridge 1958), 336ff.

18 Porter, *Reformation and reaction*, chap. 16; P.G. Lake, 'Laurence Chaderton and the Cambridge moderate puritan tradition', Cambridge Univ., Ph.D. Thesis, 1978, 236ff.

19 Porter, *Reformation and reaction*, 374.

20 For a copy of the Lambeth Articles see Schaff, *Creeds of the protestant churches*, 523f.; they were included in Irish Articles 12, 14, 15, 32, 37, 38.

21 Bicknell, *Thirty-Nine Articles*, 209; though the extended treatment of justification in the Irish Articles was also derived from the English Homily on salvation: Hardwick, *Articles of religion*, 377; Knox, 'Ecclesiastical policy of Ussher', 73.

22 For a more detailed examination of the Irish church's stance upon predestination, see below, pp. 164ff.

By giving the Lambeth Articles the status of articles of faith, the Irish church did not take itself outside the contemporary Calvinist consensus. Nevertheless, within that consensus, it took a clearly defined stance, and did what both Elizabeth and James had refused to do – officially defined the nature of predestination in a rigorously Calvinist way. Indeed, the Irish formulary was sufficiently rigorous to provide the basis for the teaching of the Westminster Assembly on the subject of predestination.[23]

One obvious explanation for the preciseness of the Irish Articles on this issue was the influence of the puritan element of the Irish church. The Irish church had provided refuge for English puritans early in Elizabeth's reign, and filled a similar role for some of the presbyterian activists after the English authorities broke up the classis movement in the late 1580s.[24] Trinity College Dublin was greatly indebted in its early years to these exiles. Walter Travers, a major figure in the English presbyterian movement, became the first full time provost of Trinity in 1594.[25] Instrumental in bringing him to Trinity was one of the College's first fellows, Mathias Holmes, who had fled to Ireland to escape the wrath of the English bishops.[26] At Trinity, Travers entertained another prominent presbyterian, Humphrey Fenn, whilst the latter preached in Dublin.[27] As provost Travers was succeeded by Henry Alvey, another presbyterian, who, as a fellow of St John's College, Cambridge, had been a close associate of William Whittaker, Master of St John's and one of the chief movers behind the composition of the Lambeth Articles.[28] The influence of these fellows and provosts was not to turn Trinity into a puritan bastion – the distinction between puritan and conformist was not a particularly important one in the Irish church at this time – but rather to shape the theological outlook of the new College along firmly predestinarian lines. This can be seen, for instance, in the sermons preached in the College chapel around the turn of the century.[29]

Nevertheless, the teaching of the Irish Articles on predestination was not *necessarily* a product of puritan theological concerns, since it represented a view also held by conformists. Elsewhere in the Irish confession, however, the desire of Convocation to accommodate puritan opinions was given more unequivocal expression, in the addition of an article on the observance of the

23 A.F. Mitchell, J. Struthers (eds.), *The minutes of the sessions of the Westminster assembly of divines* (Edinburgh 1874), pp. xlvii–xlviii, lii–liv.

24 H. Robinson (ed.), *Epistolae Tigurinae* (Parker Society, 1845), 99; S.P. 63/22/35, 63/20/17, 63/20/41, 63/30/88.

25 S.J. Knox, *Walter Travers: paragon of Elizabethan puritanism* (London 1962).

26 Ibid., 128; H.M.C. *Calendar of the Salisbury Manuscripts*, vi, 460, 531.

27 T.C.D. MS 1210, MS 357, MS 2640.

28 Porter, *Reformation and reaction*, chap. 9; T.C.D. MS 233, fols 62r–90r.

29 T.C.D. MS 1210.

sabbath, and, most especially, in the one English Article that was omitted.[30] E.A. 36 was concerned with the consecration of bishops affirming the fitness and legality of such ordination. Its omission did not imply that the church of Ireland was opposed to, or even lukewarm in its adherence to episcopal government: rather it represented a judicious compromise which left the way open for those who held different views, as, obviously, many puritans like Travers did, to remain within the established church and accept its articles.[31] A final and important concession to puritan taste ensured that if there were any elements of the Irish Articles to which they objected, it was nevertheless still possible for them to enter the Church of Ireland and conscientiously serve in its ministry, since no provision was made for ministers in Ireland to subscribe to the Articles as they had to in England.[32]

In its lenity towards precisians, the Irish church was reflecting its overwhelming concern with the need for internal unity and lack of dissension in the face of what was seen as the most serious threat of all, the Catholic church. This is the third element which so strongly influenced the Irish confession. Not only does it explain the willingness to tolerate precisians, but it also underlay the explicitness of the Irish Articles on predestination. One of the concerns of the Cambridge Heads in the 1590s had been to guard against what they saw as virtually a 'papist' doctrine, as advocated by Baro. In Ireland the incentive to adopt the unequivocal statement on predestination contained in the Lambeth Articles did not arise from the strength of Arminianism within the Church of Ireland – that was minimal until the early 1620s.[33] Rather, it was a reaction against the extensive 'papist' criticism coming from outside the protestant church – from Catholic writers and polemicists – and directed specifically at the church's views on predestination. In particular, Catholic writers seized upon the licentiousness they saw as following from the protestant claim

30 I.A. 10; Heylin, *Aerius redivivus*, 394 Mant, *History of the Church of Ireland*, 385f.; Knox denies that this article reflects puritan influence: *James Ussher*, 17, and 'Ecclesiastical policy of Ussher', 74, 90.

31 I.A. 71 did include E.A. 23, which stated that ministers had to be 'lawfully called … by men who have public authority given to them in congregation', but this was not sufficient compensation for the omission of E.A. 36, since the latter had originally been added to the Thirty-Nine Articles in 1563, specifically to rebut puritan objections to the ordinal, which E.A. 23, with its 'colourless tone and weakness in positive statement' was not sufficient to do: Bicknell, *Thirty-Nine Articles*, 321f.

32 The 'Decree of the synod' annexed to the Irish Articles simply provided that no minister 'shall publicly teach any doctrine contrary to these Articles'; on subscription in Ireland, see above, p. 76.

33 U.W., xvi, 403–6. Kilroy, 'Sermon literature', 118 makes the mistaken claim that Stephen Jerome was the Arminian referred to in this letter. The minister referred to is in fact George Stuke: Brady, *Clerical records of Cork, Cloyne and Ross*, ii, 318. For an earlier hostile reference (from 1618) to Arminianism see U.W. xv, 141f.

that justification was by faith alone, without good works, and also condemned the doctrine of double predestination as making God the author of sin.[34] The Irish Articles therefore represented a comprehensive restatement of protestant doctrine on the issue. The determination to refute Catholic criticism was specifically reflected in I.A. 28, not found in either the Lambeth or the Thirty-Nine Articles, which stated categorically that 'God is not the author of sin … '[35] The concern of the Church of Ireland to define its position in relation to Catholicism and thereby consolidate its claim to be the rightful church in Ireland, was also manifested in several other new Irish Articles which had no parallels in the English confession. Articles 59 and 60 tackled the major debate in political theory between protestants and Catholics over the deposing power of the Pope, denying that the latter could 'depose the King, or dispose of any of his Kingdoms … or … authorise any other prince to invade … or … discharge any of his subjects of their allegiance and obedience to his majesty …'[36] The Catholic practice of avoiding oaths of loyalty and legal efforts to enforce conformity by resorting to the doctrine of equivocation was condemned in I.A. 67. The final and most important addition was I.A. 80, which identified the Pope as 'that man of sin' foretold in the bible, Antichrist.

One of the reasons of the greater explicitness of the Irish confession on these matters was, of course, the fact that it was composed so much later than the English Articles, thereby coming after the Bull of excommunication in 1570, and the deterioration in relations between England and Rome.[37] But this is merely a partial explanation, for the additions also had a special relevance for the Church of Ireland, in its peculiar position of being an established reformed church in a Catholic country. John Vesey, writing later in the seventeenth century, ascribed the strongly Calvinist tone of the Irish church at the beginning of the century to the ever-present fear of Catholicism by Irish churchmen who, 'like burnt children', 'so much dread the fire, that they think they can never be far enough from their fear.'[38] As shall be seen, the

---

34 [Paul Harris] 'An answar unto an epistle written by James Usher to Sr Christopher Sibthorp', N.L.I. MS 18,647, fols 36r–51r; H. Fitzsimon, *A Catholike confutation of M. John Riders clayme of antiquitie* (Rouen 1608), 140, 160f.; J. Coppinger, *A mnemosynum or memoriall to the afflicted Catholikes in Irelande* (?Bordeaux 1606), 246.
35 For further evidence of protestant concern to rebut the Catholic claim see: H. Leslie, *A treatise tending to unitie* (Dublin 1623), 14; C. Sibthorp, *A friendly advertisement to the pretended Catholickes of Ireland* (Dublin 1622), 153ff.; Bodleian MS Rawlinson C 919, p. 765; W. Ince, *Lot's little one, or meditations on Gen. 19. Vers. 20* (London 1640), 125 (recte 126), 127; Andrews, *Quaternion of sermons*, 62.
36 I.A. 36.
37 Knox, *James Ussher*, 16f., and 'Ecclesiastical policy of Ussher', 80 explains the addition wholly in these terms.
38 J. Vesey, *Life of Bramhall* (Dublin 1676), sig. i1r.

identification of the Pope with Antichrist played a very important role in defining and shaping the protestant church's attitude towards Catholicism in Ireland.[39]

The Irish Articles, then, were considerably more than an updated version of the 1562 Articles by an 'anglican' cleric, or a puritan-inspired plot to subvert the Irish church. They reflected the firmly Calvinist consensus of the Irish church, within which both puritan and conformist elements can be discerned. They were also a product of the independence of the Church of Ireland, and of the particular challenges that it faced in Ireland.

PREDESTINATION AND CONVERSION

The Calvinist stance on predestination which the Irish Articles took was not merely of academic significance, but had a direct bearing upon the way in which clergy viewed and conducted their pastorate. Not only did the view of predestination which clergy espoused influence the way in which they approached the task of converting people, but the intellectual tradition within which the Irish church operated on this issue sought specifically to relate theological concerns to practical divinity. To use the term Calvinist to describe this intellectual tradition is to do something of an injustice to Calvin, since a considerable difference existed between Calvin and those who were subsequently labelled Calvinists on the issue of predestination.[40] Calvin had not placed overwhelming emphasis upon predestination in his theology, and when he did examine the subject, he differed from his later followers in several ways: in his premise that Christ died for all mankind, and not just the elect; in his concentration upon election at the expense of reprobation; in his lack of interest in the question of assurance; and finally, in his failure to stress preparation for faith, which led him to minimalise the role of the preaching of the law. Beza and the Heidelberg theologians, however, made predestination central to their theology. Beza believed in limited atonement, focused attention on the fate of the reprobate in the system of double predestination, saw the preaching of the law as preceding grace in the *ordo salutis*, and emphasised the need for close examination of the question of assurance.[41]

39 See below, pp. 182–90; the reference to Antichrist may also reflect the influence of the puritan element in the Church of Ireland: on the importance of this point for puritans see P.G. Lake, 'The significance of the Elizabethan identification of the Pope as Antichrist', *Journal of Ecclesiastical History*, xxxi (1980) 178.
40 B. Hall, 'Calvin against the Calvinists', in G.E. Duffield (ed.), *John Calvin* (Abingdon 1966).
41 J. Calvin, *Concerning the eternal predestination of God*, ed. J.K.S. Reid (London 1961); B.G. Armstrong, *Calvinism and the Amyraut heresy: protestant scholasticism*

William Perkins, the Cambridge theologian, combined Bezan theology with the already existing tradition of English practical divinity which sought to interpret for the faithful the implications of predestination, and thereby create a 'theoretically sound understanding of conversion that could effectually be preached.'[42] By the time of his death in 1602, Perkins had laid the foundations for what has been labelled the 'experimental predestinarian' tradition.[43] Perkins's primary achievement was to investigate the nature of conversion from the standpoint of predestinarian theology, and then to expound it in a form which could serve as the basis of the everyday ministry of clergy seeking to effect the conversion of their parishioners. Naturally, the basis was God's decree of election, by which he destined those whom he chose for salvation. There could be no question of the reasons for election, or the number God had chosen, being revealed to people: man could not hope to investigate God's secret will, his *voluntas beneplaciti*. However, it was possible for men to attempt to understand God's *voluntas signi*, his revealed will, the signs by which He indicated to man that he was chosen. The most obvious manifestation of this was God's grace, and the effect it had upon those on whom God chose to bestow it. Perkins examined and expounded the way in which God called a miserable sinner, and granted him grace, so that he could proceed from an initially weak faith, through justification and adoption, to the working out of sanctification, and the granting of assurance of salvation. Though it would be inaccurate to describe it as a practical morphology of conversion, Perkins's treatment made it possible for the more recondite aspects of predestinarian theology to be made real in terms of everyday Christian experience. Through following his *Armilla aurea*, people could, with the help of God's grace, move from sinfulness to assurance of salvation.

Perkins thus concentrated people's attention upon what he saw as the most important question anyone could pose himself: 'whether he be a child of God or no'. The vital text for Perkins and his followers was 2 Pet. 1. 10: 'Give diligence to make your calling and election sure: for if ye do these things, ye shall never fall.' The duty of ministers was, therefore, to urge, and help, their parishioners to look into their own hearts, and try to ascertain whether they

and humanism in seventeeth century France (Madison, Wisconsin 1969), 130–60; R.T. Kendall, *Calvin and English Calvinism to 1649* (Oxford 1979), 13–41; L.B. Tipson, 'The development of a puritan understanding of conversion', Yale Univ., Ph.D. Thesis, 1972, 108–28.

42 Tipson, 'Puritan understanding of conversion', 262, 155ff.; Kendall, *English Calvinism*, 43–7.

43 Kendall, *English Calvinism*, 8f., 51; on Perkins see: T.F. Merrill, *William Perkins* (Nieuwkoop 1966); I. Breward (ed.), *The work of William Perkins* (Abingdon 1970); Porter, *Reformation and reaction.*

had true saving faith; if they did, then they could hope that they were indeed amongst those chosen by God.[44]

The Irish Articles of 1615 committed the church to a predestinarian system which was ultimately derived from the Heidelberg theologians.[45] Much greater emphasis was placed upon the doctrine of predestination, and the investigation of its nature and effects, than had been done in the English Articles. The latter in this respect had been closer to Calvin: the Irish confession was more 'Calvinist'. E.A. 17, for instance, echoed Calvin's warning about the danger of the doctrine of predestination leading to excessive introspection.[46] Whilst it was accepted that contemplation of the doctrine could have joys for the godly, the Article also warned that

> for curious and carnal persons ... to have continually before their eyes the sentence of God's predestination, is a most dangerous downfall, whereby the devil doth thrust them either into desperation, or unto wretchlessness of most unclean living ... [47]

In I.A. 16, whilst the E.A. was quoted fully on the benefits of the doctrine, the complementary warning on its dangers was cut short:

> for curious and carnal persons ... to have continually before their eyes the sentence of God's predestination, is very dangerous.

Though the Irish Articles cannot be said to commit the church explicitly to the experimental predestinarians' approach to conversion, nevertheless they were closely linked to the approach of Perkins.[48] They gave a systematic exposition of the way in which a Christian proceeded from sin to salvation which,

44 W. Perkins, *The workes of that famous and worthy minister ... William Perkins*, 3 vols (London 1608–10); Tipson, 'Puritan understanding of conversion', 199ff.; Kendall, *English Calvinism*, 51–76.
45 The sequence of topics at the start of the Irish confession follows the order of another Heidelberg divine, Zanchius, in his *De religione christiana* (London 1605).
46 Kendall, *English Calvinism*, 26.
47 E.A. 17.
48 It has been suggested that the Irish Articles were directly influenced by Perkins, through the influence he exerted upon their author, James Ussher: Breward (ed.), *Work of William Perkins*, 102; Kendall, *English Calvinism*, 80n. Neither element of this argument stands up, however. The ascription of the Articles to Ussher is dubious. Furthermore, the work of Ussher cited by Breward to support his claim that he was directly influenced by Perkins, *A body of divinity* (London 1645), was published without Ussher's permission and consisted merely of youthful notes from Perkins and other authors: R. Parr, *The life ... of James Ussher, late lord Archbishop of Armagh* (London 1686), 62.

though not as clear-cut as that adumbrated by Perkins, nevertheless, could easily be assimilated to it. They certainly set out the 'working theology' for protestant pastors in the Church of Ireland: when a minister strayed in his preaching from Calvinist orthodoxy, it was to the teaching of the 1615 Articles that he was ordered to return.[49]

However, the working theology of Irish clergy cannot merely be inferred from the Irish Articles. In order to examine the way in which predestinarian theology influenced the ministry of the Irish church, and trace how it was adapted to Irish conditions, one must turn to the hitherto neglected writings and sermons of Irish churchmen. Four authors in particular will be used to try to gain some impression of the Church of Ireland's working theology: John Hull, Henry Leslie, Stephen Jerome and Richard Olmstead.

John Hull was born in Cambridge, and educated at Caius, gaining his B.D. in 1630, and serving as a fellow 1595–1602.[50] Some time after, he emigrated to Munster, where by 1615 he held two rectories and three vicarages 'in the diocese of Cloyne, where he remained until his death in 1627.[51] Before he came to Ireland, he published two religious works.[52] After his arrival, he wrote two more, a commentary on Jeremiah, finished at Cork in October 1617, and a work on salvation.[53] Since the commentary bears witness to its origin, including comments upon Hull's new homeland, it provides valuable evidence of his ministry in Ireland.

Henry Leslie was a Scot, educated at St Andrew's, where he graduated with a doctorate in divinity. Thanks to his kindred with Robert Echlin, Bishop of Down and Connor, he obtained a benefice in Down, and soon became chaplain to Archbishop Hampton of Armagh. After serving in Meath he gained the favour of Laud and Bramhall, and was in 1635 entrusted with the task of reforming the sees of Down and Connor as Bishop. He fled after the rising, and died in 1661, a short while after he had been appointed bishop of Meath.[54] After Ussher, he was one of the most prolific authors in the Church of Ireland in the early seventeenth century: of most interest here are three sermons he preached in the 1620s. The first was delivered in 1622, before the Commissioners, the

49 U.W., xvi, 439; the letter was probably addressed to the Arminian, George Stuke, mentioned in an earlier letter to Ussher, ibid. 403–6.
50 *Al. Cantab.*; some of his correspondence from this period survives in B.L. Add. MS 24,191.
51 B.L. Add. MS 19,336, fol. 68r; Brady, *Clerical records of Cork, Cloyne and Ross*, ii, 73, 306, 395.
52 *The arte of Christian sayling* (London 1602); *St Peters prophesie* (London 1610).
53 *An exposition upon a part of the Lamentations of Ieremie: lectured at Cork in Ireland* (London 1608), 2nd ed. (London 1620); *Christ his proclamation to salvation* (London 1613).
54 Ware, *Bishops*, 208f.; Bodleian, MS Rawlinson letters 57, fols 25r *et seq.*

other two in 1625, one before the King at Windsor, the other in Dublin before the Lord Deputy.[55]

Stephen Jerome was English, educated at St John's College, Cambridge, where he gained his M.A. in 1607.[56] He first came to Ireland with Lord Beaumont, Viscount Swords, probably early in the 1620s, and like Hull he obtained preferment in the Munster plantation, at Tullow, subsequently becoming chaplain to the Earl of Cork.[57] In 1632 he moved to Dublin where he preached in St Brigid's.[58]

The final member of the quartet is Richard Olmstead, who came from a puritan background in England, graduating with an M.A. from Emmanuel in 1600, and entering the ministry in Suffolk, where he became a friend of the Winthrop family, who had close family connections in Ireland. It may well have been because of this connection that Olmstead decided in 1622 to emigrate to Ireland with his wife and children.[59] He settled in Queen's County, at Clonenagh, where he was supported as a minister by Sir Charles Coote, a prominent English colonist, and where he also acquired three vicarages and one rectory in the adjacent dioceses of Ossory and Leighlin.[60] There, by his own account, he cared assiduously for his flock, preaching and catechizing weekly. It was from his sermons there that his two books came, both printed in Dublin, the second with the encouragement of Archbishop Ussher.[61]

Of the four writers, Olmstead was the most directly influenced by Perkins and the experimental predestinarian tradition. The remaining three were simply straightforward Calvinists in their approach to predestination and conversion. Before examining the relationship between their theology and their approach to their ministry, however, one point must be investigated: how representative were they of the Irish church? In the first place, it is possible that

55 Leslie, *Treatise tending to unitie; a sermon preached before his Majesty at Windsore* (Oxford 1625); idem, *A warning for Israel, in a sermon preached at Christ Church, in Dublin* (Dublin 1625).
56 *Al. Cantab.*.
57 Ware, *Writers*, 334; S. Jerome, *Irelands jubilee, or joyes Io-paen, for Prince Charles his welcome home* (Dublin 1624), sig. 3r–3v; S.I., *The haughty heart humbled: or, the penitents practice* (London 1627), sig. A2r.
58 T.C.D. MS 6404, fol. 84v.
59 *Al. Cantab.*; W.C. Pearson,'Archdeaconry of Suffolk. Mandates for induction, 1526–1629', *The East Anglian*, 3rd ser., viii (1900), 362f.; 'Winthrop papers', *Massachusetts Historical Society*, 5 vols (1929–47), i, 68, 72, 89, 95, 139, 272, 275.
60 R. Olmstead, *A treatise of the union betwixt Christ and his church, or mans felicitie and happinesse. First preached in several sermons* (Dublin 1627), sig. A3r–A3v; idem, *Sions teares leading to joy: or the waters of Marah sweetned* (Dublin 1630), sig. A2r, B1r–B2r; B.L. Harleian MS 4297, fol. 16r.
61 Olmstead, *Sions teares*, sig. A2v, B1r.

they were untypical of the corpus of printed sources for Irish theology. Perusal of the other works of Church of Ireland clergy disposes of this difficulty since, where it is possible to judge, the other writers also fall within the Calvinist consensus on theological matters.[62] Secondly, it can be objected that all four writers were émigré clergy – what of the theology of the native ministers? It cannot be denied that the existing sources, especially those that are printed, overwhelmingly reflect the views of English and Scottish clergy: some were even published when the clergy were still serving in their homeland. Nevertheless, the sources that exist – the works of James and Ambrose Ussher, of William Daniel – suggest that those indigenous clergy who were theologically trained were Calvinist. This is hardly surprising, since the only theological seminary for such clergy in Ireland, Trinity College, was quite clearly Calvinist. The sources that survive, therefore, suggest that the Irish Articles were a fair reflection of the views of native protestants within the Church of Ireland, as well the émigré clergy.[63] Thus it is justifiable to take the sermons and writings of Hull, Leslie, Jerome and Olmstead as falling within the mainstream of the Church of Ireland.[64] It is therefore proposed to examine the 'working theology' of these ministers as revealed in their works.

Olmstead explained the purpose of his preaching as being 'to make an experiment ... to stir up and provoke this frozen age to humble themselves before God'.[65] His hope was that he might direct his hearers, through an awareness of their sinful state, to seek the true way to salvation.[66] In effect, this 'true way' as mapped out by Olmstead was that originally detailed by Perkins. Accepting that it was dangerous to be 'over curious in searching into the secret things that belong to God', Olmstead instead directed his attention to examining God's *voluntas signi*, revealed to us in signs of His grace and favour, such as good works.[67] Olmstead and other writers all, of course, thought man by himself incapable of good, unable to seek his own conversion: 'The natural man perceiveth not the things that be of God, neither can he; because they

---

62 J. Hill, *The penitent sinners entertainement (London 1614), 38; Andrews, Quaternion of sermons*, 62; C. Hampton. *An inquisition of the true church and those that revolt from it* (Dublin 1622), 24f.; J. Richardson, *A sermon on the doctrine of justification* (Dublin 1625); Sibthorp, *Friendly advertisement*, 153–203; Sibthorp was strongly influenced by Perkins and the experimental predestinarian tradition in his treatment of election and reprobation: ibid., 157, 160.

63 See above, pp. 156, 161.

64 One element of the Church of Ireland which has been excluded from this study is the presbyterians in the north-east of Ireland, which form a distinct and separate group with their own particular identity.

65 Olmstead, *Sions teares*, sig. A3r–A3v.

66 Olmstead, *Union*, 13f.

67 Ibid., 2f.

are spiritually discerned.'[68] As Leslie observed, 'there is nothing in our corrupt nature that hath affinity with the divine nature'.[69] Since 'thou canst do nothing in thyself', man had to wait upon God's grace, which was the essential and only means whereby he could transcend his natural sinfulness.[70] God, said Hull, 'gives a will to desire grace, grace works the will.'[71]

Yet the reliance wholly upon God's grace in no way minimised the role of the minister, or reduced him to waiting passively upon God's grace to do its work, since God had chosen the ministry of the word as the external means through which his grace should be conveyed to the elect. The preacher had a dual role – first to preach the Law, then the gospel. The preaching of the Law – the spiritual Law of the old testament, summarised in the ten commandments – prepared the hearers for God's grace. The preacher must make them aware of their sinfulness and their fallen state, as an essential first step towards conversion: 'it is absolutely necessary that a man see and feel his wretchedness before his soul can be possessed of Christ.'[72] When the preacher had preached the Law, and his hearers were at their wits' end, then they were ready to be moved seriously to consider and desire God's mercy 'which is the first wheel of all ... opening ... the door of the heart to let in the Lord Jesus into the soul.'[73] This effectual calling, the moment or beginning of conversion, was solely the work of God's grace. But the grace was transmitted through the preaching of the word, through the minister's second and most important duty – that of proclaiming the gospel. This was the main function of the clergy – 'They are the spiritual fathers to beget men to God by the effectual and powerful preaching of the gospel.'[74] As Leslie emphasised, 'these exhortations are the means, without which ordinarily no man is, or can be converted'.[75]

The initial infusion of God's grace, however, did not end the minister's role. For the Christian now began the difficult process of making sure that he really was chosen by God. Through the administration of the sacraments, prayer, and above all preaching, the pastor comforted and exhorted and taught the elect during their progress through justification to the attaining of assurance, as they struggled with doubt and despair and the wiles of the devil, trying to discover whether they were truly called. The progress was far from easy. For Perkins's theology stressed that it was often possible for the repro-

68 Ibid., 191.
69 Leslie, *A sermon preached before his Majesty at Windsore* (Oxford 1625), 8.
70 Olmstead, *Union*, 38, 48.
71 Hull, *Christ his proclamation*, 74.
72 Olmstead, *Union*, 70.
73 Olmstead, *Sions teares*, 40.
74 Ibid., 68, 99.
75 Leslie, *Warning for Israel*, 25.

bate to appear to have grace just like the elect. As Olmstead warned, 'Be diligent to know the difference betwixt counterfeit graces and true saving graces for the devil and man's corruption hath framed a counterfeit and shadow of every virtue.'[76] Such was the closeness of the resemblance between effectual and ineffectual calling, and the difficulty of discerning the true marks of grace, that the individual needed considerable help and instruction from the minister. Meticulous self-examination was called for, since God marked his adopted children

> with certain graces, as faith, love, godly sorrow, repentance and such like ... Oh brethren ponder and consider these things, and God give you understanding and grace to find all these branches of holy sorrow in your souls.[77]

Good works, then, were not a means of attaining salvation, but a sign that God had sent his grace. By carefully watching for such signs, the Christian could assure himself that he was of the elect. Olmstead, with Perkins's *Armilla aurea* in mind, urged his hearers 'to make your calling sure, and then ye make your election sure, for these graces are like a golden chain, that one link depends upon another.'[78]

Despite the earnest preaching of Olmstead and his fellow clergy, it is possible that an inherent contradiction existed between his ministry and his theology. It has been suggested that the Calvinist system of predestination inevitably had a restrictive effect upon pastoral activity: 'the very activities of an intensely proselytizing and evangelical church ... are directly contradictory, in terms of simple logic, to strict predestinarian doctrine.'[79] Superficially at least, the predestinarian stance of the Church of Ireland posed some apparent problems for the church's universal mission. Firstly, there was a tendency towards determinism, where, since God was the sole efficient cause of conversion, man's independence was denied. If God had predestined some to salvation, and others to reprobation, then it was easy to slip into a resigned fatalism which made pastoral work irrelevant. Secondly, from the minister's point of view, through the emphasis upon reprobation as the opposite of election, a temptation existed to define those who appeared to reject the gospel as destined for damnation. In a missionary setting, where the native population was hostile, such a tendency could have unfortunate consequences,

76 Olmstead, *Sions teares*, 230.
77 Ibid., 146f.
78 Ibid., 162f.
79 C.H. George, K. George, *The protestant mind of the English reformation, 1570–1640* (Princeton 1961), 58.

with the elect being identified with the missionaries, and the reprobate with the indigenous population. Finally, there was an apparent conflict between the dominical command to preach the gospel universally, and the doctrine of limited atonement – that Christ died for the elect only. Though an offer of salvation was made to all, ultimately salvation was restricted to the elect.

The Georges noted that despite these handicaps, English protestantism exhibited a ministerial enthusiasm for proselytization 'which seems constantly to be overstepping the limits which logically it has set for itself'.[80] In fact, the Georges have to a large extent reversed the truth. For it was Perkins's achievement to give to predestinarian theology a coherent and logical exposition which fitted the pastoral context. Theoretically at least, he solved problems such as determinism to his own satisfaction; and where ministers followed his reasoning, there was little danger that their ministry would be limited or diminished.[81]

Thus the apparent conflict between the command to preach the gospel universally and limited atonement was resolved through a distinction between God's *voluntas beneplaciti*, which was that only the elect would be saved, and his *voluntas signi*, which was that the gospel was to be preached to all. Since it was only the latter which was revealed to man, 'no particular person can justly think himself exempted.'[82] For, as Olmstead went on,

> Christ bade his disciples Math. 28.19, Go teach all nations, whosoever believes and is baptised shall be saved. And that he excludes none but includes every mother's child ... So that wheresoever the sound of the gospel comes, there by the ministry of it tender is made to every soul of Christ and all his benefits.[83]

Grace, of course, was not universal. As Hull put it, it is true that all can hear the word, but 'to hear is one thing, to hear unto repentance is another ... This is a grace only special to same, not common to all'.[84] From this arose two very important questions. Firstly, what of those who heard the gospel and were not converted? And secondly, what of those who never heard the word?

Preachers in Ireland were certainly acutely aware of what they saw as the stubbornness of the Irish people. Leslie devoted a whole sermon to the text Hebrews 3.8: 'Harden not your hearts'.[85] Jerome looked back to the efforts to enforce conformity in Ireland by both coercion and persuasion:

80 George and George, *Protestant mind of the reformation*, 58.
81 Tipson, 'Puritan understanding of conversion, 236, 315, 332.
82 Olmstead, *Union*, 94.
83 Ibid., 95.
84 Hull, *Christ his proclamation*, 76.
85 Leslie, *Sermon preached before his Majesty*.

> Hath there not been means used, both by word and sword, to purge their popish leaven, to bring them (as once the Gentiles) out of the power of darkness ... to bring them to the knowledge of the truth, but all in vain? Have we not lost our oil and labour? Are they not settled worse than Moab in their popish dregs. Are they not like Babel incurable? Do they not yet ... stop their ears with the deaf adder, and will not hear the voice of the charmer, charm he never so wisely? Do they not fly our churches and congregations ... as though there were some serpentine venom in our doctrine or discipline? Can they be brought into our spiritual feasts by any reasonable compulsion? Are not their hearts (like clay in summer) grown harder and harder, even as Pharaoh's? As their eyes more blind? Their wills more perverse? Their minds more malignant?[86]

The crucial matter was the way in which such obduracy was interpreted. In some cases God sent his grace to convert the hard of heart. The problem was to distinguish such temporary obduracy 'from that hardness which is in reprobates'.[87] Was it not natural to assume that at least some of those who proved obstinate were in fact reprobate? Though tempting such an assumption was not theologically justified, since it would be presuming upon God's own secret decree of election. One cannot say that those who are obstinate and remain so are reprobate, since 'We may not prescribe any time to God, as the wind bloweth as it listeth'.[88] As Olmstead further remarked, the word, though sown, can often lie fallow for up to thirty years, before the soul is finally awakened.[89]

Nevertheless, the neglect of the word when offered was dangerous. As Ambrose Ussher, a fellow of Trinity, stressed in a sermon on Romans 10.17: 'So then faith cometh by hearing, and hearing by the word of God': the means of conversion must not be ignored. We must hear the word *now*. If it be ignored, and 'if the neglect be general', then surely God will either remove the word, or remove the people from the word.[90] Lurking at the back of the minds of Irish ministers was the possibility which Olmstead had expressed: even where the word was preached, God might nevertheless choose not to grant His grace at all –

> it is possible that [if] men living under a powerful ministry of the word ... shut their ears against it, resist the motions of the blessed spirit ... that that curse may be set upon ... man's soul (and I verily believe it is

86 Jerome, *Irelands jubilee*, 41f.
87 Olmstead, *Sions teares*, 84.
88 Olmstead, *Union*, 96.
89 Olmstead, *Sions teares*, 71f.
90 T.C.D. MS 287, fol. 25v.

upon the souls of many living under the gospel) which our saviour set upon the fig tree, *Never fruit grow on thee hereafter* ... [91]

What about those who never heard the word? All four writers emphasised the primary importance of preaching as the means whereby grace was obtained. The obvious conclusion was drawn by Olmstead: people could not hope to be saved without the ministry of the word.[92] Hence the dangerous position of the Church of Ireland, with its lack of sufficient preaching ministers. God had, Olmstead admitted, 'vouchsafed some prophets scattered here and there' in Ireland, whose preaching and teaching 'ring sweetly amongst the people'. But otherwise darkness was everywhere prevalent.[93] As Hull pointed out, this could be seen as a judgement of God. Sometimes, he warned,

> for the people's faults are persons and ministers (I would I could not say, bishops) oftentimes set over churches; (God forbid such a pattern and example should be in Ireland) under whom the people suffers ... that direful famine of the word of God.[94]

What, then, was the fate of the mass of ignorant Irishmen in 'this profane and idolatrous kingdom', who never heard the word? Their very ignorance was a bar to conversion, since, as has been noted, conversion, for protestant preachers, involved the direct confrontation between the individual and God's grace, and demanded much effort and discernment on the part of the individual Christian. This rigorous idea of the conversion process was contrasted by protestant writers with the Catholic concept, where man's own efforts were assisted by the intercession of saints, the affective devotion inspired by images, and other mediatory means, and where 'implicit faith' enabled ignorant men to assent to the church's teachings without understanding them.[95] For protestant writers, justification was by faith alone – man must fly to God in all necessities.[96]

The emphasis upon man's direct relationship with God demanded of the believer, and the potential convert, a substantial degree of knowledge and self-awareness. The failure of the protestant school system in Ireland therefore had a direct impact upon the protestant ministry, since education had a role in

---

91 Olmstead, *Sions teares*, 180f.
92 Ibid., 27f.
93 Ibid., 4; and see also Hull, *Lamentations*, 241.
94 Hull, *Lamentations*, 51.
95 Leslie, *Treatise tending to unitie*, 27; Sibthorp, *Friendly advertisement*, 78; Hull, *St Peters prophesie*, 89; Hull, *Lamentations*, 26off.; G. Downham, *A treatise concerning Antichrist* (London 1603), Book I, 63.
96 Olmstead, *Union*, 31.

preparing for conversion something akin to the preaching of the Law. Just as universities were seen as seminaries for the training of the clergy, so the purpose of schools was 'to prepare children for conversion by teaching them the doctrines and moral precepts of Christianity.'[97] Potential converts had to be versed in the basic protestant precepts, so that they could use their knowledge to examine themselves and their consciences. For though conversion was worked by God's grace, grace in fact operated through the human will and understanding. Consequently, there was little point in preaching the word to the ignorant, and waiting for God's grace to effect their conversion. As James Ussher warned: 'For let us preach never so many sermons unto the people, our labour is but lost, as long as the foundation is unlaid, and the first principles untaught'.[98]

For conversion, therefore, there had first to be an awareness of sinfulness, which was the product of the preaching of the Law working upon the individual's understanding. In addition, however, that understanding had to be illuminated by knowledge – for, according to Olmstead, knowledge of the mystery of salvation was 'so necessary' that there was 'no salvation without it'.[99] A crucial text, which he twice quoted, was Proverbs 19.2: 'That a soul be without knowledge, it is not good'.[100] He likewise warned of the dangers of 'careless ignorance' as expounded in Hosea 4.6. The implications for Ireland were disturbing. Examining the fate of 'those ignorant persons that live in that palpable darkness', Olmstead lamented:

> Oh the woes that belong to such, and you the poor natives of this kingdom, what will become of your poor souls misted in the darkness of superstition by those locusts come out of the bottomless pit, the priests and Jesuits ... Your devotions (which you say) ignorance is the mother of, doth hasten you into sin and to damnation ... [101]

The obduracy of those who had heard the word preached, and the ignorance and idolatry of those who had not, did not bode well for the Irish people's prospects of salvation in the eyes of protestant preachers. In theory, it must be stressed, they could never despair of any soul, since God might choose to send His grace at any time. According to predestinarian theology, the min-

---

97 E.S. Morgan, *The puritan family. Religious and domestic relations in seventeenth century New England*, 2nd ed. (New York 1966), 90.

98 *U.W.*, ii, 500.

99 Olmstead, *Union*, 85.

100 Ibid., 85, 133.

101 Ibid., 3, 85f.; see also Hull, *Lamentations*, 210, 295; for further treatment of this topic, see below, pp. 188f.

ister was required to make the practical assumption that all might be saved,
since God's choice of the elect was hidden. In practice, however, clergy were
sometimes tempted by the difficulties and setbacks they encountered in Ireland
to despair about the people's salvation. As Perkins had been aware, a super-
ficial understanding, or a misapplication of predestinarian doctrine could be
dangerous, since the seeds of despair were latent in the system.[102] Firstly, ministers knew that the preaching of the word was the essential means through
which God chose to send his grace: yet in many areas of Ireland the word was
not preached. Secondly, God's grace, where it was sent, could be apprehended
by its fruits: where were the good works and godliness which were the signs of
God's elect? Finally, a tendency existed within predestinarian theology to minimise the number of the elect, and portray them as an elite group set amongst
the mass of unregenerate humanity. Such an approach was attractive for protestant clergy engaged upon the hapless task of evangelization in Ireland. Stephen
Jerome, having lamented the lack of signs of grace among the ordinary people
in Ireland, proceeded –

> I know God hath his elected ones in every place and people, chiefly where
> the means be planted ... I know God hath his Lot in Sodom, his Noah
> amongst the worldlings ... but alas these godly ones are thin sown, here
> one and there one ... Alas, the true Nathaniels ... are so few that thus
> shine as stars in this our dark night of popery and profaneness ... But
> as David complains in the Psalms, we may say ... *That all are gone out of
> the way, all, for the generality are corrupt and become abominable* ... [103]

Olmstead echoed Jerome's verdict. Those who manifested the fruits of God's
grace in Ireland were almost as rare as black swans. 'I fear there are but a few,
yea very rare, scarce one of a family, or ten of a tribe' fully saved.[104]

When a Calvinist cleric such as Andrew Knox, Bishop of Raphoe, came to
Ireland with the intention to 'resist the adversary and win home out of their
claws at the least the chosen of Jesus Christ himself', he could easily, when
faced with the recalcitrance of the native Irish, conclude that perhaps not many
of the Irish had been chosen by Christ, if indeed any at all.[105] It was bad
theology, but appeared to make practical sense. Similarly, Bishop Lyon, when
looking for an explanation for the withdrawal of the Irish clergy and the
consequent shortage of native ministers in 1595, feared that their aloofness
might be a 'token' that 'God hath cast them off'.[106] And Olmstead, when faced

102 Tipson, 'Puritan understanding of conversion', 236.
103 Jerome, *Irelands jubilee*, 88–90.
104 Olmstead, *Sions teares*, 5, 117; see also, Andrews, *Quaternion of sermons*, 87.
105 S.P. 63/231/26B (1611–14, 26).
106 S.P. 63/183/47 (1592–6, 396).

with the ignorance, profanity and stubbornness of the Irish, concluded that they were obviously led, not by the spirit, but 'by the devil and every base lust, a certain sign of the state of reprobation.'[107]

Essentially, the temptation to which these clergy were succumbing was one which had always been present in the Calvinist system of double predestination: that of turning it on its head and, instead of concentrating upon the positive assumption that all might be saved, giving greater emphasis to the fact that many might be damned. The likelihood of such an inversion was of course greater in the Bezan system of double predestination to which the Irish church was committed by its confession. At its most extreme, in the works of the soldier, writer and amateur theologian (amongst many other things), Barnaby Rich, it led to an attempt to define those who were destined for damnation in Ireland by race.[108]

Rich ascribed the failure of the gospel to gain adherents in Ireland not to the weakness of the protestant ministry, but to the obduracy of the people. Even in the late 1580s he contrasted the plentiful preaching in the major towns with the meagre results.[109] By 1610 the point had merely been reinforced: in Dublin the pulpits had been well supplied with preachers for a considerable time, learned men, who admonished the Catholics 'to desist from their blind fantastical follies'. 'But neither preaching nor teaching can ... prevail amongst them'.[110] Rich ascribed their failure to the strength of Catholicism and the power of Antichrist, devoting almost a whole book to demonstrating that the Pope was that man of sin of Revelation.[111] Rich stressed that he did not wish to decry the chances of salvation of the Irish – 'there is as near a highway to go to heaven from out of Ireland, as there is from any part of England'.[112] However, though the *potential* for salvation was present in Ireland, the reception which the preaching of the gospel received did not bode well for the *achievement* of salvation there. 'Where the love of the word and the gospel is contemned and despised, and utterly set at naught, as we see at this day (but especially here in Ireland) let them assure themselves that it is the work of the devil'.[113] Rich condemned the Catholic approach to conversion, and instead emphasised the primacy of God's grace. Yet, his extensive experience of Ireland

107 Olmstead, *Union*, 256.
108 On Rich see, T.M. Cranfill, D.H. Bruce, *Barnaby Rich; a short biography* (Austin, Texas 1953).
109 S.P. 63/144/35 (1588–92, 182f.: not fully calendared).
110 B. Rich, *A new description of Ireland* (London 1610), 55; idem, *A true and kind excuse written in defence of that book, entitled A new description of Ireland* (London 1612), sig. D2r.
111 Rich, *True and kind excuse*, sig. B4v; idem, *A short survey of Ireland* (London 1609).
112 Rich, *New description*, sig. B1r–v.
113 Rich, *True and kind excuse*, sig. G1r–G1v.

had shown him how seldom God had granted His grace. And, in these circumstances, when the word of God is preached 'unto men that be wicked unto whom God hath given no grace to receive it, then are they nothing thereby amended, but their hearts are the rather the more obdured'.[114] Rich's experience was evidently shared by Stephen Jerome: 'Convince their conscience we may, as Christ convinced the scribes and Pharisees ... Augustine the Manichees and Pelagians ... but till God give the grace, we cannot convert them.'[115] However, only Rich took this to its facilely logical conclusion – that the Catholics were, because of their manifest lack of grace, reprobate. Referring to 2 Corinthians 13.5, he wrote:

> Now the spirit of God is the only mark that is given to those that are elect, now the papist that hath not this feeling, if St Paul's words be true, is a reprobate, for he hath not the mark ... Then what are the papists but the destroyers of the kingdom of Christ, and the builders up of the kingdom of the devil.[116]

Rich may appear somewhat extreme. But his application – or, rather, misapplication – of current soteriological doctrine has a believable logic about it that might have appealed to some of those not expert in theology.

It is evident that historians can no longer ignore the mutuality of faith and practice in the Church of Ireland. Theology was not a remote academic exercise, of real interest only to Oxford or Cambridge fellows; it impinged directly upon the ministry of Irish churchmen. However, it cannot be assumed that a straightforward relationship existed between the church's predestinarian theology and its missionary failure. Far from restraining evangelical zeal, predestinarian theology in fact contained an inner insistence upon the need to preach both the Law and the gospel. The causes of the failure of the Church of Ireland lay in the immense practical difficulties it faced, both within the established church, and from the Catholic church outside, and in the church's commitment to an anglicizing reformation policy. Where theology served the ministers was in providing a means of explaining why they failed, why their preaching was so ineffective. The attractiveness of such an explanation lay in the fact that it placed the onus for failure not upon the protestant church or ministry, but upon the sinfulness of the people and the reluctance of God to send His grace to them.

114 Ibid., sig. C2v.
115 Jerome, *Irelands jubilee*, 75.
116 Rich, *True and kind excuse*, sig. G1r-v.

PROTESTANTISM AND CATHOLICISM

The intellectual framework within which the Church of Ireland viewed Catholicism was derived from the hostile English, and ultimately continental protestant tradition. The Pope was seen as the head of a corrupt church, which debased and defiled true religion, and exploited popular ignorance and superstition to lead its adherents into idolatry and even political disloyalty.[117]

Though not without its populist aspect, anti-Catholicism was founded upon a firm intellectual basis. In the latter part of the sixteenth century the major activity of many English theologians was anti-Catholic polemic. Most particularly in Cambridge, considerable academic effort and energy was devoted to defending protestant and rebutting Catholic claims.[118] Nor was the activity confined to the finer points of divinity and doctrine. The conflict between Catholic and protestant was placed within a wider historico-theological context, derived from Revelation and other apocalyptic books in the bible. Foxe, in his *Acts and monuments* indelibly imprinted upon the English mind an interpretation of Christian history which saw events since the coming of Christ in terms of the gradual unfolding of the battle between the forces of light and darkness, Christ and Antichrist. The antichristian corruptions which the papacy had gradually imposed upon the Catholic church had first been opposed by mediaeval heretics such as the Waldensians and the Lollards, and then been openly denounced by the protestant reformers. Whatever the contemporary sufferings, persecutions and difficulties of the protestant cause, its identification with the forces of truth ensured it of ultimate victory in the fight against Antichristian error.[119]

117 R. Clifton, 'Fear of popery', in Russell (ed.), *Origins of the Civil War*, 146–9; John Miller., *Popery and politics in England 1660–1688* (Cambridge 1973), 68f.; C.Z. Wiener, 'The beleaguered isle. A study in Elizabethan and early Jacobean anti-Catholicism', *Past & Present*, li (1971).

118 P. Milward, *Religious controversies of the Elizabethan age. A survey of printed sources* (London 1978), 127–56; P.G. Lake, 'Laurence Chaderton and the Cambridge moderate puritan tradition', Cambridge Univ., Ph.D. Thesis, 1978, 79ff.; R. Bauckham, 'The career and thought of Dr William Fulke (1537–1589)', Cambridge Univ., Ph.D. Thesis, 1973, 140ff.

119 Clifton, 'Fear of popery', 149–51; W. Haller, *Foxe's 'Book of martyrs' and the elect nation* (London 1963) – but see also K.R. Firth, *The apocalyptic tradition in reformation Britain 1530–1645* (Oxford 1975), chap. 3, especially pp. 106–8; R. Bauckham, *Tudor apocalypse. Sixteenth century apocalypticism, millenarianism and the English reformation: from John Bale to John Foxe and Thomas Brightman* (Abingdon 1978); P. Toon ed., *Puritans, the millennium and the future of Israel: puritan eschatology 1600 to 1660* (Cambridge 1970); P. Christianson, *Reformers and Babylon: English apocalyptic vision from the reformation to the eve of the civil war* (Toronto 1978); Lake, 'Elizabethan identification of the Pope as Antichrist'.

In the sixteenth century, neither the preoccupation with religious polemic, nor the apocalyptic interpretation of Christian history, were particularly notable features of the Church of Ireland. The vast majority of the native clergy were little concerned with such academic novelties, whilst those indigenous ministers who were aware of current protestant intellectual trends were hardly likely to embrace with enthusiasm an apocalyptic interpretation of history which implied that their Catholic kinsmen and friends were antichristian. Initially, only a few isolated English clergy, most especially Bishop Bale of Ossory, and also Archbishop Loftus and Bishop Jones, accepted the equation of the Pope with Antichrist, and sought to assert the implications of such an equation.[120] It was not until the growth of a more doctrinally conscious church after the 1590s that the anti-Catholic ethos of contemporary protestantism emerged clearly amongst the clergy of the Church of Ireland.

On the one hand, the influx of clergy from England and Scotland brought into the ministry of the Irish church clergy who brought with them the anti-Catholicism which they had assimilated on the other side of the Irish sea. On the other hand, the new university in Dublin soon demonstrated that not only was it to serve as a theological seminary, but its theology was also to have a strong polemical emphasis. Graduate studies were wholly devoted to divinity, and the holder of the chair of divinity was entitled 'Professor of Theological Controversies'.[121] The two figures who held the chair between 1607 and 1641 certainly lived up to their title. A dominant theme in the work of James Ussher, the first Professor, was controversy with Catholicism, even from his student days, when he set himself the task of reading the whole of the church fathers, so as to be better equipped to demonstrate the rectitude of the protestant position.[122] His lectures as Professor consisted largely in the detailed refutation of the foremost Catholic apologist of the time, Cardinal Bellarmine.[123] Joshua Hoyle, Ussher's successor, provided the students with a similar diet, spending sixteen years refuting Bellarmine in detail during his weekly lecture.[124]

Trinity's emphasis upon controversial theology led to the growth of public debate between Catholic and protestant in Ireland over doctrinal issues. Though long a feature of the English scene, until the first years of the seventeenth

---

120 Firth, *Apocalyptic tradition in Britain*, chap. 2; the difference of opinion between Sir Nicholas White and Bishop Jones in 1586 on the issue of toleration can be seen as resting upon whether one sees Catholicism as Antichristian or not: S.P. 63/125/12 (1586–8, 101f.); Brady, *State papers*, 113ff.

121 J.E.L. Oulton, 'The study of divinity in Trinity College, Dublin since the foundation', *Hermathena*, lviii (1941), 3.

122 Knox, *James Ussher*, chap. 10.

123 U.W., xiv.

124 J. Hoyle, *A rejoynder to the Master Malones reply concerning reall presence* (Dublin 1641), sig. C 3v, [a4r].

century Ireland lacked the crucial conjunction of trained protagonists and a means of dissemination. The foundation of Trinity in 1592, together with the influx of English clergy and Catholic seminarists provided the former, whilst the establishment of Frankton as official printer, and the presses of the Catholic colleges on the continent, supplied the latter. In 1602 Frankton took time off from his labours with the printing of Daniel's translation of the new testament to produce John Rider's *A friendly caveat to Irelands Catholikes*. Rider, who had close connections with Trinity, declared it his intention to proselytize the Queen's Irish subjects and show them how they had 'been so long deceived by Romish priests'.[125] The best means of achieving this, he felt, was to controvert the priests in their own country, and thus to 'discover the weakness of popery to the best minded Catholics'. To this end, Rider claimed that he had 'gone home with them to their own doors, fought with them in their own lists ... in the presence of their best friends'.[126]

Rider's main opponent was the prominent Jesuit, Henry Fitzsimon. Though a protestant in his youth, Fitzsimon had been converted to Catholicism, and subsequently became a missionary in Ireland.[127] For his pains he was imprisoned in Dublin, and during his imprisonment, he made his first venture into controversy with the youthful Ussher, in 1600.[128] The dispute with Ussher was broken off, and never entered into print, but a subsequent encounter with Rider led to a more public and long-lasting debate, stretching from 1600 to 1614, and producing five published works.[129] This was the first of regular encounters between Irish Catholic and protestant disputants, some of which survive only in manuscript, others of which were printed in Britain and Europe.[130] The lengthiest was between James Ussher and the Jesuit William Malone (alias Browne). Malone's original challenge to the protestant side to

125 Rider, *Friendly caveat*, sig. A3r.
126 Ibid., sig. A3v.
127 Anon., 'Father Henry Fitzsimon, S.J.', *Irish Ecclesiastical Record*, viii (1872), ix (1873).
128 For Fitzsimon's account see his *Words of comfort*, ed. Hogan, and his *Britannomachia ministrorum in plerisque et fidei fundamentis et fidei articulis dissidentium* (?Douai 1614), 14; for protestant accounts, see *Collectione Batesiana* (London 1681), 737; Parr, *Life of Ussher*, 6ff.; and a letter in Ussher's own hand in Bodleian MS Barlow 13, fols 80r–83v. The best summary of the dispute is in *Biographia Britannica*, 6 vols (London 1747–66), vi, 4063.
129 H. Fitzsimon, *A Catholike confutation of M. John Riders clayme of antiquitie* (Rouen 1608); idem, *A reply to M. Riders rescript. And a discoverie of puritan partialitie in his behalfe* (Rouen 1608); idem *Britannomachia ministrorum*; Rider, *Friendly caveat; idem, A rescript*, published in 1604, according to Fitzsimon, *Reply to M. Riders rescript*, 41, but no copy known to have survived.
130 Amongst the MSS sources: Bodleian Library, MS Barlow 13, fols 22r–25r, 210r–225r; N.L.I. MS 18,647; T.C.D. MSS 285–7, 291.

prove that the fathers did not support Catholic doctrine was made in 1619, and briefly answered by Ussher.[131] In 1624 Ussher published a longer reply, which elicited a further response from the Jesuit.[132] To it Ussher did not respond, but three other Irish clergy undertook the task, two Trinity graduates, Joshua Hoyle and Roger Puttock, and George Synge, an English minister beneficed in Ireland.[133] In addition, a lay protestant controversialist, Christopher Sibthorpe, a judge, also replied to Malone, though his work was never published.[134]

The controversial endeavours of Irish protestants were important less for their outward effectiveness in converting Catholics, than in their internal impact upon the Church of Ireland. No matter how diverse their views on other matters, all members of the church could agree upon the necessity for unity in the face of the Catholic challenge.[135] Even more than this, however, the polemicists, in the process of refuting Catholic claims, helped create for the Church of Ireland a consciousness of its own beliefs, and their distinctiveness, which helped to turn the church into a protestant and doctrinally aware body. Thus, when a minister such as Edward Warren was asked to deal with a difficult point in theology by a member of his Kilkenny parish, it was to his memories of Ussher's lectures as Professor of Theological Controversies that he turned in order to answer.[136]

The apocalyptic context within which controversial theology was commonly placed in England exerted an increasing influence upon Irish churchmen after the 1590s. Even in England the apocalyptic perception of history gave rise to

131 U.W., iii, pp. xi, 3–5; Bodleian Library, MS Barlow 13, fols 393r–499r.
132 *An answer to a challenge made by a Jesuit in Ireland* (Dublin 1624) W. Malone, *A reply to Mr James Ussher his answere* (?Douai 1627).
133 Hoyle, *Rejoinder to Malones reply*; R. Puttock, *A rejoynder unto W. Malones reply to the first article* (Dublin 1632); G. S[ynge] *A rejoynder to the reply published by the Jesuites* (Dublin 1632).
134 'An answere to so much as Mr Malone the Jesuite his reply ... as concerneth mee', Bodleian Library, MS Rawlinson C 849, fols 294r–302r; and written in Sibthorp's hand at the end of an annotated copy of his *A reply to an answere, which a popish adversarie made to two chapters conteined in the first part of that booke ... A friendly advertisement to the pretended Catholickes of Ireland*, T.C.D. Library, BB.11.28.
135 See Ussher's response to Jacob Whitehall, a minister who came to Ireland having been censured for his deviant opinions concerning Judaism by the Archbishop of Canterbury. Ussher was perfectly prepared to accept Whitehall as a minister in the Church of Ireland, but sought to direct his academic energy along different lines: 'I counselled him rather to spend his pains in setting down the history of purgatory, or invocation of saints, or some of the other points in controversy betwixt the Church of Rome and us.' U.W., xv, 162.
136 U.W., xvi, 342f.; and see also ibid., 407f.

a certain psychological tension. Although people could be confident of the ultimate victory of Christ and the forces of light, nevertheless, such optimism was often offset by the knowledge that they were currently living during the last days when Antichrist was at his strongest, and the threat he posed to the godly greatest. Optimism about the ultimate victory was therefore constrained by fear of the intervening sufferings and persecutions. Hence the pessimistic aspect of apocalyptic foreboding was often strong, England being seen as a beleaguered isle beset by the forces of evil. In Ireland, with its history of rebellion and religious recalcitrance, protestant pessimism about the Catholic threat was still more vivid. The protestants were not merely an isolated island community, they were an isolated minority within an island. To them Revelation appeared to speak directly. Founded upon the premise that these were the last times, given over to Satan and his angels, Revelation stressed the need for true Christians to separate themselves from Antichristian idolatry. Any compromise with the forces of evil would threaten their role as God's Israel, and forfeit their chances of ultimate, and possibly imminent, salvation. For, in contrast to the remainder of the new testament, Revelation stressed the difficulty of achieving salvation and victory in the present, tending to postpone them until the future, when they had been earned by human effort and self-denial. Revelation reminded people that in addition to the new testament God of love offering his grace to save them, there was also the old testament God of vengeance and terrible punishment who condemned many to damnation.

Revelation also offered, of course, a framework within which history could be explained. James Ussher was the first Irish churchman to devote himself to the historical interpretation of Revelation and other apocalyptic books of the bible. In his *Gravissimae quaestionis, de Christianarum ecclesiarum, continua successione historica explicatio*, published in London in 1613, the model of church history which he set forth was largely based upon the work of Foxe and Bale. He saw the first six hundred years as relatively pure, thanks to the church's closeness to its original source of inspiration, and to the binding of Satan for a thousand years. Then corruptions crept in, until, as the millenium was reached, Satan was unbound, and the church progressively overwhelmed by Antichristian iniquity.[137]

Ussher in his *Gravissimae quaestionis* dealt generally with the first thousand years of European church history, following the example set by other exponents of the apocalyptic interpretation of history. His most original achievement was in *A discourse of the religion anciently professed by the Irish and British*, published in London in 1631, where he attempted to relate such an interpretation

---

137 U.W., ii; Knox, *James Ussher*, details the debt to Foxe. Ussher never completed the second part of this work, in which he had intended to extend his treatment up to the period of the reformation.

specifically to Irish history. He sought to prove that the Irish church in its early years was relatively free from the corruptions of Rome, and thereby managed to preserve the essentials of the faith uncorrupted. Thus the church held the same views on matters such as grace, predestination, faith and good works, as the protestant reformers. Only gradually after the millennium did corruptions grow, when, as a result of the efforts of St Malachy and others, the Irish church came under the influence of Rome. As Ussher summed up his views in the work's dedication:

> I do not deny but that in this country, as well as in others, corruptions did creep in by little by little, before the devil was let loose to procure that seduction which prevailed so generally in these last times: but ... the religion professed by the ancient bishops, priests, monks and other Christians in this land, was for substance the very same with that which now by public authority is maintained therein against the foreign doctrine brought in thither in latter times by the Bishop of Rome's followers.[138]

Ussher in effect provided a respectable historical parentage for the protestant church in Ireland, at a time when such respectability was extremely important. It was, however, considerably more than merely an exercise in legitimation, for it also made real for Irish protestants the apocalyptic interpretation of history not just in relation to the European church, but in relation to their own church and its position in Ireland as well. The influence of apocalypticism can thus be traced both in the ministry of the Irish church, and in the way in which its official attitude towards Catholicism developed in the early seventeenth century.

Amongst the quartet of preachers clear signs of eschatological foreboding can be discerned, arising both from their sense that they were living in the last days, and from their perception of the corruption and idolatry which surrounded them in Ireland. Olmstead declared that the Devil and Antichrist were everywhere in evidence in Ireland. He wished 'that they might excite the kings of the earth to that Armageddon, which, Oh our Lord hasten, and I verily believe is at hand, sin never more common; and though the Lord pronounce a woe on them yet ... men sleep and continue in sin'.[139] Both Olmstead and Leslie detailed the sins of Ireland, from idolatry to incest, and pointed to the signs which God had already given of his wrath, such as the famines of recent years. Leslie warned 'when he takes a people in hand for to school them ... he begins with mild chastisements (but if these do not prevail) he proceeds to sharper corrections.'[140] Olmstead echoed: 'What think you of this island?

138 U.W., iv, 238f.
139 Olmstead, *Sions teares*, 6f.
140 Leslie, *Warning for Israel*, 5.

Hath not the immortal God smitten it with wars and consumed them with famine, and may not we say as Jeremy, *sed non doluerunt, but they have not sorrowed* ... '[141] He went on to explore the implications of the contemporary failure of the reformation in Ireland:

> When a just and most almighty God begins to correct a nation, and they stoop not ... under His correcting hand, He will never desist till He bend or break them ... Seeing therefore these symptoms and characters of God's fearful indignation are upon us, even upon this miserable island, what cause have we to cry out with the prophet, will thine anger never cease? ... let all of us ... *turn from our evil ways*; ye natives from your idolatry, superstition, theft, ignorance and oaths; ye English from your profaneness, drunkenness, lukewarmness, and all other sins.[142]

Such exhortations, however, were fairly standard: even in England apocalyptic foreboding was often used as the natural setting for the preaching of the Law. Many contemporary preachers bewailed the sinfulness of the times with savage indictments of their fellow countrymen, urging repentance before the imminent day of judgement.[143] Olmstead and the other ministers were, it could be argued, merely indiscriminately applying this to Ireland. In fact, however, its application was not indiscriminate – Olmstead distinguishes between Irish and English sinfulness, with the former generally being seen as much the more serious. Consequently, though the diagnosis was similar in both countries – sinfulness calling for repentance – the extent and gravity of the disease was far greater in Ireland. Hull warned of the failure of Irish people to come to church: writing of Cork, he claimed, 'of ten thousand in this town, not ten frequent the church'. If, he argued, the measure of the prosperity of a kingdom was 'the flourishing of the word', then the position of Ireland was indeed perilous.[144] Leslie pointed the contrast between Ireland and England most precisely using the biblical parallel of Judah and Samaria, with the latter, as the neighbouring country sunk in a state of sin, serving as a warning to Israel.

> For ye know, Judah was the first and mother kingdom, so is England to us; Samaria was far more corrupt in religion than Judah, having only a show of truth... so is this kingdom where we live. The Samaritans were a mixed people of Jews and Gentiles; so are we here. The Samaritans had a mixed worship: for in Samaria both the God of Israel and the gods

141 Olmstead, *Sions teares*, 141.
142 Ibid., 142f.
143 Thus, even before he came to Ireland the tone of apocalyptic foreboding can be discerned in Hull's work: e.g. *St Peters prophesie*, 500ff.
144 Hull, *Lamentations*, 234f.

of the nations were worshipped: and would to God it were not so here ...
Is there not a succession of priests sacrificing upon every mountain, and
under every green tree ... ?[145]

The growth in awareness of an apocalyptic interpretation of church history
in the Church of Ireland therefore had extensive implications for the outlook
and mentality of Irish protestants, both in the way they viewed themselves,
and in the way they viewed their Catholic opponents. Since Revelation was
replete with warnings about the dangers of compromise with the forces of
Antichrist, protestants sought to separate and dissociate themselves from what
they saw as the fatal idolatry and corruption of the Catholic church.

Several Irish churchmen in the reign of James, after examining the chances
of salvation for Catholics, came to the conclusion that the difference between
the two churches could be one of (everlasting) life and death. Their starting
point was provided by I.A. 68, which stated that there was only one Catholic
church[146] 'out of which there is no salvation'. Within this Catholic church
were a wide variety of particular churches, with many different creeds, but
sharing a commitment to the essential elements of faith necessary for salvation.
These 'principles of the doctrine of Christ', as Ussher termed them, were the
foundations upon which the particular churches were built. The problem in
relation to the Church of Rome was that the Popes had erected upon those
foundations an insecure building. Ussher did not totally deny that salvation
was possible within that church. Following 2 Thessalonians 2.4, in which Paul
stated that Antichrist sat within the temple of God, he distinguished between
the particular church (= temple of God) and the papacy (= Antichrist) which
occupied it.[147]

The crucial question that remained, however, was to what extent did the
presence of Antichrist threaten the status of the Roman Church as a true church:
was it merely corrupted, or was it totally apostatical? Ussher certainly felt that
as corruptions had grown in the years after the millennium, the very foundations of the Roman Church had been threatened. Only those whose ignorance
freed them from understanding the malignant popish innovations, allowing
them to retain the essentials of the faith uncorrupted, could be saved within the
church of Rome.[148] But Ussher was not hopeful about the fate of those who
espoused such innovations – 'For popery itself is nothing else but the botch
or plague of that church; which hazardeth the souls of those it seizeth upon'.[149]

145 Leslie, *Warning to Israel*, 10.
146 In the sense that it is used here, of course, 'Catholic' refers to the invisible church
   which cannot err, and which contains the particular churches.
147 U.W., ii, 476ff.
148 Ibid., 492, 496.
149 Ibid., 493.

The conclusion was that God's appeal in Rev. 18.4: 'Come out of her my people', was directed against those who, like the Roman Catholics, lived under Antichrist in the city of Babylon.[150]

Nevertheless, because of 2 Thessalonians 2.4, Ussher was hesitant about asserting categorically that the Church of Rome had forfeited its title of a true particular church. As another unnamed Irish protestant argued:

> If in popery there were nothing else but a dunghill or brothelhouse of Satan: if there were no fashion of church left there ... Antichrist should not sit in the temple of God ... But the question is how may it be called a church that is a den of so many superstitions? ... it is so called not because it holdeth all the qualities and conditions of a church, but because it hath some remainder ... Maugre Satan's malice that church hath retained the principles and foundations of faith albeit blemished with human doctrines ... [151]

A similar position was taken by Archbishop Hampton of Armagh (1613–25), who thought that the Church of Rome was, just, a true church. It possessed some graces and signs of a true church, such as baptism, although their purity had almost vanished under the manifold corruptions – 'I account it a church, but miserably deformed, and infected with infinite errors.'[152]

However, Ussher represented but one strand of thought on this question in the Church of Ireland. As he was fully aware, some held that the Church of Rome was not a visible church of God, not even 'a stained, corrupted and unsound church; but flatly no church ... at all.'[153] Amongst the Irish churchmen who claimed that it was a false church were Walter Travers, Provost of Trinity, George Andrews, Dean of Limerick, and Bishop Downham of Derry.[154] Downham's view of the Church of Rome was founded upon his apocalyptic interpretation of history. He accepted that the Church had been a true church before 607, but 'after that the church became apostatised and adulterous'.[155] Thus, in treating of 2 Thessalonians 2.4, he differed from

150 Ibid.

151 Bodleian Library, MS Barlow 13, fol. 481v.

152 C. Hampton, *An inquisition of the true church, and those that revolt from it* (Dublin 1622), 19.

153 Entry in Ussher's commonplace book, Bodleian Library, MS Rawlinson C 919, p. 1027.

154 Andrews, *Quaternion of sermons*, 50; W. Travers, *An answere to a supplicatorie epistle, of G.T. for the pretended catholiques: to the Privy Councell* (London 1583), 280–2, 305; R. Bauckham, 'Hooker, Travers and the Church of Rome in the 1580s', *Journal of Ecclesiastical History*, xxix (1978), 43; Rider, *Friendly caveat*, sig. W2r.

155 Downham, *Treatise concerning Antichrist*, Book II, 105.

Ussher. The church in which Antichrist sits had once been a true church, but no longer: now it was 'the whore of Babylon, an adulterous, and idolatrous, and apostatical church, which once was Rome ... now Babylon ... once the church of Christ, now the church of Antichrist'.[156] Downham conceded that the church possessed some 'notes and signs' of a true one, but such was its idolatry and corruption that it had only the name of a church, being in fact Babylon.[157] Since the Pope was Antichrist, and the Roman church apostatical, Downham unhesitatingly concluded that all who joined themselves to that church were destined for hell. To remain within Antichrist's church 'wilfully after he is discovered ... is a fearful sign of reprobation. For it is impossible that the elect should finally be seduced by Antichrist. Math. 24 v.24'[158] Rev. 18.4 commanded us to separate from the Church of Rome, Downham argued: therefore all who remained in it were disobeying God's commandment, and were destined for damnation. They were those of whom Paul observed in 2 Thessalonians 2.10–12 that Antichrist would effectively deceive them because they received not the love of truth: 'And for this cause God shall send them strong delusion, that they should believe a lie: that they all might be damned who believed not the truth'. To emphasise his point, Downham quoted St Jerome: 'They shall be seduced by the lies of Antichrist, who are prepared unto perdition.'[159]

Downham therefore came to Ireland already convinced of the iniquity of the Roman Church, and the impossibility of salvation within it. Thirteen years experience as a bishop in Ireland in no way changed his opinions: as he wrote to a Catholic in his Derry diocese in 1629, 'your religion of popery is superstitious and idolatrous, your faith erroneous and heretical, your church in respect of both apostatical, your deified Pope the head of that Catholic apostasy, and consequently Antichrist'.[160] In the case of those such as Ussher who were reluctant to argue from first principles that the Roman church was apostatical, and salvation within it impossible, woeful experience of their ministry in Ireland could ultimately lead them to the same conclusions as Downham. Ussher had allowed that those who, through ignorance, did not espouse popish corruptions could be saved within the Church of Rome. But, in the predestinarian system of salvation, the possession of a certain amount of knowledge was an essential precondition for conversion. And those Irish Catholics who were ignorant of popish corruptions were generally also ignorant of the essentials of the faith, without which there was no salvation. Consequently, Ussher

156 Ibid., 129.
157 Ibid., 130.
158 Ibid., 190.
159 Ibid.
160 Bodleian Library, MS Chatsworth 78, p. 55; S.P. 63/250/22ii (1625–32, 511f.).

in practice shared the pessimistic conclusion which Downham had arrived at theoretically.

In a sermon preached before the King in 1624 Ussher demonstrated that ignorance of the basics of salvation was 'not only perilous, but damnable'. Hence Ireland's condition was to be lamented, since 'the people generally are suffered to perish for want of knowledge; the vulgar superstition of popery not doing them half that hurt, that the ignorance of those common principles of faith doth'.[161] Ussher's pessimism was also evident in the very work in which he sought to open the eyes of the Irish people and show them the extent to which they had been corrupted and misled by Antichrist. He was not optimistic that his exegetic endeavours would in fact 'induce my poor country-men to consider a little better of the old and true way from whence they have hitherto been misled.'[162] The reaction of the Irish to the protestant gospel inescapably reminded him of the warning given in Luke 16.31: 'If they hear not Moses and the prophets neither will they be persuaded, though one rose from the dead.' Referring to the familiar text of 2 Thessalonians 2.10–11, Ussher remarked:

> The woeful experience whereof, we may see daily before our eyes in this poor nation: where, such as are slow of heart to believe the saving truth of God delivered by the apostles and prophets, do with all greediness embrace ... those flying legends, wherewith their monks and friars in these latter days have polluted the religion and lives of our ancient saints.[163]

The contrast between the theory and the practice of predestinarian theology has already been commented upon.[164] The theory called for a vigorous campaign of evangelism, to bring the word to the people. Since it was impossible for man to know whom God had chosen, ministers had therefore to proceed upon the assumption that all might be called. In practice, however, the joys of elections were not always emphasised, but the dangers of reprobation; not the possibility that all might attain salvation, but the probability that many would not. Similarly, the apocalyptic outlook had both positive and negative aspects. In theory, it provided an incentive for clergy to go out and preach the word, not only to those in the protestant church, but also those in the Catholic church whom God had commanded 'Come out of her'. In their mission, clergy could be sustained by the hope of ultimate victory over the

161 U.W., ii, 499.
162 Ibid., iv, 237.
163 Ibid., 238; and see also Jerome, *Irelands jubilee*, 182.
164 See above, pp. 171ff.

forces of Antichrist. In practice, however, the difficulties which clergy encountered in their ministry, and the reception of their attempts to preach the word
in Ireland led them towards the more pessimistic aspect of the apocalyptic
interpretation in order to explain their failure. Rather than the hope of ultimate victory, it was the awareness of the sufferings and persecution which the
godly would receive at the hands of Antichrist in the intervening period which
was uppermost in the minds of Irish churchmen. The negative aspects of both
predestinarianism and apocalypticism were combined by Olmstead. In examining the rightfulness and justice of God punishing the sinfulness of the Irish
nation, he pointed to the most notable example of such righteousness, God's
'foredamning and reprobating ... infinite millions of people following Adam'.[165]
In Ireland, he warned, 'the time is coming and hastens apace when the mighty
God will manifest this to the full.'[166]

It would be erroneous to suggest that the theological and intellectual outlook of Irish preachers was the primary cause of the failure of their ministry
in Ireland.[167] The difficulties of the reformation predate the creation of a doctrinally aware and intellectually coherent ministry. Rather, the pessimism was
a product of their experience in Ireland, as in the case of Ussher, with the
apocalyptic and predestinarian tradition providing a rationale within which
their failure could be explained by reference to forces entirely outside their
control. However, though initially a means of explaining why the reformation
had failed in Ireland, subsequently this intellectual outlook served further to
restrict and diminish the Church of Ireland's missionary élan.

165 Olmstead, *Sions teares*, 135.
166 Ibid., 137f.
167 See above, p. 178.

CHAPTER 9

The protestant church and the protestant state

Theology did more than merely while away the leisure time of Irish church-men in academic speculation. It provided them with a coherent explanation of their experiences in Ireland and their role there, both on an overarching level, in terms of the apocalyptic interpretation of history, and at the practical level of the parochial ministry. The growth of a truly protestant church was therefore of major significance, since it created a body of ministers who were united by a shared view of their position and duties in Ireland. Yet this very solidarity had within it scope for friction and conflict. For, as has been demon-strated, their claims in the religious field were absolute, positing the rectitude of the protestant position as a basis for political as well as religious policy. Within the ministry this served as a centripetal force, binding the disparate elements of Irish protestantism together. But it remains to be seen how it influ-enced the relation of the ministry to the wider protestant community and the state. For these bodies existed in a far more accommodating and relativist atmosphere: protestant settlers, whatever their opinions on the sinfulness of recusancy, needed labourers and tenants, and were unwilling to see them imprisoned to further the enforcement of conformity; the state had, whatever its views on the antichristian nature of Catholicism, perforce to reach an accom-modation with the majority of the Irish population, if the Irish polity was to function effectively. In short, scope existed for considerable conflict between the identity and responsibilities of the protestant population and the protestant state as seen from the ideological standpoint of the church, and as seen from the pragmatic standpoint of profit-seeking settlers or harassed secular officials.

THE CREATION OF A PROTESTANT IDENTITY

The doctrinal and ideological unity of the Church of Ireland in the early sev-enteenth century played an important role in fostering a distinct protestant 'self-image'. Pragmatic pressures and developments had of course shaped Irish protestantism in such a way that by the 1620s and 1630s it was largely iden-tified with the new English and settler interest – protestant strongholds were in effect areas of English or Scots settlement. This simple demographic fact, however, was assimilated into the broader historical and theological perspec-tives of the protestant preachers in Ireland. They sought to create a distinct

identity for protestants which recognised their minority status and gave rise
to a sense of communal solidarity. The means used by the preachers was biblical analogy: the old testament in particular provided obvious parallels and
lessons for minorities faced with a hostile environment. Henry Leslie, as has
been seen, used the example of Judah and Samaria to define the relative posi-
tions of England and Ireland. Other clergy identified the English in Ireland
with the Israelites, God's chosen people. The metaphor was illuminating and
very useful for the preachers, since it enabled them to place the English protestants and the Irish Catholics in exact and clearly defined perspective. The Irish
could be castigated as worshippers of false Gods, like the other nations which
the Israelites encountered in the chosen land. Equally, the English could be
admonished for their sins, yet without detracting from their special position
– for the Israelites, despite their chosen status, had on occasions failed to fulfil their duties towards God.

The old testament also provided unequivocal guidance on the relationship
between these two groups. Even before he came to Ireland, Hull bracketed
Catholics with 'Jews and heretics, Turks and infidels' as little better than
heathens.[1] Since the new English dwelt amongst Catholics in Ireland, they
were obviously in a similar position to the Israelites, who had lived among
heathens too. Hence the English had to pay special attention to the warnings
and instructions which God had given the Israelites, and take note of the anger
which the Israelites had provoked by taking heathen Gods and wives. For, as
God's wrath had consumed the Israelites, 'so will it our English-Irish [by this
Hull meant the new English], if they do not speedily repent; neither covenant
nor marriage must be made with idol worshippers.'[2] Though Hull conceded
that the Israelites were meant to serve as an example of the better way to the
heathens, essentially his argument was not missionary in its implications, or
outward looking, but concerned with making the English in Ireland aware of
their separate role and identity. The main function of the heathens was to
serve as a warning to the godly of the inherent sinfulness of man.[3] A similarly defensive moral was drawn by George Andrews in an assize sermon preached
in Limerick in 1624, when he warned of the dangers of intermarriage with
Catholics. Such alliances were, he claimed, forbidden by God in Deuteronomy.
In that book the Israelites had been instructed on their behaviour in the
promised land towards the seven other nations that dwelt there:

> thou shalt smite them, and utterly destroy them; thou shalt make no
> covenant with them, nor show mercy unto them: neither shalt thou make

---

1 Hull, *Christ his proclamation*, 50f.
2 Hull, *Lamentations*, 197f.
3 Ibid., 198.

marriages with them ... For they will turn away thy son from following me, that they may serve other gods: so will the anger of the Lord be kindled against you, and destroy thee suddenly.[4]

Stephen Jerome also identified the English nation with Israel. God had entered into a covenant with the Jews, and elected them of all nations to have his church and receive his laws. In return he expected obedience.[5] The English nation was similarly chosen by God to be a church for 'the propagation and profession of true religion': 'hath not the Lord sequestrated and separated us from pagans and heathens ... whom for a time He hath rejected for their un-belief, to be a church unto himself, and people jealous of good works.'[6] Jerome sought to apply this to his English auditors in Ireland – 'to bring our English-Irish Israel parallel with David's Israel', by making them aware of their sin-fulness, and the responsibilities that lay upon them as God's chosen people.[7] 'If ever nation and people ... had cause and occasion to act the part of David and his worthies ... we are the people.'[8] The difficulty, as Jerome saw it, was that though they now possessed more means to grace than there had been in Judea, 'yet we make less use of them'.[9] The English in Ireland were guilty of the sin of ingratitude to God, a dangerous failing, since lack of gratitude was a sign of a graceless heart.[10] They therefore must take heed of the danger of falling into idolatry like the Israelites did, and instead repent of their sins: 'Oh that my words, like spurs ... might excite and stir you to this neglected ... duty!'[11]

Preachers such as Jerome, Hull, Olmstead and Leslie saw their task in just such a light – to bear witness to the truth in a heathen land, and awaken those chosen by God, the protestant laity, to an awareness of their sacred task there. Hence Leslie's choice of text for his sermon published in 1625 – Hosea 14.2: 'O Israel, return unto the Lord thy God; for thou hast fallen by thy iniqui-ties.' Hull's treatment of the parallel between the English in Ireland and the Israelites also arose from an Old Testament text, Lamentations 1.3: 'Judah is gone into captivity because of affliction, and because of great servitude: she dwelleth among the heathen, she findeth no rest'.[12] Hull with his lengthy def-inition of the word nation, and Jerome with his exposition of the covenant

---

4 Deuteronomy 72–4; Andrews, *Quaternion of sermons*, 36.
5 Jerome, *Irelands jubilee*, 152.
6 Ibid., 153f.
7 Ibid., 115; see also 90f.
8 Ibid., 151.
9 Ibid., 76 (recte, 80).
10 Jerome, *Irelands jubilee*, 92–99.
11 Ibid., 139.
12 Hull, *Lamentations*, 151ff.

God had entered into with the English nation, were both seeking to foster a sense of collective identity amongst the protestants in Ireland.

How did their fellow protestants, clerical and lay, react to their efforts? Amongst the protestant clergy, the vision of English settlers as chosen people amongst the heathen Irish obviously placed the native clergy in an anomalous position. How could thee identify with the self-image projected by the English preachers? Many could not: hence the falling away of native clergy unable to find a niche in the reformed ministry. Some of those who remained may have done so for financial motives, anxious to retain their livings, and little concerned with theology or collective identity. However, there was a third group – those native clergy who were doctrinally aware, and had received a protestant education: their reaction to the new intellectual ethos of the Church of Ireland pointed to a significant change in the attitudes of indigenous protestants.

The change was closely linked to the increasing association between protestantism and anglicization, which put those members of the established church who favoured the old persuasive indigenous protestant tradition under increasing pressure. This commitment to anglicization was a crucial element in ensuring that it was not the outward-looking and missionary aspects of protestant theology which were emphasised in Ireland, but the pessimistic and introspective elements. Rather than seeking to accommodate the native Irish and their Gaelic culture within the Church of Ireland, protestant clergy expected native clergy to espouse and assimilate the anglicized values of the established church. Where a protestant minister was using the Irish language in his work, as in the case of William Daniel, an inherent conflict existed between the means of conversion and the ultimate end. Daniel was prepared to use the Irish language for proselytization; but he was seeking converts to a church which ultimately believed in the anglicization of the native Irish.

The protestant understanding of conversion served to strengthen the presumption that native members of the church had to change their style of life. Conversion involved the sinner abandoning his previous ways, and finding a new identity in Christ – implicit in this was the assumption that one's previous pattern of life would be transformed. Conversion was not simply a matter of changing one's faith in a formal manner, but involved the whole human being – 'whoever one was, religion was the way one lived, not merely what one professed to believe.'[13] A Catholic convert to protestantism would, through God's grace, gain the will to regenerate himself, and attain a new and 'lively' faith; he would also, in the process, cleave to an anglicized church, cast off his previous idolatrous behaviour, and accept the supremacy and God-given power of the King. In the sixteenth century these choices had been blurred and unclear, since the Church of Ireland was an amorphous and ill-defined

13 D.C. Stineback, 'The status of puritan-Indian scholarship', *New England Quarterly*, li (1978), 84; A.J. Krailsheimer, *Conversion* (London 1980), 5f.

body of ministers and people. But the protestant church of the early seventeenth century developed a clear self-image, and a coherent ideology. In order to become full members of this protestant church, the indigenous population had in some respects to reject their cultural heritage, forsake their family loyalty, and renounce traditional beliefs.

This was especially difficult for the native Irish, since their culture and beliefs were so different from those of the anglicized church. Sometimes, when they did become protestant, the change of allegiance was symbolized in the abandonment of their Gaelic surname. Two members of the O'Gowans, a Cavan family, conformed and entered the ministry of the Church of Ireland.[14] One, presumably locally educated, was a convert from the Catholic priesthood, and he retained his Irish name, Shane O'Gowan, and served his one cure in Kilmore.[15] The other, however, Nicholas O'Gowan, received a protestant education at Trinity, graduating with a B.A. in 1602 as Nicholas Smith. He held two benefices in Kilmore as a non resident in 1622, together with another six in the diocese of Meath, where he resided.[16] The MacCrossan family had traditionally been bards to the O'Moores in Laois. In the late sixteenth century two members of the family conformed, one entering the government service, the other, Sean MacCrossan, becoming a minister in the established church. The latter anglicized his name to John Crosby, and became Bishop of Ardfer.[17] The process of acculturation was obviously satisfactory to English eyes, since Crosby received special mention in the 1615 regal visitation: 'homo admodum civilis, coram nobis bene se gessit' – a marked contrast to the visitors' verdicts on other native Irish bishops.[18] One feature of the native ministry which aroused considerable criticism from English bishops and officials was the number of clergy who married recusant wives. Common in the sixteenth century, the habit persisted in the seventeenth, especially in the west. Such clergy were generally despised by English bishops serving in Ireland. The accepted pattern was rather that of Trinity graduates such as Barnabas Bolger and Neale Malloy, who demonstrated their assimilation by marrying the daughters of new English settlers. Indeed, concern about the low standard of native ministers led the Scottish Archbishop of Cashel to suggest in 1628 that natives should not be admitted to the ministry unless they had been suitably trained in a university in Ireland, England or Scotland.[19]

14 See above, p. 143.
15 T.C.D. MS 550, pp. 148–9.
16 U.W., i, App. V, p. lxix; A.D.
17 *Burke's Irish family records* (London 1976), 297f.; J. Maclean (ed.), 'Letters from Sir Robert Cecil to Sir George Carew', *Camden Society*, o.s., lxxxviii (1884), 35f.; Morrin (ed.), *Patent rolls*, ii, 560 (inaccurately transcribed, see S.P. 63/213/60 (Add. 1565–1654, 622).
18 B.L.Add. MS 19,826, fol. 94r.
19 T.C.D. MS 1188, fol. 11r.

The 1641 rising demonstrated how native clergy were torn between conflicting loyalties. Considerable pressure was put upon native Irish protestants
by the rebels, and many native clergy were unable to resist the pressure to
apostatize.[20] On the other side, a rare example of the way in which protestant
ties could outweigh racial loyalty was the case of Owen O'Connolly who first
gave warning to the Lords Justices of the plot to seize Dublin Castle in 1641.
O'Connolly was a servant of Sir John Clotworthy, a puritan planter, and had
married an Englishwoman.[21] When he heard of the plot, he had been faced
with a choice between loyalty to his fellow countrymen (in this case, his fos-
ter-brother), and his religious duty, with the concomitant political loyalty which
that implied. As Henry Jones, Dean of Kilmore, explained his decision: 'the
good man [was] moved with the fear of God, love for his King and country,
and commiseration for his fellow subjects, Christians and protestants'.[22]

The element of choice between two sets of values and beliefs was also
apparent amongst the Anglo-Irish community, though in a more complicated
and straightforward way than with the native Irish. Traditionally, as the proud
descendants of the Norman conquerors, the Anglo-Irish had had an innate
sympathy with the anglicized approach to Gaelic Ireland. This could lead
naturally to the espousal of protestant reform: an Anglo-Irish protestant of the
sixteenth century, like Rowland White, could marry his religious convictions
to anglicizing reforms in the secular and cultural spheres.[23] In the early seventeenth century, the persistence of an indigenous ministry in the Pale can
also partly be seen as a product of Anglo-Irish willingness to accept an anglicizing reformation. Nevertheless, the vast majority of the Anglo-Irish remained
loyal to the Catholic church.[24] Such devotion to Catholicism would appear to
form a natural bond between the Anglo-Irish and the native Irish. Identification
with the latter, it has been argued, was strengthened by the growth in the later
sixteenth century of an Irish patriotism which transcended the previous narrow,
Pale-based ethnic identity of the Anglo-Irish. Emerging patriotism, growing
cultural intercourse, common distaste for the increasing dominance of the new
English, and a shared religion, all tended to draw the Anglo-Irish towards their
countrymen.[25] Arguing along similar lines, the career of Richard Stanyhurst
suggests that immersion in Irish religious nationalism could lead to a muting
of traditional Anglo-Irish hostility towards Gaelic culture.[26]

20 See the example of Thomond: Frost, *History and topography of Clare*, 357, 360,
    361, 365.
21 Moody, Martin, Byrne (eds.), *New history of Ireland*, iii, 291.
22 *A perfect relation of the beginning and continuation of the Irish rebellion* (London
    1641), 14.
23 N.P. Canny (ed.), 'The dysorders of the Irishery 1571', *Studia Hibernica*, xix (1979).
24 See above, p. 19.
25 Bradshaw, *Irish constitutional revolution*, 276ff.
26 C. Lennon, 'Richard Stanyhurst (1547–1618) and Old English identity', *Irish*

Yet, if such a shift in Anglo–Irish commitments occurred, it might be expected that more would have found common ground with the protestant church, because of a shared preference for anglicization, and a distaste for the shift towards the native Irish. One reason why this was not the case was the profound political alienation of the Anglo–Irish in the later sixteenth century, which turned them against the new English elite. A second element may be the nature of Irish Catholicism's transition from survivalism to the counter-reformation. As it developed in Old English areas, amongst orders like the Jesuits, the counter-reformation in Ireland accommodated and adopted the old English assumption that reform was to be placed in an anglicizing context. The common religious bond between native Irish and old English was more apparent than real as a culturally unifying force. In consequence, the nascent political nationalism of the later sixteenth century did not in the early years of the following century replace the more narrow group loyalty of the old English.[27]

Where did this place the old English protestants? Clearly, they were not faced with the same stark conflict of cultural loyalties as were the native Irish converts. Was there, then, only a religious divide? In fact protestantism separated them from their fellow old English in two further ways. Firstly, they had a totally different education, at a diocesan school, and then at Trinity College, where there was a predominantly new English tone. More importantly, protestantism implied a political loyalty to the crown which was far more complete than that which followed from Catholic political theory.[28] The Catholic old English sought strenuously to deny this, or minimise its significance, asserting that political loyalty was perfectly consonant with their religious allegiance. But this was simply not true: ultimately the old English commitment to the counter-reformation was incompatible with their loyalty to the English crown, as James brought home to them in the second decade of the seventeenth century.[29] The loyalty of the old English protestants to the crown, together with their anglicized education, inevitably brought them closer to the position of the new English bishops and clergy in Ireland. Their protestant training taught them that Catholicism was idolatrous; their political theory showed them that the King had a duty to extirpate idolatry; therefore they were able to give their wholehearted support to the enforcement of conformity amongst the recusant old English by civil means – a step which their predecessors in the sixteenth century Church of Ireland, whether through their commitment to persuasion, or their racial solidarity, had drawn back from. In

Historical Studies, xxi (1979).
27 A. Clarke, 'Colonial identity in early seventeenth century Ireland', *Historical Studies*, xi (1978).
28 J.P. Sommerville, 'Jacobean political thought and the controversy over the oath of allegiance', Cambridge Univ., Ph.D. Thesis, 1981.
29 Clarke, 'Colonial identity in Ireland'.

this respect, therefore, seventeenth century Anglo-Irish bishops such as Ussher, Daniel and Anthony Martin were little different from their fellow new English prelates. Daniel's views were perfectly compatible with those of Loftus or Jones: a fundamental and uncompromising distaste for Catholicism; an identification of the Pope with Antichrist; a firm belief in a state aided reformation, and enthusiasm for Chichester's efforts to enforce conformity in particular; support for the plantation in Ulster; and criticism of the barbarity of the native Irish.[30]

PROTESTANT IDENTITY: CHURCH AND PEOPLE

Though there was, as far as can be judged from the surviving sources, unanimity amongst the protestant ministry, founded upon their concern to fight the antichristian enemy, no similar consensus existed within the broader protestant community, between ministers and planters, or between church and state. The church's relations with its protestant parishioners were often far from cordial, on one notable occasion degenerating into open warfare.[31] Some of the tension can be attributed to the familiar conflict of interests between clergy and laity over issues such as tithes. Yet there was another contributory factor. As has been seen, the clergy sought to create among the protestants of Ireland a sense of their collective identity, devoting much effort to admonishing the new English to fulfil their religious obligations. Implicit in the fact that preachers had thus to exhort their fellow protestants was a reluctance by the latter to fulfil the role demanded by the clergy.

The church urged the protestants to be aware of their calling, the task for which God had placed them in a heathen land. Settlers in particular had been sent to Ireland by James with the primary duty of reducing the country to civility and religion. Such grandiose aims, as has been noted, did not long survive the arrival of the planters in Ireland. Settlers perforce compromised with the native population, employing them as labourers and tenants, and ignored the official insistence that such employment be conditional on religious conformity. Against such *de facto* toleration of Catholicism even the thunderings of Bishop Downham proved ineffective.[32] The settlers' lack of care for religion therefore added to the irritation which churchmen already felt over the lay predacity towards church possessions. Nor were the ordinary run of settlers any better than the leading undertakers in terms of the example they set to the native population. In Ulster there were many complaints about

30 Daniel, *Leabhar*, [fols 2v–3r]; S.P. 63/193/38 (1596, 121); T.C.D. MS 2158, fol. 87r; Armagh Public Library, 'Returnes of the bishops', fol. 44v.
31 Perceval-Maxwell, *Scottish migration*, 263f.; P. Kilroy, 'Bishops and ministers during the primacy of Ussher', *Seanchas Ardmhacha*, viii (1977), 288.
32 See above, pp. 153f.

the low standards of behaviour and morality of the mass of the planters.[33] Neither were those in Munster any more suitable to serve as examples of civility and protestantism, according to Sir Parr Lane: 'The meaner sort of the English who have resided there any time are the worst part of the venom that the country yields'.[34] If these judgements are accurate, then the aspersions so frequently cast upon protestants by Catholic writers – that their religion gave rise to all kinds of licentiousness, vice and immorality by the nature of its doctrine of predestination – can be seen to have been accurate in relation to fact, if not cause.

Though there was clearly scope for division between protestant clergy and their parishioners, the extent of their conflict, and its reasons, are not always apparent from the surviving sources. More information is available, however, about an even more serious rift within the protestant community – that between protestant church and protestant state, over the policy to be followed towards the Catholic majority in Ireland.

CONFORMITY AND CONVERSION: STATE AND CHURCH

Even in Germany, where there was a popular reformation movement, the assistance of the secular power was soon found to be essential to support and further the spread of protestantism. In England and Ireland, on the other hand, the reformation was from the start imposed from above, through the supreme authority of the monarch. This Erastian settlement laid down the basic pattern of church-state relations throughout our period in both Ireland and England.[35]

The clearest exposition of the relationship by an Irish churchman was given by James Ussher, who followed the standard protestant formulation of John Jewell. His starting point was the royal supremacy 'in all causes whatsoever'.[36]

33 Perceval-Maxwell, *Scottish migration*, 279ff.; N.P. Canny, 'Dominant minorities: English settlers in Ireland and Virginia 1550–1650', in A.P. Hepburn ed., *Minorities in history* (London 1978), 53; id., 'The permissive frontier: social control in English settlements in Ireland and Virginia, 1550–1650', in Andrews, Canny, Hair (ed.), *Westward enterprise*, 21–3.
34 Bodleian Library, MS Tanner 458, fol. 33v.
35 G.R. Elton, *The Tudor constitution* (Cambridge 1963), 333ff.; *idem, Policy and police*; J.W. Allen, *A history of political thought in the sixteenth century* (London 1957), 171ff.; C. Cross, *The royal supremacy in the Elizabethan church* (London 1969), 23ff.; *idem*, 'Churchmen and the royal supremacy', in F. Heal, M.R. O'Day ed, *Church and society in England: Henry VIII to James I* (London 1977).
36 U.W., ii, 461; for a fuller exposition of Ussher's views on kingship, see U.W., xi, 223ff.

Supremacy, however, though it extended to both civil and ecclesiastical cases, dealt only with external jurisdiction. A different power had been ordained by God to minister to the inner man. Whilst the power of the sword had been entrusted to the magistrate, the power of the keys, of loosing and binding consciences, was committed to the church.[37] Both church and state sought to bring men to obey the first table of the ten commandments, concerning piety and religious duties, and the second, concerning moral honesty. But the church worked upon the inner man, by preaching and exhortation, whilst the magistrate used his power of civil jurisdiction to enforce outward obedience. This was not, of course, to conflate the two powers: 'For though the matter wherein their government is exercised may be the same, yet is the form and manner of government therein always different'.[38] Despite the distinction, scope for tension nevertheless existed between the royal supremacy in external jurisdiction, and the church's separate and God-given power in spiritual matters. In theory, bishops and ministers were entrusted with the power to decide questions of doctrine and ceremony: as Ussher explained, quoting Jewell and Alexander Nowell,

> It is necessary that a godly ministry should decide these matters, and ...
> it belongeth to the bishop's office to do so: (not the magistrate's: who
> are yet to judge of civil causes properly). It is necessary that the prince
> should do these things by the discretion of the priests and bishops ... [39]

In practice, however, the chief governor's powers in England extended considerably beyond that of external jurisdiction, and Elizabeth exerted much influence over issues of doctrine and ceremony, albeit officially with the advice and consent of the church. Provided churchmen never reached the point where they felt they had to place their obedience to God above their loyalty to the chief governor, conflict could be avoided; but the possibility of such conflict was present within the existing framework of church-state relations.[40]

To a certain extent, the possibility of such a confrontation occurring between the King and the Irish bishops was lessened by the distance of Ireland from England, and the consequent weakness of royal control. This can be seen in the enforcement of conformity in Ireland, or in the independence of convocation in 1613 in including the Lambeth Articles in the Irish confession. Yet,

37 U.W., ii, 462.
38 Ibid., 464.
39 Bodleian Library, MS Rawlinson C 919, p. 571.
40 Cross, 'Churchmen and the royal supremacy', 20–3, 25–7; P. Collinson, 'If
    Constantine, then also Theodosius: St Ambrose and the integrity of the Elizabethan
    Ecclesia Anglicana', *Journal of Ecclesiastical History*, xxx (1979).

in another respect, the Church of Ireland was considerably more dependent upon the state than the English church. In England, church and state could be merged in the wider identity of the Christian commonwealth, with the church as an inclusive body including most of the King's subjects. In Ireland, however, the protestant church was in a far more exposed position – no correlation existed between its membership and the King's subjects. In consequence, when the church asked the magistrate to enforce outward conformity to the religion established by law, it was asking the civil authorities to act against a substantial proportion of the King's subjects, with obvious implications for the political cohesion of the commonwealth.

The King and his advisers in England were, as has been seen, fully aware of these implications, and counselled moderation to civil and church leaders in Ireland. But the church leaders in Ireland saw the role of the magistrate as clear and incontrovertible, and availed of every opportunity to spell out just what his duty was in relation to the establishing of true worship and the extirpation of heresy. Using both old testament and historical examples, they sought not just to rebut Catholic claims that the magistrate had no God-given authority in such matters, but also to remind the civil authorities of their duty, always seeking, by their eisegetic approach to their texts, to relate them to the particular problem of obdurate recusancy in Ireland. The first place to which they turned for inspiration and guidance was the relationship between the kings of Israel and the church portrayed in the old testament. Ussher twice took the text 2 Chronicles 34.33, which described how King Josias 'took away all the abominations' from the country of Israel, and made the people serve the Lord their God.[41] The first lesson which he drew was that the king indeed had the power to decide in matters ecclesiastical. The second concerned the king's power to remove abominations. What were these abominations, and could they be equated with Catholic worship in Ireland? Ussher had little hesitation in identifying the 'idolatries of the Roman church' as abominations: 'I dare truly affirm that Jereboam's calves and idolatries were not so sinful as theirs is.'[42]

The implication for Ireland was that the magistrate had a duty to force all Catholics to give up their idolatry. Nor could the magistrate tolerate Catholics if they were otherwise loyal to the established order – for Ussher stated that idolatry could not be allowed by any godly prince, not even if those who practised it were in other matters quiet and loyal.[43] The third conclusion that Ussher drew from the text was that, in addition to suppressing idolatry, the King also had a duty to establish the true service of God through compelling all to follow the true religion. This was a crucial issue for the Church of

---

41 U.W., xiii, 567–79; Bodelian Library, MS Rawlinson C 919, pp. 579–82.
42 U.W., xiii, 573–5; Bodleian Library, MS Rawlinson, C 919, p. 581.
43 U.W., xiii, 573.

Ireland, since it had been the subject of the clash between English and Irish authorities at the start of James's reign.

A second way in which Irish churchmen approached the issue of the state's responsibility in religious matters was through historical precedent, from the time of the early church. The most popular example was that of the Donatists, the North African schismatics of the fourth and fifth centuries, whose stubbornness in the face of efforts to win them over had led to Augustine's conversion to the use of secular power to enforce conformity.[44] To the protestants, it served as ideal analogy for their position in Ireland. They knew that they were the true church; the Catholics were schismatics, obdurate heretics who refused to listen to the truth. As Leslie argued, in his sermon before the 1622 Commissioners, it was this obduracy and 'long continuance in error' of the Irish Catholics that formed the main impediment to protestant success,

> there being nothing harder than to break an ignorant man of his custom ... This is noted by that father [Augustine] to have hindered the reformation of the Donatists: 'Some were bound not by truth, but by the hard knot of obdurate custom ... '[45]

The way to overcome this, Leslie felt, was compulsion – 'fear is that which will overcome custom'.[46] Indeed, fear was the *only* way: instruction and persuasion were useless, merely exacerbating the problem. Here Leslie quoted Augustine again, using a passage which was a favourite with Irish churchmen:

> 'si doceantur et non terreantur, vetustate consuetudinis obdurati, ad capescandam salutis viam pigrius aurgent.' You [the Commissioners] are the second servants of the Lord, sent with this commission, 'Compel them to come in, that my house may be full.' Ye must compel them by laws and punishments.[47]

He pointed to the methods of Constantine and Theodosius the Younger. The latter

> set a fine of ten pounds of gold upon the Donatists who were the recusants of that age: which had very good success. For ... thereby many of them were moved to profess religion, and though at first they did profess

---

44 P.R.L. Brown, *Augustine of Hippo* (London 1967); W.H.C. Frend, *The Donatist church* (London 1952).
45 Leslie, *Treatise tending to unitie*, 42.
46 Ibid., 44.
47 Ibid., 45.

it merely by compulsion: yet afterwards they professed only for devotion.[48]

The obvious criticism of this policy was that it required the magistrate to force the consciences of recusants, something which most agreed was not possible. Sir Christopher Sibthorp, the theologically minded judge, expounded the standard protestant answer to such an objection. He began by quoting St Augustine's letter to Boniface:

'Where you think ... that none must be forced to truth against their wills, you be deceived, not knowing the scriptures, nor the power of God; which maketh them willing afterward which were unwilling at the first ... Princely power and authority giveth many men occasion to be saved'.[49]

Kings, Sibthorp went on to argue, had a *duty* to compel their subjects

although not to faith, yet to the outward means of faith, which is coming to the church and assemblies of God's people, there to hear the word of God read and preached. For howsoever it be granted, that God only worketh faith in men's souls, and not men, nor the power of kings; yet thereupon it followeth not, but that a king may nevertheless command and compel them to external obedience, and cause them to present their bodies in those churches and assemblies where the ordinary means of faith and salvation is to be had. And as for God's inner working, upon their souls, and his blessing upon that outward means, when they be in those assemblies, kings and princes do, and must, leave those things unto God alone ... [50]

A similar point was made by Ussher when he tackled the question: 'Will you make a papist come to church against his conscience?'[51] He argued that, since the Catholic sins in not coming to hear the ministry publicly established by the King, the magistrate had a duty to act against him, both to reprove sin, and to enable the sinner to repent. The latter point was extremely important, since it reflected the theological underpinning behind the insistence of Ussher, Loftus, Jones, and other Irish churchmen that the magistrate must enforce

---

48 Ibid.; other Irish protestants followed Leslie in applying the Donatist analogy to such recusancy: see Sibthorp, *Reply to an answere*, 56; Rich, *True and kind excuse*, sig. B1v; Hull, *St Peters prophesie*, 84.
49 Sibthorp, *Friendly advertisement*, 8f.
50 Ibid., 9.
51 U.W., xiii, 577.

conformity. As they saw it, all that they were asking was that the magistrate should put the people into a position where they were able to be converted, by the operation of God's grace through the preaching of the word. In answer to the claim that they were trying to force consciences, they pointed to the distinction between conformity and conversion. The former was the duty of the magistrate to enforce – to ensure outward attendance at church. Conversion was the sphere of the clergy and, as Jones admitted, 'must be free from the heart and without compulsion'.[52] The urgency with which the protestant leaders demanded that the civil authorities fulfil their duty in this regard resulted from their conviction that without such help their preaching would be useless. Given the distinction between the two powers, the church could not itself force people to come to church – it could only preach and teach. The relationship between the spiritual and temporal powers in this regard was thus almost a mirror image of their respective responsibilities in excommunication. In the latter, the church authorities dealt with the spiritual matter, and then handed the person over to the secular authorities to be dealt with by the temporal sword; in this case, the temporal authorities were to use their power to hand people over to the church, so that they could be subject to the *gladium spiritus* – the word of God.

In this light the policy so strenuously advocated by Loftus and Jones in 1603–4 assumes a new importance. In their view conformity was an essential prerequisite for conversion. For the first time, the state was in a position to ensure that conformity was enforced. It was essential that this be done. If it were not, the preaching of the gospel would be of little use. Like Barnaby Rich, Loftus and Jones compared the many years of preaching in Dublin with the paucity of the results, since only the English attended the services. Knowing as they did 'the wilfulness of this people and the induration of their hearts against the true religion', they could see no other course than coercion, if these latter-day Donatists were to be 'reclaimed from their idolatry to come to hear the glad tidings of the truth and of their salvation.'[53] If this were not done, then 'the preachers shall but lose their labours (few or none will come to hear them)'.[54]

Ussher too thought that 'the case is plain': a recusant must be forced by the civil power. 'For let him be left to his own conscience, and he will continue in sin all the days of his life'.[55] He granted, of course, that many would remain hard-hearted, but some, he claimed, had been converted by these means.[56] In any case, to argue from success or failure was to intrude into the

52 Huntingdon Library, San Marino California, MS EL 1148, p. 197.
53 S.P. 63/216/8 (1603–6, 151–3).
54 S.P. 63/215/68 (1603–6, 60).
55 U.W., xiii, 577.
56 Ibid., 578.

area of God's secret will, by which some were inevitably destined for everlasting hardness of heart and consequent damnation. The church's duty was
merely to preach God's revealed will, that salvation was offered to all; the
magistrate's duty was merely to see that the people heard this preaching.

The rejection by the King and his advisers of the policy of enforced conformity in 1606–7 did not reflect any disagreement over the nature of the ultimate relationship between *regnum* and *sacerdotium*. However, in practice, the
King and the leaders of the Irish church saw the relative responsibilities of
state and church in a markedly different fashion. James, whilst he accepted
that the monarch had a duty to enforce outward conformity to the true religion, was content to do so moderately, without too much rigour. As he
explained to the English parliament of 1621, he was content with the laws then
in force against recusants in England: the problems arose, not from their inadequacy, or lack of enforcement, but from the failure of the church to play its
part in winning over Catholics.[57] James's similar insistence upon the pastoral
role of the Irish church was incomprehensible to Irish church leaders. The
King's exhortations to greater missionary endeavour seemed to them to miss the
whole point: he was leaving out the essential first step – conversion could not
come without conformity first being rigorously enforced by the magistrate.

The climax to Irish churchmen's disillusionment with royal policy came in
the 1620s. Ussher preaching before the House of Commons in 1620, restated
the uncompromising protestant attitude towards Catholicism:

> Their blindness I do much pity: and my heart's desire ... is that they
> might be saved. Only this I must say, that ... I cannot preach peace unto
> them. For, as Jehu said to Joram, 'What peace, so long as the whore-
> doms of thy mother Jezebel, and her witchcrafts are so many?' ... Let
> her put her whoredoms out of her sight ... or rather, because she is past
> all hope, let those that are seduced by her, cease to communicate with
> her ... and we shall be all ready to meet them and rejoice ... for their
> conversion. In the mean time, they who sit at the helm and have the
> charge of our church and commonwealth ... must provide by all good
> means that God be not dishonoured by their open idolatries, nor our
> King and state endangered by their secret treacheries. Good laws there
> are already enacted to this purpose: which, if they were duly put in exe-
> cution, we should have less need to think of making new.[58]

57 W. Notestein, F.H. Relf, H. Simpson ed., *Commons debates*, 1621, 7 vols (New
   Haven 1935), ii, 6f.; v, 471; it should be noted that English anti-recusancy legislation was considerably tougher than the Irish.
58 U.W., ii, 456f.

The suspension of even the limited enforcement of conformity in Ireland in 1621 did not bode well for Ussher's plea,[59] but the despatch of the 1622 Commissioners gave the opportunity for Irish churchmen to press their case for a return to a rigorous policy. The Irish bishops stressed to the Commissioners that before the reformation could make any progress, the state must first banish all Catholic priests.[60] In giving evidence privately to the Commissioners, Archbishop Hampton claimed that before the suspension of the recusancy proceedings, most Catholics had been forced to come to church. Pointing to the judgement of Augustine on the civil enforcement of conformity, Hampton stated that he was opposed to the use of the church's power of excommunication in so general a disease, and urged instead that the 'pecuniary mulct' was the proper course.[61] Leslie, in his sermon before the commissioners, repeated this advice, and his plea was echoed later in 1622 when James Ussher preached at Christ Church on the occasion of the new Deputy, Lord Falkland, receiving the sword of state. He chose as his text Romans 13.4: 'He beareth not the sword in vain', and expounded the 'duty of the magistrate in seeing those laws executed that were made for the furtherance of God's service'.[62]

The pressure achieved its immediate aim. The Commissioners recommended that a greater effort be made to enforce conformity through the banishment of priests and the imposition of recusancy fines, and these proposals were put into effect.[63] In January 1624 an enthusiastic Lord Falkland issued a proclamation ordering priests to leave Ireland within 40 days.[64] Bishops and sheriffs were instructed to institute proceedings against recusants. But it was not to be. Less than a month later the English Privy Council ordered the suspension of proceedings in view of the proposed match with Spain. Falkland was left with the embarrassing task of writing to the bishops and sheriffs rescinding his earlier orders.[65] Repeated demands from the Dublin officials, supported by Chichester and Grandison in England, that the action against recusants should go ahead as originally planned were finally rejected by the English Privy Council in January 1625 for 'reasons of state'.[66] The progress of the Spanish alliance was, as a result, watched with concern in Ireland.[67] Yet

59 P.R.O.I., M 2452 (unfoliated), Instructions for assize judges 1621.
60 Bodleian MS Carte 30, fol. 127r–v.
61 N.L.I. MS 8014, ii; 8014, iii, 5; 8014, iv, 4; 8014, v, 10.
62 U.W., xvi, 180.
63 B.L. Add. MS 4756, fols 22v–23v; S.P. 63/237/35, fol. 74v (1615–25, 418).
64 S.P. 63/238(pt 1)/10–11 (1615–25, 458ff.); Grosart (ed.), *Lismore papers*, 2nd ser., iii, 86ff.
65 S.P. 63/238(pt 1)/22 (1615–25, 464); Bodleian Library, MS Rawlinson C 439, fols 28v–29v.
66 S.P. 63/238(pt 2)/72 (1615–25, 511); S.P. 63/238(pt 2)/99 (1615–25, 538); S.P. 63/239/8 (1615–25, 557).
67 Grosart (ed.), *Lismore papers*, 2nd ser., iii, 66ff., 71ff., 93, 97ff.; U.W., xv, 201.

even its failure did not further protestant demands. Instead, as England moved towards war with Spain, it became imperative to reach some agreement with the Irish Catholics, both to preserve England's 'back door', and to provide money for the raising and support of more troops. One of the bargaining counters which the new King sought to use in negotiating with Irish Catholics was the promise of religious toleration.

TOLERATION: STATE VS CHURCH

Throughout the first two decades of the seventeenth century the Church of Ireland felt strongly that it needed more consistent and rigorous support from the secular sword. However, their disappointment at the King's refusal to provide such support did not lead them into open criticism of the role of the King, or the established subjection of the church to state in jurisdictional matters. Leslie, in his sermon before the 1622 Commissioners, stressed that he sought not 'to prescribe rules to authority' in his treatment of the ways in which godly kings had forced people to the true worship of God. Ussher in his sermon in Christ church accepted that the chief magistrate had the power to limit the activities of the lower at his pleasure.[68] Leslie and Ussher were not merely uttering pious platitudes – there was a strong and genuine protestant commitment to the ideal of the godly prince, which was more than just loyalty to one's secular ruler. The monarch was chosen by God to wield the sword, and though he had a moral obligation to heed the advice of pious clergymen in the exercise of his jurisdiction, the clergy had no desire or capacity to force their views on the prince in such matters.[69] As Archbishop Hampton explained to a somewhat impatient Ussher in 1623, re the suspension of the laws against recusancy because of the impending Spanish match,

> Seeing it hath pleased God (whose councils may be secret, but not unjust) to exercise us with this mixture, let us remember how dangerous it is to provoke princes with too much animosity, and what hazard Chrysostom brought to religion in that way. The gospel is not supported with wilfulness, but by patience and obedience.[70]

Nevertheless, the innate assumption behind the contemporary acceptance of royal supremacy was that the ruler would act in a godly manner. The

68 Leslie, *Treatise on unitie*, 46; U.W., xv, 180.
69 Sommerville, 'Jacobean political thought and the oath of the allegiance', 369.
70 U.W., xv, 199.
71 Downham, *Treatise concerning Antichrist*, Bk II, 190f.; W.K. Jordan, *The development of religious toleration in England, 1603–40* (London 1936), 143ff., totally mistakes

possibility remained, however, that he might use his power in a way which seemed to the churchmen ungodly, or tending to weaken the standing of true religion. If such an issue arose, the Irish bishops in particular, with their strong belief in the absolute rectitude of their theological position, might prove unwilling to allow compromise on issues which they thought basic to the safety of the protestant religion in Ireland, however strong were the political reasons for compromise.

One such issue was toleration. This aroused united and strong opposition in the Church of Ireland as soon as it became evident that Charles was considering it as a possible bargaining counter in his negotiations with the Irish Catholics. The strength of the opposition to toleration can be seen from the writings of two bishops, Ussher and Downham. The latter's opposition was firmly rooted in his identification of the Pope as Antichrist. Since recusants were by definition followers of Antichrist, there could be no question of there being 'favoured or spared in a Christian commonwealth … And surely if not their persons, then much less ought their antichristian religion be tolerated … For what fellowship can there be between light and darkness'. In sum, reconciliation between the two churches was inconceivable, since one was the true church, the other the church of Antichrist.[71] An identical position was taken by Loftus and Jones in 1603. When they heard rumours that James was intending to tolerate Catholicism they wrote to him, stating their confidence that the rumours were false, since, they averred, no man in Christendom was better equipped to judge 'what agreement there is like to be between light and darkness, between God and Belial, and between the glorious gospel of Christ, and the superstitious idolatry of Antichrist … '[72]

The Irish bishops stuck to their position throughout the early seventeenth century with determination, much to the embarrassment of the state, which found the total rejection of toleration a severe handicap in its dealings with the majority of the Irish population. The conflict between principle and *Realpolitik* came to a head when Charles offered limited toleration to the Catholics in the negotiations leading to the graces in 1628.[73] Already concerned at the lack of official sympathy and help for the church in its efforts to recover its property, and dissatisfied with the failure to enforce conformity, ministers and bishops saw the proposal to 'put religion to sale' as the last straw. Dean John Hill of

the attitudes of Ussher and Downham towards toleration. In the latter case, he derives his opinion of Downham as 'the great liberal Irish prelate', whose 'remarkable position' on toleration 'went further than anglican thought in general', from a work written, not by Downham, but by a considerably younger Arminian namesake.

72 S.P. 63/215/58 (1603–6, 59f.).

73 A. Clarke, *The Old English in Ireland 1625–42* (London 1966), 28–59; idem, *The graces, 1625–41* (Dundalk 1968); Moody, Martin, Byrne (eds.), *New history of Ireland*, iii, chap. 8.

Kilmore, who wrote to Ussher in 1626, when he first got wind of the proposal, begged him to 'stand up for the Lord Christ' and ensure that any toleration of popery was resolutely opposed – 'The Lord knows we are miserable enough already'.[74] The threat of toleration stung Ussher into action. He called a meeting of Irish prelates at his house in Drogheda in November 1626, at which they drew up a declaration.[75] Their premise was that Roman Catholicism was 'superstitious and idolatrous'; Catholics' faith and doctrine were therefore 'erroneous and heretical; their church in respect of both, apostatical.' Thus, to grant them toleration in return for political and financial concessions was a grievous sin, on two counts. It made the state an accessory to the perdition of those Irish people who died in the catholic faith; and it set religion to sale, 'and with it, the souls of the people'.[76]

For the while, the bishops refrained from the momentous step of making their opposition public. Ussher was aware that the Catholic side had considerable reservations about the proposals, and hoped that negotiations would in consequence break down.[77] Yet at the same time he begged Archbishop Abbot to advise the King to follow a policy which 'may be more for his honour and the good of the church.'[78] But Abbot was not an influential figure. The negotiations continued and when, in April 1627, the 'great assembly' met to discuss the proposals, the prelates reconvened and determined to make their opposition known. They chose one of the most public of occasions – a sermon before the Lord Deputy in Christ Church on 23 April, preached by George Downham on the text Luke 1[74]: 'That he would grant unto us, that we being delivered out of the hand of our enemies might serve him without fear.'[79] Downham used the text to make a plea against the toleration of 'false religion' which 'many among us for gain and outward respects' were willing to grant.[80] To judge from the reported reaction of his auditory, Downham was expressing the fears of many other protestants, and was perhaps even giving voice to the real opinion of the Lord Deputy.[81] Nor was Downham's sermon

---

74 U.W., xvi, 435f.
75 U.W., xv, 366.
76 The declaration was signed by twelve of the Irish bishops; one bishop, James Spottiswood, was present but did not sign. Of the nine bishops who did not attend old age and unavailability are as likely explanations for their absence as disagreement with the sentiments of the declaration. Bernard, *Life of Usher*, 6off.; Parr, *Life of Ussher*, 8; U.W., i, 73f.; U.W., xv, 366; A.B. (ed.), *A brief memorial of the life and death of Dr James Spottiswood* (Edinburgh 1811), 113.
77 U.W., xv, 366.
78 Ibid.
79 S.P. 63/244/693 (1625–32, 240); Bernard, *Life of Usher*, 64, gives the text as Luke 1.23–35, which makes no sense in the context.
80 Bernard, *Life of Usher*, 62; Parr, *Life of Ussher*, 29; S.P 63/244/693 (1625–32, 239f.).
81 Ibid.; S.P. 63/246/32 (1625–32, 304).

the end of the Irish bishops' public protest. The following week, two archbishops, Ussher, and Malcolm Hamilton of Cashel, preached again at Christ
Church in opposition to toleration, Ussher warning of the inevitability of divine
punishment if it were granted.[82] Hamilton, a royal chaplain, sought to bring
his opposition specifically to the notice of his royal master the following year
when he presented to Charles a petition from the Munster clergy, adding to
it a composition of his own – 'Overtures ... relating to things general for the
good of the church'.[83]

Hamilton began his treatise by pointing out the practical implications of
toleration. If granted it would give immense support to the Catholic cause,
and much discomfit the protestants. The Catholics could claim that the protestants had admitted that their own religion was false, 'or else we would never
have yielded to any toleration'.[84] 'Favour and connivency' had in the past only
made Catholicism the more strong and obdurate.[85] Far from being a threat to
the stability of the commonwealth, the rigorous enforcement of recusancy legislation ultimately would benefit it immensely.[86]

In the final part of his treatise, Hamilton tackled the general question of
the objections to toleration from a biblical and theological standpoint, pointing in particular to the similarities between the situation of the Israelites and
the experience of Irish protestants. He first dealt with the politic evasion of
those who claimed that the time was not yet ripe for the civil magistrate to
enforce conformity. Such as claimed this were, Hamilton suggested, like those
mentioned in Haggai 1 who, when commanded by God to rebuild His temple,
said that it was not the right moment to do so. As punishment, God sent them
scanty harvests. If He was so angry with those who did not build a house for
His worship, 'What shall we expect whereas the service and worship of God
itself is neglected, idolatry and idolators not curbed'.[87] Nor was fear of rebellion any excuse for leniency, any more than Saul's explanation that fear
prevented him from carrying out God's command to kill King Agag and his
cattle. On that occasion the prophet Samuel had warned Saul that because of
his lack of obedience the Lord would reject him as king. Saul's response was
perfectly apposite for Hamilton's purpose: he replied contritely 'I have sinned:
for I have transgressed the commandment of the Lord ... because I feared the
people and obeyed their voice.'[88]

82 Bernard, *Life of Usher*, 64; Parr, *Life of Ussher*, 29; T.C.D. MS 6404, fol. 65v.
83 T.C.D. MS 1188; S.P., Signet office 1/1, pp. 308f. (1625–32, 365).
84 T.C.D. MS 1188, fol. 2r.
85 Ibid., fol. 2v.
86 Ibid., fols 7v–8v.
87 Ibid., fol. 8v.
88 Ibid.; 1 Samuel 15.23–24.

The history of the Israelites afforded Hamilton with abundant proof of the danger of tolerating idolatry. He then applied this lesson directly to Charles's policy in Ireland:

> Above all things, I your Majesty's loyal subject and faithful hearted chaplain exhort your sacred person to have a special care of the suppression of idolatry in all your Majesty's kingdoms, but in special in Ireland where it reigns as a sin that rent the kingdom of David in sunder.[89]

Hamilton adduced many more old testament examples in support of his claim that the toleration of idolatry led inevitably to divine punishment. If God unleashed His anger against the whole ten tribes of Israel for the rebellion of two tribes and their erection of altars to idols, 'what shall we then fear against the whole kingdom of Ireland, where all the realm is full of altars not to the worship of God but to Baal.'[90] After further extensive reference to the growth of idolatry in Israel, he concluded by examining the situation in Ireland:

> what growth hath idolatry taken within this 24 years or thereabouts? Go to the chief city of Dublin, there is here in the city some present who have seen all the aldermen of Dublin come to church ... Now the case is altered, all goes to mass for the most part, and the city, yea the whole realm, swarms with priests.[91]

When examining the prospects of the protestant church in Ireland, however, Hamilton did not despair. He was sure that if the magistrate forced people to attend church and hear the word, conversion would follow. He acknowledged that at first such efforts would be mocked,

> yet at the last I doubt not but a number will come to our church; and when they have tasted of the sweetness of ... the word of truth one shall draw another as Philip did Nathaniel ... I put no question if this secondary means be used but God hath decreed in his own time to call a number to himself in Ireland by the preaching of the word.[92]

At first sight, Hamilton's appraisal was more optimistic than Olmstead's gloomy speculations about the number of the elect in Ireland. But Hamilton too had a sense of apocalyptic foreboding: 'are not these things written for our examples

89 T.C.D. MS 1188, fol. 9r; see 1 Kings 11.11.
90 T.C.D. MS 1188, fol. 9v.
91 Ibid.
92 Ibid., fol. 10r.

to admonish us upon whom the ends of the world are come'.[93] All depended upon the important *caveat* 'if this secondary means be used'. If the people were not made to come to church, then it was probable that they would not find salvation. Hence his concluding appeal to King Charles, in which he urged him to remember Christ's words in Luke 14.21: 'Compel them ... to come in', and demanded that 'if they will not come', then the 'statute may take hold of them' and force them to attend church.[94]

Though, as Ussher had hoped, the proposal to grant toleration subsequently foundered, the protest of the Irish bishops was of more than passing interest. In the context of the Irish church, the declaration of 1626, and the sermons and treatises of Ussher, Downham, Hamilton and Leslie, demonstrated how deep the belief in the antichristian nature of Catholicism was, and how far the churchmen were prepared to go to defend the implications which followed from this belief. In the broader context of the 1620s and 1630s in both England and Ireland, the declaration of 1626 remained important as a public and prescient statement of concerns which were increasingly to trouble Calvinist clergy in the face of 'Arminian' trends in royal ecclesiastical policy. Looking back from the 1630s and early 1640s, the declaration could appear as a brave attempt by the Irish bishops to remind the King of his duty towards (Calvinist) orthodoxy. Both Downham and Hamilton explicitly based their opposition to royal policy upon their duty to defend the honour of true religion. The former, in his sermon of 27 April 1627, tactfully stated that he did not wish 'that what is spoken for the maintenance of religion, and the service of God, should be thought to be a hindrance of the King's service'. Nevertheless, he proceeded to demand that the offer of toleration be withdrawn.[95] Hamilton was equally forthright. It was the duty of bishops to speak up for the true religion against heresy, even if it meant opposing kings and emperors, as had happened in the early church, when the emperors were tempted to compromise with heresies such as Arianism – 'If the emperors did seem to yield, for policy sake, yet the true orthodox bishops did stoutly defend both against the heretics and against the emperors'.[96] Hence the significance of Hamilton's reference to 1 Samuel 15.23–24 – in this text it was the prophet who admonished the king; and the king, fearful of the wrath of God, admitted his sin, and sought to follow God rather than the dictates of popular pressure. Such opposition, viewed from the perspective of the early 1640s, seemed to those on the parliamentarian side almost prophetic, in view of the subsequent dangerously Romanizing trends of Charles's reign.[97]

93 Ibid., fol. 9v; see 1 Cor.10.11.
94 Ibid., fol. 10v.
95 Bernard, *Life of Usher*, 63.
96 T.C.D. MS 1188, fol. 2v.
97 *The protestatation of the archbishops and bishops of Ireland against the toleration of*

CALVINIST CONSENSUS: CHALLENGE AND VINDICATION

Some Irish protestants expected that once the fuss over toleration had died away, there would be a return to the penal measures of the years before the Spanish match. The two Irish Lords Justices, Loftus and Cork, who succeeded Falkland, set about the suppression of Catholic religious houses and the reintroduction of recusancy fines with genuine enthusiasm. Hopes were entertained that Wentworth when he finally took over from Loftus and Cork would prove similarly rigorous. As John Ridge, an English puritan minister beneficed in Connor, wrote *c.*1632 about Wentworth:

> divers hope that he shall come better furnished than some have been before him for restraining of these vile idolatries and abominations in the kingdom; men say that he hath done good that way in his former government, the papists are somewhat afraid of him already; it might be a great blessing to them if some care now at length might be taken of them, for they are exceeding ignorant, yea very brutes in the things of God and their salvation; and yet very obstinate and perverse, as all ignorant ones usually are; howsoever, were their lords called over and kept a while in England, their priests restrained, and some fine laid upon the people, in all likelihood they would soon be reclaimed ... [98]

Another protestant minister, the Trinity educated Roger Puttock, also demonstrated that the approach of Loftus and Jones was far from dead. He dedicated his attack upon the Jesuit Malone, published in Dublin in 1632, to Wentworth, expressing the hope that the new Lord Deputy would defend by the sword that faith which the author upheld with his pen: 'There is no cause to complain of evil government, for there hath been more teaching than terror: but we have cause to pray, that terror may expel that hard and evil custom, which by teaching will not be removed.'[99]

By the 1630s, however, such hopes were unrealistic. In practical terms, the task of enforcing conformity was formidable and daunting. The Catholic church had in the previous two decades been substantially reorganized, and most dioceses now had resident bishops or vicars apostolic. Even the most zealous of

popery agreed upon, and subscribed by them at Dublin (London 1641); *A declaration of the commons assembled in parliament; concerning the rise and progress of the grand rebellion in Ireland* (London 1643), 24; W. Prynne, *Canterburies doome* (London 1646), 434.

98 N.L.I. MS 8014, i: not dated, but the reference to the metropolitan visitation by the Archbishop of Armagh dates it to 1632.

99 Puttock, *Rejoynder unto Malones reply*, sig. q5r; the quotation is, of course, from St Augustine; see above, p. 203.

protestant officials could not but accept that the strength of the Catholic hierarchy and priesthood, and their hold upon the affections of the people, made
it impossible to advocate coercion with the same optimism and confidence that
it offered a complete solution to the problem of recusancy which had been
evinced by civil and ecclesiastical officials some twenty years earlier. Sir Francis
Annesley, for example, in 1629 lamented the inexcusable lethargy of the Irish
authorities and their 'too long permissiveness and connivency', and urged that
'something must be done for the advancement of God's glory and the defence
of true religion'. However, faced with the effects of that long connivency,
Annesley accepted that 'moderation and forbearance' would have to be used.
There was, he felt, no point in acting against the large majority of loyal and
quiet Catholics, thereby alienating them from the government.[100] A similar
realism was also evident in other proposals for the enforcement of penal legislation, which distinguished between the regular priests and other aggressive
upholders of papal jurisdiction on the one hand, and the 'loyal Catholics' on the
other hand.[101] Consequently, a more pragmatic approach to recusancy developed. Fines on the Catholic laity were discussed in terms of their revenue,
usually with a view to supporting the army, rather than, as before, in terms
of their effectiveness in eradicating recusancy once and for all.

If the strength of the Catholic church made the thoroughgoing enforcement
of conformity appear an increasingly unattractive political proposition, the
change in the political and ideological climate in the 1630s made doubly sure
that the Dublin administration had little enthusiasm for such a policy.
Previously, Loftus and Jones and their successors had been able to rely upon
a sympathetic hearing from the secular officials in Dublin for their pleas for
firmness towards recusancy, since both sides shared common ideological and
theological assumptions about the role of coercion. The new administration
led by Wentworth, however, had little sympathy for such an approach. The
new Lord Deputy refused to accept the assumption that the first step in spreading the reformation must firm action against Catholics. Furthermore, Bramhall,
and the other clergy associated with the new administration, did not share the
ideological assumptions which the earlier generation of Calvinist Irish clergy
had so unhesitatingly avowed.

As Bramhall, Laud and Wentworth saw it, the main problem for the Church
of Ireland was not the Catholic threat, or recusancy, but the non-conformity,

100 S.P. 63/248/45 (1625–32, 441f.).
101 S.P. 63/245/884 (1625–32, 297f.); S.P. 63/246/7 (1625–32, 324); on policy towards
     Catholics in this period see R.D. Edwards, 'Church and state in the Ireland of
     Míchél Ó Cléirigh 1626–1641', in Sylvester O'Brien (ed.), *Measgra i gcuimhne
     Mhichíl Uí Chléirigh. Miscellany of historical and linguistic studies in honour of Brother
     Michael Ó Cleirigh, O.F.M. chief of the four masters 1643–1943* (Dublin, 1944).

theological extremism, abuses and poverty of the established church itself. The new administration therefore set in train a whole series of reforms, designed to reform the Irish church according to its preferred policy. The Church of Ireland in Convocation in 1634–5 adopted both the English Canons of 1604 and the Thirty-Nine Articles. The latter reflected the desire of Bramhall and Laud to move the church away from the Calvinist extremes of its earlier confession; the former similarly was directed at weeding out the precisian and presbyterian elements which had, through the absence of such canons, been able to flourish within the established church.[102] The disciplinary framework, as well as the power of Wentworth and Bramhall, was further strengthened by the resuscitation of the Ecclesiastical Commission.[103] Thus puritan and presbyterian clergy were weeded out, especially in the dioceses of Down and Connor, whilst Arminian clerics from England were favoured with Irish preferments.[104] Attention was also paid to the Irish seminary. Laud himself composed new statutes for Trinity, and an Arminian provost and fellows were appointed.[105] Finally, a serious effort was made to tackle one of the fundamental weaknesses of the Church of Ireland. Under Wentworth's firm, sometimes Draconic hand, the church regained many endowments and possessions which had previously rested in the hands of laymen, thus increasing the income available to support ministers.[106]

The move away from previous policies was most evident in the new administration's approach to recusancy. Wentworth's and Bramhall's first priority was not the enforcement of conformity, but internal reform of the Church of Ireland.[107] Their policy echoed that advocated by the English Privy Council in 1606–7, when it had been suggested that, rather than concentrating upon forcing the Catholics to church, the Church of Ireland would be better occupied in setting its own house in order so that it could effectively evangelise

102 T.C.D. MS 1038, fols 112v–117r; T.C.D. MS 1062, pp. 6off.; Scott, Bliss ed., *Works of Laud*, vi, 396f.; vii, 78, 98f., 117f., 132; H.M.C., *Hastings MSS*, iv, 61–6; Knowler ed., *Strafford's letters*, i, 342f., 378f.; Sheffield City Library, Strafford MSS, vol 5, pp. 56, 100, 106; Shirley (ed.), *Papers relating to the Church of Ireland*, 43f.
103 Marsh's Library, MS Z4.2.1, 6–9; Sheffield City Library, Strafford MSS, vol. 6, pp. 51, 56; 20/149; Scott, Bliss (eds.), *Works of Laud*, vii, 75.
104 Sheffield City Library, Strafford MSS, 20/179; S.P. 63/254/185 (1633–47, 88); S.P. 63/256/35 (1633–47, 160f.); S.P. 63/256/41 (1633–47, 164); Shirley (ed.), *Papers relating to the Church of Ireland*, 41ff.; on the preferment of Arminians, see Scott, Bliss ed., *Works of Laud*, iv, 288; vi, 324, 386, 416; vii, 321f.; Sheffield City Library, Strafford MSS, vol. 6, p. 180; S.P. 63/256/84 (1633–47, 186).
105 Scott, Bliss (eds.), *Works of Laud*, vi, 355f., 399, 487f.; S.P. 63/255/142–3, 146–7 (1633–47, 140f.); Mahaffy, *Epoch*, chap. 6.
106 See above, p. 68.
107 Sheffield City Library, Strafford MSS, vol. 6, pp. 4, 26, 44; Scott, Bliss (eds.), *Works of Laud*, vi, 324f.

the native population.[108] Wentworth also restated the Privy Council's earlier desire for persuasive methods. In his speech to the Irish parliament in 1634 Wentworth referred to the possibility of levying the 12*d*. fine on Irish recusants, but explained that the King had rejected this course since he 'held it more natural in cases of conscience and religion to soften and incline the hearts of men by ... the sound persuasive doctrine of his clergy than by constraint to enforce a seducing conformity'.[109]

The previous orthodoxy had been founded upon the Calvinist theological consensus, most notably expounded in the 1615 Articles: this too was challenged by the new administration. The overwhelming concern with the antichristian threat posed by the Church of Rome was not shared by Arminian clerics. Rather, 'the practical implications of the new position was a truce with Roman Catholicism'.[110] This undermined the whole basis of the church policy of Calvinist clerics such as Loftus, Jones or Downham. Nor did the Arminians share the Calvinist concern with the rigours of double predestination – they did not see conversion as a stark confrontation between man and grace, between a helpless sinner and the destiny chosen for him by God. Instead, they placed more emphasis upon man's free will, and his capacity to perform good works, and the role of the sacraments as vehicles of grace.[111] Again, this constituted a direct challenge to the working theology of Calvinist clergy in Ireland.

Ideally, such a theological outlook should in theory have provided a far better basis for the evangelization of the Irish population than did Calvinism. The approach to Catholicism was less hostile, and the view of conversion closer to traditional Catholic doctrine, and less open to misinterpretation by ministers driven to pessimism by their experience of evangelism in Ireland. A willingness to question and move away from existing orthodoxies could certainly substantially change a minister's approach to reformation policy and to his ministry in Ireland, as can be seen in the case of William Bedell.[112] Though from an impeccably puritan background, Bedell, as has been seen, was far more willing than his Calvinist contemporaries to adapt the gospel to Irish conditions, and take into account the peculiar difficulties which the reformation faced in Ireland. He shared the conviction of Wentworth that the immediate enforcement of penal legislation against Catholics was pointless, and even dangerous. As he explained in 1633, the poverty and discontentment of the people, the power exerted over them by the priests, and the sheer number of

108 See above, pp. 57f.
109 B.L. Harleian MS 7004, fols 261v–261xr; for a discussion of Wentworth's policy towards Catholicism see Clarke, *Old English*, 116f.
110 Tyacke, 'Arminianism in England', 80.
111 Ibid., 77ff.
112 See above, pp. 124f.

recusants, all suggested that it would be counterproductive to impose the 12*d.* fine. For, unless these impediments were removed, 'to impress the form presently by pecuniary mulcts would but breed a monster'.[113]

This reflected Bedell's generally temperate attitude towards the Catholic church, a product both of his experience, as a chaplain to the English Ambassador to Venice 1607–10, and of his theology. As he explained in a series of letters to a friend who had been converted to Catholicism, he accepted that the Church of Rome was a true church, though corrupted.[114] On the identification of the Pope with Antichrist he was ambivalent. While he felt that protestants could hardly avoid coming to such a conclusion in the light of the biblical texts, he noted that this 'commonly received opinion' was nevertheless 'no part of the doctrine of our church' (i.e. it was not included in the Thirty-Nine Articles).[115]

The way in which Bedell's attitude towards Catholicism developed during his time in Ireland can be seen in a sermon he preached before the state in Christ Church in 1634, on Revelation 18.4.[116] This was the classic text for protestant preachers who wanted to demonstrate that the Roman church was a false one, which all true Christians, in answer to God's call to come out from it, were duty bound to abandon. Bedell began by admitting what most of his audience would have implicitly assumed, that Rome was indeed Babylon, the seat of Antichrist, to which Rev. 18.4 referred. For Bedell, like Ussher, this suggested that the Roman church was a true church; unlike Ussher, however, he went on to conclude that within it there lived many good Christians, 'not redeemed only, but in the possession of the grace of our Lord Jesus Christ'.[117] Such an emphasis reversed that generally made by Irish protestants. Bedell thus rejected the pessimistic estimates about the number of elect within the Church of Rome which were made by several protestant preachers in Ireland. Instead, he claimed that there were many potential converts. The problem, he claimed, was not the obduracy of the Catholics, but the lack of protestant evangelism. Bedell was sure that if only the message of Rev. 18.4 were carried to the people of Ireland, many would hear and obey.[118]

Bedell's gentle approach to Catholicism, and his theological moderation, provided him with an essential intellectual underpinning for his ministry to

---

113 Sheffield City Library, Strafford MSS, 20/115; Knowler ed., *Strafford's letters*, i, 148.

114 W. Bedell, *The copies of certain letters which have passed between Spain and England in matters of religion* (London 1624), 75f., 82.

115 Ibid., 77, 81f.

116 Bodleian Library, MS Tanner 458, fols 161r–186v; printed in N. Bernard, *The judgement of the late Archbishop of Armagh*, 2nd ed. (London 1659), pagination irregular.

117 Bernard, *Judgement*, 61ff.

118 Ibid., 94ff.

the native Irish in Kilmore. The old saw, that a minister, however Calvinist
in his study, had perforce to be an Arminian in the pulpit, though, as has been
seen, theoretically inaccurate, in fact caught an important practical distinction.
The Calvinism and apocalypticism of the Irish preachers, though in theory an
activist and missionary ideology, in practice tended to serve as a ready framework within which the failure of the ministry of the clergy could be explained.
Bedell avoided these pitfalls, and was therefore able to expand the limited
horizons of the protestant ministry in Ireland.

However, Bedell was an idiosyncratic figure in the Church of Ireland,
distinct from the Arminians as well as the Calvinists. For, though they shared
some of his intellectual assumptions, the Arminian clergy who came to Ireland
in the 1630s differed from Bedell on two important issues. First, they did not
share his primary commitment to missionary evangelism: the primary concern
of the Arminians in the 1630s was with the reform of abuses within the Church
of Ireland. Second, they remained committed to an anglicizing reformation.
The clergy were not to seek to adapt to the culture and demands of the native
population; the latter must rather be acculturated and brought up to English
norms of civility. Thus, when Bedell pressed in the 1634 Convocation for
divine service to be provided in Irish, Bramhall opposed such an approach on
the familiar basis that it contravened the provisions of 28 Henry VIII *c*.15, the
'Act for the English order, habit and language'.[119]

Calvinists within the Church of Ireland opposed the new orthodoxy where
they could. Ussher had always been a firm and, at times in the 1620s, out-
spoken opponent of Arminianism. By the 1630s his disagreement was expressed
more circumspectly, but nevertheless, quite plainly, in his decision in 1631 to
publish an edition of the work of Gotteschalk of Orbais, a ninth century predestinarian whom Ussher viewed as a Calvinist *avant la lettre*.[120] Bishop
Downham joined in the defence of the Calvinist consensus, with his *Covenant
of grace*, published in Dublin in 1631. But this more open dissent was quashed
by Bishop Laud, who ordered that the book be withdrawn. A hint of lay opposition to Arminian innovations in church ceremonies is contained in a letter
written by Sir John Clotworthy, a northern puritan planter, in 1635: 'We want
no new addition that the wit of man can invent, to make the worship of God
pompous in outward but penurious in inward part.'[122] The most persistent
critic of Arminian innovations was the indefatigable puritan professor of
theology at Trinity, Joshua Hoyle. He engaged in a lengthy battle with Bedell

---

119 Barnard, *Cromwellian Ireland*, 173.
120 *Gotteschalci, et praedestinatione controversiae ab eo motae, historia* (Dublin 1631);
    and see U.W., xvi, 9.
121 *The covenant of grace* (Dublin 1631); D.N.B., s.v. Downham, George.
122 'Winthrop papers', iii (1943), 193.

during the latter's provostship, at one time publicly voicing his disagreement with Bedell's interpretation of Rev. 18.4, seeking instead to show that the Church of Rome was not a true church, and going on to refute 'all the points of Arminianism'.[123] Hoyle pursued his opposition to Arminianism even after the fall of Wentworth and Laud, giving evidence at the latter's trial on how he had perverted the Church of Ireland.[124] In particular, Hoyle complained about the Arminian provost of Trinity, William Chappel, who, he claimed, suggested that priests should not be subject to the secular power.[125]

Though the demolition of the Calvinist consensus aroused disquiet among protestants in Ireland, opposition to the policy of Wentworth and Bramhall was muted, never attaining the cohesion and outspokenness which the Irish Bishops had shown in 1626. There were several reasons for this. Firstly, the English king was for the first time in the seventeenth century in a position where he had a strong Lord Deputy who could impose royal policy upon the Church of Ireland. Under Wentworth the church was, as has been observed, brought directly into line with the Church of England. This ended its previous independence and relative freedom of action. Secondly, churchmen had little difficulty in supporting the efforts of the authorities in one sphere – that of the recovery of impropriations and alienated endowments. Thirdly, support for the policy of reform instituted by Wentworth and Bramhall could further be justified on the grounds that it represented a necessary interlude before the previous reformation policy could be resumed. Archbishop Ussher, a firm supporter of the civil coercion of Catholics, thus indicated after Strafford's fall that the Lord Deputy had, he believed, fully intended that conformity should be enforced in Ireland, but had felt that the way would first have to be prepared by reforming the Church of Ireland.[126] Finally, it must be remembered that there was a large body of the protestant laity who probably cared little about official theological doctrine, so long as they were left free to pursue their practical interests as planters, tenants, etc.

Apocalyptic concern about the consequences of tolerating Catholicism and encouraging the forces of Antichrist could therefore safely be ignored by Wentworth and Bramhall in the 1630s. Yet ultimately such fears were validated in the eyes of Irish churchmen in the most scarifying manner possible. Seen in the context of earlier warnings by Ussher, Hamilton and Downham about the danger of divine judgement if toleration were granted, the rising of

---

123 McNeill (ed.), *Tanner letters*, 100; Shuckburgh (ed.), *Two biographies*, 27.
124 H.M.C., *The manuscripts of the House of Lords*, xi (1962), 438ff.; J.H., *Jehojadahs justice against Mattan, Baal's priest; or, the covenanters justice against idolaters. A sermon preached upon occasion of a speech utter'd upon Tower Hill* (London 1645).
125 H.M.C., *House of Lords MSS*, xi (1962), 440.
126 B.L.Add. MS 34,253, fol.3r.

1641 could be interpreted as the almost inevitable commination which Ussher and his fellow clerics had foretold. The inattention and sinfulness of the protestants, the idolatry and antichristianity of the Catholics, had brought down God's just anger upon the people of Ireland.

At the time, not all saw it in such a light. Many protestants, having come to terms with the *de facto* toleration of the 1630s, complained of the ungratefulness of the Catholics, rebelling despite the generous treatment they had received.[127] But in retrospect, the apocalyptic interpretation had considerable appeal, since it provided a ready-made and familiar frame of reference within which the outbreak of the rebellion, its causation, and its savagery, could be interpreted. Hence Ussher was elevated to the status of a prophet. In January 1603, after Mountjoy had suspended the proceedings against recusants ordered by Loftus during the Lord Deputy's absence, Ussher had preached in Christ Church against this dereliction of duty on the part of the magistrate, taking as his text Ezekiel 4.6: 'And thou shalt bear the iniquity of the house of Judah forty days: I have appointed each day for a year.' According to Bernard, he then directly applied the text to the recent 'connivance of popery' ordered by Mountjoy, stating: '"From this year will I reckon the sin of Ireland, that those whom you now embrace shall be your ruin and you shall bear this iniquity."'[128] Bernard claimed that Ussher had written this prophetic utterance into his bible which had been published in 1601, exactly forty years before the rising.[129]

A similarly apocalyptic interpretation was given by Leslie, after the rising had taken place. Preaching at Oxford in 1643 on the text Jeremiah 5.9: 'Shall I not visit thee for these things, saith the Lord: and shall not my soul be avenged on such a nation as this?', Leslie detailed the punishment of evil nations:

---

127 M.S. *A discourse concerning the rebellion in Ireland* (London 1642), 7; *A manifestation directed to the honourable Houses of Parliament in England* (London 1644); *A perfect relation of the beginning and continuation of the Irish rebellion from May last to this present 12th January 1641* (London 1641), 13: *Remonstrance of divers remarkable Passages concerning the church and kingdome of Ireland* (London 1642), sig. B1r; N. Bernard, *The whole proceedings of the siege of Drogheda in Ireland* (London 1642), sig. A3v.

128 Bernard, *Life of Usher*, 39.

129 Ibid.; Ussher was also reported to have made apocalyptic prophecies concerning the future of the protestant faith and its struggle with Antichrist, during the time when he was in England, after 1641: N.L.I. MS 17,853. These, together with Ussher's prophecy of the 1641 rebellion, were issued under his name in the 1680s when the accession of James II again made the issue pertinent: *Prophecies concerning the return of popery into England, Scotland and Ireland* (London 1682); *Bishop Usshers second prophesie* (London 1681); *The prophecy of James Ussher* (London 1687).

Yea almighty God hath already begun to visit; he is come down to execute vengeance upon our sinful nation. In Ireland there is nothing but ruin, desolation, and woe ... we of that sinful land did provoke God, and he hath stretched over us the line of Sodom, the plummet of Samaria.[130]

Two Irish ministers further spelt out the reasons why God had chosen to vent his wrath upon the people of Ireland. As Daniel Harcourt, who had served in Down and Connor before the rising, explained, the English in Ireland had made the mistake of advancing 'politic ends before pious'.[131] Now they had found 'how dearly the Israelites paid for their cruel mercy in not extirpating the idolatrous Canaanites ... teaching us ... that policy without piety is a damnable discretion.'[132] Had the protestants of Ireland followed such a pious course, 'it had not been in the power of these reprobates, thus to have profaned the holy food or the feeders thereon.'[133] Roger Puttock, who in 1632 had asked Wentworth to use his sword to extirpate Catholicism, in 1642 reflected that the sufferings of the protestants in Ireland might serve a useful purpose, since 'We were doting before on Rome and her idolatries'.[134]

With its atrocities real and imagined, the 1641 rising fixed in the protestant mind this apocalyptic interpretation of their position in Ireland, and impressed upon them the need to remain separate from the treacherous Irish. It was thus not the scepticism of lay protestants, or the efforts of the government to reach an accommodation with the Catholics, nor the working relations which some settlers established with the native Irish, that was remembered from the early seventeenth century, but the prophetic warnings uttered by protestant clergy mindful of the need to refrain from contact with and contamination by the forces of Antichrist.

130 H. Leslie, *A sermon preached at the public fast the ninth of Feb. in St Mary's Oxford, before the great assembly of the members of the honourable House of Commons there assembled* (Oxford 1643), 29.
131 D. Harcourt, *A new remonstrance from Ireland* (s.l. 1643), 3.
132 Ibid.
133 Ibid., 4.
134 R. Puttock, *Good and true newes from Ireland being the copy of a letter sent from Mr Roger Buttock, one of the chief ministers in the city of Dublin, to a brother of his a merchant living in ... London* (London 1642), sig. A2v.

Conclusion

Between 1590 and 1641 the Church of Ireland was transformed. The most significant change was in the nature of its ministry. The clergy of the established church in the late sixteenth century were largely conformist, traditionally minded, native reading ministers with little ideological commitment to the reformation. Over the next four decades, during the 'second reformation', these ministers were gradually replaced by university educated, English speaking, clearly protestant preachers. The amorphous church of the 1590s was succeeded by the tightly knit, firmly Calvinist institution of the early seventeenth century, with its own confession and distinct ideological outlook.

The most important point about this transformation, however, was that it was not linked with any similar change in the religious allegiance of the Irish people. It was evident by the 1630s that this new protestant church had made little progress in winning over the Anglo-Irish or the native Irish to protestantism. Indeed, if anything, the church of the 1630 attracted even fewer of the native population than that of the 1590s. Reasons for this are not difficult to find. The church in the 1590s had inherited severe financial and institutional problems which were to cripple it for many decades to come. The poverty of benefices and the dilapidation of the churches, together with the extent of lay control, had effectively spancelled reform in the sixteenth century. They continued to limit any ambitions the established church had in the following century to support a preaching ministry in every parish in Ireland.

Part of the reason for the failure of the second reformation to attract popular support lay in the fact that it followed so long after the first legal establishment of the reformed church in Ireland. The gap between the declaration of royal supremacy and the effective creation of a protestant church afforded a crucial breathing space to the Catholic church in Ireland. Moreover, during the hiatus, the practical difficulties facing the established church, far from disappearing, actually in many cases grew worse. Thus, for instance, the Nine Years War at the end of the century increased the financial problems of the church and added to the number of ruined churches. To a certain extent, therefore, the action of the civil and ecclesiastical authorities in the 1590s and early seventeenth century, sprang, not from a sense of the opportuneness of the moment, but from a realisation of the mounting pressures upon the Church of Ireland by forces outside it. Had not some action been taken to attract trained English preachers, the ministry of the Church might simply have melted away. The difficulty was, of course, that action was being taken at the very time when the Catholic church was beginning to realise and assert its growing strength. When the protestant preachers finally began to bring the reformed gospel to the townspeople of the Pale they found that the leading elites so crucial to the success of the reformation had already been won over by the mendicants and seminary priests. At the same time, the background and outlook of the new preaching ministers was such that they were in no position to take the reformation to the mass of people who lived outside the towns. A few exceptional preachers sought to instruct the native Irish in their own language; in some dioceses there existed a sub-stratum of native reading ministers who could be used to interpret the protestant service to native congregations. But generally the ethos of the second reformation was firmly English. Reformation and anglicization would, it was assumed, go hand in hand. The Irish people must be made 'civil' so that they could receive the gospel from the English-speaking ministers.

Some of the difficulties encountered by protestant preachers trying to spread the gospel in Ireland derived from the nature of their message. Protestantism was, first and foremost, a literate, bibliocentric religion, relying heavily upon an educated, usually urban elite. It had little appeal for the traditionally minded rural inhabitant. This was especially true in Ireland, where the established church was committed to a view of salvation which placed great emphasis upon the self-awareness of the individual Christian. The personal confrontation between man and God, and the need for rigorous self-examination to discover whether one was truly in receipt of God's grace, left little place for affective piety, devotion to saints, or any other mediatory and less intellectual aids to faith. Indeed, protestant preachers in emphasising the need to 'fly to God in all necessities', specifically attacked Catholic piety and its emphasis upon simple faith inspired by images. It is not difficult to see which approach would appeal to the mass of the Irish people still following the traditional religious practices of their forefathers.

The efforts of the protestant ministers to win over the Irish population were further hampered by the weakness of the educational system. As Montgomery, Chichester, and many other civil and church leaders realised in the early seventeenth century, an effective state controlled system of schooling, leading on to Trinity College, was of vital long-term importance if the reformation was to take root in Ireland. Political, financial and organizational problems prevented much progress being made in this sphere in the sixteenth century, and it was not until the first three decades of the following century that protestant schools began to be established in most Irish dioceses. But by then, of course, they were faced with a rival system of non-conformist pedagogy. One protestant schoolmaster complained that he was unable to obtain financial support from the inhabitants of Ossory in 1634 for the diocesan school 'because they would rather maintain the Popish schoolmasters to whom they send their children'.[1] As a result, the protestant schools catered largely for the protestant, new English inhabitants' children.

As seen by protestant churchmen at the time, one of the main reasons for the failure of the reformation to gain widespread support was the reluctance of the civil authorities to enforce conformity. Loftus and Jones, at the beginning of James's reign, were quite clear in their minds about the correct reformation policy, on both theoretical grounds, and based on their experience of Ireland. But the only time when they and the Dublin authorities were allowed free rein to implement this policy, in 1605, had ambiguous results. To the church leaders and civil officials the experiment had only failed because of a lack of nerve on the part of the King and his advisers in England. For the Irish Catholics, the policy was a serious misjudgement, both of the resilience of Catholicism, and of the economic and social consequences of enforcing conformity through legal means. It is conceivable that the view of Loftus and Jones was correct: had the rigorous policy been enforced consistently over a period of years, and had the authorities been prepared to take some short term political and economic risks and disruption, then widespread conformity might have been achieved. But, in the view of the government in London, the risks of the policy were too great – there was no guarantee that it would in the end succeed. And, in ordering a change of policy in 1606–7, the English Privy Council pointed to one of the basic difficulties in the strategy of Loftus and Jones – their concentration upon the towns to the exclusion of the countryside. This might have been a viable policy some decades earlier (had the central government then had the power to enforce it) before the political and religious alienation of the Anglo-Irish and burgher classes in the towns. In the early years of James's reign, however, it brought the state into conflict with the very class and the very areas where Catholicism was at its strongest and most resilient. In short, just as the protestant schools when they were finally established found that the rival Catholic system was already entrenched, so too the protestant church leaders early in James's reign when they finally were able to call upon the civil arm for support in the enforcement of conformity, found that their belated efforts could not make up for earlier inactivity.

Disappointed in their hopes of firm action by the civil authorities, unable to communicate with the native Irish, their churches and schools shunned by native and Anglo-Irish alike, and beset by financial difficulties, the clergy of the Church of Ireland were in no position to contemplate or undertake missionary work or evangelism amongst the Irish population. They saw their task in Ireland in more limited terms – as being to serve the existing new English or Scottish protestant population. Hence in Ulster the clergy lived

1 B.L. Harleian MS 4297 fol. 2r.

and ministered for the most part in the settled lowland areas. Similarly in Munster and Leinster the outlying parishes with few protestants were generally neglected by protestant preachers. Thus the basic paradox about the growth in the number of preachers in the Church of Ireland – the increase in preaching clergy could, in many areas, lead to a reduction in the geographical extent of the church's ministry.

The restricted and limited view taken by protestant clergy of their role in Ireland was primarily a product of the severe practical difficulties which the reformation encountered in Ireland, and the inability of the Church of Ireland to adapt its message and its policy to suit Irish conditions. However, it is notable that their continued failure to win over the Irish population did not result in protestant ministers questioning their approach to their pastorate. This was because they had few doubts about the rectitude of their approach. Whatever the practical problems they might encounter, their theology and ideology provided them with a crucial intellectual underpinning which could be used to explain and make palatable their difficulties and their failures.

The predestinarian theology which the Church of Ireland so firmly espoused in its confession of 1615 could be twisted in such a manner that it provided an elitist colonial ideology for the Church of Ireland. Few writers or preachers were as crude as Barnaby Rich in identifying the Irish natives with the reprobate and the new English with the chosen. But there were hints in the sermons of Olmstead and the writings of Leslie, Hull and Ussher that they too were on occasions, when they beheld the failure of the protestant gospel in Ireland, tempted by such a neat dichotomy. So too Irish churchmen, beset on all sides by Catholic priests and parishioners, naturally looked to the apocalyptic books of the bible for an historico-religious explanation for their position in Ireland. And in Revelation they found exactly what they were looking for: an interpretation of history as a battle between the beleaguered forces of light and the ever threatening powers of darkness. With the help of James Ussher it was easy to trace this battle in, and apply it to, Irish history.

The major achievement of the second reformation during the period 1590–1641 did not lie in spreading protestantism – in missionary terms, the Church of Ireland was a failure. Rather, it lay in the creation of a protestant church and a protestant community with a clearly defined sense of identity. It was, in fact, during these four decades that Irish protestantism as a distinctive entity was born, with its potent blend of religious and racial attitudes. And though many aspects of its subsequent history remains to be written, it is possible to discern in this period the origins of certain themes which were later to feature prominently in the protestant tradition: the ambivalent relationship with the authorities in England; the hostility towards, and neglect of, Gaelic culture; the identification of Catholicism with disloyalty; a visceral fear of the threat posed by the Catholic majority; and a determination to impose upon

Catholics penal legislation. In such matters, not in its effectiveness in converting the native population, lay the longer term importance of the protestant church and ideology which was created during the late sixteenth and early seventeenth centuries in Ireland.

Bibliography

1. MANUSCRIPTS

Public Library, Armagh
W. Daniel, Expositio prophetiae Zechariae (1594)
W. Daniel, Sermon upon 1 Timothy 2.8
T. Haynes, Certaine principall matters concerning the state of Ireland (1600)
Orders of council and other documents relative to the diocese of Meath
The returnes of the bishops of Ireland to his Majesties Commissioners in May,
    June and July 1622.

All the above MSS are stored in the fireproof press on the ground floor.

Public Record Office of Northern Ireland, Belfast
D 683   Ellis documents.

University Library, Cambridge
Add. 4344   Disputation between Bishop Leslie and the presbyterians,
                     1636.

Archbishop Marsh's Library, Dublin
Z3.1.3   Copy of returns of bishops in 1622.
Z3.1.14   Book of precedents, Archdiocese of Armagh.
Z3.1.19   Thomas Jones, Answer of a faithful servant to his sover-
                     eign prince.
Z3.2.7   Dudley Loftus's annals.

National Library of Ireland, Dublin
643   Translation of part of Rothe's *Analecta*.
8013–4   Papers of the 1622 Commissioners.
13,236–7   Lismore papers.
13,240, 13,256   Lismore papers.
13,901   Rent roll of bishopric of Cloyne, 1605.
16,085   Edmund Sexton's notebook.
16,250   Paul Harris, An Answar unto an epistle written by James
                     Usher to Sr Christopher Sibthorp.
17,853   Report of conversation with Ussher on the doom of the
                     church.
18,282   Temporalities of the see of Limerick, 1622.
18,637, 18,643   Manchester manuscripts re Ulster plantation.
18,646, 18,648   Ibid.
18,650, 18,651   Ibid.

Public Record Office of Ireland, Dublin

Record Commissioners MSS:
RC 4	Repertories to Chancery inquisitions.
RC 6	Repertories to Chancery decree rolls.
RC 9	Repertories to Exchequer inquisitions.
RC 12/1	Repertory to Exchequer decrees.
RC 15	Regal visitation books, copies.
RC 17/4	Calendar of fiants, James I.
1A.49.102–8	Acta regia.

Ferguson MSS:
1A.49.141	Abstracts of revenue, Exchequer orders.
1A.49.143	Abstracts of equity, Exchequer orders.
1A.49.144	Abstracts of equity, Exchequer orders.

Chancery pleadings, salved:
1C.2.144–186	Parcels A–Z.
1C.3.83–104	Parcels AA and BB.

Representative Church Body Library, Dublin
Libr. 32	Tenison Groves MSS

Trinity College, Dublin Library, Dublin
180	Mathias Holmes, An answer to the Jesuits annotations on the four gospels.
221	Notes by Ambrose Ussher on sermons by various preachers.
217	William Daniel's notebook, 1592.
285–6	Works by Ambrose Ussher.
287	Sermons by Ambrose Ussher.
295	Notes by Mathias Holmes.
357–8	Luke Challoner's commonplace books and notes.
550	Copy of bishops returns for Ulster in 1622.
566	Visitations of dioceses, 1590s, 1610, 1615.
582	Dispute re primacy between Armagh and Dublin.
786	Parr Lane, News from the holy isle.
808	Documents re the 1622 Commissioners.
809–41	1641 rebellion: depositions.
843	State of diocese of Dublin, 1630.
865	Copy of 1622 return for Armagh.
1038	Dean Andrews's notes on proposed canons, 1634.
1062	W. Reeves, History of Irish Convocation.
1065	Reeves's collections on Archbishop Loftus.
1066	Reeves's copy of 1615 visitation.
1067	Reeves's copy of 1634 visitation.
1073–4	U.W., i, xv, xvi, annotated by Reeves.

1188	M. Hamilton, Overtures ... relating things generall for the good of the church.
1210	Sermons in Trinity in 1590s.
6404	J. Ware, Annals.

Register House, Edinburgh

| N 2/3 | Documents re Haberdashers' proportion in Londonderry. |

British Library, London
Additional:

3827	Letters to Falkland.
4274	Letter from Ussher to Lady Vere, 1624.
4756	Entry book of 1622 Commissioners.
4780	Papers re Ironmongers' plantation in Londonderry.
4792	Extracts from irish Council Book.
11,402	Abstract of English Council register, 1601–10.
19,836	Regal visitation 1615.
19,837–42	Recognizances in Chancery.
19,865	Edmund Sexton's notebook.
24,191	Letters to John Hull.
34,253	Ussher's evidence to the House of Lords, 1641.
35,830–2	Miscellaneous state papers.
35,842	Bacon on Ireland.
39,853	Cornwallis's comments on Ireland 1613.
47,142	Papers of Irish court of Castle Chamber.

Cottonian:
Titus B X,

| B XII, CVII | Various documents. |

Harleian:

697	Munster Council Book.
4297	Orders of Commissioners of Ecclesiastical Affairs.
6842	Miscellaneous state papers.
7004	Miscellaneous papers.

Royal:

| 18 A LVI | Tract by Sir John Dowdall. |
| 17 A XVIII | Theological treatise by Robert Marchall. |

Egerton:

| 80 | Transcript of letters by Richard Boyle. |

Lansdowne:

| 156, 159, 984 | Various documents. |

Lambeth Palace Library, London
2013   Return of the Bishop of Ossory to 1622 Commissioners.

Public Record Office, London
31/8/199–202   Philadelphia papers.
46/90   De Renzi papers.
14   State papers, domestic.
63   State papers, Ireland.
SO/1   Signet office: Irish letter book.

Chetham Library, Manchester
6701   Dudley Loftus's collection of state papers.

Bodleian Library, Oxford
Laud 612   Various documents.
Barlow 13   Papers collected by Ussher.
Carte: Official papers of sixteenth and seventeenth centuries.
Clarendon 1, 2   Papers of Sir Humphrey May.

Rawlinson:
A 491   Taxation of Irish dioceses
C 439   Falkland letter book.
C 849   Ussher notebook.
C 850   Transcript of part of Raphoe register.
C 919   Ussher commonplace book.
C 1290   Notes by Ussher.

Tanner:
72   Irish bishops on toleration
75   Sancroft's notes on ecclesiastical letters patent; letter of
                          George Montgomery.
281   Ussher's judgement on episcopacy and ordination.
458   Parr's Character of the Irish; Bedell's sermon on Rev. 18 4.

Rawlinson letters 57 Life of Henry Leslie.
Sancroft 18   Sancroft's notes on Ussher's letters.

Exeter College Library, Oxford
95   Letter book of the 1622 Commissioners.

Huntingdon Library, San Marino
EL 1148   Thomas Jones, The church faulte.
EL 335   Letter re state of Ireland, by E.S., 1615.

Sheffield City Libraries, Sheffield
Strafford MSS.

2. CONTEMPORARY WORKS

A brefe declaration of certein principall articles of religion (Dublin 1567)

A declaration of the commons assembled in parliament; concerning the rise and progress of the grand rebellion in Ireland (London 1643)

A manifestation directed to the honourable Houses of Parliament in England ... (London 1644)

G. Andrews, *A quaternion of sermons preached in Ireland in the summer season 1624* (Dublin 1625)

A perfect relation of the beginning and continuation of the Irish rebellion from May last, to this present 12th January, 1641 (London 1641)

Articles of religion agreed upon by the archbishops and bishops, and the rest of the cleargie of Ireland, in the convocation holden at Dublin in the yeare of our Lord God 1615: for the avoidance of diversities of opinions: and the establishing of consent touching true religion (Dublin 1615)

W. Barlow, *The summe and substance of the conference* ... *at Hampton Court, January 14 1603* (London 1604)

W. Bedell, *The copies of certaine letters which have passed between Spaine and England in matter of religion* (London 1624)

—, *The A.B.C., or the institution of a Christian* (Dublin 1631)

N. Bernard, *The life and death of* ... *Dr James Usher* (Dublin 1656)

—, *The judgement of the late Archbishop of Armagh*, 2nd ed. (London 1659)

—, *Clavi trabales; or, the nailes fastned by some great masters of assemblyes* (London 1661)

—, *The whole proceedings of the siege of Drogheda in Ireland* ... (London 1642)

J. Coppinger, *A mnemosynum or memoriall to the afflicted Catholickes in Irelande* ([?Bordeaux] 1606)

Constitutions and canons ecclesiastical (Dublin 1635)

R. Daborn, *A sermon preached in the cathedral church of the cittie of Waterford* (London 1618)

W. Daniell, *Tiomna nuadh* (Dublin 1602)

—, *Leabhar na nurnaightheadh gcomhchoidchiond* (Dublin 1608)

G. Downham, *A treatise concerning Antichrist* (London 1603)

—, *Two sermons, the one commending the ministerie in generall: the other defending the office of bishops in particular* (London 1608)

—, *The covenant of grace* (Dublin 1631)

H. Fitzsimon, *A Catholike confutation of M. John Riders clayme of antiquitie; and a caulming comfort against his Caveat* (Rouen 1608)

—, *A replie to M. Riders Rescript. And a discourse of puritan partialitie in his behalf* (Rouen 1608)

—, *The justification and exposition of the divine sacrifice of the masse* ([Douai] 1611)

—, *Britannomachia ministrorum in plerisque & fidei fundamentis & fidei articulis dissidentium* (Douai 1614)

C. Hampton, *Two sermons preached before the Kings most exc. majesty* (London 1609)

—, *A sermon preached in Glasco in Scotland, June 10, 1610, at the holding of a general assembly there* (London 1611)

—, *An inquisition of the true church, and those that revolt from it* (Dublin 1622)

—, *A sermon preached before the Kings Majestie, in the church of Beauty in Hampshire ... An addition to the former treatise of soveraignetie* (Dublin 1620)

D. Harcourt, *The clergies lamentation* ([London] 1644)

—, *A new remonstrance for Ireland* (s.l. [1643])

P. Heylin, *The history of the sabbath* (London 1636)

—, *Aerius redivivus: or, the history of the presbyterians* (Oxford 1670)

J. Hill, *The penitent sinners entertainement* (London 1614)

J. Hopkins, *A sermon preached before the Kinges maiestie by J. Hopkins one of highnesse chaplaines* (London 1604)

J. Hoyle, *A rejoynder to the Master Malones reply concerning reall presence* (Dublin 1641)

J. H[oyle], *Jehojadahs justice against Mattan, Baal's priest; or, the covenanters justice against idolaters. A sermon preacht upon the occasion of a speech utter'd upon Tower Hill* (London 1645)

J. Hull, *The arte of Christian saylinge* (London 1602)

—, *St Peters prophesie* (London 1610)

—, *An exposition upon a part of the Lamentations of Jeremie: lectured at Corke in Ireland* (London 1618); 2nd ed. (London 1620)

—, *Christ his proclamation to salvation* (London 1613)

S. J[erome], *The soules centinell ringing an alarum against impietie and impenitencie* (Dublin 1631)

—, *The haughty heart humbled: or, the penitents practice* (London 1628)

S. Jerome, *Irelands jubilee, or Irelands joyes lo-paen, for Prince Charles his welcome home* (Dublin 1624)

—, *Irelands jubilee, or Irelands joyes lo-paen, for King Charles his welcome home* (London 1625)

W. Ince, *Lot's little one. Or meditations on Gen. 19 Vers. 20* (London 1640)

H. Jones, *A remonstrance of divers remarkable passages concerning the church and kingdome of Ireland* (London 1642)

H. Leslie, *A sermon preached before his Majesty at Windsore* (Oxford 1625)

—, *A warning for Israel, in a sermon preached at Christ Church, in Dublin* (Dublin 1625).

—, *A sermon preached before his Majesty at Wokin* (London 1627)

—, *A sermon preached at the public fast in the ninth of Feb. in St Mary's Oxford, before the great assembly of the members of the honourable House of Commons there assembled* (Oxford 1643)

—, *A treatise tending to unitie: in a sermon preached at Droghedah, June 9, 1622, before the King's Majesties Commrs* (Dublin 1623)

F. Lopez de Gomara, *The pleasant historie of the conquest of the weast India atchieved by H. Cortes*, transl. T.N. (London 1578).

W. Malone, *A reply to Mr James Ussher his answere* (s.l. 1627)

F. Moryson, *An itinerary* (London 1617)

R. Olmstead, *Sions teares leading to joy: or the waters of Marah sweetned. First preached at Clonenagh in the Queenes County in severall sermons* (Dublin 1630)

—, *A treatise on the union betwixt Christ and the church: or mans felicitie and happinesse. First preached in several sermons* (Dublin 1627)

R. Parr, *The life of the most reverend father in God, James Ussher, late Lord Archbishop of Armagh* (London 1686)

W. Perkins, *The workes of that famous and worthy minister of Christ in the universitie of Cambridge, Mr William Perkins,* 3 vols (Cambridge 1608–9)

W. Prynne, *Hidden workes of darknes brought to publike light, or, a necessary introduction to the history of the Archbishop of Canterburie's triall* (London 1645)

—, *Canterburies doome* (London 1646)

R. Puttock, *A reioynder unto W. Malone's reply to the first article* (Dublin 1632)

—, *An abstract of certain depositions* (London 1642)

R. Puttock, *Good and true news from Ireland being the copy of a letter sent from Mr Roger Buttock, one of the chief ministers in the city of Dublin to a brother of his a merchant, living in ... London* (London 1642)

Remonstrance of divers remarkable Passages concerning the church and kingdome of Ireland (London 1642)

B. Rich, *Greenes newes from both heaven and hell* (London 1593)

—, *The Irish hubbub, or the English hue and crie* (London, 1617)

—, *A short survey of Ireland. Truely discovering who hath armed that people with disobedience* (London 1069 (sic))

—, *A new description of Ireland: wherein is described the disposition of the Irish* (London 1610)

—, *A true and kinde excuse written in defence of that booke, intituled A newe description of Irelande* (London 1612)

J. Richardson, *A sermon on the doctrine of justification* (Dublin 1625)

J. Rider, *The coppie of a letter sent from M. Rider, concerning the newes out of Ireland* (London 1601)

—, *A friendly caveat to Irelands catholickes* (Dublin 1602)

D. Rothe, *Analecta sacra nove et mire de rebus Catholicorum in Hibernia ... gestis* (Cologne 1616–19)

T. Ryves, *The poore vicars plea. Declaring that a competencie of meanes is due to them out of tithes notwithstanding the impropriations* (London 1620)

—, *Regiminis anglicani in Hibernia defensio, adversus Analecten* (London 1624)

G.S., *A briefe declaration of the barbarous and inhumane dealings of the northern Irish rebels* (London 1641)

—, *Sacrae heptades, or seaven problems concerning Antichrist* (Amsterdam 1625)

M.S., *A discourse concerning the rebellion in Ireland* (London 1642)

C. Sibthorp, *A friendly advertisement to the pretended catholickes of Ireland ... in the end whereof is added an epistle written to the author by ... James Vssher Bishop of Meath* (Dublin 1622)

—, *A reply, to an answere, which a popish adversarie made to two chapters conteined in the first part of that booke, which is intituled A friendly advertisement*

(Dublin 1625); a 'second edition', with additions and deletions in the hand of Sibthorp, dated 1627, in in T.C.D. Library at BB.11.28.

—, *A surreplication to the reioynder of a popish adversarie* (Dublin 1627)

A. Spicer, *Nebuchadonosor at Rome, or the Pope at Babylon. A sermon preached ... at Coleraine in the north of Ireland* (London 1617)

G. S[ynge], *A rejoynder to the reply published by the Jesuites under the name of William Malone* (Dublin 1632)

The protestation of the Archbishops and bishops of Ireland against the toleration of popery agreed upon, and subscribed by them at Dublin, the 26 of November (London 1641)

W. Travers, *An answere to a supplicatorie epistle, of G.T. for the pretended Catholiques* (London [1583])

—, *A full and plain declaration of ecclesiastical discipline* ([Heidelberg] 1574)

J. Ussher, *Gotteschalci, et praedestinatianae controversiae ab eo motae, historia* (Dublin 1631)

—, *Strange and remarkable prophesies and predictions of the holy, learned and excellent James Ussher* (London 1678)

—, *Bishop Ushers second prophesie* (London 1681)

—, *An answer to a challenge made by a Jesuit in Ireland* (Dublin 1624)

—, *Prophecys concerning the return of popery into England, Scotland and Ireland* (London 1682)

—, *The prophecy of James Ussher* (London 1687)

3. PRINTED SOURCES

A.B. (ed.), *A brief memorial of the life and death of Dr James Spottiswood* (Edinburgh 1811)

I. Breward (ed.), *The work of William Perkins* (Abingdon 1970)

E.S. Byam, *Chronological memoir of the three clerical brothers ... Byam*, 2nd ed. (Tenby 1862)

Calendar of the state papers relating to Ireland, of the reigns of Henry VIII, Edward VI, Mary, and Elizabeth, preserved in the State Paper Department of Her Majesty's Public Record Office, 11 vols (London 1860–1912)

Calendar of the state papers relating to Ireland, in the reign of James I, preserved in Her Majesty's Public Record Office and elsewhere, 5 vols (London 1872–80)

Calendar of the state papers relating to Ireland, of the reign of Charles I, preserved in the Public Record Office (London 1900–3)

Calendar of the state papers and manuscripts relating to English affairs, existing in the archives and collections of Venice, and in other libraries in northern Italy, vol. 10 (London 1893)

Calendar of the Carew manuscripts preserved in the archiepiscopal library at Lambeth, 6 vols (London 1867–73)

N.P. Canny (ed.), 'The dysorders of the Irishery, 1571', *Studia Hibernica*, xiv (1979)

D.A. Chart (ed.), *Londonderry and the London companies 1609–1629 being a survey and other documents submitted to King Charles I by Sir Thomas Phillips* (Belfast 1628)

T.F. Colby (ed.), *Ordnance survey of the County of Londonderry ... parish of Templemore* (Dublin 1837)

Collectione Batesiana (London 1681)

R.D. Edwards (ed.), Letter book of Sir Arthur Chichester 1612–1614', *Analecta Hibernica*, viii (1938)

C.L. Falkiner (ed.), 'Barnaby Rich's "Remembrances [sic, recte 'Remonstrances'] of the state of Ireland, 1612'", *Proceedings of the Royal Irish Academy* xxvi (1906)

—, 'William Farmer's *Chronicles of Elizabeth Quene of Ireland*', *English Historical Review*, xxii (1907)

A.B. Grosart (ed.), *Lismore papers*, 10 vols (London 1886–8)

W. Herbert, *Croftus sive de Hibernia liber*, (ed.) W.E. Buckley (London 1887)

E. Hogan (ed.), *Hibernia Ignatiana seu Ibernorum Societas Iesu patrum monumenta* (Dublin 1880)

— (ed.), H. Fitzsimon, *Words of Comfort* (Dublin 1881)

G. Hand, V.W. Treadwell (eds.), 'His majesty's directions for ordering and settling the courts within his kingdom of Ireland, 1622', *Analecta Hibernica*, xxvi (1970)

M. Hickson (ed.), *Ireland in the seventeenth century or the Irish massacres of 1641–2*, 2 vols (London 1884)

E.M. Hinton (ed.), 'Rych's *Anothomy of Ireland*, with an account of the author', *Publications of the Monder Language Association*, IV (1940)

Historical Manuscripts Commission:

    Calendar of the manuscripts of the ... Marquis of Salisbury ... preserved at Hatfield House, Hertfordshire, 19 vols (London 1883 – in progress)

    The manuscripts of the House of Lords, vol. xi (London 1962)

    Report on the manuscripts of the earl of Egmont, vol. i (London 1905)

    Report on the Laing manuscripts, preserved at the University of Edinburgh, vol. i (London 1914)

    Report on the manuscripts of the late Reginald Rawdon Hastings esq., 4 vols (London 1928–47)

Inquisitionum in officio rotulorum cancellariae hiberniae asservatarum, repertorium, 2 vols (Dublin 1826–9)

Journals of the House of Commons of the kingdom of Ireland, vol i (Dublin 1796)

T.W. Jones (ed.), *A true relation of the life and death of William Bedell* (London 1872)

W. Laud, *The works of Archbishop Laud*, (ed.) W. Scott and J. Bliss, 7 vols, (Oxford 1847–60)

J. Livingston, 'A brief historical relation of his life written by himself', *Woodrow Society* (Edinburgh 1847)

W. Knowler (ed.), *The Earl of Strafford's letters and despatches*, 2 vols (London 1799)

[D. Laing (ed.)], *Original letters relating to the ecclesiastical affairs of Scotland*, Bannatyne Club, 2 vols (Edinburgh 1851)

R. Lascelles, *Liber munerum publicorum Hiberniae*, 2 vols (London 1824–30)

W. Lithgow, *The totall discourse of the rare adventures, and painefull peregrinations of long nineteene yeares travells*, (ed.) G. Phelps (London 1974)

H.H.G. MacDonnell, *Chartae et statuta Collegii sacrosanctae et individuae Trinitatis reginae Elizabethae, juxta Dublin* (Dublin 1844)

J. Maclean (ed.), 'Letters from Sir Robert Cecil to Sir George Carew', *Camden Society*, lxxxviii (1884)

C. McNeill (ed.), *The Tanner letters* (Dublin 1943)

—, 'Harris: collectanea de rebus Hibernicis', *Analecta Hibernica*, vi (1934)

J.P. Mahaffy (ed.), *The particular book of Trinity College, Dublin* (London 1904)

C. Maxwell, *Irish history from contemporary sources, 1509–1610* (London 1923)

T.W. Moody, 'The revised articles of the Ulster plantation, 1610', *Bulletin of the Institute of Historical Research*, xii (1935)

—, J.G. Simms (ed.), *The bishopric of Derry and the Irish Society of London 1602–1705* (Dublin 1968)

J. Morrin (ed.), *Calendar of the patent and close rolls of chancery in Ireland*, 3 vols (Dublin 1861–3)

H. Morley (ed.), *Ireland under Elizabeth and James I* (London 1890)

K.W. Nicholls, 'The episcopal rentals of Clonfert and Kilmacduagh', *Analecta Hibernica*, xxvi (1970)

—, 'Visitations of the dioceses of Clonfert, Tuam and Kilmacduagh, c.1565–67', *Analecta Hibernica*, xxvi (1970)

W. Notestein, F.H. Relf, H. Simpson (eds.), *Commons debates*, 1621, 7 vols (New Haven 1935)

G. O'Brien (ed.), *Advertisements for Ireland* (Dublin 1923)

D.J. O'Doherty, 'Students at the Irish College, Salamanca (1595–1619)', *Archivium Hibernicum*, ii (1913)

—, 'Students at the Irish College, Salamanca (1619–1700)', *Archivium Hibernicum*, iii (1914)

'O'Kane papers', *Analecta Hibernica*, xii (1943)

The register of the Privy Council of Scotland, 14 vols (Edinburgh 1877–98)

J. Perrott, *The chronicle of Ireland, 1584–1608*, (ed.) H. Wood (Dublin 1933)

Report of the Deputy Keeper of the public records of Ireland, xv–xvi (1884–5)

Report of her Majesty's commissioners on the revenues and condition of the established Church of Ireland (Dublin 1868)

W.A. Reynell (ed.), '"The estate of the diocese of Derry" compiled by Dr. George Downham', *Ulster Journal of Archaeology*, i–ii (1895–96)

H. Robinson (ed.), *Epistolae tigurinae* (Parker Society, 1845)

M.V. Ronan (ed.), 'The regal visitation of Dublin, 1615', *Archivium Hibernicum* viii (1941)

—, 'Archbishop Bulkeley's visitation of Dublin, 1630', *Archivium Hibernicum*, viii (1941)

W. Row (ed.), *The life of Mr Robert Blair, minister of St Andrews, containing his autobiography, from 1593 to 1636* (s.l. 1848)

P. Schaff, *The creeds of the evangelical protestant churches* (London 1877)

E.P. Shirley (ed.), *Original letters and papers in illustration of the history of the Church of Ireland during the reigns of Edward VI, Mary and Elizabeth* (London 1851)

—, *Papers relating to the Church of Ireland (1631–9)* (London and Dublin [1874])

E.S. Shuckburgh (ed.), *Two biographies of William Bedell Bishop of Kilmore with a selection of his letters* (Cambridge 1902)

R.C. Simington (ed.), *Books of survey and distribution* (Dublin 1944–67)

J.S. Spedding (ed.), *The letters and life of Francis Bacon*, 7 vols (London 1861–74)

E. Spenser, *A view of the present state of Ireland*, (ed.) W.L. Renwick (Oxford 1970)

'State of Ireland, 1611', *Archivium Hibernicum*, ii (1913)

The statutes at large passed in the parliaments held in Ireland, 3 vols (Dublin 1786)

J. Strype, *Annals of the reformation and establishment of religion … during Queen Elizabeth's happy reign*, 4 vols (Oxford 1824)

J.W. Stubbs (ed.), *Archbishop Adam Loftus and the foundation of Trinity College, Dublin: speeches delivered by him on various occasions* (Dublin 1892)

W.C. Trevelyan, C.E. Trevelyan (eds.), 'Trevelyan papers, part III', *Camden Society*, cv (1872)

J. Ussher, *The whole works of … James Ussher*, (ed.) C.E. Elrington, J.H. Todd, 17 vols (Dublin 1847–64)

J. Ware, *The whole works of Sir James Ware*, (ed.) W. Harris, 2 vols (Dublin 1847–60)

'Winthrop papers', *Massachusetts Historical Society*, i–v (1929–47)

4. REFERENCE WORKS

D.A. Beaufort, *A new map of Ireland civil and ecclesiastical* (London 1792)

H.F. Berry, 'Probable early students of Trinity College, Dublin (being wards of the crown), 1599–1616', *Hermathena*, xvi (1911)

Biographica Britannica (London 1747–66)

Burke's Irish family records (London 1976)

G.D. Burtchaell, T.U. Sadleir (eds.), *Alumni Dublinenses* (Dublin 1935)

C.H. Cooper, T. Cooper, *Athenae Cantabrigienses*, 3 vols (Cambridge 1858–1913)

H. Cotton, *Fasti ecclesiae Hibernicae*, 6 vols (Dublin 1845–78)

Dictionary of National Biography, 63 vols (London 1885–1900)

E.R. McC.Dix, *Catalogue of early Dublin printed books 1601 to 1700*, 2 vols repr. (New York 1971)

J. Foster, *Alumni Oxonienses*, 1500–1714, 4 vols (Oxford 1891)

J.B. Leslie, *Ardfert and Aghadoe clergy and parishes* (Dublin 1940)

—, *Armagh clergy and parishes* (Dundalk 1911)

—, *Clogher clergy and parishes* (Enniskillen 1929)

—, H.B. Swanzy, *Biographical succession lists of the clergy of the diocese of Down* (Enniskillen 1936)

—, *Derry clergy and parishes* (Enniskillen 1937)

—, *Ferns clergy and parishes* (Dublin 1936)

—, *Ossory clergy and parishes* (Enniskillen 1933)

—, *Raphoe clergy and parishes* (Enniskillen 1940)

J. Lodge, revised M. Archdall, *The peerage of Ireland*, 7 vols (London 1789)

A.G. Mathews, *Calamy revised* (Oxford 1934)

P. Milward, *Religious controversies of the Elizabethan age. A survey of printed sources* (London 1978)

J. Peile (ed.), *Biographical register of Christ's College, Cambridge*, 2 vols (Cambridge 1910)

St J.D. Seymour, *The succession of parochial clergy in the united dioceses of Cashel and Emly* (Dublin 1908)

W.H. Rennison, *Succession list of the dioceses of Waterford and Lismore* (Waterford 1920)

J. Venn, J.A. Venn, *Alumni Cantabrigienses*, part I, 4 vols (Cambridge 1922–27)

A. Wood, *Athenae Oxoniensis*, (ed.), P. Bliss, 4 vols (London 1815–20)

5. SECONDARY WORKS

W.M. Abbott, 'James Ussher and "Ussherian" episcopacy, 1640–1656: the primate and his *Reduction* manuscript' in *Albion*, xxii (1990)

G.B. Adams, 'Aspects of monoglottism in Ulster', *Ulster Folklife*, xxii (1976)

J.W. Allen, *A history of political thought in the sixteenth century* (London 1957)

K.R. Andrews, N.P. Canny, P.E.H. Hair (eds.), *The westward enterprise: English activities in Ireland, the Atlantic and America, 1480–1650* (Liverpool 1978)

B.G. Armstrong, *Calvinism and the Amyraut heresy. Protestantism and scholasticism in seventeenth century France* (Madison 1969)

R.G. Asch, 'Antipopery and ecclesiastical policy in early seventeenth century Ireland' in *Archiv für Reformationsgeschichte*, lxxxiii (1992)

N.D. Atkinson, 'The plantation of Ely O'Carroll 1619–1693', Dublin University M.Litt Thesis, 1958

W.D. Baillie, *The Six Mile Water revival of 1625* (Newcastle Co. Down 1976)

John Bale, *The vocacyon of Johan Bale* (1990)

T.C. Barnard, *Cromwellian Ireland* (Oxford 1975)

—, 'Crises of identity among Irish protestants 1641–1685' in *Past & Present*, cxxvii (1990)

—, 'Protestants and the Irish language, c.1675–1725' in *Journal of Ecclesiastical History*, xliv (1993)

—, 'The Protestant interest, 1641–1660', in J.H. Ohlmeyer (ed.), *Ireland from independence to occupation 1641–1660* (Cambridge 1995)

D.M. Barratt, 'Conditions of the parish clergy from the reformation to 1660 in the dioceses of Oxford, Worcester and Gloucester', Oxford Univ., D. Phil. Thesis, 1950

R. Bauckham, 'The career and thought of Dr William Fulke (1537–1589)', Cambridge Univ., Ph.D. Thesis, 1973

—, *Tudor apocalypse. Sixteenth century apocalypticism, millenarianism and the English reformation: from John Bale to John Foxe and Thomas Brightman* (Abingdon 1978)

—, 'Hooker, Travers and the church of Rome in the 1580s', *Journal of Ecclesiastical History*, xxix (1978)

E.J. Bicknell, *A theogical introduction to the Thirty-Nine Articles of the Church of England*, 3rd ed. (London 1955)

F.R. Bolton, 'Griffith Williams, Bishop of Ossory (1641–72)' in *Journal of the Butler Society*, ii 3 (1984)

J. Bossy, 'The counter-reformation and the people of Catholic Ireland, 1596–1641', *Historical Studies*, viii (1971)

K.S. Bottigheimer, 'The failure of the reformation in Ireland: *une question bien posée*' in *Journal of Ecclesiastical History*, xxxvi (1985)

C.R. Boxer, 'The problem of native clergy in the Portuguese and Spanish empires', *Studies in Church History*, vi (1976)

—, *The church militant and Iberian expansion 1440–1770* (Baltimore 1978)

B.I. Bradshaw, 'Fr Wolfe's description of Limerick, 1574', *North Munster Antiquarian Journal*, xvii (1975)

—, 'George Browne, first reformation Archbishop of Dublin', *Journal of Ecclesiastical History*, xxi (1970)

—, *The dissolution of the religious orders in Ireland under Henry VIII* (Cambridge 1974)

—, 'The Edwardian reformation in Ireland', *Archivium Hibernicum* ssvi (1976–7)

—, 'The Elizabethans and the Irish', *Studies*, xlvi (1977)

—, 'Sword, word and strategy in the reformation in Ireland', *Historical Journal*, xxi (1978)

—, 'Edmund Spenser on justice and mercy', in Tom Dunne (ed.), *The writer as witness: literature as historical evidence* (Historical Studies, xvi, Cork, 1987)

—, 'The reformation in the cities: Cork, Limerick and Galway, 1534–1603', in John Bradley (ed.), *Settlement and society in medieval Ireland: studies presented to Francis Xavier Martin, O.S.A.* (Kilkenny, 1988)

—, 'Robe and sword in the conquest of Ireland', in Claire Cross, David Loades and J.J. Scarisbrick (eds.), *Law and government under the Tudors* (Cambridge 1988)

—, 'The wild and woolly west: early Irish Christianity and Latin orthodoxy', in W.J. Shiels and Diana Wood (eds.), *The churches, Ireland and the Irish: studies in church history* (Studies in Church History, xxv, Oxford 1989)

—, 'Geoffrey Keating: apologist of Irish Ireland', in B.I. Bradshaw, Andrew Hadfield and Willy Maley (eds.), *Representing Ireland. Literature and the origins of the conflict, 1534–1660* (Cambridge 1993)

—, Andrew Hadfield and Willy Maley (eds.), *Representing Ireland. Literature and the origins of conflict, 1534–1660* (Cambridge 1993)

C.F. Brady, 'Conservative subversives: the community of the pale and the Dublin administration, 1556–1586' in *Historical Studies*, xv (1985)

—, 'Spenser's Irish crisis: humanism and experience in the 1590s' in *Past & Present*, cxi (1986)

— and Raymond Gillespie (eds.), *Natives and newcomers. Essays on the making of Irish colonial society* (Dublin 1986)

B. Brook, *Lives of the puritans*, 3 vols (London 1813)

P.R.L. Brown, *Augustine of Hippo* (London 1967)

G. Burnett, *The life of William Bedell* (London 1685)

Marc Caball, 'Providence and exile in early seventeenth-century Ireland' in *Irish Historical Studies*, xxix (1994)

N.P. Canny, *The formation of the Old English elite in Ireland* (Dublin 1973)

—, *The Elizabethan conquest of Ireland: a pattern established 1565–76* (Hassocks 1976)

—, 'The ideology of English colonization from Ireland to America', *William and Mary Quarterly*, xxx (1973)

—, 'Why the reformation failed in Ireland: *Une question mal posée*', *Journal of Ecclesiastical History*, xxx (1979)

—, 'Dominant minorities: English settlers in Ireland and Virginia, 1550–1650', in A.C. Hepburn (ed.), *Minorities in history* (London 1978)

—, *The upstart earl: a study of the social and mental world of Richard Boyle, first earl of Cork, 1566–1643* (Cambridge 1982)

—, 'Edmund Spenser and the development of Anglo-Irish identity' in *Yearbook of English Studies*, xiii (1983)

—, 'The formation of the Irish mind: religion politics and Gaelic Irish literature, 1580–1750', in C.H.E. Philpin (ed.), *Nationalism and popular protest in Ireland* (Cambridge 1987)

—, *From reformation to restoration: Ireland 1534–1660* (Dublin 1987)

—, 'Identity formation in Ireland: the emergence of the Anglo-Irish', in N.P. Canny and Anthony Pagden (eds.), *Colonial identity in the Atlantic world, 1500–1800* (Princeton 1987)

—, *Kingdom and colony: Ireland in the Atlantic world 1560–1800* (Baltimore 1988)

—, 'In defence of the constitution? The nature of the Irish revolt in the seventeenth century', in L. Bergeron and Louis Cullen (eds.), *Culture et pratiques politiques en France et en Irlande XVI–XVIIIᵉ siècle: Actes du Colloque de Marseille* (Paris 1991)

—, 'The marginal kingdom: Ireland as a rpoblem in the first British empire', in Bernard Bailyn and P.D. Morgan (eds.), *Strangers within the realm. Cultural margins of the first British empire* (Chapel Hill 1991)

—, 'The 1641 depositions: a source for cultural and social history' in *History Ireland*, i no. 4 (1993)

—, 'The attempted anglicization of Ireland in the seventeenth century: an exemplar of "British history"', in J.F. Merritt (ed.), *The political world of Thomas Wentworth, Earl of Strafford, 1621–1641* (Cambridge 1996)

Amanda Capern, '"Slipperye times and dangerous dayes": James Ussher and the Calvinist reformation of Britain, 1560–1660', University of New South Wales, Ph.D. thesis, 1991

—, 'The Caroline church: James Ussher and the Irish dimension' in *Historical Journal*, xxxix (1996)

Charles Carltron, *Archbishop William Laud* (London 1987)

P.R.N. Carter, 'Royal taxation of the English parish clergy, 1535–58', University of Cambridge, Ph.D thesis, 1994

P. Christianson, *Reformers and Babylon: English apocalyptic vision from the reformation to the eve of the Civil War* (Toronto 1978)

—, 'Reformers and the Church of England under Elizabeth I and the early Stuarts', *Journal of Ecclesiastical History*, xxxi (1980)

A. Clarke, *The Old English in Ireland, 1625–42* (London 1966)

—, *The graces, 1625–41* (Dundalk 1968)

—, 'Colonial identity in early seventeenth century Ireland', *Historical Studies*, xi (1978)

—, 'Ireland, 1534–1660', in J. Lee (ed.), *Irish historiography* (Cork 1981)

—, 'The 1641 depositions', in Peter Fox (ed.), *Treasures of the Library: Trinity College Dublin* (Dublin 1986)

—, 'Sir Piers Crosby, 1590–1646: Wentworth's "tawney ribbon"' in *Irish Historical Studies*, xxvi (1988)

—, 'Bishop William Bedell (1571–1642) and the Irish reformation', in C.F. Brady (ed.), *Worsted in the game: losers in Irish history* (Dublin 1989)

—, 'Varieties of uniformity: the first century of the Church of Ireland', in W.J. Shiels and Diana Wood (eds.), *The churches, Ireland and the Irish: studies in church history* (*Studies in Church History*, xxv, Oxford 1989)

—, 'Colonial constitutional attitudes in Ireland, 1640–1660' in *Proceedings of the Royal Irish Academy*, xc, Sect. C 11 (1990)

S.J. Clausen, 'Calvinism in the Anglican hierarchy, 1603–1643: four episcopal examples', Vanderbilt, Ph.D. thesis, 1989

Helen Coburn Walsh, 'Enforcing the Elilzabethan settlement: the vicissitudes of Hugh Brady, bishop of Meath, 1563–84' in *Irish Historical Studies*, xxvi no. 104 (1989)

—, 'Responses to the protestant reformation in sixteenth century Meath' in *Riocht na Midhe*, viii (1987)

Thomas Cogswell, *The blessed revolution. English politics and the coming of war 1621–1624* (Cambridge 1989)

J. Collier, *An ecclesiastical history of Great Britain* (London 1840)

P. Collinson, *The Elizabethan puritan movement* (London 1967)

—, 'If Constantine, then also Theodosius: St Ambrose and the integrity of the Elizabethan *Ecclesia Anglicana*', *Journal of Ecclesiastical History*, xxx (1979)

T.L. Cooke, *The early history of the town of Birr, or Parsonstown* (Dublin 1875)

T. Corcoran (ed.), *State policy in Irish education A.D. 1536 to 1816* (Dublin 1916)

P.J. Corish (ed.), *A history of Irish Catholicism* (Dublin 1967–9)

—, *The Catholic community in the seventeenth and eighteenth centuries* (Dublin 1981)

—, *The Irish Catholic experience: a historical survey* (Dublin 1985)

Des Cowman, 'The reformation bishops of the diocese of Waterford and Lismore' in *Decies*, xxvii (1984)

T.M. Cranfill, D.H. Bruce, *Barnaby Rich; a short biography* (Austin 1953)

C. Cross, *The royal supremacy in the Elizabethan church* (London 1969)

B. Cunningham, 'Political and social change in the lordships of Clanrickard and Thomond, 1569–1641', M.A. Thesis, University College Galway, 1979

— (ed.), 'A view of religious affiliation and practice in Thomond, 1591' in *Archivium Hibernicum*, xlviii (1994)

—, 'Seventeenth–century interpretations of the past: the case of Geoffrey Keating' in *Irish Historical Studies*, xxv (1986)

—, 'Geoffrey Keating's Eochair Sgiath an Aifrinn and the Catholic reformation in Ireland', in W.J. Shiels and Diana Wood (eds.), *The churches, Ireland and the Irish* (*Studies in Church History*, xxv, Oxford 1989)

— and Raymond Gillespie, '"Persecution" in seventeenth-century Irish' in *Éigse*, xxvii (1987)

— and Raymond Gillespie, '"The most adaptable of saints": the cult of St Patrick in the seventeenth century' in *Archivium Hibernicum*, xlix (1995)

M.H. Curtis, 'The alienated intellectuals of early Stuart England', *Past & Present*, xxiii (1962)

Julian Davies, *The Caroline captivity of the church. Charles I and the remoulding of Anglicanism 1625–1641* (Oxford 1992)

J.E.A. Dawson, 'Two kingdoms or three? Ireland in Anglo-Scottish relations in the middle of the sixteenth century', in R.A. Mason (ed.), *Scotland and England 1286–1815* (Edinburgh 1987)

B. Dickins, 'The Irish broadside of 1571 and Queen Elizabeth's types', *Transactions of the Cambridge Bibliographical Society*, i (1949)

D.M. Downey, 'Culture and diplomacy. The Spanish-Habsburg dimension in the Irish Counter-Reformation movement, *c.*1529–*c.*1629', Cambridge University, Ph.D. thesis, 1994

J.I. Dredge, *Dr George Downame, Bishop of Derry* (Manchester 1881)

—, *The writings of Richard Bernard. A bibliography* (Horncastle 1890)

T.J. Dunne, 'The Gaelic response to conquest and colonisation: the evidence of the poetry' in *Studia Hibernica*, xx (1990)

P. Dwyer, *History of Killaloe from the reformation to the close of the eighteenth century* (Dublin 1978)

R.D. Edwards, 'The history of the penal laws against Catholics in Ireland from 1534 to the treaty of Limerick 1691', London Univ., Ph.D. Thesis, 1933.

—, *Church and state in Tudor Ireland* (Dublin 1935)

—, 'Church and state in the Ireland of Michael O'Clerigh', in S. O'Brien (ed.), *Miscellany in honour of Michael O'Clerigh* (Dublin 1944)

—, 'Ireland, Elizabeth I, and the counter-reformation', in S.T. Bindoff, J. Hurstfield, C.H. Williams (ed.), *Elizabethan government and society* (London 1961)

S.G. Ellis, 'John Bale, Bishop of Ossory, 1552–3' in *Butler Society Journal*, ii (1984)

—, *Tudor Ireland. Crown, community and the conflict of cultures 1470–1603* (London 1985)

—, 'Economic problems of the church: why the reformation failed in Ireland' in *Journal of Ecclesiastical History*, xli (1990)

— and Sarah Barber (eds.), *Conquest and union. Fashioning a British state, 1485–1725* (London 1995)

G.R. Elton, *Policy and police. The enforcement of the reformation in the age of Thomas Cromwell* (Cambridge 1972)

J.C. Erck, *An account of the ecclesiastical establishment in Ireland, as also, an ecclesiastical register* (Dublin 1830)

Kenneth Fincham and P.G. Lake, 'The ecclesiastical policy of James I' in *Journal of British Studies*, xxxiv 2 (1985)

'Father Henry Fitzsimon, S.J.', *Irish Ecclesiastical Record*, viii (1872)

K.R. Firth, *The apocalyptic tradition in reformation Britain 1530–1645* (Oxford 1975)

Alan Ford, 'The protestant reformation in Ireland', in Ciaran Brady and Raymond Gillespie (eds.), *Natives and newcomers: essays on the making of Irish colonial society 1534–1641* (Dublin 1986)

—, 'Correspondence between Archbishops Ussher and Laud' in *Archivium Hibernicum*, xlvi (1991–2)

—, 'The Church of Ireland 1558–1641: a puritan church?', in Alan Ford, James McGuire and Kenneth Milne (eds.), *As by law established. The church of Ireland since the reformation* (Dublin 1995)

—, 'Dependent or independent: the Church of Ireland and its colonial context, 1536–1647' in *The Seventeenth Century*, x (1995)

—, 'The reformation in Kilmore to 1641', in Raymond Gillespie (ed.), *Cavan: an Irish county history* (Dublin 1995)

—, '"Standing one's ground": religion, polemic and Irish history since the reformation', in Alan Ford, James McGuire and Kenneth Milne (eds.), *As by law established. The church of Ireland since the reformation* (Dublin 1995)

—, 'Reforming the holy isle: Parr Lane and the conversion of the Irish', in T.C. Barnard, Dáibhí Ó Cróinín and Katharine Simms (eds.), *The transmission of learning in Ireland* (Aldershot 1996)

—, James McGuire and Kenneth Milne, *The Church of Ireland: a critical bibliography 1536–1992* (Antrim 1993)

—, 'The religious role of Trinity College, Dublin, 1591–1630', Dublin University, Moderatorship dissertation, 1978

W.H.C. Frend, *The Donatist church* (London 1952)

J. Frost, *The history and topography of Clare* (Dublin 1893)

Declan Gaffney, 'The practice of religious controversy in Dublin, 1600–1641', in W.J. Sheils and Diana Wood (eds.), *The churches, Ireland and the Irish* (*Studies in Church History*, xxv, Oxford 1989)

H. Gallwey, *The Wall family in Ireland, 1170–1970* (Naas 1970)

J.R. Garstin, *The Book of Common Prayer in Ireland: its original and history* (Dublin 1871)

C.H. George, K. George, *The protestant mind of the English reformation* (Princeton 1961)

Raymond Gillespie, *Colonial Ulster: the settlement of east Ulster, 1600–1641* (Cork 1985)

—, 'Funerals and society in early seventeenth century Ireland' in *Journal of the Royal Society of Antiquaries of Ireland*, cxv (1985)

—, 'Catholic religious practices and payments in seventeenth-century Ireland' in *Archivium Hibernicum*, xlvii (1993)

—, *The sacred in the secular: religious change in Catholic Ireland, 1500–1700* (Colchester, Vermont 1993)

— (ed.), *The proctor's accounts of Peter Lewis 1564–65* (Dublin 1995)

J. Graves, J.G. Primm, *The history, architecture and antiquities of the cathedral of St Canice* (Dublin 1857)

I. Green, 'Career prospects and clerical conformity in the early Stuart church', *Past & Present*, xc (1981)

S.C. Greenslade (ed.), *The Cambridge history of the bible*, 3 vols (Cambridge 1963)

D. Gregory, *The history of the western highlands and isles of Scotland*, 2nd ed. (Edinburgh 1881)

Andrew Hadfield, 'The English view of Ireland c.1540–c.1600', New University of Ulster at Coleraine, Ph.D. thesis, 1988

—, 'Briton and Scythian: Tudor representations of Irish origins' in *Irish Historical Studies*, xxviii 112 (1993)

—, 'English colonialism and national identity in early modern Ireland' in *Eire-Ireland*, xxviii (1993)

—, 'Translating the reformation: John Bale's Irish *Vocacyon*', in B.I. Bradshaw, Andrew Hadfield and Willy Maley (eds.), *Representing Ireland. Literature and the origins of the conflict, 1534–1660* (Cambridge 1993)

— and John McVeagh (eds.), *Strangers to that land: British perceptions of Ireland from the reformation to the famine* (Gerrard's Cross 1992)

—, 'The course of justice: Spenser, Ireland and political discourse' in *Studia Neophilologica*, lxv (1993)

—, 'Spenser, Ireland and sixteenth-century political theory' in *The Modern Language Review*, lxxxix (1994)

—, 'The "sacred hunger of ambitious minds": Spenser's savage religion', in D.B. Hamilton and Richard Strier (eds.), *Religion, literature, and politics in post-reformation England, 1540–1688* (Cambridge 1996)

C. Haigh, *Reformation and resistance in Tudor Lancashire* (Cambridge 1975)

H. Hajzyk, 'The church in Lincolnshire c.1595–c.1640', Cambridge Univ., Ph. D. Thesis, 1980

B. Hall, 'Calvin against the Calvinists', in G.E. Duffield (ed.), *John Calvin* (Appleford 1966)

W. Haller, *Foxe's 'Book of martyrs' and the elect nation* (London 1963)

J. Hardiman, *History of the town and county of Galway* (Dublin 1820)

C. Hardwick, *A history of the articles of religion*, 3rd ed. (London 1895)

G.A. Hayes McCoy, 'Sir John Davies in Cavan in 1606 and 1610', *Breifne*, i (1960)

F. Heal, R. O'Day (ed.), *Continuity and change. Personnel and administration of the Church of England 1500–1642* (Leicester 1976)

J. Healy, *History of the diocese of Meath*, 2 vols (Dublin 1908)

G. Hill, *An historical account of the plantation in Ulster ... 1608–20* (Belfast 1877)

J.E.C. Hill, *Economic problems of the church. From Archbishop Whitgift to the Long Parliament*, repr. (London 1971)

R.J. Hunter, 'The Ulster plantation in the counties of Armagh and Cavan, 1608–41', M.Litt. Thesis, Dublin University, 1969

J.L. Hurstfield, *Freedom corruption and government in Elizabethan England* (London 1973)

W.R. Jacobs, *Dispossessing the American Indian: Indians and whites on the colonial frontier* (New York 1972)

F.G. James, *Lords of the ascendancy. The Irish House of Lords and its members 1600–1800* (Dublin 1995)

H.A. Jefferies, 'The Irish parliament of 1560: the anglican reforms authorised' in *Irish Historical Studies*, xxvi (1988)

F. Jennings, *The invasion of America. Indians, colonialism and the cant of conquest* (Williamsburg 1975)

F.M. Jones, *Mountjoy, 1563–1606: the last Elizabethan deputy* (Dublin 1958)

W.K. Jordan, *The development of religious toleration in England 1603–40* (New York 1936)

H.F. Kearney, *Strafford in Ireland, 1633–41: a study in absolutism* (Manchester 1959)

R.T. Kendall, *Calvin and English Calvinism to 1649* (Oxford 1979)

W.D. Killen, *The ecclesiastical history of Ireland*, 2 vols (Belfast 1875)

P. Kilroy, 'Division and dissent in the Irish reformed church, 1615–1634', University College Dublin, M.A. Thesis, 1973

—, 'Sermon and pamphlet literature in the Irish reformed church, 1613–1634', *Archivium Hibernicum*, xxxiii (1975)

—, 'Bishops and ministers in Ulster during the primacy of Ussher', *Seanchas Ardmhacha*, viii (1977)

R.B. Knox, 'The ecclesiastical policy of James Ussher, Archibshop of Armagh', London Univ., Ph.D. Thesis, 1956

—, *James Ussher, Archbishop of Armagh* (Cardiff 1967)

S.J. Knox, *Walter Travers: paragon of Elizabethan puritanism* (London 1962)

A.J. Krailsheimer, *Conversion* (London 1980)

K.O. Kupperman, 'British attitudes towards the American Indian 1580–1640', Cambridge Univ. Ph.D. Thesis, 1977

P.G. Lake, 'Anti-Popery: the structure of a prejudice', in Richard Cust and Ann Hughes (eds.), *Conflict in early Stuart England: studies in religion and politics 1603–42* (1989)

—, 'Laurence Chaderton and the Cambridge moderate puritan tradition', Cambridge Univ. Ph.D. Thesis, 1978

—, 'The significance of the Elizabethan identification of the pope as Antichrist', *Journal of Ecclesiastical History*, xxxi (1980)

Anne Laurence, 'The cradle to the grave: English observations of Irish social customs in the seventeenth century' in *The Seventeenth Century*, iii no. 1 (1988)

H.J. Lawlor, 'Two collections of visitation reports in the library of Trinity College', *Hermathena*, xxxi (1905)

Joseph Leerssen, 'Archbishop Ussher and Gaelic culture' in *Studia Hibernica*, xxii–xxiii (1982–3)

—, *Mere Irish and Fíor Gael: studies in the idea of nationality, its development and literary expression prior to the nineteenth century* (Amsterdam and Philadelphia 1986)

C. Lennon, 'Richard Stanyhurst (1547–1618) and Old English identity', *Irish Historical Studies*, xxi (1979)

—, 'The Counter-Reformation in Ireland 1542–1641', in C.F. Brady and Raymond Gillespie (eds.), *Natives and newcomers. Essays on the making of Irish colonial society* (Dublin 1986)

—, *The lords of Dublin in the age of reformation* (Dublin 1989)

—, 'The bowels of the city's bounty': the municipality of Dublin and the foundation of Trinity College in 1592' in *Long Room*, xxxvii (1992)

—, *Sixteenth-century Ireland: the incomplete conquest* (Dublin 1994)

Joseph Liechty, 'The popular reformation comes to Ireland: the case of John Walker and the foundation of the Church of God, 1804', in R.V. Comerford, Mary Cullen, J.R. Hill and Colm Lennon (eds.), *Religion, conflict and co-existence in Ireland* (Dublin, 1990)

—, *Roots of sectarianism in Ireland. Chronology and reflections* (Belfast 1993)

Rolf Loeber, *The geography and practice of English colonization from 1534 to 1609* (Athlone 1991)

A.J. Loomie, 'Toleration and diplomacy. The religious issue in Anglo-Spanish relations, 1603–1605', *Transactions of the American Philosophical Society*, n.s; liii (1963)

E.W. Lynam, 'The Irish character in print', *The Library*, 4th ser., iv (1924)

H.R. McAdoo, 'The Irish translation of the Book of Common Prayer', *Éigse*, ii (1940)

John McCafferty, 'God bless your free Church of Ireland': Wentworth, Laud, Bramhall and the Irish convocation of 1634', in J.F. Merritt (ed.), *The political world of Thomas Wentworth, Earl of Strafford, 1621–1641* (Cambridge 1996)

—, 'John Bramhall and the reconstruction of the Church of Ireland, 1633–1641', University of Cambridge, Ph.D. thesis, 1996

Mícheál MacCraith, 'Ireland and the Renaissance', in Glanmor Williams and R.O. Jones (ed.), *The Celts and the Renaissance: tradition and innovation* (Cardiff 1990)

—, 'The Gaelic reaction to the reformation', in S.G. Ellis and Sarah Barber (eds.), *Conquest and union. Fashioning a British state, 1485–1725* (London 1995)

T.P. McCaughey, *Memory and redemption: church, politics and prophetic theology in Ireland* (Dublin 1993)

John McCavitt, 'The Lord Deputyship of Sir Arthur Chichester in Ireland, 1605–16', Queen's University Belfast, Ph.D. thesis, 1988

—, '"Good planets in their several spheares" – the establishment of the assize circuits in early seventeenth century Ireland' in *Irish Jurist*, n.s., xxiv (1989)

—, 'Lord Deputy Chichester and the English government's "mandates policy" in Ireland, 1605–7' in *Recusant History*, xx (1991)

—, 'The flight of the earls, 1607' in *Irish Historical Studies*, xxix (1994)

R.B. McDowell and D.A. Webb, *Trinity College Dublin 1592–1952* (Cambridge 1982)

P. McGrath, *Papists and puritans under Elizabeth I* (London 1967)

T.J. McKenna, 'The Church of Ireland clergy in Cork: an analysis of the 1615 regal visitation', *Journal of the Cork Historical and Archaeological Society*, lxxvii (1972)

W.C. MacKenzie, *The highlands and isles of Scotland* (Edinburgh 1937)

R.E.W. Maddison, 'Robert Boyle and the Irish bible', *Bulletin of the John Rylands Library*, xli (1958)

E. Maguire, *A history of the diocese of Raphoe*, 2 vols (Dublin 1920)

J.P. Mahaffy, *An epoch in Irish history: Trinity College, Dublin, 1591–1640* (London 1903)

Willy Maley, 'Spenser's Irish English: language and identity in early modern Ireland' in *Studies in Philology* (1994)

W.T. Maley, 'Edmund Spenser and cultural identity in early modern Ireland', Cambridge University, Ph.D. thesis, 1989

R. Mant, *History of the Church of Ireland from the reformation to the revolution*, 2 vols (London 1840)

R.A. Marchant, *The puritans and the church courts in the diocese of York 1560–1642* (London 1960)

H.J.M. Mason, *The life of William Bedell, D.D. Lord Bishop of Kilmore* (London 1843)

T.F. Merrill, *William Perkins* (Nieuwkoop 1966)

P.G.E. Miller, *The New England mind. The seventeenth century*, 2nd ed. (Harvard 1954)

S.A. Millsop, 'The state of the church in the diocese of Down and Connor during the episcopate of Robert Echlin 1613–35', Queen's Univ. Belfast, M.A.Thesis, 1979

Anthony Milton, *Catholic and reformed. The Roman and Protestant churches in English Protestant thought, 1600–1640* (Cambridge 1994)

—, 'Thomas Wentworth and the political thought of the personal rule', in J.F. Merritt (ed.), *The political world of Thomas Wentworth, Earl of Strafford, 1621–1641* (Cambridge 1996)

T.W. Moody, 'The treatment of the native population under the scheme for the plantation in Ulster', *Irish Historical Studies*, ii (1938–9)

—, *The Londonderry plantation* (Belfast 1939)

C. Mooney, 'The church in Gaelic Ireland: thirteenth to fifteenth centuries', in P.J. Corish (ed.), *A history of Irish Catholicism*, ii (1969), fascicle 5

E.S. Morgan, *The puritan family. Religion and domestic relations in seventeenth century New England*, 2nd ed (New York 1966)

John Morgan, *Godly learning. Puritan attitudes towards reason, learning and education, 1560–1640* (Cambridge 1986)

J.P. Morgan, 'Godly learning: puritan theories of the religious utility of education 1560–1640', Cambridge Univ., Ph.D. Thesis, 1977

S.E. Morison, *The founding of Harvard College* (Cambridge Mass. 1935)

J.S. Morrill, 'A British patriarchy? Ecclesiastical imperialism under the early Stuarts', in Anthony Fletcher and Peter Roberts (eds.), *Religion, culture, and society in early modern Britain* (Cambridge 1994)

H.L. Murphy, *A history of Trinity College Dublin* (Dublin 1951)

D. Neal, *The history of the puritans or protestant nonconformists*, 2nd ed., 2 vols (London 1754)

K.W. Nicholls (ed.), *The O'Doyne (Ó Duinn) manuscript* (Dublin 1983)

D. O'Brien, *History of the O'Briens from Brian Boroimhe* (London 1949)

Breandán Ó Buachalla, 'James our true king: the ideology of Irish royalism in the seventeenth century', in D.G Boyce, Robert Eccleshall and Vincent Geoghegan (eds.), *Political thought in Ireland since the seventeenth century* (London 1993)

M.R. O'Day, 'Clerical patronage and recruitment in England during the Elizabethan and early Stuart periods', Ph.D. Thesis, London Univ., 1972

—, 'The ecclesiastical patronage of the Lord Keeper, 1558–1642', *Journal of Ecclesiastical History*, xxvi (1975)

J. O'Donoghue, *Historical memoirs of the O'Briens* (Dublin 1860)

Mary O'Dowd, *Power, politics and land: early modern Sligo 1568–1688* (Belfast 1991)

W.N. Osborough, 'Canon law in protestant lands', in R.H. Helmholz (ed.), *Canon law in protestant lands* (Berlin 1992)

M.D. O'Sullivan, *Old Galway* (Cambridge 1942)

William O'Sullivan (ed.), 'Correspondence of David Rothe and James Ussher, 1619–23' in *Collectanea Hibernica*, xxxvi–xxxvii (1994–5)

J.L. Oulton, 'The study of divinity in Trinity College, Dublin since the foundation', *Hermathena*, lviii (1941)

H.S. Pawlisch, *Sir John Davies and the conquest of Ireland. A study in legal imperialism* (Cambridge 1985)

A.F.S. Pearson, 'Alumni of St Andrews and the settlement if Ulster', *Ulster Journal of Archaeology*, 3rd ser., xiv (1941)

R.H. Pearce, *The savages of America: a study of the Indians and the idea of civilization*, rev. (ed.) (Baltimore 1965)

M. Perceval-Maxwell, *The Scottish migration to Ulster in the reign of James I* (London 1973)

—, 'Ireland and the monarchy in the early Stuart multiple kingdom' in *Historical Journal*, xxxiv (1991)

—, *The outbreak of the Irish rebellion of 1641* (Dublin 1994)

W.A. Phillips (ed.), *History of the Church of Ireland*, 3 vols (London 1933–4)

H.C. Porter, *Reformation and reaction in Tudor Cambridge* (Cambridge 1958)

—, *The inconstant savage: England and the north American Indian, 1500–1600* (London 1979)

M. Quane, 'Cavan Royal School', *Journal of the Royal Society of Antiquaries of Ireland*, c (1970)

D.B. Quinn, 'Information about Dublin printers, 1556–1573, in English financial records', *Irish Book Lover*, xxviii (1941)

—, 'Anglo-Irish local government, 1485–1534', *Irish Historical Studies*, i (1939)

J. Quigley, 'The history of the Irish bible', *The Irish Church Quarterly*, x (1917)

J. Rabbitte, 'Alexander Lynch, schoolmaster', *Journal of the Galway Archaeological and Historical Society*, xvii (1936)

O.P. Rafferty, *Catholicism in Ulster 1603–1983, an interpretative history* (London 1994)

T.O. Ranger, 'The career of Richard Boyle, first Earl of Cork, in Ireland 1588–1643', Oxford Univ., D.Phil. Thesis, 1959

L.J. Reeve, 'The Secretaryship of State of Viscount Dorchester', Cambridge, Ph.D. thesis, 1984

J.S. Reid, *History of the presbyterian church in Ireland*, (ed.) W.D. Killen, 3 vols (Belfast 1967)

P. Ricard, *The spiritual conquest of Mexico. An essay on the apostolate and the evangelizing methods of the mendicant orders in New Spain: 1523–1572*, transl. L.B. Simpson (Los Angeles 1966)

J. Richardson, *A short history of the attempts ... to convert the popish natives of Ireland* (London 1712)

P.S. Robinson, *The plantation of Ulster. British settlement in an Irish landscape, 1600–1670* (Dublin, 1984)

—, 'The plantation of County Tyrone in the seventeenth century', Queen's Univ. Belfast, Ph.D. Thesis, 1974

H.H.W. Robinson-Hammerstein, 'Aspects of the continental education of Irish students in the reign of Queen Elizabeth I', *Historical Studies*, viii (1971)

—, 'Erzbischof Adam Loftus und die elizabethanische Reformationspolitik in Irland', Marburg Univ., Dr Phil. Thesis, 1976

—, *Archbishop Adam Loftus. The first provost of Trinity College, Dublin* (Dublin, 1993)

S.H. Rooy, *The theology of missions in the puritan tradition* (Delft 1965)

C. Russell (ed.), *The origins of the English Civil War* (London 1973)

—, 'The British background to the Irish rebellion of 1641' in *Historical Research*, lxi (1988)

—, *The fall of the British monarchies 1637–1642* (Oxford 1991)

—, 'Composite monarchies in early modern Europe: the British and Irish example', in Alexander Grant and K.J. Stringer (eds.), *Uniting the kingdom? The making of British history* (London 1995)

B.W. Sheahan, *Savagism and civility. Indians and Englishmen in colonial Virginia* (Cambridge 1980)

F.H. Shriver, 'The ecclesiastical policy of James I: two aspects: the puritans (1603–1605) – the Arminians (1611–1625)', Cambridge Univ., Ph.D. Thesis, 1968

E.S. Shuckburgh, *Emmanuel College* (London 1904)

J. Simon, *Education and society in Tudor England* (Cambridge 1966)

J.P. Sommerville, 'Jacobean political thought and the controversy over the oath of allegiance', Cambridge Univ., Ph.D. Thesis, 1981

W.B. Steele, 'The sept of Mac-I-Brien Arra', *Journal of the Cork Historical and Archaeological Society*, 2nd ser., iii (1897)

D.C. Stineback, The status of puritan-Indian scholarship', *New England Quarterly*, li (1978)

J. Sweet, *Revelation* (London 1979)

W.J. Tighe, 'William Laud and the reunion of the churches: some evidence from 1637 and 1638' in *The Historical Journal*, xxx (1987)

L.B. Tipson, 'The development of a puritan understanding of conversion', Yale Univ., Ph.D. Thesis, 1972

R.J. Tollefson, 'A study of the church in the life and thought of Archbishop James Ussher', Iowa Univ., Ph.D. Thesis, 1963

P. Toon (ed.), *Puritans, the millenium and the future of Israel: puritan eschatology 1600–1660* (Cambridge 1970)

V. Treadwell, 'The Irish court of wards under James I', *Irish Historical Studies*, xii (1960)

Hugh Trevor-Roper, 'James Ussher, Archbishop of Armagh', in *Catholics, Anglicans and puritans* (London 1989)

N.R.N. Tyacke, 'Arminianism in England, in religion and politics, 1604–1640', Oxford Univ., D.Phil. Thesis, 1968

—, 'Puritanism, Arminianism and counter-revolution', in C. Russell ed., *The origins of the English Civil War* (London 1973)

W. Urwick, *The early history of Trinity College, Dublin 1591–1660* (London 1891)

Norman Vance, *Irish literature: a social history. Tradition, identity and difference* (Oxford 1990)

A.T. Vaughan, *New England frontier: puritans and Indians, 1620–1675* (Boston 1965)

J. Vesey, *Life of Archbishop Bramhall* (Dublin 1676)

F.X. Walker, 'The implementation of the Elizabethan statutes against recusants, 1580–1603', London Univ., Ph.D. Thesis, 1961

J.A. Watt, *The church and the two nations in mediaeval Ireland* (Cambridge 1970)

M.J. Westerkamp, *The triumph of the laity. Scots-Irish piety and the great awakening, 1625-1760* (Oxford 1988)

N.J.D. White, *Four good men* (Dublin 1927)

C.Z. Wiener, 'The beleaguered isle. A study of Elizabethan and early Jacobean anti-Catholicism', *Past & Present*, li (1971)

Avihu Zakai, *Exile and kingdom: history and apocalypse in the puritan migration to America* (Cambridge 1992)

Index